★ BETTER HOMES AND GARDENS ★

HERITAGE OF AMERICA COOKBOOK

BETTER HOMES AND GARDENS® BOOKS
Des Moines

BETTER HOMES AND GARDENS BOOKS®
An Imprint of Meredith® Books

President, Book Group: Joseph J. Ward
Vice President and Editorial Director: Elizabeth P. Rice
Executive Editor: Connie Schrader
Art Director: Ernest Shelton
Test Kitchen Director: Sharon Stilwell

HERITAGE OF AMERICA COOKBOOK

Project Managers/Editors: Jennifer Darling and Shelli McConnell
Project Art Director/Designer: Lynda Haupert

Recipe Writers: Linda J. Henry,
  Marge Steenson, Linda Woodrum
Test Kitchen Product Supervisor:
  Marilyn Cornelius
Recipe Copy Editor: Jennifer Speer
  Ramundt
Consultant Editor: Lorna J. Sass, Ph.D.
Contributing Writer: Jane Horn
Text Copy Editor: Judith Dunham
Production Editor: Paula Forest
Production Manager: Douglas Johnston

Food Photographer: Steven Mark
  Needham
Food Stylist: Anne Disrude
Prop Stylist: Betty Alfenito
Assistant to the Photographer:
  Petra Henttonen
Cover Photographer: Lyne Neymeyer
Cover Food Stylist: Janet Pittman
Historical Picture Research:
  Gillian Speeth
Picture Research: Alisa Guttman

©Copyright 1993 by Meredith
Corporation, Des Moines, Iowa.
All Rights Reserved.
Printed in China
First Edition. Printing Number and Year:
5 4 3 2   97 96 95 94 93
Library of Congress Catalog Card
  Number: 93-77081
ISBN: 0-696-01995-7

Co-Produced by Weldon Owen Inc.
President: John Owen
Publisher: Jane Fraser
Editorial Assistant: Jan Hughes
Production: James Obata,
  Stephanie Sherman

Manufactured by Mandarin Offset

MEREDITH CORPORATION

Corporate Officers: Chairman of Executive Committee: E. T. Meredith III
Chairman of the Board, President, and Chief Executive Officer: Jack D. Rehm
Group Presidents: Joseph J. Ward, Books; William T. Kerr, Magazines;
Philip A. Jones, Broadcasting; Allen L. Sabbag, Real Estate
Vice Presidents: Leo R. Armatis, Corporate Relations;
Thomas G. Fisher, General Counsel and Secretary; Larry D. Hartsook, Finance;
Michael A. Sell, Treasurer; Kathleen J. Zehr, Controller and Assistant Secretary

Our seal assures you that every recipe in the *Heritage of America Cookbook* has
been tested in the Better Homes and Gardens® Test Kitchen. This means that each
recipe is practical and reliable, and meets our high standards of taste appeal.
We guarantee your satisfaction with this book for as long as you own it.

WE CARE!

All of us at Better Homes and Gardens® Books are dedicated to providing
you with the information and ideas you need to create tasty foods. We welcome your
comments and suggestions. Write us at: Better Homes and Gardens® Books,
Cookbook Editorial Department, BB-117, 1716 Locust St., Des Moines, IA 50309-3023

If you would like to order additional copies of any of our books,
call 1-800-678-2803 or check with your local bookstore.

Cover: Apple-Cherry Pie
Page 1: Pralines, top left, Huguenot Apple-Pecan Torte, top right, and Southern Pecan Pie
Right: The Rio Grande cuts through Big Bend National Park, Texas.
Pages 4-5: Beef Pot Roast, left, Cream of Chicken and Wild Rice Soup, right, and
  Black Walnut-Wild Raspberry Bread
Pages 6-7: A windmill stands in isolation on the wide-open prairies of the Midwest.
Pages 10-11: Hot German Potato and Pea Salad, top, Corn on the Cob, left, and KC Barbecued Ribs
Page 12: Fried Green Tomatoes and Catfish Pecan

CONTENTS

Preface

The editors of Better Homes and Gardens® Books are proud to present the Better Homes and Gardens® *Heritage of America Cookbook,* a grand history of our country and its favorite foods.

Much more than a collection of recipes, this spectacular volume is brimming with lively historical details about the origins of our kitchens, cookbooks, restaurants, and traditional meals. Beginning with the pilgrims' landing, it tells the story of our nation's great waves of immigrants and their impact on American cuisine, and it traces our westward expansion, from the survival techniques of prairie cooking to the introduction of chuck wagons and hot chilies. Above all, in describing the evolution of such favorites as Dutch doughnuts, southern barbecue, and kosher corned beef, this book captures the melting pot of flavors and aromas that represent American cookery at its best.

Of course, you'll find exceptional recipes, too—more than 300 of them, all tested by the home economists in our own kitchens to ensure your success. With each recipe you'll find a tempting photo and additional historic detail, making this a book to use and enjoy time and time again.

We think the *Heritage of America Cookbook* will become one of your favorites, both as a cookbook and as an entertaining and informative glimpse at our nation's past. Come explore with us, region by region, as we present the best of our country's culinary history, all in this one special volume.

To all who love cooking and America's cuisine, we dedicate this book.

Introduction

The first English colonists set down roots in Jamestown, Virginia, almost four hundred years ago. Those early days were fraught with peril, but freedom and determination acted as fertilizer, and before long, hard work was rewarded with an abundant harvest and sufficient know-how to make life livable in the New World.

And a brave New World it was. Everything—from trees to game, from climate to soil—was totally new. To these tradesmen and farmers, the wilderness and its inhabitants offered no familiar comfort of home, and potential danger lurked beyond every hill and dale. This scenario of challenge and uncertainty was repeated decade after decade as settlers expanded westward, each group seeking to experience the life, liberty, and pursuit of happiness that America had to offer.

In the late eighteenth century, approximately ninety-five percent of Americans lived on farms and provided for the majority of their own basic needs by the sweat of their own brows. If they could afford it, frontier settlers purchased a few specialty items—such as sugar, coffee beans, and spices—from the general store, but the basic menu was composed of whatever wild foods and game were available, salted meat, and fruits and vegetables that had been put up by the overworked housewife.

In reality, however, travelers reported that there was rarely that much variety. Indeed, most typical frontier families ate a monotonous diet of cornmeal mush and a long-cooked stew flavored with bits of salt pork, cured ham, or bacon. More often then not, a makeshift coffee was made of roasted rye.

In his 1845 novel *The Chainbearers*, James Fenimore Cooper describes the typical fare of early Kentucky pioneers: "I hold a family to be in a desperate way when the mother can see the bottom of the pork barrel. Give me the children that's raised on good sound pork afore all the game in the country. Game's good as a relish and so's bread; but pork is the staff of life."

As each new wave of settlers and immigrants moved westward, they brought with them the recipes and cooking techniques of their childhood, adapting favorite dishes to locally grown foods and to the exigencies of life on the frontier. Over the years, as their lives moved beyond absorption with the basic necessities, regional styles of cooking evolved. Indeed, it can be said that the most characteristic dishes of a given area are chapters in the edible history of that place.

We've come a long way from the survival cooking of the early frontiersmen to the supermarket aisles overflowing with choice. Our original English culinary heritage has been blended into a complex "curry" with the spices of many nations. We have embraced with open arms not only French fries, but Italian pizzas and pastas, Swiss cheeses, Chinese wonton soup, and Japanese sushi. And when we take a break from cheering at that all-American game called baseball, it's a frankfurter we reach for, rarely remembering that this treat is in fact a German sausage.

The melting pot of American cookery has always been democratic, allowing every influence the right to make itself heard. The particular ingredients that get stirred into each regional cauldron are detailed in the chapters that follow.

Technology Takes Command

Over the course of the nineteenth century, America transformed from a nation of self-sufficient farmers to a nation with large and concentrated urban areas. By 1930, only

The early settlers found New England a hard garden to tend, with its rocky soil and harsh winters. But they adapted, and the land flourished.

The rise of commercial canning made home preserving less critical, but cooks still "put up" because it was economical and satisfying.

forty-five percent of our population remained on farms. This shift could not have taken place without technology: mechanization made it possible for the few to produce food for the many.

Numerous inventive geniuses made major contributions to this transformation. First there was Oliver Evans, a Delaware farmer's son who, in 1783, invented the fully mechanized grain mill. Evans also developed three types of conveyors which led to fully mechanized assembly-line production. Although the dehumanizing aspect of this system was ridiculed by Charlie Chaplin in the movie Hard Times, the assembly line ultimately enabled American consumers to enjoy the tremendous variety of packaged foods available today.

In 1802 in France, Nicholas Appert discovered the revolutionary process of preserving food by canning. Within two decades, the Englishman William Underwood brought this technique to our shores and opened America's first canning company on Boston's waterfront. Underwood's company began to "devil" its canned meats and seafood by adding special seasonings, and in

1867 registered the first American food trademark—Red Devil.

In 1833, Cyrus Hall McCormick brought forth his mechanical reaper, a machine that replaced the labor-intensive sickle and scythe. Over the next few decades, McCormick's factory produced thousands of reapers, the single

implement that opened up the American plains to large-scale farming. Many of the laborers displaced by the reaper turned from farm work to industry, many of them in turn becoming involved with the processing and distribution of food.

Early Entrepreneurs

When the California Gold Rush struck in 1849, San Francisco's population jumped from five thousand to thirty-five thousand in one year. The scramble for food brought out the competitive spirit in many an entrepreneur. One was Francis Cutting, who began packing pickles, and canning fruits and vegetables for hungry miners. His thriving company eventually came under the label of Del Monte.

Another purposeful businessman was Gail Borden, who first developed a highly portable concentrated meat extract called the Meat Biscuit. In 1858, Borden founded the New York Condensed Milk Company, producing concentrated milk in cans for those who no longer had access to the fresh product.

When the Civil War broke out in 1861, men like Borden were prepared to supply the Union Army with canned goods, and the entire industry expanded dramatically to meet the needs of troops on the move. When the war finally ended in 1865, the taste for canned goods continued to grow as urban cooks began turning away from home-processed foods to store-bought items.

Quick to jump on the convenience bandwagon was Joseph Campbell, who in 1869 began canning tomatoes in Camden, New Jersey. Before long, the company's line was expanded to include a range of condensed soups. Campbell's contemporary, the young Henry Heinz, took food manufacturing in a slightly different direction when he began bottling

From Hearth to Cookstove:
The Evolution of the American Kitchen

Colonial housewives and early frontier cooks had no choice but to endure the dangers and back-breaking work characteristic of open-hearth cooking (for a detailed description, see page 29). Among the earliest innovations was the cookstove, whose design was set in motion during the late eighteenth century by Benjamin Thompson, better known as Count Rumford. The Rumford stove was a primitive boxlike unit set over the fire, and Rumford's main contribution was the notion that efficiency of time and fuel was gained by containing the heat source in a restricted space. His original ideas were improved upon over the next century so that by the 1860s a stovetop and oven unit had replaced fireplace cooking in many parts of the United States.

The space and time efficiency of the stove inspired numerous female writers to extol its virtues and to introduce American women to the general concept of domestic science. In *Housekeeper and Healthkeeper*, published in 1874, Catherine Beecher claims, "After extensive inquiry and many personal experiments, the author has found a cooking-stove constructed on true scientific principles, which unites convenience, comfort, and economy, in a remarkable manner." Beecher describes the stove's workings in detail and diagrams the proper placement of sink, workspace, and storage areas for optimum efficiency. While the earliest cookstoves were fueled by wood and then by coal, by the 1930s cleaner fuels such as gas and electricity had become available.

The availability of refrigeration was also a great boon to the home cook. Although wealthy colonists like George Washington and Thomas Jefferson used ice for cooling drinks and preparing ice cream, few Americans in those early years could afford this luxury. A Maryland farmer named Thomas Moore patented the design for a refrigerator in 1803. This was actually an insulated ice box with room for food storage. As ice became more readily available, the concept of home refrigeration grew so rapidly that Eliza Leslie wrote in her 1840 *House Book* that refrigerators are "conveniences which no family should be without." Indeed, she recommends that if possible a family have two, one for meats and the other for dairy products. By the early 1900s, the fuss of dealing with ice was eliminated with the introduction of gas and electric models. By the 1940s, a refrigerator was as common in American kitchens as was running water.

As technology advanced, so did the lot of the American home cook. Appliances became more and more affordable and were streamlined to offer maximum service while taking up minimal space. Refrigerators and stoves were given porcelain enamel finishes, making them much easier to clean.

And there were gadgets galore! A few decades into this century, many middle-class housewives could boast of owning electric corn poppers, pop-up toasters, and electric waffle makers, coffee makers, and frying pans. Seeing all of these small electrical appliances on display at the New York electric exhibition of 1911, one observer commented, "The housewife and cook of the future, instead of feeling like a drudge in a smoky, smelly, overheated kitchen, will have the dignity of workers in a cool, clean laboratory for the scientific preparation of savory food and the abolition of dyspepsia."[1]

A nineteenth-century coal-fueled cookstove.

pickles, and horseradish in his Pittsburgh factory.

Meanwhile, during the final quarter of the century, following the completion of the transcontinental railroad in 1869, the improved efficiency of refrigerated railroad cars made it possible to supply the nation with perishable food. The men most responsible for providing fresh meat to the masses were two Chicago competitors named Gustavus Swift and Philip Armour. In addition, farmers on the West Coast began shipping fruits and vegetables to the East.

"TESTED"
for Every Baking Purpose

During this same period, advanced manufacturing and packaging technology gave birth to dozens of products that have since become household words. Minnesota millers at Pillsbury and Gold Medal sent forth premium flours in huge quantity all across the nation. R. T. French bottled his prepared mustard and Thomas Lipton boxed up his imported teas. Oscar Meyer began distributing old-world sausages and Joel Cheek presented Americans with his preblended Maxwell House coffee.

Rows of canned goods line the shelves of this general store. One of the first successful canned convenience products was baked beans in tomato sauce, developed by the Van Camp brothers in 1861. Bulk foods, like beans and pickles, sat in barrels and sacks. Top: This Gold Medal Flour advertisement appeared in a 1913 magazine.

From General Store to Supermarket

During most of the nineteenth century, Americans had purchased what they needed from bulk bins in a general store. As the century drew to a close, with the ever-increasing number of packaged foods, brand loyalty was born. To provide an animated link to factory-produced foods, clever manufacturers created such American icons as the Baker's Chocolate bonneted damsel (1892), Aunt Jemima (1893), Mr. Peanut (1918), and the Jolly Green Giant (1925). Perhaps the most famous icon of them all was the one invented by the advertising department of the Washburn Crosby company. Since Betty Crocker's "birth" in 1936, her portrait has been updated five times to stay in keeping with the times.

These attractively packaged foods were advertised in newspapers and the growing number of ladies' magazines. They began to sell themselves, obviating the need for any help from the local grocer. This fact was noticed by Memphis grocer Clarence Saunders, who opened the first chain of self-service Piggly Wiggly stores in 1916. This concept of retailing quickly attracted imitators, and within a few decades most Americans were doing their food shopping in supermarkets.

As a result, the American menu has irrevocably changed from a diet of salt pork and cornmeal mush to one of ever-increasing variety. Adding even further to the roster of consumer choice are the "frosted foods" developed by Clarence Birdseye and marketed as early as 1929. All of these boxed, canned, and frozen foods make out-of-season ingredients available year-round. While the advantages are obvious, a growing uniformity in the American diet has created a serious threat to our nation's fine heritage of regional cookery.

It is precisely to honor this fine heritage that this volume has been written.

Americans at the Table

After cutting each piece of meat, Americans have the peculiar habit of setting down their utensils and switching hands to lift the food to their mouths. While many explanations have been offered for this idiosyncrasy, the final answer may by revealed by an exploration of our early table manners.

When the colonists left England, even the most genteel of them were not in the habit of using that newfangled invention known as a fork. Like their ancestors back home, the early settlers relied upon the knife both to cut food and to convey it to their mouths.

Over the next two centuries, the fashion in England changed, and the fork gained almost universal acceptance. Therefore, when English travelers passed through the United States during the nineteenth century, they invariably expressed shock at the crudeness of American manners. One traveler described how Americans "plunged into their mouths enormous wedges of meat and pounds of vegetables, perched on the ends of their knives."[2]

The earliest forks had only two tines, then three, then four. By the time most Americans had the four-tined fork to deal with, they had found a way to incorporate this implement into their polite eating styles. But because the habit of cutting meat and raising food to the mouth with the right hand was already so firmly entrenched, they maintained the same practice for the cutting and switched hands and utensils for the lifting.

It's cumbersome, but it does get the job done.

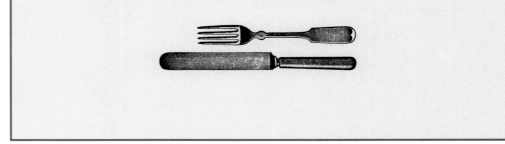

New England

hen the colonists first stepped onto Cape Cod shores in November 1620, they were arriving in a land of plenty. But the exhausted Pilgrims saw nothing more than "a hideous and desolate wilderness, full of wild beasts and wild men." Such was the description of Plymouth in those early years by William Bradford, later to become the town's governor. It was a description born of ignorance and short-lived, for by the time one year had passed, the newcomers were moved to express their gratitude for the New World's bounty at a Thanksgiving feast.

Like the majority of people, our founding fathers were not particularly eager to change their eating habits. Had they been able to continue enjoying a steady diet of roast beef and plum pudding, they would happily have done so. But America had neither cows nor wheat to offer, and with the threat of starvation ever present, the colonists of necessity began learning how to cultivate and prepare the unfamiliar foods they encountered — Indian corn, beans, pumpkins, cranberries, and maple syrup, to name but a few.

Previous pages: The white clapboard architecture of Marlow, New Hampshire, is typical of New England villages. One building was usually a church, another the town hall. Above: New England's rocky coast offered the Pilgrims their first glimpse of shore. The granite cliffs of Acadia National Park in Maine display their rugged beauty.

Since most of the first settlers had been tradesmen and artisans in England, they knew little to nothing about providing for their own sustenance. In a remarkable twist of fate, there appeared before them an Indian named Squanto who had learned English during a sojourn in Europe as an indentured servant. Squanto taught the pilgrims how to hunt for venison and wildfowl and showed them where to dig along the sandy beaches for the local clams, *poquauhocks,* which they came to call quahogs.

Perhaps even more important, Squanto demonstrated to them the sophisticated Native American way of cultivating rocky New England soil and maximizing the relatively short growing season. His method

involved embedding corn kernels in little mounds of earth and fertilizing each mound with small herringlike fish. In an early example of companion planting, navy (pea) beans were planted just to the side of the corn and their vines encouraged to grow around the stalks. This born-in-the-garden combination of beans and corn, flavored with a bit of nut oil or bear grease, was called succotash, derived from the Algonquian Indian word *sukquttahash.*

The three vegetables most common in Indian cooking—sometimes referred to as the "sacred sisters"—were beans, corn, and squash. Indian legends commemorating the miraculous powers of these foodstuffs are legion, and the Native Americans performed ritual corn dances during the growing season to implore benevolent spirits to grant them bountiful crops.

A staple of the Indian diet was the hoecake, a small brittle biscuit made of cornmeal and water that was baked in hot ashes (later on the blade of a hoe) until dry and brittle. Some historians believe that the colonists dubbed this long-lasting biscuit a journey cake since it was ideal travelers' fare. Over time, the name shifted to johnnycake and

Artist Jennie Brownscombe's 1914 impression of the first Thanksgiving at Plymouth, Massachusetts.

Thanksgiving

The tradition of celebrating the fall harvest was as familiar to the Pilgrims as it was to Chief Massasoit, the Wampanoag Indian chief who befriended the settlers during that first harsh winter in Plymouth.

The Pilgrims had come to America with memories of the Harvest Home Festival, an age-old celebration described by the sixteenth-century English farmer Thomas Tusser as a time when "harvest folk, servants and all . . . make all together good cheer in the hall." Such cheer was created by singing, demonstrating skills with firearms, and feasting on boiled or roasted beef, Yorkshire pudding, apple pies, cakes, and ale.

The Native Americans had a more solemn approach to the harvest. They held an eight-day corn festival to offer thanks to the Earthmother for her bounty. During this time, tribesmen brought gifts to their chief and contributed corn to the village granary.

Although different in approach, both celebrations shared the expression of gratitude for the harvest and the assurance it provided for sustenance during the long winter months ahead. In much the same spirit, it was quite natural for the Pilgrims and Chief Massasoit's tribe to join in offering thanks for the successful corn crop of 1621.

In truth, very little is known about what was actually eaten at this first Thanksgiving meal in America. Thanks to the diary of Pilgrim Edward Winslow, we do know that Chief Massasoit arrived with ninety men and was feted and feasted for three days. The menu included a wide variety of wildfowl and five deer. It is very likely that the roasted meat was accompanied by cornmeal porridge, sweetened with maple syrup and dotted with cranberries. Squash and beans probably played a significant role in the feast, and perhaps a simple quahog clam chowder provided warming sustenance on that cold November day.

As years went on, the colonists adapted these basic regional ingredients to their own tastes: they stuffed the turkey with breadcrumbs and oysters; stewed the cranberries with sugar for a sweet relish; and added milk, eggs, and maple syrup to the stewed pumpkin and created pumpkin pie. Indeed, by the time President Abraham Lincoln proclaimed Thanksgiving a national holiday on October 3, 1863, the Thanksgiving meal was well on the way to looking and tasting very much as it does today.

Thanksgiving Day card, circa 1900.

Above: Corn was a staple in the diet of Native Americans in New England. A bountiful harvest was cause for celebration.
Right: Most of New England is woodland, like this Vermont forest. Broad-leafed trees blaze with autumn color.
Below: Cooking implements like this spider pot were designed for hearth cooking. It stood on long legs above glowing coals scattered across the hearth floor.

the biscuit evolved into a pancake enriched with milk and sometimes sweetened with molasses. To this day, johnnycakes remain a popular Rhode Island specialty which connoisseurs insist be made only with local, stone-ground white flint corn.

Indian pemmican was another staple, both for travelers and for basic sustenance during the long winter months. An early regional form of jerky, pemmican was prepared by pounding salt-dried venison or other game with berries and melted fat, which acted as a preservative. The mixture was formed into coils and stored in animal skins until it was needed.

Such food was practical and well suited to the Native American way of life, but for the colonists the tastes were strange and the preparations unsophisticated. As soon as they were able, the early settlers established dairy herds to provide them with their dearly beloved butter and cheese. They coaxed the soil into producing their highly esteemed wheat and rye, grown from imported seed. And before long their kitchen gardens boasted a wide range of culinary herbs. Those who could afford them purchased expensive, imported spices — peppercorns, cinnamon, nutmeg, cloves, and ginger — to help

re-create the flavors of home.

Drawing from a cornucopia of local and imported ingredients, the colonial cook gradually transformed the simple foods of the northeastern Indians into the more complex dishes that have become trademarks of New England's regional cuisine. Succotash was embellished with some cubed squash and a dollop of butter, and seasoned with salt and pepper. A simple "mush" of cornmeal and water became a rich "hasty pudding" when some milk or cream was stirred into it. With the addition of rye or wheat flour and a dollop of molasses, the pudding was steamed in a cloth to create the famous Boston brown bread. Then, after the addition of a few eggs and a sprinkling of cinnamon — followed by a sojourn in the oven — Indian pudding was born.

Beyond a doubt, corn was a staple of the early American kitchen, but it must have come as a shock to the colonial housewife when she

The best home cooks didn't always write down their favorite recipes except in barest outline form, as they often knew them by heart.

The Cook's Library

It took a full twenty years after the signing of the Declaration of Independence for America to proclaim any form of culinary independence through the publication of a cookbook written by an American author—proof positive that political allegiances are more readily changed than gastronomic ones.

Before Connecticut-based Amelia Simmons wrote *American Cookery* in 1796, all of the cookbooks printed in the colonies and early republic were editions of titles written and published in England. For example, the first cookbook to come off American printing presses was the 1742 edition of Eliza Smith's *The Compleat Housewife.* Other titles soon followed, including Susannah Carter's *The Frugal Housewife,* brought out in Boston in 1772.

In addition to these early printed cookbooks, many a New England housewife kept her own handwritten "Book of Receipts." One such manuscript cookbook that survived the perils of the hearth fire is Mrs. Anne Gibbons Gardiner's collection of recipes, dated 1763. Mrs. Gardiner, the wife of a Boston doctor who divided his time between that city and central Maine, includes recipes for such typical English dishes of the period as mutton broth, anchovy sauce, pickled nasturtium buds, English "catchup," and "artichoak" pie. An occasional bow to the fact that she is west of the Atlantic—"In this Country, Bass and white, or silver Perch, seem to be as proper as any Sort of Fish to caveach [pickle]"—does not detract from the fact that hers is essentially an English cookbook.

Although Amelia Simmons's *American Cookery* also contains a vast majority of English recipes, it is clear that she wrote her slim volume to address the needs of the average cook of modest means, still struggling to make the best use of readily available (therefore inexpensive) Native American fare. To this end, she includes the following instructions for making pumpkin pie: "One quart stewed and strained [pumpkin], 3 pints cream, 9 beaten eggs, sugar, mace, nutmeg, and ginger, laid into paste [pastry crust] . . . and with a dough spur, cross and chequer it, and bake [it] in dishes three quarters of an hour." Amelia Simmons also offers recipes for winter squash pudding, "a nice Indian pudding," Indian slapjack, and johnnycake or hoecake.

Of fascination to food historians is the fact that her cookbook is the first to use culinary terms that clearly begin to distinguish American cooking from its English ancestry. She borrows the anglicized word *squash* from the Indians and uses it instead of the English *marrow.* She calls preserved watermelon rinds *American citron,* uses the term *molasses* instead of *treacle,* and refers to pancakes as *slapjacks.*

Amelia Simmons's is also the first cookbook to use an ingredient called pearlash in her cookie and gingerbread recipes. Pearlash, derived from the ashes of burned plants, is an ancestor to our modern-day baking powder. It produces the lightness in baking that we've come to associate with cookies, quick breads, and biscuits. In part through *American Cookery,* word of its use reached England and caused quite a stir—in the newspapers as well as in the batter!

Above: Mystic Seaport, Connecticut, a re-creation of a nineteenth-century New England coastal village, celebrates the region's seafaring past. Below: An early nineteenth-century watercolor, typical of New England folk art.

discovered that cornmeal did not yield a well-bred loaf no matter how hard she kneaded. (It is impossible to create a yeast bread of cornmeal because it lacks gluten.) Undaunted, she blended Native American know-how with Yankee ingenuity, and evolved a medley of corn-based baked goods. Anadama bread was a blend of wheat flour and cornmeal, with a healthy dose of molasses, while rye 'n' Injun was a yeasted loaf of cornmeal, wheat, and rye flours.

Two factors imposed culinary limits on all of this Yankee ingenuity. One was the austere influence of the Puritan founding fathers, and the other was the fact that the New England house-wife—unlike her south-ern sister—rarely had any household help. As a

result, the regional cookery of New England is characterized by frugali-ty and a pragmatic, no-nonsense attitude. It is food made delicious by the less-is-more approach, allow-ing the simple and direct flavors of quality regional ingredients to play center stage.

Traditional baked beans are sea-soned with just a bit of salt pork and molasses and slow-cooked in an

earthenware pot over Saturday night—originally prepared this way so that the Puritans could observe a labor-free Sabbath and still enjoy a hearty and nutritious Sunday meal. Then there is a clambake, a boiled Maine lobster, or a simple fish chowder that has the vibrant taste of the sea. Or there might be cod-fish cakes (salt cod, eggs, and breadcrumbs) and New England boiled dinners (corned beef and root vegetables), both of which make tasty use of foods that have skillfully been stored to last the long, cold winter.

And desserts, with fan-ciful names like grunts, slumps, and pandowdies, are really nothing more than fresh fruit baked into various forms of deep-dish pies. What could be simpler and more delicious?

At Plimoth Plantation, left, in Plymouth, Massachusetts, the Pilgrim's first settlement is reproduced down to a blazing hearthfire. During colonial times, pots hung at a distance above the fire for slow cooking, or sat directly over the coals for more intense heat. Above: A long-handled wooden peel was used to slide baked goods in and out of the deep recesses of colonial ovens.

The Early American Hearth

For those of us who turn a dial or press a button to cook dinner, it is difficult to imagine the hard labor involved in preparing a meal over a hearth fire. For the colonial American family, the kitchen was at the heart of the home, and it is no wonder! Not only did the fire provide needed warmth, but the cook no doubt had to do her mothering with one hand while stirring the pot with the other.

The first task was to light the fire under the chimney and wait for the coals to be red-hot enough to spread them out in little piles across the expanse of the brick or granite hearth. It is over these live coals that the skillful cook placed her three-legged Dutch ovens and spider frying-pans. Alternatively, if she wished to cook food over a very slow fire, she could reduce the heat's intensity by hooking the pot from an adjustable chain to a crane attached to the inside wall of the chimney. This crane operated like a gate, swinging to and fro over the hearth, allowing maximum flexibility for the placement of the pots. In this way, the cook could regulate heat by adjusting the pot's proximity to the glowing coals.

The hearth cook had various other time-tested tools at her disposal. She used firedogs fitted with iron spits of various sizes for roasting either a small pullet or a sizable joint of beef. Under the roasting meat, she would always place a dripping pan to catch the fat, and in this fat she might pour a frothy batter made of eggs, milk, and wheat flour to create a sizzling-hot Yorkshire pudding.

For even roasting, spits had to be rotated at even intervals and were therefore equipped with a handle at one end. In the more sophisticated colonial kitchens, mechanical devices were available for turning the spit. One was the clock jack, attached to the wall beside or above the fireplace. This was a type of vertical dangle spit with a large hook at one end for attaching the meat. The spit was rotated by the unwinding of a cord slowly released by the clock jack mechanism.

Lobster buoys decorate a shingled boathouse in Bernard, Maine, on Mount Desert Island. Lobster was once so plentiful that it was considered ordinary fare — the 1906 edition of Fannie Farmer's The Boston Cooking-School Cook Book *listed thirty-eight ways to prepare lobster.*

For roasting small birds, there was also a tin or copper reflector oven, shaped like an open half-cylinder, with a spit set horizontally in the middle. When in use, the open side of the roaster faced the fire so that the bird was quickly cooked by direct heat on the one side and reflected heat on the other. A little door on the closed side enabled the cook to see if the bird was "done to a turn" without moving the oven away from the fire.

Since hearth cooking was accompanied by a great risk of burning, the colonial housewife made certain that her long skirt was made of flame-resistant wool. To guarantee a safe distance from red-hot pots, all of her tools had long handles, including a wooden peel. Resembling the pizza peel used today, it was used to set breads and pies into the beehive-shaped oven built about six feet deep into the wall next to the chimney.

This oven was lit once or twice a week by burning wood inside it until the brick-lined walls were good and hot. The skillful cook judged the precise temperature according to the length of time she was able to hold her bare hand in the oven, and when the moment was right, she quickly swept out the ashes and used the peel to shove in the breads and pies for baking. She extracted a use for every last bit of heat, drying out fruit as the oven cooled and perhaps even baking some sugar-laced meringue kisses at the very end.

"Save your kisses for a slack fire," as the saying goes.

Fine Dining
At Boston's Parker House

*H*arvey Parker had a great love of fine food, and when he first opened the giant bronze doors of Parker House in 1855, he shocked proper Bostonians by importing a chef from France and paying him five hundred dollars per week. This was an exorbitant sum of money in the nineteenth century and easily twelve times more than any respectable chef was being paid at the time.

Parker lost no time introducing the new chef to a curious public—a public that before long included Henry Wadsworth Longfellow, John Greenleaf Whittier, Nathaniel Hawthorne, and Oliver Wendell Holmes. These distinguished gentlemen, all members of the Saturday Club, met weekly to discuss their literary concerns, to dispute the merits of the chef's aspic of oysters, and eventually to found *Atlantic Monthly* magazine.

Here are some of the dishes they might have sampled on a Saturday afternoon in the mid–nineteenth century: Wellfleet oysters, turtle soup, baked cod in claret sauce, leg of mutton with caper sauce, partridges with truffles and jelly, lobster salad, and Charlotte russe for dessert.

Noticeable by their absence are two New England classics often associated with the hotel's name: Parker House rolls and Boston cream pie. The precise origin of the rolls is lost in the mists of time, but the great event certainly occurred before 1865. Around that time, a baker named Ward brought to Parker's attention the plump, yeasty rolls that now go by the hotel's name. Anyone who has eaten a hot Parker House roll just out of the oven knows how memorable the experience can be, and the American public clearly agreed, for by the 1870s, the rolls were being shipped all over the country. (Indeed, a case can be made that Parker House rolls contributed to the American preference for soft, doughy white breads.)

*P*arker House on School Street in 1925.

And Boston cream pie? Parker House probably did not invent this well-known confection—not a pie at all, but two sponge cakes held together by a layer of rich custard. A recipe for sponge cake for cream pies appears in the *Boston Cook Book* of 1887 written by Mrs. D. A. Lincoln (Fannie Farmer's predecessor as principal of the Boston Cooking School). In 1932, however, Parker House improved upon the recipe by spreading a layer of chocolate icing on top, and dessert lovers have owed a debt of gratitude to this famous Boston hotel ever since.

Flavors from New England

Rhode Island

CLAMBAKE

Colonists cooked clams, lobsters, and oysters in rock-lined pits on the beach, a technique that hasn't changed much in three centuries. The modern clambake has expanded the menu to include chicken, corn, potatoes, and fish. This version bakes on a grill.

16   **large *or* 20 small clams in shells**
4   **9-ounce frozen lobster tails, thawed**
4   **cups parsley sprigs**
4   **large fresh ears of corn, halved, *or* 8 small ears of corn**
    Clarified Butter

Thoroughly wash, drain, and rinse clams in salt water (⅓ cup salt to 1 gallon water) three times. With kitchen shears, cut down both undersides of lobster tails; pull off thin underside membranes.

Tear off eight 2½-foot lengths of wide, heavy foil. Use 2 pieces of foil for each packet. Place *1 cup* parsley in center of each packet. Arrange one lobster tail, four large clams, and the corn on top of bed of parsley. Repeat with remaining ingredients. Drizzle Clarified Butter evenly over lobster, clams, and corn in the packets. Sprinkle lightly with salt. Seal tightly.

Place packets, seam side up, on grill directly over coals. Cover and grill over *medium-hot* coals for 20 to 25 minutes or till lobster is bright red and cooked and clams are opened. (Discard any unopened clams.) To serve, remove lobster, clams, and corn from packets to serving plates. Spoon juices over the seafood and corn. Serves 4.

Clarified Butter: In a saucepan melt ½ cup *butter* without stirring. When the butter is completely melted, slowly pour the clear, oily, top layer into a dish. Discard the milky layer left in the pan.

Nutrition information per serving: 500 calories, 35 g protein, 31 g carbohydrate, 28 g total fat (16 g saturated), 169 mg cholesterol, 852 mg sodium, 1,138 mg potassium

Maine

BOILED LOBSTER

Lobster was so plentiful in the earliest days of this country, that some settlers eventually refused to eat it. In fact, a group of Maine colonists called a strike in 1608 to protest the monotony of their diet: lobster, lobster, and more lobster.

6   **cups water**
1½   **teaspoons salt**
4   **6-ounce lobster tails**
    Clarified Butter (see recipe, above)

In a 3-quart saucepan bring water and salt to boiling. Add lobster tails; return to boiling. Simmer, uncovered, for 6 to 10 minutes or till shells turn bright red and meat is opaque; drain. Serve with Clarified Butter. Makes 4 servings.

Nutrition information per serving: 295 calories, 17 g protein, 1 g carbohydrate, 24 g total fat (15 g saturated), 124 mg cholesterol, 529 mg sodium, 289 mg potassium

Boiled Lobster, top, and Clambake

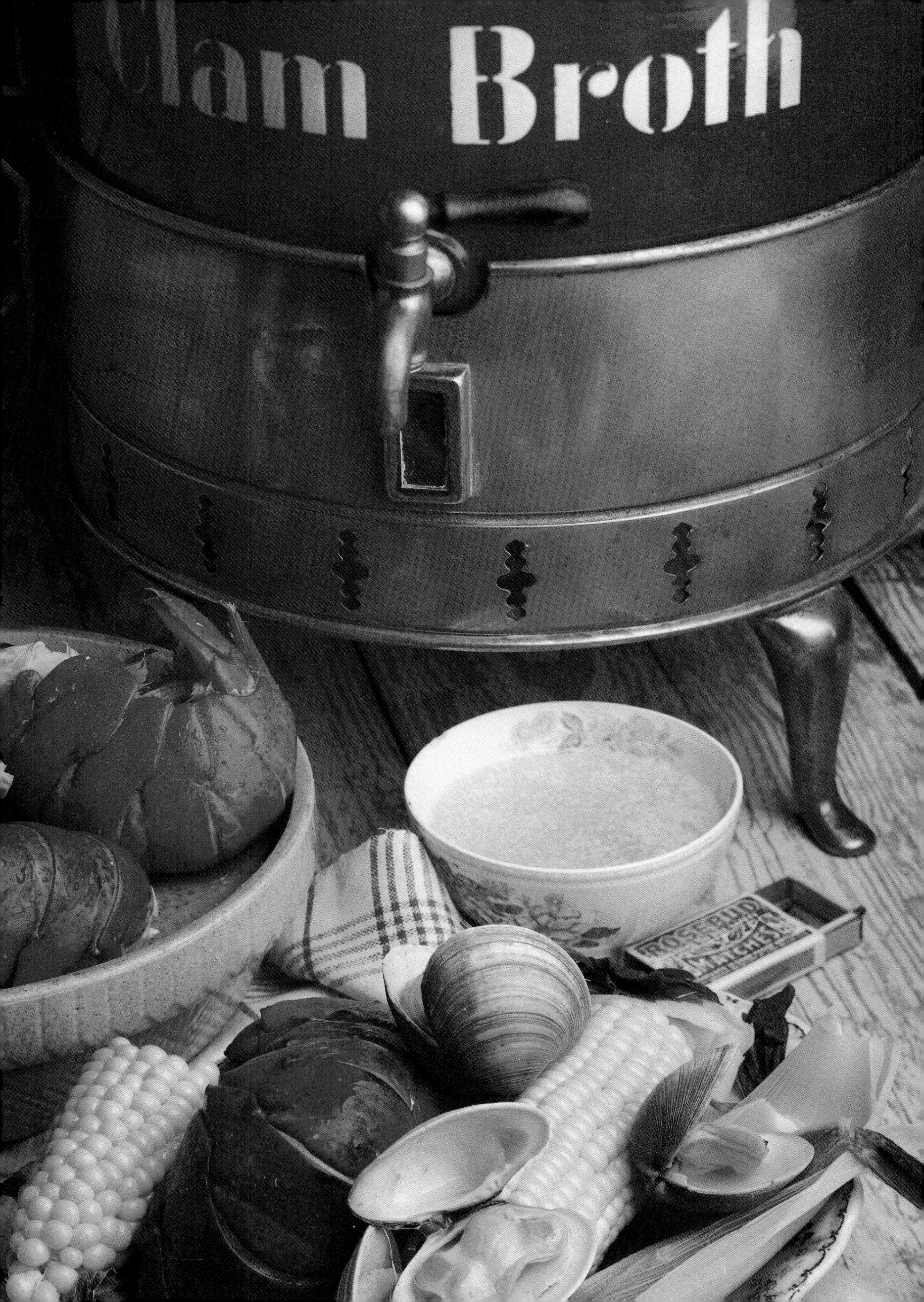
Clam Broth
ROSEBUD
MATCHES

Roasted Chestnuts

open. Discard any clams that do not open. Serve with sauce. Makes 8 servings.

Nutrition information per serving: 82 calories, 4 g protein, 2 g carbohydrate, 6 g total fat (3 g saturated), 22 mg cholesterol, 32 mg sodium, 133 mg potassium

New Hampshire

ROASTED CHESTNUTS

"Under the spreading chestnut tree the village smithy stands," wrote Henry Wadsworth Longfellow in 1842. These graceful trees, now diminished in number by disease, once flourished throughout New England. The nuts were roasted and eaten, and the wood was used for building.

Whole fresh chestnuts

Using a sharp knife, cut an X in the flat side of each chestnut. (This allows the shell to peel easily and prevents the nut from exploding during cooking.) Arrange nuts in a single layer in an ungreased baking pan. Bake in a 425° oven for 15 minutes, tossing once or twice. Cool slightly; peel and serve while warm.

Nutrition information per chestnut: 22 calories, 0 g protein, 5 g carbohydrate, 0 g total fat (0 g saturated), 0 mg cholesterol, 0 mg sodium, 53 mg potassium

Massachusetts

STEAMED CLAMS WITH HORSERADISH-DILL SAUCE

"Clams should boil about fifteen minutes in their own water; no other need be added, except a spoonful to keep the bottom shells from burning."
These simple directions appeared in The American Frugal Housewife, *a cookbook by a Boston woman named Child. The year was 1836, so it couldn't have been Julia; in fact, it was Lydia Maria Child.*

24   live clams
12   quarts cold water
1   cup salt
1   8-ounce carton dairy sour cream
2   tablespoons snipped fresh chives
1   tablespoon milk
1   tablespoon snipped fresh dill *or* 1 teaspoon dried dillweed
1   teaspoon prepared horseradish
    Snipped fresh chives (optional)

To clean clams, scrub them under cold running water. In a 4-quart Dutch oven combine *4 quarts* of the water and *⅓ cup* of the salt. Add clams and soak for 15 minutes. Drain and rinse. Discard water. Repeat twice. Rinse clams well.

Meanwhile, for sauce, in a small mixing bowl stir together sour cream, chives, milk, dill or dillweed, and horseradish. Cover and chill till serving time. Garnish with snipped fresh chives, if desired.

To steam clams, in the same Dutch oven add water to ½-inch depth; bring to boiling. Place clams in a steamer basket. Place basket of clams in Dutch oven. Cover and steam for 5 minutes or till clams

Maine

LOBSTER RISOTTO

Native Americans taught early New Englanders how to steam the huge lobsters that were so easily pulled from the Atlantic. The region's cooks continue to create new ways to enjoy this favorite shellfish.
(Pictured on page 36)

½   cup chopped onion
2   cloves garlic, minced
1   tablespoon olive oil *or* cooking oil

Steamed Clams with Horseradish-Dill Sauce

1   cup Arborio rice *or*
      long grain rice
3   cups vegetable broth *or*
      chicken broth
1   cup bite-size asparagus
      pieces *or* small broccoli
      flowerets
12 ounces cooked lobster,
      cut into bite-size pieces
¼   cup grated Parmesan cheese
3   tablespoons snipped fresh
      basil *or* parsley

In a medium saucepan cook onion and garlic in hot oil till onion is tender. Stir in rice. Cook and stir for 5 minutes to brown. Meanwhile, in another saucepan bring vegetable or chicken broth to boiling; reduce heat and simmer. Slowly add *1 cup* of the broth to the rice mixture, stirring constantly. Continue to cook and stir till liquid is absorbed. Add *½ cup* broth and the asparagus or broccoli to the rice mixture, stirring constantly. Continue to cook and stir till liquid is absorbed. Add

1 cup more broth, ½ cup at a time, stirring constantly till the broth has been absorbed. This should take about 15 to 20 minutes.

Stir in the remaining broth. Cook and stir till rice is slightly creamy and just tender. Stir in lobster, Parmesan cheese, and basil or parsley. Heat through. Serve immediately. Makes 4 servings.

Nutrition information per serving: 358 calories, 28 g protein, 43 g carbohydrate, 7 g total fat (2 g saturated), 66 mg cholesterol, 1,025 mg sodium, 654 mg potassium

Lobster Risotto, top (see recipe, page 34), Skewered Scallops and Swordfish with Fennel

---

Massachusetts

BROILED SCROD WITH LEMON BUTTER

Scrod is a young cod, under two pounds. "Scrod are always broiled, spread with butter, and sprinkled with salt and pepper," wrote Bostonian Fannie Farmer in The Boston Cooking-School Cook Book. *The simplest preparation is still the best for this very New England fish.*
(Pictured on page 40)

1½ **pounds fresh *or* frozen scrod fillets, cut 1 inch thick**
2 **tablespoons butter *or* margarine, melted**
1 **to 2 tablespoons lemon juice**
 Snipped parsley
 Lemon wedges
 Hot boiled potatoes (optional)

Thaw fish fillets, if frozen. Place in a single layer on a greased rack of an unheated broiler pan. Tuck under any thin edges.

Combine butter and lemon juice; brush fillets. Sprinkle with salt and pepper.

Broil fish 4 inches from the heat for 10 to 12 minutes or just till fish begins to flake easily, brushing occasionally with lemon-butter mixture. Brush again before serving. Garnish with parsley and lemon wedges. If desired, serve with hot boiled potatoes. Makes 6 servings.

Nutrition information per serving: 124 calories, 19 g protein, 0 g carbohydrate, 5 g total fat (2 g saturated), 57 mg cholesterol, 150 mg sodium, 219 mg potassium

Maine

SKEWERED SCALLOPS AND SWORDFISH WITH FENNEL

Although best known for lobster, Maine waters are a prime source for large-shell, succulent sea scallops. They're harvested all year, but are abundant in the warm months. Swordfish is strictly a warm-weather catch in New England.

½	pound fresh *or* frozen scallops
½	pound fresh *or* frozen swordfish steaks, cut 1 inch thick
1	fennel bulb, trimmed and cut into thin wedges
¼	cup olive oil *or* cooking oil
2	tablespoons lime juice *or* lemon juice
2	tablespoons finely chopped green onion
1	tablespoon snipped fresh thyme *or* ½ teaspoon dried thyme, crushed
1	teaspoon fennel seed, crushed
1	medium red sweet pepper, cut into 1-inch squares
8	small fresh mushrooms

Thaw scallops and swordfish, if frozen. Cut swordfish into 1-inch cubes. Cook fennel in boiling water for 4 minutes; drain and cool.

For marinade, in a plastic bag mix oil, lime juice, onion, thyme, fennel seed, and ¼ teaspoon *pepper.* Add scallops, swordfish, fennel, sweet pepper, and mushrooms. Seal bag. Refrigerate 1 hour, turning bag occasionally to distribute marinade.

Drain fish and vegetables, reserving marinade. On eight 12-inch skewers, alternately thread scallops, swordfish, fennel, sweet pepper, and mushrooms, leaving about ¼ inch between pieces. Place on the greased unheated rack of a broiler pan. Broil 4 inches from the heat for 5 minutes. Turn kabobs over and brush with reserved marinade. Broil 4 to 5 minutes more or till fish flakes easily with a fork and scallops are opaque. Serves 4.

Nutrition information per serving: 273 calories, 22 g protein, 7 g carbohydrate, 18 g total fat (3 g saturated), 38 mg cholesterol, 346 mg sodium, 797 mg potassium

Massachusetts

NEW ENGLAND CLAM CHOWDER

Clam chowder is one of the great dishes of this region, beloved by New Englanders since colonial days. In Moby Dick, *Herman Melville described its satisfactions: "the chowder being surpassingly excellent, we dispatched it with great expedition...."* (Pictured on page 42)

1	pint shucked clams *or* two 6½-ounce cans minced clams
2	slices bacon, halved
2½	cups finely chopped, peeled potatoes
1	cup chopped onion
1	teaspoon instant chicken bouillon granules
1	teaspoon Worcestershire sauce
¼	teaspoon dried thyme, crushed
2	cups milk
1	cup half-and-half
2	tablespoons all-purpose flour

Chop shucked clams, reserving juice; set clams aside. Strain clam juice to remove bits of shell. (Or, drain canned clams, reserving juice.) If necessary, add water to clam juice to equal *1 cup.* Set aside.

In a saucepan cook bacon till crisp. Remove bacon, reserving 1 tablespoon drippings. Drain bacon on paper towels; crumble. Set aside.

In the same saucepan combine reserved bacon drippings, reserved clam juice, potatoes, onion, bouillon granules, Worcestershire sauce, thyme, and ⅛ teaspoon *pepper.* Bring to boiling; reduce heat. Cover and simmer about 10 minutes or till potatoes are tender. With the back of a fork, mash potatoes slightly against the side of the pan.

Combine milk, half-and-half, and flour till smooth. Add to potato mixture. Cook and stir till bubbly. Stir in clams. Return to boiling; reduce heat. Cook 1 to 2 minutes more. Sprinkle with bacon. Serves 4.

Nutrition information per serving: 487 calories, 31 g protein, 43 g carbohydrate, 21 g total fat (11 g saturated), 112 mg cholesterol, 494 mg sodium, 1,276 mg potassium

Vermont

NEW ENGLAND CHEESE SOUP

The Vermont cheese industry dates at least to 1822, when the Crowley Cheese Company opened for business in rural Healdville. The state's justly famous cheddars have been used in soups like this one to satisfy Yankee appetites during the long, dreary New England winters. (Pictured on page 42)

½	cup chopped carrot
½	cup sliced celery
½	cup chopped red sweet pepper
¼	cup sliced green onion
¼	cup margarine *or* butter
⅓	cup all-purpose flour
½	teaspoon instant chicken bouillon granules
¼	teaspoon ground white pepper
2½	cups milk
1	cup water
2	cups shredded sharp cheddar cheese (8 ounces)
2	cups shredded American cheese (8 ounces)

In a saucepan cook carrot, celery, sweet pepper, and onion in margarine till tender. Stir in flour, bouillon granules, and white pepper. Add milk and water all at once. Cook and stir till bubbly. Cook and stir 1 minute more. Stir in cheddar cheese and American cheese till cheese melts. Makes 4 servings.

Nutrition information per serving: 697 calories, 34 g protein, 26 g carbohydrate, 51 g total fat (27 g saturated), 125 mg cholesterol, 1,488 mg sodium, 714 mg potassium

Irish Stew with Mint Sour Cream

In a small bowl stir together beer or water and flour. Stir into meat mixture. Cook and stir till thickened and bubbly. Cook and stir 1 minute more.

To serve, stir together the sour cream and mint. Dollop each serving with sour cream mixture. Makes 4 servings.

Nutrition information per serving: 327 calories, 23 g protein, 35 g carbohydrate, 10 g total fat (4 g saturated), 65 mg cholesterol, 625 mg sodium, 857 mg potassium

Massachusetts

PORTUGUESE SAUSAGE SOUP

Portuguese fishermen and sailors settled in New England coastal towns like New Bedford, Massachusetts, before the Civil War. They brought with them their spicy Iberian cuisine. Sausage soup is one of the best known of these recipes. (Pictured on page 42)

4	ounces hot Italian sausage links, sliced ¼ inch thick
4	ounces sweet Italian sausage links, sliced ¼ inch thick
½	cup chopped onion
2	medium potatoes, peeled and sliced
2	14½-ounce cans chicken broth *or* vegetable broth
1	10-ounce package frozen chopped spinach
½	cup beer *or* water
¼	teaspoon pepper

In a large saucepan cook the hot sausage, sweet sausage, and onion till sausage is browned and onion is tender. Drain fat. Add the potatoes, chicken or vegetable broth, spinach, beer or water, and pepper. Bring to boiling; reduce heat. Cover and simmer about 20 minutes or till potatoes are tender. Makes 6 side-dish servings.

Nutrition information per serving: 163 calories, 10 g protein, 14 g carbohydrate, 7 g total fat (2 g saturated), 18 mg cholesterol, 698 mg sodium, 504 mg potassium

Massachusetts

IRISH STEW WITH MINT SOUR CREAM

In the nineteenth century, Boston was the port of entry for untold numbers of European immigrants, particularly from Ireland, who fled poverty and starvation in hope of a better life. This famous meat-and-potato stew fortified the Irish of Boston and was adopted by New England as its own.

12	ounces lean, boneless lamb, cut into 1-inch cubes
2	cups beef broth
¼	teaspoon salt
⅛	teaspoon pepper
1	bay leaf
3	medium potatoes, peeled and cut into 1-inch chunks
2	medium onions, cut into wedges
1½	cups sliced carrots
½	teaspoon dried thyme, crushed
½	teaspoon dried basil, crushed
½	cup cold beer *or* water
2	tablespoons all-purpose flour
⅓	cup dairy sour cream
2	teaspoons snipped fresh mint

In a large saucepan or Dutch oven combine lamb, broth, salt, pepper, and bay leaf. Bring to boiling; reduce heat. Cover and simmer for 30 minutes. Skim fat off meat mixture. Add potatoes, onions, carrots, thyme, and basil. Cover and simmer for 30 minutes more or till vegetables are tender. Discard bay leaf.

Anadama Bread, left (see recipe, page 45), and New England Boiled Dinner

Massachusetts

NEW ENGLAND BOILED DINNER

A dinner of meat and vegetables boiled together became a New England tradition because it "cooked itself." Colonial women would let the combination simmer in an iron pot all day while they went on with other chores.

2   bay leaves
2   tablespoons snipped fresh
     thyme *or* 2 teaspoons
     dried thyme, crushed
1   teaspoon whole cloves
½   teaspoon whole black
     peppercorns
1   3- to 3½-pound corned beef
     brisket
8   cups water
3   small onions, halved
4   medium carrots *or* parsnips,
     quartered crosswise
3   small potatoes
     (about 12 ounces)
3   stalks celery, quartered
     crosswise
½   of a small head cabbage,
     cut into 6 wedges
     Mustard Glaze
     Snipped fresh thyme
     (optional)

For the spice bag*, cut a double thickness of 100 percent cotton cheesecloth into a 6- or 8-inch square. Place bay leaves, thyme, cloves, and peppercorns in the center of the cheesecloth. Bring up the corners and tie with a clean string.

Place corned beef in a 4- to 6-quart Dutch oven. Add spice bag and the water to corned beef. Bring to boiling; reduce heat. Cover and simmer for 2½ hours.

Add onions, carrots or parsnips, potatoes, and celery to corned beef. Return to boiling. Cover and simmer for 10 minutes. Add cabbage wedges; simmer, covered, about 10 minutes more or till meat and vegetables are tender.

Meanwhile, prepare Mustard Glaze. Drain meat and vegetables; discard the spice bag. Arrange meat and vegetables on a serving platter. Spoon Mustard Glaze over meat and vegetables. If desired, garnish with fresh thyme. Slice the corned beef across the grain. Serves 6 to 8.

*Note: If a spice packet is provided with the corned beef, use it instead of the bay leaves, thyme, cloves, and peppercorns.

Mustard Glaze: In a medium saucepan combine ⅔ cup packed *brown sugar,* ½ cup *vinegar,* ½ cup *prepared mustard,* and ½ teaspoon *garlic powder.* Bring to boiling, stirring till sugar dissolves. Cook, uncovered, for 5 minutes. If necessary, beat smooth with a wire whisk or rotary beater. Makes about 1 cup.

Nutrition information per serving: 487 calories, 27 g protein, 39 g carbohydrate, 26 g total fat (8 g saturated), 125 mg cholesterol, 1,755 mg sodium, 752 mg potassium

RATATOUILLE-TOPPED COD

The codfish is so intertwined with Massachusetts history that it appears on the state seal, and a wooden replica of the "Sacred Cod" has hung in the statehouse since 1784. Of course, Cape Cod got its name because so many of the fish swam in local waters.

1½	cups cubed, peeled eggplant
½	cup chopped green pepper
½	cup chopped red sweet pepper
½	cup chopped yellow sweet pepper
½	cup chopped onion
½	cup sliced zucchini
½	cup sliced mushrooms
3	cloves garlic, minced
2	tablespoons olive oil *or* cooking oil
3	medium tomatoes, seeded and chopped
½	teaspoon salt
1	tablespoon snipped fresh basil *or* ½ teaspoon dried basil, crushed
1½	teaspoons snipped fresh oregano *or* ¼ teaspoon dried oregano, crushed
¼	teaspoon pepper
1	pound cod fillets, cut into 2-inch chunks
¼	cup snipped fresh basil *or* parsley
¼	cup coarsely shredded Parmesan cheese

Broiled Scrod with Lemon Butter, left (see recipe, page 36), and Ratatouille-Topped Cod

In a large skillet cook eggplant, green pepper, red sweet pepper, yellow sweet pepper, onion, zucchini, mushrooms, and garlic in hot oil till tender. Stir in the tomatoes, salt, basil, oregano, and pepper. Cook, uncovered, for 15 minutes more, stirring occasionally.

Arrange fish chunks in the bottom of a greased 2-quart rectangular baking dish. Sprinkle lightly with salt and pepper. Spoon vegetable mixture over fish. Cover with foil. Bake in a 450° oven for 15 to 20 minutes or till fish flakes easily with a fork. Remove from oven and sprinkle with the ¼ cup basil or parsley and Parmesan cheese. Makes 4 servings.

Nutrition information per serving: *225 calories, 24 g protein, 12 g carbohydrate, 10 g total fat (2 g saturated), 52 mg cholesterol, 461 mg sodium, 704 mg potassium*

MAPLE-GLAZED TURKEY BREAST WITH ORANGE-PARSLEY STUFFING

Americans so appreciated the native wild turkey that Benjamin Franklin wanted to make it, rather than the eagle, the national bird. He described the turkey as "respectable" but dismissed the eagle as a "Bird of bad moral Character." (Pictured on page 43)

shredded *orange peel*; 2 teaspoons *dried marjoram*, crushed; 1 teaspoon *dried thyme*, crushed; 2 cloves *garlic*, minced; ½ teaspoon *salt*; and ¼ teaspoon *pepper*. Mix well. In a small mixing bowl stir together ¼ cup *margarine or butter*, melted; 2 slightly beaten *eggs*; ⅓ cup *orange juice*; and ½ cup *water*. Toss with bread mixture; if necessary, add more water for desired moistness. Spoon stuffing into a 3-quart casserole. Cover and bake in a 325° oven for 45 to 50 minutes or till heated through. Makes 9½ cups.

For a whole stuffed turkey: Prepare stuffing as directed, *except* do not bake in the 3-quart casserole. Double the amounts for the glaze and prepare as directed.

Rinse one 12- to 14-pound *turkey*, then pat dry. Season body cavity with salt. Spoon some of the stuffing loosely into neck cavity. Skewer neck skin to back. Spoon more of the stuffing loosely into body cavity. (Do not pack stuffing too tight or it will not get hot enough by the time the turkey is cooked.) Tuck drumsticks under tail skin or tie to tail. Twist wing tips under the back. Transfer any remaining stuffing to a casserole; cover and chill.

Place turkey, breast side up, on a rack in a shallow roasting pan. Insert a meat thermometer into the center of one of the inside thigh muscles. The bulb should not touch the bone. Cover turkey loosely with foil. Roast turkey in a 325° oven for 4½ to 5½ hours or till thermometer registers 180° to 185°. Cut band of skin between legs after 3½ hours. During the last 30 minutes of roasting, uncover turkey and brush turkey with maple glaze.

Bake casserole of stuffing alongside turkey the last 40 to 45 minutes of cooking time. When done, remove turkey from oven; cover. Let stand 20 minutes before carving.

To serve, remove the stuffing from turkey; transfer it to a serving bowl. Carve the turkey and serve warm. Makes 12 to 14 servings.

Nutrition information per serving: 576 calories, 41 g protein, 40 g carbohydrate, 27 g total fat (6 g saturated), 145 mg cholesterol, 782 mg sodium, 514 mg potassium

⅓ cup maple syrup
3 tablespoons Dijon-style mustard
1 tablespoon margarine *or* butter
2 teaspoons Worcestershire sauce
1 4- to 5-pound fresh *or* frozen whole turkey breast with bone, thawed
Orange-Parsley Stuffing

For glaze, in a small saucepan combine maple syrup, mustard, margarine or butter, and Worcestershire sauce. Cook and stir over medium heat till margarine melts. Set aside.

Rinse turkey; pat dry. Place turkey, skin side up, in a shallow roasting pan. Bake, uncovered, in a 325° oven for 2 to 2½ hours or till a meat thermometer inserted in thickest part registers 170°. Brush with glaze during the last 30 minutes of roasting.

While turkey breast is baking, prepare Orange-Parsley Stuffing. Bake stuffing, uncovered, alongside turkey during the last 50 minutes of roasting or till stuffing is heated through. Makes 8 to 10 servings.

Orange-Parsley Stuffing: In a large mixing bowl combine 10 cups *dry bread cubes*; 1 cup snipped *parsley*; ½ cup chopped *onion*; 4 teaspoons

Massachusetts

CRANBERRY-MAPLE SAUCE

Not only did Native Americans teach the Europeans to enjoy the meat of the wild turkey, but they also showed them that cranberries could be sweetened by boiling them with maple syrup, an approach which inspired the ultimate creation of cranberry sauce.

½   cup packed brown sugar
½   cup maple syrup *or*
     maple-flavored syrup
2   cups cranberries (8 ounces)
1   tablespoon shredded orange
     peel *or* lemon peel

In a saucepan mix brown sugar, maple syrup, and ½ cup *water.* Bring to boiling, stirring to dissolve sugar. Reduce heat; simmer, uncovered, for 5 minutes, stirring occasionally.

Add cranberries. Return to boiling; reduce heat. Simmer for 3 to 4 minutes or till cranberry skins pop, stirring occasionally. Remove from heat. Stir in orange peel. Serve warm or chilled with roast poultry, pork, or ham. Makes about 1¾ cups.

Nutrition information per tablespoon: 28 calories, 0 g protein, 7 g carbohydrate, 0 g total fat (0 g saturated), 0 mg cholesterol, 1 mg sodium, 26 mg potassium

Vermont

MASHED MAPLE SWEET POTATOES

In many areas of New England, maple syrup was often the only sweetener available to the colonists. Two common uses were to dress up sweet potatoes and to add flavor to beans. Today, Vermont leads the country in maple syrup production.

 New England Cheese Soup, top (see recipe, page 37), New England Clam Chowder, center (see recipe, page 37), and Portuguese Sausage Soup, (see recipe, page 38)

Maple-Glazed Turkey Breast with Orange-Parsley Stuffing (see recipe, page 40), Mashed Maple Sweet Potatoes, and Cranberry-Maple Sauce

3   medium sweet potatoes,
     peeled and quartered
¼   cup maple syrup *or*
     maple-flavored syrup
2   tablespoons margarine *or*
     butter
¼   teaspoon salt
¼   to ⅓ cup half-and-half,
     light cream, *or* milk

In a medium saucepan cook potatoes, covered, in a small amount of boiling water for 30 to 35 minutes or till very tender; drain. Mash with a potato masher or beat with an electric mixer on low speed.

Add maple syrup, margarine or butter, and salt. Gradually beat in enough half-and-half, light cream, or milk to make potato mixture light and fluffy. Pipe or spoon potato mixture onto serving plates. Makes 6 servings.

Nutrition information per serving: 151 calories, 2 g protein, 25 g carbohydrate, 5 g total fat (1 g saturated), 4 mg cholesterol, 166 mg sodium, 278 mg potassium

Connecticut

WHOLE WHEAT POPOVERS WITH SHALLOTS

In the nineteenth century, glazed ovenproof pottery molds known as Boston cups were manufactured for baking popovers. They resemble what we would call a custard cup today. (Pictured on page 44)

¼   cup minced shallots
1   tablespoon margarine *or*
     butter
     Shortening *or* **nonstick**
     spray coating
2   beaten eggs
1   cup milk
⅔   cup all-purpose flour
⅓   cup whole wheat flour
¼   teaspoon salt

In a small skillet or saucepan cook shallots in margarine or butter till tender. Set aside.

Using *½ teaspoon* shortening for each cup, grease the bottom and sides of six 6-ounce custard cups or the cups of a popover pan. Or, spray cups with nonstick coating. Place the custard cups on a 15x10x1-inch baking pan; set aside.

In a mixing bowl combine beaten eggs, milk, and shallot mixture. Add all-purpose flour, whole wheat flour, and salt. Beat with a rotary beater or wire whisk till the mixture is smooth. Fill the greased cups *half* full. Bake in a 400° oven about 40 minutes or till very firm.

Immediately after removal from the oven, prick each popover with a fork to let steam escape. If crisper popovers are desired, return popovers to oven for 5 to 10 minutes more or to desired crispness (be sure the oven is turned off). Serve hot. Makes 6 popovers.

Nutrition information per popover: 140 calories, 6 g protein, 19 g carbohydrate, 5 g total fat (1 g saturated), 74 mg cholesterol, 147 mg sodium, 128 mg potassium

Whole Wheat Popovers with Shallots (see recipe, page 43), and Cream of Baked Squash and Garlic Soup

Maine

CREAM OF BAKED SQUASH AND GARLIC SOUP

The colonists watched Native Americans rotate their crops to avoid depleting the soil. They followed suit: rather than planting only corn in the same field season after season, they alternated it with another vegetable, usually squash.

2 **medium acorn squash (about 3 pounds total)**

2 **to 4 tablespoons maple syrup *or* maple-flavored syrup**

4 **teaspoons margarine *or* butter**

1 **head garlic, cloves separated and peeled**

1 **carrot, cut into 1-inch pieces**

1 **onion, cut into wedges**

4 **cups chicken broth**

1 **cup whipping cream**
   Whole *or* snipped fresh basil leaves *or* Italian parsley sprigs (optional)

Cut each squash in half lengthwise. Scoop out and discard seeds. Place squash halves, cut side up, in a shallow roasting pan. Place *one-fourth* of the maple syrup and *1 teaspoon* margarine or butter in the cavity of each squash half. Arrange garlic, carrot, and onion around squash. Pour *2 cups* of the chicken broth in pan; cover tightly with aluminum foil. Bake in a 350° oven for 2 hours or till vegetables are very tender.

Remove pan from oven; let vegetables cool slightly. Scoop pulp from squash shells and stir into vegetable mixture.

Place *half* of the squash mixture in a blender container or food processor bowl. Cover and blend or process till smooth. Repeat with remaining squash mixture. Transfer entire squash mixture to a large saucepan; stir in remaining chicken broth. Heat and stir till mixture boils. Stir in whipping cream. *Do not boil.* Season to taste with salt and pepper. If desired, garnish each serving with basil or parsley. Makes 6 servings.

Nutrition information per serving: 305 calories, 6 g protein, 32 g carbohydrate, 18 g total fat (10 g saturated), 54 mg cholesterol, 608 mg sodium, 930 mg potassium

44

Massachusetts

ANADAMA BREAD

Was Anna a lazy wife who forced her fisherman husband to bake his own bread? As he slipped the loaf into the oven, he was said to have muttered, "Anna, damn 'er!" Or at least that's the story repeated most often about this famous recipe.
(Pictured on page 39)

½   cup cornmeal
⅓   cup packed brown sugar
1   teaspoon salt
1   cup boiling water
⅓   cup cooking oil
4½   to 5 cups all-purpose flour
1   package active dry yeast
1   8¾-ounce can cream-style
     corn

In a medium bowl stir together the cornmeal, brown sugar, and salt. Stir in the boiling water and oil. Cool mixture till warm (120° to 130°), stirring occasionally (allow approximately 15 to 20 minutes).

In a large mixing bowl stir together *1 cup* of the flour and the yeast. Add cornmeal mixture and cream-style corn. Beat with an electric mixer on low speed for 30 seconds, scraping the sides of the bowl constantly. Beat on high speed for 3 minutes. Using a spoon, stir in as much of the remaining flour as you can. Turn out onto a lightly floured surface. Knead in enough of the remaining flour to make a moderately stiff dough that is smooth and elastic (6 to 8 minutes total).

Shape dough into a ball. Place in a lightly greased bowl; turn once to grease surface. Cover and let rise in a warm place till double (about 1 hour).

Punch dough down. Turn out onto a lightly floured surface. Divide dough in half. Cover and let rest for 10 minutes. Lightly grease two 1-quart casseroles or a large baking sheet.

Shape each half of the dough into a round loaf. Place loaves in prepared casseroles or 3 inches apart on the baking sheet. Cover and let rise in a warm place till nearly double (about 40 minutes). Bake in a 375° oven about 40 minutes or till bread sounds hollow when lightly tapped. If necessary, loosely cover the bread with foil the last 20 minutes to prevent overbrowning. Remove bread from casseroles or baking sheet immediately. Cool on wire racks. Makes 2 loaves (32 servings).

Nutrition information per serving: 104 calories, 2 g protein, 18 g carbohydrate, 2 g total fat (0 g saturated), 0 mg cholesterol, 90 mg sodium, 42 mg potassium

Massachusetts

PARKER HOUSE ROLLS

Boston's Parker House was an instant success when it opened in 1855 because it introduced a radical concept: diners could eat there when they pleased, not just at specified hours. These soft yeast rolls that look like little purses are associated with this famous hostelry.
(Pictured on page 48)

3½   to 4 cups all-purpose flour
1   package active dry yeast
1   cup milk
¼   cup sugar
¼   cup margarine *or* butter
½   teaspoon salt
3   egg yolks
     Melted margarine *or* butter

In a large mixing bowl combine *1½ cups* of the flour and the yeast; set aside. In a medium saucepan heat and stir the milk, sugar, margarine or butter, and salt just till warm (120° to 130°) and margarine almost melts. Add to the flour mixture. Then add the 3 egg yolks. Beat with an electric mixer on low to medium speed for 30 seconds, scraping the sides of the bowl. Beat on high speed for 3 minutes. Stir in as much of the remaining flour as you can.

On a lightly floured surface, knead in enough of the remaining flour to make a moderately stiff dough that is smooth and elastic (6 to 8 minutes total). Shape into a ball. Place in a greased bowl; turn once to grease surface. Cover; let rise in a warm place till double (about 1½ hours).

Lightly grease baking sheets. On a lightly floured surface, roll dough to ¼-inch thickness. Cut with a 2½-inch round biscuit cutter, dipping the cutter into flour between cuts. Brush with melted margarine or butter. To shape, use a wooden spoon handle to make a slight off-center crease in each round. Fold large half over small half, overlapping slightly. Press folded edge firmly. Place 3 inches apart on the baking sheets. Let rise in a warm place till nearly double (about 30 minutes).

Bake in a 375° oven for 10 to 12 minutes or till golden. Remove rolls from baking sheets and cool on a wire rack. Makes 24 rolls.

Nutrition information per roll: 113 calories, 3 g protein, 17 g carbohydrate, 4 g total fat (1 g saturated), 27 mg cholesterol, 75 mg sodium, 45 mg potassium

Massachusetts

BOSTON BROWN BREAD

The Puritans served this steamed bread as a Sabbath dish along with baked beans, an inseparable combination for New Englanders even today. It is another of those early American "rye 'n' Injun" mixtures: cornmeal, wheat, and rye flours.

½   cup cornmeal
½   cup whole wheat flour
½   cup rye flour
½   teaspoon baking powder
¼   teaspoon baking soda
¼   teaspoon salt
1   cup buttermilk *or* sour milk
⅓   cup light molasses
2   tablespoons brown sugar
1   tablespoon cooking oil
¼   cup raisins *or* chopped
     walnuts
     Soft-style cream cheese *or*
     **flavored soft-style cream
     cheese (optional)**

In a large mixing bowl stir together cornmeal, whole wheat flour, rye flour, baking powder, baking soda, and salt.

In a mixing bowl combine buttermilk or sour milk, molasses, brown sugar, and oil. Gradually add milk mixture to flour mixture, stirring just till combined. Stir in raisins or chopped walnuts. Pour into a well-greased 7½x3½x2-inch loaf pan. Grease a piece of foil. Place the foil, greased side down, over the loaf pan. Press foil around edges to seal.

Place loaf pan on a rack in a 4- or 5-quart Dutch oven. Pour hot water into the Dutch oven around the loaf pan till water covers 1 inch of the loaf pan. Bring water to boiling; reduce heat. Cover and simmer for 2 to 2½ hours or till a toothpick inserted in the center comes out clean. Add additional boiling water to the Dutch oven as needed.

Boston Baked Beans with Pancetta, and Boston Brown Bread

Remove loaf pan from the Dutch oven; let stand 10 minutes. Remove bread from the pan. Serve warm. If desired, serve with cream cheese. Makes 1 loaf (14 servings).

Nutrition information per serving: 95 calories, 2 g protein, 19 g carbohydrate, 1 g total fat (0 g saturated), 1 mg cholesterol, 87 mg sodium, 204 mg potassium

Massachusetts

BOSTON BAKED BEANS WITH PANCETTA

While Boston gets the credit for this dish, it was actually popular throughout all the colonies. Since it could be made a day ahead, it was a favorite with those whose religion restricted work on the Sabbath. For a more traditional dish, use salt pork instead of pancetta or bacon.

1   **pound dry navy beans** *or*
     **dry great northern beans
     (2⅓ cups)**
8   **cups cold water**
6   **ounces pancetta
     (Italian bacon)** *or*
     bacon, cut up

1   cup chopped onion
¼   cup packed brown sugar
¼   cup molasses
¼   cup maple syrup *or*
     maple-flavored syrup
¼   cup Worcestershire sauce
1   teaspoon dry mustard
½   teaspoon salt
¼   teaspoon pepper
4   ounces pancetta *or* bacon,
     cooked crisp and drained
     (optional)

Rinse beans. In a 4½-quart Dutch oven combine beans and cold water. Bring to boiling; reduce heat. Simmer, uncovered, for 2 minutes. Remove from heat. Cover and let stand for 1 hour. (*Or*, skip boiling the water and soak the beans overnight in a covered pan.) Drain and rinse beans.

In the same pan combine beans and 8 cups *fresh water.* Bring to boiling; reduce heat. Cover and simmer about 1¼ hours or till tender, stirring occasionally. Drain beans, reserving liquid. In the same pan cook the 6 ounces pancetta or bacon over medium heat till slightly crisp. Add onion to bacon and drippings; cook and stir till tender. Add brown sugar. Cook and stir till sugar dissolves. Stir in molasses, maple syrup, Worcestershire sauce, dry mustard, salt, and pepper. Add drained beans and *1 cup* of the reserved bean liquid. If desired, transfer to a bean pot.

Cover and bake in a 300° oven for 2¼ to 2½ hours or to desired consistency, stirring occasionally. If necessary, add additional reserved bean liquid. If desired, sprinkle with cooked pancetta or bacon before serving. Makes 10 to 12 servings.

Nutrition information per serving: 239 calories, 10 g protein, 45 g carbohydrate, 3 g total fat (1 g saturated), 3 mg cholesterol, 241 mg sodium, 635 mg potassium

Creamed Succotash, left, Hearty Corn Chowder, top center (see recipe, page 48), and Cheesy Creamed Corn

Maine

CREAMED SUCCOTASH

Following Native American guidelines, the Pilgrims grew beans and corn so that the vines of one plant twined around the stalks of the other for support. The colonists borrowed from the Algonquian word sukquttahash *to give this dish its name.*

1   10-ounce package frozen
    succotash
1   tablespoon margarine *or*
    butter
1   tablespoon all-purpose flour
¾   teaspoon instant chicken
    bouillon granules
¼   teaspoon onion powder
½   cup milk
    Cracked black pepper

Cook succotash according to package directions; drain. Stir in margarine or butter till melted. Stir in flour, bouillon granules, and onion powder. Add milk all at once. Cook and stir till thickened and bubbly. Cook and stir 1 minute more. Sprinkle with pepper. Serves 3 or 4.

Nutrition information per serving: 154 calories, 6 g protein, 23 g carbohydrate, 6 g total fat (1 g saturated), 3 mg cholesterol, 320 mg sodium, 320 mg potassium

Connecticut

CHEESY CREAMED CORN

Corn graters were folk implements devised to speed up the job of removing the milky pulp from the kernels. With their rows of nails pounded into boards, they looked more like instruments of torture than kitchen helpers.

2   slices bacon, cut up
3   medium ears of fresh corn *or*
    1½ cups loose-pack, frozen
    corn
3   tablespoons water
2   tablespoons finely chopped
    onion
    Dash pepper
½   of a 3-ounce package cream
    cheese, cubed
1   tablespoon milk (optional)

In a small saucepan cook bacon till crisp. Remove bacon, reserving *1 tablespoon* drippings in saucepan. Drain bacon and set aside.

If using fresh corn, with a sharp knife cut corn from cobs about two-thirds down the kernels; do not scrape cob. (You should have about 1½ cups of corn.) Add the fresh or frozen corn, water, onion, and pepper to the saucepan. Bring just to boiling. Reduce heat. Cover and simmer for 5 to 7 minutes or till corn is crisp-tender.

Add the cream cheese to the undrained corn mixture in the saucepan. Stir over low heat till melted. If necessary, stir in the milk to make corn mixture of desired consistency. Sprinkle with reserved bacon. Makes 4 servings.

Nutrition information per serving: 138 calories, 4 g protein, 11 g carbohydrate, 10 g total fat (4 g saturated), 21 mg cholesterol, 126 mg sodium, 192 mg potassium

If using fresh corn, use a sharp knife to cut off just the kernel tips, then scrape the cobs with the dull edge of the knife. (You should have 3 cups corn.)

Place *1¾ cups* corn in a food processor bowl. Cover and process till smooth; set aside.

In a large saucepan cook onion and celery in hot oil till onion is tender but not brown. Stir in chicken broth and potato. Bring to boiling; reduce heat and simmer, covered, for 10 minutes. Stir in the corn purée and the remaining corn. Cook, uncovered, about 10 minutes more or till potato and corn are tender, stirring occasionally.

In a small bowl combine milk, flour, pepper, and ground red pepper; stir into corn mixture. Cook and stir till thickened and bubbly. Cook and stir 1 minute more. Stir in ham and cheese; cook and stir till cheese melts and soup is heated through. Garnish with parsley. Makes 5 servings.

Nutrition information per serving: 274 calories, 14 g protein, 36 g carbohydrate, 10 g total fat (4 g saturated), 23 mg cholesterol, 571 mg sodium, 604 mg potassium

Parker House Rolls (see recipe, page 45), Beet and Apple Salad, and Spiced Blueberry Jam

Rhode Island

HEARTY CORN CHOWDER

Like settlers in other regions, New Englanders noticed that the Native Americans used fresh corn for its meat and its liquid. Corn, a prime ingredient in substantial soups like this one, both thickened and extended the broth. (Pictured on page 47)

6   fresh medium ears of corn *or* 3 cups frozen whole kernel corn, thawed

½   cup chopped onion
½   cup chopped celery
1   tablespoon cooking oil
1   14½-ounce can chicken broth
1   cup cubed, peeled potato
1   cup milk
4   teaspoons all-purpose flour
⅛   teaspoon pepper
    Dash ground red pepper
½   cup diced, fully cooked ham
½   cup shredded sharp cheddar cheese (2 ounces)
2   tablespoons snipped fresh parsley

Maine

SPICED BLUEBERRY JAM

Maine is a prime supplier of both wild and cultivated blueberries. Of the two, the wild berry is smaller, with a more intense flavor. It also grows on bushes in mountain areas of New Hampshire and Vermont, there for the picking.

6   cups blueberries
2   tablespoons lemon juice
½   teaspoon ground cinnamon
¼   teaspoon ground allspice
    Dash ground cloves
7   cups sugar
1   6-ounce package (2 foil pouches) liquid fruit pectin

Crush blueberries. (You should have 4½ cups blueberries.) In an 8- or 10-quart kettle combine crushed blueberries, lemon juice, cinnamon, allspice, and cloves. Stir in sugar.

Bring to a full rolling boil, stirring constantly. Stir in pectin. Return to a full rolling boil. Boil hard for 1 minute, stirring constantly. Remove from heat; quickly skim off foam with a metal spoon. Ladle at once into hot, sterilized, half-pint jars, leaving ¼-inch headspace. Adjust lids. Process in a boiling-water canner for 5 minutes. Makes 9 half-pints.

Note: If you would like to use antique canning jars, ladle the hot jam into sterilized, half-pint jars, leaving ¼-inch headspace. Adjust lids; cool and then store in the refrigerator.

Nutrition information per tablespoon: 41 calories, 0 g protein, 11 g carbohydrate, 0 g total fat (0 g saturated), 0 mg cholesterol, 1 mg sodium, 9 mg potassium

Vermont

BEET AND APPLE SALAD

Beets turn up in many New England recipes, including the famous side dishes named after both Harvard and Yale and beet-tinted red flannel hash. Yankees also love apples of all varieties.

3   **medium beets (about 1 pound)** *or* **one 16-ounce can julienne beets, rinsed and drained**
3   **tablespoons salad oil**
3   **tablespoons white wine vinegar**
1   **teaspoon shredded orange peel**
2   **tablespoons orange juice**
2   **tablespoons sliced green onion**
1   **tablespoon snipped fresh mint** *or* **1 teaspoon dried mint, crushed**
1   **teaspoon honey**

Hot Buttered Cider Sipper (see recipe, page 51), and Cranberry-Banana Bread with Orange Butter

2   **cups torn romaine lettuce**
1   **coarsely chopped tart green apple (about 1 apple)**
    Fresh mint (optional)

In a medium saucepan cook fresh whole beets, covered, in boiling water for 40 to 50 minutes or till tender; drain. Cool slightly; slip off skins and cut into thin strips.

Meanwhile, for dressing, in a screw-top jar combine salad oil, white wine vinegar, orange peel, orange juice, green onion, mint, and honey. Cover and shake well.

In a mixing bowl combine beets and *half* of the dressing. Cover and refrigerate the beet mixture and the remaining dressing 2 to 24 hours.

To serve, in a mixing bowl combine torn romaine and chopped apple. Toss apple mixture with the remaining dressing. Using a slotted spoon, spoon beet mixture over apple mixture. If desired, garnish with fresh mint. Makes 4 servings.

Nutrition information per serving: 136 calories, 1 g protein, 11 g carbohydrate, 10 g total fat (1 g saturated), 0 mg cholesterol, 36 mg sodium, 258 mg potassium

Massachusetts

CRANBERRY-BANANA BREAD WITH ORANGE BUTTER

Cranberries were probably first known as "crane berries" because cranes living near cranberry bogs fed on the fruit. Later they were dubbed "bounce berries" because of the way ripe berries jump if dropped (bruised ones stay put). The marshy waters of Cape Cod are a prime source of this native wetland berry.

1½   **cups all-purpose flour**
¾   **teaspoon ground cinnamon**
½   **teaspoon baking soda**
¼   **teaspoon salt**
¼   **teaspoon ground nutmeg**
2   **beaten eggs**
1   **cup sugar**
¾   **cup coarsely chopped cranberries**
⅔   **cup mashed ripe banana**
¼   **cup cooking oil**
1   **teaspoon finely shredded orange peel**
     Orange Butter

In a mixing bowl combine flour, cinnamon, baking soda, salt, and nutmeg. In another bowl stir together eggs, sugar, cranberries, banana, oil, and orange peel. Add to flour mixture, stirring just till combined. Pour into a greased 9x5x3-inch loaf pan.

Bake in a 350° oven for 50 to 60 minutes or till a toothpick inserted near the center comes out clean. Cool 10 minutes. Remove from pan; cool on a wire rack. Wrap and store overnight. Serve with Orange Butter. Makes 1 loaf (18 servings).

Orange Butter: In a small mixing bowl beat ½ cup *margarine or butter* with an electric mixer till softened. Add 1 tablespoon *powdered sugar*, 1 teaspoon finely shredded *orange peel*, 1 tablespoon *orange juice*, and ¼ teaspoon *vanilla*. Beat till smooth.

Nutrition information per serving: 173 calories, 2 g protein, 22 g carbohydrate, 9 g total fat (1 g saturated), 24 mg cholesterol, 103 mg sodium, 53 mg potassium

BANANA-CINNAMON WAFFLES

In areas where sugar maples grew, colonists made maple syrup according to instructions from local Native Americans. Trees were tapped in the spring when the sap began to rise. Some of the syrup was allowed to crystallize into sugar, while another portion was reserved for maple syrup.

1¾ cups all-purpose flour
1 tablespoon baking powder
¾ teaspoon ground cinnamon
¼ teaspoon salt
2 egg yolks
1½ cups milk
⅔ cup mashed ripe banana
½ cup cooking oil
2 egg whites
   Warm maple syrup *or*
      maple-flavored syrup

In a large mixing bowl combine flour, baking powder, cinnamon, and salt. In another mixing bowl beat egg yolks slightly; beat in milk, banana, and oil. Add egg yolk mixture to flour mixture all at once. Stir just till combined but still slightly lumpy.

In a medium mixing bowl beat egg whites till stiff peaks form (tips stand straight). Gently fold beaten egg whites into flour-egg yolk mixture, leaving a few fluffs of egg white. *Do not overmix.*

Pour 1 to 1¼ cups batter onto grids of a preheated, lightly greased waffle baker. Close lid quickly; do not open during baking. Bake according to manufacturer's directions. When done, use a fork to lift waffle off grid. Repeat with remaining batter. Keep waffles warm in a 300° oven while cooking remaining waffles. Serve with maple syrup. Makes 4 or 5 waffles.

Nutrition information per waffle: 874 calories, 12 g protein, 137 g carbohydrate, 32 g total fat (6 g saturated), 113 mg cholesterol, 458 mg sodium, 627 mg potassium

Autumn Cider Syrup, Red Flannel Hash, Banana-Cinnamon Waffles, and Chunky Applesauce with Brandy (see recipe, page 52)

AUTUMN CIDER SYRUP

In rural New England, especially Vermont, sweet cider was boiled down into a syrup for many cooking uses, the most notable being cider pie.

2 tablespoons sugar
2 tablespoons brown sugar
¼ teaspoon ground cinnamon
⅛ teaspoon ground nutmeg
   Dash ground cloves
¾ cup apple cider *or* apple
      juice
2 teaspoons lemon juice
¼ cup apple jelly

In a small saucepan stir together sugar, brown sugar, cinnamon, nutmeg, and cloves. Stir in apple cider or apple juice and lemon juice. Cook and stir over medium heat till sugars dissolve. Stir in apple jelly. Bring to boiling. Reduce heat and boil gently, uncovered, about 25 minutes or to desired consistency. Serve warm with pancakes or waffles. Makes about ⅔ cup.

Nutrition information per tablespoon: 39 calories, 0 g protein, 10 g carbohydrate, 0 g total fat (0 g saturated), 0 mg cholesterol, 3 mg sodium, 30 mg potassium

8 to 10 minutes or till browned on bottom, turning occasionally. Stir in milk, and, if desired, hot pepper sauce. Makes 4 servings.

Nutrition information per serving: 290 calories, 13 g protein, 22 g carbohydrate, 17 g total fat (5 g saturated), 56 mg cholesterol, 887 mg sodium, 579 mg potassium

Rhode Island

HOT BUTTERED CIDER SIPPER

Most of colonial New England's apple crop went into cider, a very popular beverage. In the early days of this country cider meant hard cider, and every member of the family drank it. Cider mixed with rum was called a stonewall.
(Pictured on page 49)

1	quart apple cider *or* apple juice
3	tablespoons honey
2	tablespoons lemon juice
1	teaspoon whole cloves
1	teaspoon whole allspice
4	inches stick cinnamon, broken
¼	to ⅓ cup brandy
3	teaspoons butter *or* margarine
	Cinnamon sticks (optional)

In a medium saucepan combine apple cider or apple juice, honey, and lemon juice. For spice bag, place the cloves, allspice, and stick cinnamon in a double thick, 6-inch-square piece of 100 percent cotton cheesecloth. Bring the corners of the cheesecloth together and tie them with a clean string. Add spice bag to cider mixture.

Cover saucepan, and heat through but *do not boil.* Discard spice bag and stir in brandy. Ladle hot cider mixture into mugs; float about ½ *teaspoon* butter or margarine atop each serving. If desired, serve with cinnamon sticks as stirrers. Makes 6 (6-ounce) servings.

Nutrition information per serving: 149 calories, 0 g protein, 29 g carbohydrate, 2 g total fat (1 g saturated), 5 mg cholesterol, 25 mg sodium, 210 mg potassium

Vermont

RED FLANNEL HASH

While picturesque—the hash turns a rich red from the beets—this dish is strictly utilitarian. Corned beef left over from Monday's boiled dinner appeared in Thursday's hash. It is associated with Vermont, and its famous native son, Ethan Allen, and his Green Mountain Boys.

⅓	cup finely chopped shallots *or* onions
2	tablespoons margarine *or* butter
2	cups chopped, cooked potatoes *or* loose-pack, frozen, hash brown potatoes, thawed
1	16-ounce can diced beets, drained
1½	cups finely chopped, cooked corned beef *or* beef
¼	teaspoon salt
¼	teaspoon pepper
2	tablespoons milk
	Few drops bottled hot pepper sauce (optional)

In a large skillet cook shallots or onions in margarine or butter till tender. Stir in potatoes, beets, beef, salt, and pepper. Spread evenly in skillet. Cook over medium heat for

PUMPKIN SHORTCAKE WITH FALL FRUIT MEDLEY

When Benjamin Franklin served as America's representative to France, he was criticized by Connecticut newspapers for his reported extravagance. In reply, Franklin wrote in 1784 that plain Connecticut food like pumpkin, if available to him, would be better than "all the luxuries of Paris."

1¼	cups all-purpose flour
½	cup packed brown sugar
1	teaspoon pumpkin pie spice
½	teaspoon baking powder
½	teaspoon baking soda
⅓	cup buttermilk *or* sour milk
¼	cup shortening, margarine, *or* butter, softened
½	cup canned pumpkin
¼	cup honey
1	egg
½	teaspoon finely shredded orange peel
	Fall Fruit Medley
	Pumpkin Cream

In a large mixing bowl combine flour, brown sugar, pumpkin pie spice, baking powder, and baking soda. Add buttermilk or sour milk, shortening, pumpkin, honey, egg, and orange peel. Beat with an electric mixer on low to medium speed till smooth. Pour batter into a greased and floured 8x1½-inch round baking pan.

Bake in a 350° oven for 35 to 40 minutes or till a toothpick inserted near the center comes out clean. Cool in the pan on a wire rack for 10 minutes. Remove cake from pan. Split into 2 layers. Place bottom layer on a serving plate. Spoon *half* of the Fall Fruit Medley over bottom layer of cake. Top with *half* of the Pumpkin Cream. Place remaining cake layer atop and repeat fruit layer. Dollop with remaining Pumpkin Cream. Makes 8 servings.

Fall Fruit Medley: In a large skillet melt 2 tablespoons *margarine or butter.* Stir in ¼ cup packed *brown sugar,* ½ teaspoon ground *cinnamon,* ½ teaspoon finely shredded *orange*

Pumpkin Shortcake with Fall Fruit Medley

peel, and ⅛ teaspoon ground *cloves.* Cook and stir over medium heat till sugar melts and mixture is bubbly. Stir in 1 cup chopped *green apple,* ½ cup *apple cider or apple juice,* and ¼ cup snipped pitted *prunes.* Cook and stir for 5 minutes. Stir in ¼ cup *cranberries.* Cook and stir till cranberries soften and mixture becomes syrupy. Stir in ¼ cup chopped toasted *walnuts or pecans.*

Pumpkin Cream: In a medium mixing bowl beat 1 cup *whipping cream* and 2 tablespoons *sugar* till soft peaks form. Fold in ½ cup canned *pumpkin.*

Nutrition information per serving: 449 calories, 5 g protein, 55 g carbohydrate, 25 g total fat (10 g saturated), 68 mg cholesterol, 130 mg sodium, 230 mg potassium

CHUNKY APPLESAUCE WITH BRANDY

Apples have always been a favorite fruit of Yankee cooks. They baked them, turned them into pies or pastry-topped slumps and betties, fried them as a side dish, and, of course, cooked them down for applesauce.
(Pictured on page 50)

1½	pounds cooking apples (4 to 5 medium), peeled, quartered, and cored

⅓	cup water
3	to 4 tablespoons brown sugar
3	tablespoons apple brandy *or* apple schnapps
⅛	teaspoon ground cinnamon Dash ground nutmeg
2	tablespoons apple brandy *or* apple schnapps

In a large saucepan combine apples, water, brown sugar, the 3 tablespoons apple brandy or apple schnapps, cinnamon, and nutmeg. Bring to boiling; reduce heat. Cover and simmer for 8 to 10 minutes or till tender, adding a little more water if necessary.

Remove from heat. Mash with a potato masher or process in a food processor bowl to a chunky purée. Stir in the remaining apple brandy or apple schnapps. Serve warm or chilled; stir before serving. Makes 5 or 6 servings.

Nutrition information per serving: 130 calories, 0 g protein, 25 g carbohydrate, 0 g total fat (0 g saturated), 0 mg cholesterol, 2 mg sodium, 173 mg potassium

Massachusetts

CRANBERRY FOOL

Fool, an old English dessert of stewed, puréed fruit and cream, was popular throughout the colonies. One well-known version called for swirling crushed gooseberries through a hearty dollop of whipped cream, or mixing them with a rich custard. The use of cranberries is a New England adaptation.
(Pictured on page 54)

1½	cups whipping cream
2	tablespoons sugar
1	teaspoon vanilla
1	16-ounce can whole cranberry sauce

In a mixing bowl combine whipping cream, sugar, and vanilla. Beat with an electric mixer on medium speed till soft peaks form. Place the cranberry sauce in a large mixing bowl. Using a spatula, gently fold the whipped cream into the cranberry sauce till just combined (the mixture should be red and white). Cover loosely and refrigerate till serving time. To serve, spoon mixture into sherbet dishes, parfait dishes, or wine glasses. Makes 8 servings.

Nutrition information per serving: 252 calories, 1 g protein, 26 g carbohydrate, 17 g total fat (10 g saturated), 61 mg cholesterol, 33 mg sodium, 48 mg potassium

Vermont

DEEP-DISH APPLE PIE WITH CHEDDAR CHEESE CRUST

Apple pie was a fixture on New England breakfast tables. The ultimate was apple pie served with cheddar. As the saying goes, "Apple pie without cheese is like a kiss without a squeeze."

Cheddar Cheese Pastry Crust
½   cup packed brown sugar
2   tablespoons all-purpose flour
½   teaspoon ground cinnamon
7   cups sliced, peeled cooking apples
1   teaspoon finely shredded lemon peel
     Vanilla ice cream *or* frozen yogurt (optional)

Prepare Cheddar Cheese Pastry Crust; cover and chill for 30 minutes. Meanwhile, in a large bowl stir together the brown sugar, flour, and cinnamon. Add apples and lemon peel, tossing to coat. Transfer to a 9-inch, deep-dish pie plate, a 10-inch pie plate, or a 1½-quart casserole.

On a lightly floured surface roll chilled pastry into a circle 1 inch larger than the top of pie plate or casserole. Cut slits in pastry. Place pastry atop apple mixture. Seal and

Deep-Dish Apple Pie with Cheddar Cheese Crust, and Pumpkin Pie (see recipe, page 55)

flute to rim of pie plate. Cover edges of pie with foil. Place on a baking sheet. Bake in a 375° oven for 25 minutes. Remove foil and bake for 25 to 30 minutes more or till crust is golden and apple mixture is bubbly. Serve warm or cool. If desired, serve with ice cream or frozen yogurt. Makes 8 servings.

Cheddar Cheese Pastry Crust: In a medium mixing bowl combine 1 cup *all-purpose flour* and 2 tablespoons *sugar*. Cut in ½ cup chilled *margarine or butter* till mixture resembles coarse crumbs. Add ½ cup finely shredded *sharp cheddar cheese* (2 ounces), 1 *egg yolk*, and 1 tablespoon *ice water*. Mix just till combined. Form dough into a ball; flatten slightly. Wrap dough in clear plastic wrap and refrigerate for 30 minutes.

Nutrition information per serving: 305 calories, 5 g protein, 40 g carbohydrate, 15 g total fat (4 g saturated), 34 mg cholesterol, 152 mg sodium, 172 mg potassium

PUMPKIN PIE

For the early colonists the availability of pumpkin often meant the difference between survival and starvation. At first rejected as peasant food, pumpkin became an almost daily staple for settlers in the New World. Was pumpkin pie served at the first Thanksgiving? It's uncertain, but it soon became a colonial favorite. (Pictured on page 53)

1	16-ounce can (1¾ cups) pumpkin*
⅔	cup sugar
1	teaspoon ground cinnamon
½	teaspoon ground ginger
½	teaspoon ground nutmeg
3	eggs
1	5-ounce can (⅔ cup) evaporated milk
½	cup milk
	Pastry for Single-Crust Pie (see recipe, right)
	Whipped cream (optional)

For filling, in a large mixing bowl stir together pumpkin, sugar, cinnamon, ginger, and nutmeg. Add eggs. Use a rotary beater or wire whisk to lightly beat till combined. Gradually stir in evaporated milk and milk. Mix well. Set pumpkin mixture aside.

Prepare and roll out Pastry for Single-Crust Pie as directed. Line a 9-inch pie plate with pastry. Trim and crimp the edge of the pastry. With the pie plate on the oven rack, pour the pumpkin filling into the pastry shell.

To prevent overbrowning, cover the edge of the pie with foil. Bake in a 375° oven for 25 minutes. Remove foil. Bake about 25 minutes more or till a knife inserted near the center comes out clean. Completely cool the pie on a wire rack. If desired, serve topped with

Cranberry Fool (see recipe, page 52), and Gingerbread with Lemon-Butter Sauce.

whipped cream. Store, covered, in the refrigerator. Makes 6 servings.

*Note: To substitute fresh pumpkin for canned pumpkin, cut a medium pumpkin into 5-inch-square pieces. Remove seeds and fibrous strings. Arrange pieces in a single layer, skin side up, in a large shallow baking pan. Cover with foil. Bake in a 375° oven for 1 to 1½ hours or till tender. Scoop pulp from rind. Place part of the pulp at a time in a blender container or food processor bowl. Cover; blend or process till smooth. Place in a cheese-cloth-lined strainer; press out excess liquid. Makes 1¾ cups.

Nutrition information per serving: 357 calories, 8 g protein, 47 g carbohydrate, 16 g total fat (5 g saturated), 116 mg cholesterol, 238 mg sodium, 289 mg potassium

---

PASTRY FOR SINGLE-CRUST PIE

1¼	cups all-purpose flour
¼	teaspoon salt
⅓	cup shortening *or* lard
3	to 4 tablespoons cold water

Mix flour and salt. Cut in shortening or lard till pieces are the size of small peas. Sprinkle 1 tablespoon of the water over part of the mixture; gently toss with a fork. Push to side of bowl. Repeat till all is moistened. Form dough into a ball.

On a lightly floured surface, flatten dough with your hands. Roll out dough from center to edges, forming a circle about 12 inches in diameter. Wrap pastry around a rolling pin. Unroll pastry onto a 9-inch pie plate. Ease pastry into pie plate; do not stretch pastry.

Trim to ½-inch beyond edge of pie plate; fold under extra pastry; flute edge. Do not prick pastry. Bake as directed in individual recipes.

Baked Pastry Shell: Prepare as above, except prick bottom and sides of pastry generously with the tines of a fork. Prick where bottom and sides meet all around pie shell. Bake in a 450° oven for 10 to 12 minutes or till golden. Cool on a wire rack.

GINGERBREAD WITH LEMON-BUTTER SAUCE

The earliest forms of gingerbread were made by boiling bread crumbs with honey and ginger to create a thick paste that was pressed into loaves. The first American recipe for a cakelike gingerbread appeared in American Cookery, written by Amelia Simmons in 1796 and published in Hartford, Connecticut.

1½	cups all-purpose flour
¼	cup packed dark brown sugar
¾	teaspoon ground cinnamon
¾	teaspoon ground ginger
½	teaspoon baking powder
½	teaspoon baking soda
⅛	teaspoon ground allspice
½	cup shortening
½	cup light molasses
1	egg
¼	cup finely chopped crystallized ginger
	Lemon-Butter Sauce

Mix flour, brown sugar, cinnamon, ginger, baking powder, soda, and allspice. Add shortening, molasses, egg, and ½ cup *water*. Beat with a mixer on low to medium speed till combined. Beat on high speed 2 minutes. Fold in crystallized ginger. Pour into a greased and floured 2-quart square baking dish.

Bake in a 350° oven 35 to 40 minutes or till a toothpick inserted near center comes out clean. Cool 10 minutes. Serve warm with Lemon-Butter Sauce. Makes 9 servings.

Lemon-Butter Sauce: Mix ¼ cup *sugar* and 1 tablespoon *cornstarch*; add ¾ cup *half-and-half or light cream* and 2 tablespoons *butter*. Cook and stir over medium heat till mixture is bubbly. Reduce heat; cook for 1 minute. Remove from heat. Stir in 2 tablespoons finely chopped *crystallized ginger*, ¼ teaspoon finely shredded *lemon peel*, and 3 tablespoons *lemon juice*. Serve warm.

Nutrition information per serving: 345 calories, 4 g protein, 46 g carbohydrate, 17 g total fat (6 g saturated), 38 mg cholesterol, 96 mg sodium, 337 mg potassium

Maine

INDIAN PUDDING WITH SWEETENED WHIPPED CREAM

At first, Indian pudding was a plain, stirred cornmeal mush, like Italian polenta. As America left its infancy, it became more elegant. Nineteenth-century cookbooks offered numerous recipes for baked cornmeal puddings with spices, eggs, milk, and sweeteners.

1	cup milk
⅓	cup yellow cornmeal
2	tablespoons margarine *or* butter
⅓	cup molasses
¼	cup sugar
½	teaspoon ground ginger
½	teaspoon ground cinnamon
2	beaten eggs
1½	cups milk
½	cup snipped dried apples *or* mixed dried fruit bits
	Sweetened Whipped Cream
	Ground cinnamon

In a medium saucepan combine the 1 cup milk, cornmeal, and margarine or butter. Bring to boiling, stirring constantly. Reduce heat; cover and cook over low heat for 5 minutes. Remove from heat. Stir in molasses, sugar, ginger, the ½ teaspoon cinnamon, and ¼ teaspoon *salt;* mix well. Combine eggs and the 1½ cups milk; stir into cornmeal mixture. Stir in dried fruit. Transfer mixture to a 1-quart casserole.

Bake, uncovered, in a 325° oven about 1¼ hours or till a knife inserted near the center comes out clean. Serve warm or chilled with Sweetened Whipped Cream; sprinkle with cinnamon. Serves 6.

Sweetened Whipped Cream: In a chilled bowl beat ½ cup *whipping cream* and 1 tablespoon *powdered sugar* with a rotary or electric mixer till soft peaks form.

Nutrition information per serving: 314 calories, 7 g protein, 40 g carbohydrate, 15 g total fat (7 g saturated), 106 mg cholesterol, 215 mg sodium, 495 mg potassium

Indian Pudding with Sweetened Whipped Cream, top, and Maple Crème Brûlée

Vermont

MAPLE CRÈME BRÛLÉE

Thomas Jefferson's French chef, Julien, prepared crème brûlée, *burnt cream, for him at the White House. A salamander, a heated iron plate that functioned like a broiler, was used to caramelize the sugar on the top. Maple syrup links this version with New England.*

2	eggs, slightly beaten
1	egg yolk, slightly beaten
⅓	cup maple syrup *or* maple-flavored syrup
1	teaspoon vanilla
1	cup half-and-half
2	tablespoons sugar

Mix eggs, egg yolk, maple syrup, and vanilla. Stir in half-and-half, mix well. Divide mixture among four 6-ounce ramekins or custard cups. Place ramekins in a baking dish. Pour hot water into dish until it reaches halfway up the sides of ramekins. Bake in a 350° oven 35 to 40 minutes or till a knife inserted near the center comes out clean. Remove ramekins from baking dish; cool slightly. Cover with clear plastic wrap; chill at least 2 hours.

Before serving, place sugar in a small skillet. Cook over medium-high heat till sugar begins to melt *(do not stir),* shaking skillet occasionally to heat sugar evenly. Reduce heat to low; cook till sugar is melted and golden (about 5 minutes). Stir as necessary after sugar begins to melt. Drizzle over brûlée. Serve immediately. Serves 4.

Nutrition information per serving: 224 calories, 6 g protein, 30 g carbohydrate, 11 g total fat (5 g saturated), 182 mg cholesterol, 60 mg sodium, 136 mg potassium

Massachusetts

NEW ENGLAND CHOCOLATE CHIP COOKIES

Ruth Wakefield, proprietor of the Toll House Inn in Whitman, is credited with inventing the chocolate chip in the 1930s. She experimented by chopping up a chocolate bar and blending the bits into her butter drop-cookie batter. When the chocolate bits held their shape during baking, a new industry in chocolate morsels and chocolate-chip cookies was born.

1	cup shortening
2¼	cups all-purpose flour
¾	cup sugar
¾	cup packed brown sugar
2	eggs
1	teaspoon vanilla
1	teaspoon baking soda
1	12-ounce package semisweet chocolate pieces
1	cup chopped walnuts

Beat shortening with a mixer for 30 seconds. Beat in about *half* the flour, the sugars, eggs, vanilla, soda, and ¼ teaspoon *salt*. Beat in remaining flour. Stir in chocolate and nuts. Drop dough by rounded teaspoons 2 inches apart onto an ungreased cookie sheet. Bake in a 350° oven for 10 to 12 minutes or till edges are lightly browned. Makes about 60.

Nutrition information per cookie: 106 calories, 1 g protein, 12 g carbohydrate, 7 g total fat (2 g saturated), 7 mg cholesterol, 26 mg sodium, 42 mg potassium

New England Chocolate Chip Cookies, left, Joe Froggers, top center, and Chocolate Snickerdoodle Drops

CHOCOLATE SNICKERDOODLE DROPS

Several regions claim these crinkle-top sugar-and-spice cookies, but they are as firmly rooted in New England as anywhere else. The addition of chocolate is a modern variation.

½ cup margarine *or* butter
1 cup all-purpose flour
1 cup sugar
⅓ cup unsweetened cocoa powder
1 egg
½ teaspoon vanilla
¼ teaspoon baking soda
¼ teaspoon cream of tartar
2 tablespoons sugar
1 teaspoon ground cinnamon

Beat margarine with a mixer on medium to high speed 30 seconds. Add about *half* of the flour, the 1 cup sugar, cocoa powder, egg, vanilla, soda, and cream of tartar. Beat till combined. Stir in remaining flour. Drop by slightly rounded teaspoons 2 inches apart onto an ungreased cookie sheet. Stir together remaining sugar and cinnamon. Sprinkle dough with sugar-cinnamon mixture. Bake in a 375° oven 9 to 11 minutes or till edges are firm. Cool. Makes about 30 cookies.

Nutrition information per cookie: 76 calories, 1 g protein, 11 g carbohydrate, 3 g total fat (1 g saturated), 7 mg cholesterol, 35 mg sodium, 25 mg potassium

JOE FROGGERS

Are these the first of the giant cookies? Here's the story: Uncle Joe, who lived by a frog pond in Marblehead, made wildly popular molasses cookies that were as big as lily pads. Fishermen would barter for them—offering rum for cookies—because they were good keepers on long sea voyages.

¾ cup margarine *or* butter
4 cups all-purpose flour
1 cup sugar
1 cup molasses
2 tablespoons water
2 tablespoons rum *or* milk
1½ teaspoons ground ginger
1 teaspoon baking soda
½ teaspoon ground cloves
½ teaspoon ground nutmeg
¼ teaspoon ground allspice

Beat margarine with a mixer on medium to high speed 30 seconds. Add about *half* of the flour, and all of the remaining ingredients Beat till combined. Stir in remaining flour. Divide dough in half. Cover and chill for at least 3 hours.

On a lightly floured surface, roll *half* of the dough at a time to about ¼-inch thickness. Cut into circles with a floured 4-inch round cookie cutter. Place on a greased cookie sheet. Bake in a 375° oven for 9 to 11 minutes or till edges are firm and bottoms are just lightly browned. Cool on cookie sheet 1 minute. Remove; cool on a wire rack. Makes about 24 cookies.

Nutrition information per cookie: 199 calories, 2 g protein, 34 g carbohydrate, 6 g total fat (1 g saturated), 0 mg cholesterol, 88 mg sodium, 226 mg potassium

Boston Cream Pie

Massachusetts

BOSTON CREAM PIE

This "pie" is actually a cake: two layers of yellow sponge cake with a vanilla custard filling. Boston's Parker House hotel made its version famous by icing the pie with chocolate. Other recipes use powdered sugar instead of chocolate, or raspberry preserves in place of custard which is called Washington pie.

1	cup plus 2 tablespoons sifted cake flour *or* 1 cup sifted all-purpose flour
⅔	cup sugar
1½	teaspoons baking powder
¼	teaspoon salt
½	cup milk
¼	cup cooking oil
2	egg yolks
1	teaspoon vanilla
2	egg whites
¼	teaspoon cream of tartar
	Vanilla Pudding Filling
	Chocolate Glaze

In a medium mixing bowl combine flour, sugar, baking powder, and salt. Make a well in the center of the flour mixture. Add milk, oil, egg yolks, and vanilla. Beat with an electric mixer on low to medium speed till combined. Then beat on high speed for 3 minutes. Set beaten mixture aside.

Thoroughly wash beaters. In a large mixing bowl beat egg whites and cream of tartar on medium to high speed till stiff peaks form (tips stand straight). Pour the beaten mixture over the egg white mixture and gently fold in.

Gently pour batter into an *ungreased* 9-inch springform pan. Bake in a 350° oven for 25 to 30 minutes or till top springs back when lightly touched. *Immediately* invert the pan on a wire rack. Cool completely. Remove the cake from the pan.

To assemble, cut cake horizontally in half. Place bottom layer on a serving plate or board. Spread Vanilla Pudding Filling on top. Top with second layer. Pour Chocolate Glaze over cake and down sides. Store in refrigerator. Serves 8.

Vanilla Pudding Filling: In a saucepan combine ½ cup *sugar*, 2 tablespoons *all-purpose flour*, 1 tablespoon *cornstarch*, and ⅛ teaspoon *salt*. Stir in 1¼ cups *milk*. Cook and stir till thickened and bubbly. Reduce heat; cook and stir 2 minutes more. Set aside. In a bowl slightly beat 2 *eggs*. Stir *1 cup* of hot mixture into eggs; transfer entire mixture to the saucepan. Cook and stir 2 minutes more. *Do not boil.* Remove from heat. Stir in 1 tablespoon *margarine or butter* and 1½ teaspoons *vanilla* till combined. Cover surface with plastic wrap; cool. Makes 1¾ cups.

Chocolate Glaze: In a saucepan melt 1 square (1 ounce) *unsweetened chocolate* and 1 tablespoon *margarine or butter* over low heat. Remove from heat. Stir in ¾ cup sifted *powdered sugar* and ½ teaspoon *vanilla* till crumbly. Stir in 2 teaspoons *very hot water*. Stir in 3 to 4 teaspoons additional *hot water*, 1 teaspoon at a time, to a make a glaze of pouring consistency. Makes ½ cup.

Nutrition information per serving: 366 calories, 7 g protein, 55 g carbohydrate, 14 g total fat (4 g saturated), 111 mg cholesterol, 236 mg sodium, 148 mg potassium

New Hampshire

CHERRY-RASPBERRY COBBLER

One explanation for the term cobbler *is that the biscuit crust resembles the rounded tops of cobblestones. Raspberries grow wild throughout New England, especially in Vermont and New Hampshire.*

1   cup all-purpose flour
2   tablespoons sugar
1½ teaspoons baking powder
¼   cup margarine *or* butter
⅓   cup sugar
2   tablespoons cornstarch
1   10-ounce package frozen red raspberries, thawed
¼   cup water
1   tablespoon lemon juice
4   cups frozen, unsweetened, pitted, tart red cherries
1   egg
¼   cup milk
1   tablespoon sugar
¼   teaspoon ground cinnamon
½   cup chopped pecans
    Vanilla ice cream, half-and-half, *or* light cream (optional)

For biscuit topping, in a medium mixing bowl stir together the flour, the 2 tablespoons sugar, and baking powder. Cut in margarine or butter till mixture resembles coarse crumbs. Set aside.

For filling, in a medium saucepan combine the ⅓ cup sugar and cornstarch. Add thawed raspberries, water, and lemon juice. Cook and stir till thickened and bubbly. Stir in thawed cherries; cook and stir till bubbly again. Reduce heat and keep filling hot.

In a small bowl use a fork to beat together egg and milk. Add egg mixture all at once to the biscuit topping. Using a fork, stir just till moistened.

Transfer hot filling to an ungreased 2-quart square baking dish. Immediately drop topping mixture from a teaspoon into small mounds atop filling. Combine the 1 tablespoon sugar and cinnamon; sprinkle over topping. Sprinkle

Cherry-Raspberry Cobbler, top, and Berry-Apple Slump

with pecans. Bake, uncovered, in a 400° oven 20 to 25 minutes or till cobbler tests done. If desired, Serve warm with ice cream. Serves 6.

Nutrition information per serving: 402 calories, 6 g protein, 62 g carbohydrate, 16 g total fat (2 g saturated), 36 mg cholesterol, 162 mg sodium, 267 mg potassium

Maine

BERRY-APPLE SLUMP

A slump usually consists of dumplings dropped onto hot, sweetened fruit. If you live on Cape Cod, though, a slump is a grunt. Both are cousins to cobblers, betties, and pandowdies, all part of an extended family of whimsically named pastry-topped fruit desserts.

1   cup water
1   cup chopped, peeled cooking apples
1   cup fresh *or* frozen blueberries
¾   cup cranberries
⅔   cup sugar
¾   cup all-purpose flour
¼   cup sugar
1   teaspoon baking powder
¼   teaspoon ground cinnamon
⅛   teaspoon ground nutmeg
3   tablespoons margarine *or* butter
⅓   cup milk
    Half-and-half *or* light cream (optional)

In a 3-quart saucepan combine water, apples, blueberries, cranberries, and the ⅔ cup sugar. Bring to boiling; reduce heat. Cover and simmer for 5 minutes.

Meanwhile, for topping, combine flour, the ¼ cup sugar, baking powder, cinnamon, nutmeg, and ¼ teaspoon *salt*. Cut in margarine or butter till the mixture resembles coarse crumbs. Add milk to flour mixture, stirring just to moisten. Drop topping into 6 mounds atop hot filling. Cover and simmer about 15 minutes or till a toothpick inserted in the topping comes out clean. Serve warm; if desired, top with half-and-half or light cream. Serves 6.

Nutrition information per serving: 366 calories, 7 g protein, 55 g carbohydrate, 14 g total fat (4 g saturated), 111 mg cholesterol, 236 mg sodium, 148 mg potassium

The Middle Atlantic

Internationalism is a good word to describe the culinary character of the Middle Atlantic region. From the great melting pot of New York, arriving immigrants fanned out to New Jersey, Delaware, and Pennsylvania, bringing with them the favorite dishes of their childhood. Before long, new dishes were created by substituting New World ingredients for those traditionally used back in the old country. But in many pockets of the region, the direct influence of foreign cuisines—especially Dutch and German—is still keenly felt.

One of the earliest explorers of the area was the Englishman Henry Hudson, who in 1609 sailed up the river that now bears his name. In the employ of the Dutch East India Company, Hudson bartered cloth and gin for the highly prized fur and tobacco offered by the native Algonquian Indians. Word of the New World's riches quickly traveled back to Holland, and droves of traders arrived with dispatch, followed by the first group of settlers in 1623. It took only three more years for the enterprising Dutch to purchase Manhattan Island from its native inhabitants for an estimated twenty-four dollars worth of trinkets.

Previous pages: What is now Delaware, including idyllic Trussam Pond, was once part of Pennsylvania. In 1682 Charles II of England granted this land to William Penn, who needed coastline for his colony. Above: An Amish farmer, plainly dressed in dark colors and protected from the sun with a wide-brimmed hat, plows his field behind a team of horses. His strict sect turns its back on twentieth-century technology like tractors.

As a result of Hudson's exploration, the Dutch claimed a vast tract of land that stretched from New England as far south as Virginia. Over the next sixty years, they were in constant conflict with the English over rights to this territory, until England won in 1674 and the colony called New Netherland was dissolved forever.

Despite their relatively short tenure as a political power in this country, the Dutch left a lasting impression on our kitchens. The settlers brought with them the grains and cereals they so loved to eat: wheat, rye, oats, barley, and buckwheat. They were diligent farmers and before long were harvesting fine crops for the hearty whole-grain breads that formed a staple of their diet. But some of the grain came to other ends, as nostalgically described by Washington Irving in "The Legend of Sleepy Hollow": "Fragrant buckwheat fields caused soft anticipations in the mind of dainty slapjacks, well buttered, and garnished with honey or treacle . . . by the delicate little dimpled hand of Katrina van Tassel."

Aside from pancakes, the Dutch introduced this country to a number of other grain-based specialties that we take for granted as "all-American." They arrived with waffle irons for making their beloved

Pennsylvania Dutch tinware, like this exuberantly decorated coffeepot, was both practical and whimsical.

waffles, and wafering irons for preparing thin, crisp wafers. Dutch cooks frequently prepared sweet little cakes they referred to as *koekjes,* which gave us our word *cookies.*

The Dutch were fond of desserts, and as Washington Irving reminds us in his 1809 *A History of New York,* they were responsible for bringing the doughnut to these shores: "Sometimes the table was graced with immense apple pies, or saucers full of preserved peaches and pears; but it was always sure to boast an enormous dish of balls of sweetened dough, fried in hog's fat, and called dough nuts, or oly koeks—a delicious kind of cake, at present, scarce known in this city, excepting in genuine dutch [sic] families; but which retains its pre-eminent station at the tea tables in Albany [New York]."

Like the settlers in New England, the Dutch soon learned to appreciate Indian pumpkin and corn. For a breakfast treat, they might stir stewed pumpkin into

If the original Dutch settlers could visit "New Netherland" today they would find this rural landscape somewhat familiar. On the other hand, they'd never recognize their once-bucolic Manhattan Island.

batter to make pumpkin pancakes, but an even greater favorite was the cornmeal mush they called by the Delaware Indian name *sappaen*. They often breakfasted on huge bowls of *sappaen* served with deep wells of buttermilk in the center, and contemporary travelers frequently commented on the Dutch love of milk, butter, and cheese.

The other great Dutch culinary legacy is coleslaw, or *kool sla,* as they called it. When the Swedish traveler Peter Kalm first tasted this unusual dish on his travels through America in 1749, he described it as "an unusual salad [which] tastes better than one can imagine. [It is made of] cab-bage . . . cut in long thin strips and dressed with oil, vinegar, salt, and pepper."[1] It is remarkable how little the recipe has changed over the last two hundred years.

While it was the Dutch who left a strong imprint in colonial New York, it was the Germans who had a profound effect on the cooking of eastern Pennsylvania. Known as the Pennsylvania Dutch (a corrupted form of the word *Deutsch,* which means German), these settlers were mostly Rhineland farmers whose meals were simple and hearty. Many of the staple dishes of the Pennsylvania Dutch are related to the butchering of hogs and the imagi-native use of every part of the animal's anatomy. The pigs' head and feet are put to practical use in the preparation of head cheese, a type of sausage made of the cooked meat from these parts doused with vinegar and spices and molded into a loaf.

To make a well-known regional dish called scrapple, a rich broth is thickened with cornmeal and studded with bits of pork, then left to cool. Then it is sliced and fried like sausage. Pigs' knuckles with sauerkraut dumplings is a typical soup, as is *schnitz un knepp,* made by boiling smoked ham with dried apples.

Providing a nice counterpoint to this straightforward fare were the

By the end of the eighteenth century, the farms of the Middle Atlantic states were prospering. Grist mills like this one preserved as part of the Clinton (New Jersey) Historical Museum Village were built to process the bounty. Below: As America became more urban and the railroads made coast to coast transportation of perishable goods possible, the family pantry no longer was stocked from the family farm. The demand increased for processed and packaged goods.

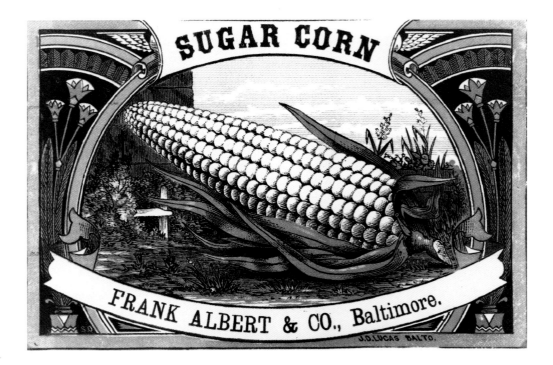

Pennsylvania Dutch sweets and sours, the pickles and preserves that traditionally accompanied the main meal. Made of both fruits and vegetables, a medley served in separate bowls might include spiced Seckel pears, pickled cantaloupe and watermelon rind, and pepper relish, a mixture of chopped green and red peppers, shredded cabbage, and onions, doused with vinegar, spices, and brown sugar.

With such a legacy offered by his countrymen, it should come as no surprise that a young man from the area began peddling his pickles and his wife's renowned catsup in the nearby city of Pittsburgh. His name was Henry Heinz.

America Dines Out

Imagine the relief of the weary colonial traveler when he came upon a sign that read "Drink for the thirsty, food for the hungry, lodging for the weary, and good keeping for horses." The earliest eating establishments in America were taverns, where the guest might enjoy a simple grilled chop or a venison stew and then run up a bill in the taproom while sipping rum punch or mulled cider. Another popular drink called flip—a combination of beer and rum—was heated by a hot poker known as a loggerhead. The loggerhead sometimes doubled as a weapon in arguments, hence the expression to be "at loggerheads" with someone. To protect against pilfering during the night, all of the alcoholic beverages in the tavern were locked behind wooden bars, which is precisely why we use the word *bar* to refer to drinking establishments today.

In the banner year of 1794, the City Hotel in New York opened its doors, offering diners the novelty of a meal without the necessity of being an overnight guest. The concept grew, and by the late 1820s, urban easterners found themselves with a wide choice of dining establishments. Most popular were chop and steak houses, a concept borrowed from the British. Oyster houses offered briny bivalves either fresh on the half shell or panfried.

The dining-out experience in American restaurants until the mid–nineteenth century was crude and boisterous, what one early observer described as an experience of "gobble, gulp, and go." The Swiss Delmonico brothers set about changing that phenomenon by teaching the public what the words *fine dining* meant. Opening their first restaurant in 1831, they hired a French chef, set the tables with impeccably clean white linen cloths and fine china, and proceeded to set

Ben Franklin at the Table

Like his contemporary Thomas Jefferson, Benjamin Franklin was interested in just about everything. Often referred to as "The Sage of Philadelphia," this author, statesman, and scientist took a keen interest in food—such a keen interest that he spent a certain amount of time examining the relationship of diet and health. For much of his life he aimed toward balance and moderation, advising his wife Deborah to "let not thy Table exceed the fourth Part of thy Income; see thy Provision be solid, and not far fetched, fuller of Substance than of Art; be wisely frugal in thy Preparation, and freely chearful in thy entertainment."[2]

In *Poor Richard's Almanac*, he returns to the subject with regularity, suggesting the following in the year 1742:

★ Eat and drink such an exact Quantity as the Constitution of thy Body allows of, in reference to the Services of the Mind.

★ They that study much, ought not to eat so much as those that work hard, their Digestion being not so good.

★ The exact Quantity and Quality being found out, is to be kept to constantly.

★ Youth, Age, and Sick require a different Quantity . . .

★ The Measure of Food ought to be (as much as possibly may be) exactly proportionate to the Quality and Condition of the Stomach, because the Stomach digests it . . .

★ The Difficulty lies, in finding out an exact Measure; but eat for Necessity, not Pleasure, for Lust knows not where Necessity ends.[3]

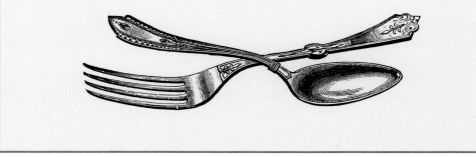

Jewish delicatessens flourished in urban centers like New York's Lower East Side.

The Great Nosh

Between 1880 and 1924, more than 2 million Jews left Germany and eastern Europe for the United States, and the great majority of them settled in New York. They left a unique and enduring gastronomic legacy fondly referred to as the New York Deli.

Dining in an authentic New York kosher deli was a unique experience. Of course, you can order what the late comedian Sam Levenson referred to as Yiddish K rations: kasha (buckwheat groats), kugel (noodle or potato pudding), kishke (stuffed cow's intestine), and knaidel soup (chicken broth with matzoh ball dumplings). But more likely you'll have a corned beef or a hot pastrami sandwich on rye and wash it down with Dr. Brown's Cel-Ray soda. But what makes eating that sandwich truly memorable is the sixty-year-old Jewish waiter who shuffles on tired feet, wears grease-smudged glasses, and barks in your ear with a strong Yiddish accent.

He commands you where to sit ("That's the only table we got left; you want to eat, or don't you?"), stands as the moral arbiter of right and wrong ("If you want sauerkraut on your pastrami sandwich, you'll have to put it on yourself; it makes the bread soggy"), slides the sandwich-laden plates to you as if he were practicing for the bowling league, and then tells you when it's time to leave ("Did you come to eat or to sit?").

This kind of banter was what the old-timers affectionately referred to as the corned beef cabaret. For example, once a customer in the Stage Delicatessen was overheard complaining to a waiter, "I don't like the looks of this whitefish." "You want looks," quipped the waiter, "order a goldfish." Another time, a group of tourists ordered sandwiches and coffee. One man commanded, "And make sure that my coffee is in an absolutely clean cup." When the waiter returned with the order, before placing the sandwiches and coffee on the table, he inquired, "Now which one of you gets the clean cup?"[4]

Although you can still get a mighty fine corned beef sandwich in many New York delis—so stuffed it will be hard to get your jaw around it—it's the old Yiddish waiters and their chutzpah that have gone the way of the hula-hoop.

standards of elegance for this country. Delmonico's menu from the start was à la carte and within a decade was offering more than 350 entrées.

The Delmonico's steak had special renown. It was prepared by pounding and then coating a two-inch-thick sirloin with melted butter and a sprinkling of salt. The steak was broiled for a precise fourteen minutes, but the secret of success was as much due to the fine quality and aging of the meat as it was to the proper cooking. (To this day sirloins are often called New York steaks on menus throughout the country and are distinguished by their taste and tenderness.)

Educated by Delmonico's to enjoy the most sophisticated continental

Pennsylvania Dutch dish, circa 1785.

cuisine that money could buy, an eager public entered the portals of the new Waldorf-Astoria in 1893. In the dining room, the snobbish maître d', Oscar Tschirky, maintained an extraordinary level of service, training his waiters to carve roasts tableside and

ceremoniously ignite flambés for dessert. The Waldorf had numerous signature dishes, among them lobster Newburg (which was actually invented at Delmonico's) and the apple-celery salad with mayonnaise dressing that bears the hotel's name today.

Although there were a handful of memorable restaurants in nineteenth-century New York, there was only one diner who became a legend, and that was Diamond Jim Brady. On an average day, he breakfasted on eggs, grits, pancakes, steaks, chops, and fried potatoes, all washed down with a few jugs of orange juice. A midmorning snack might include a few dozen oysters, followed by a multicourse restaurant lunch of turtle soup, a dozen crabs and a half-dozen lobsters, an

The first Delmonico's restaurant opened in 1831. In one location or another, it catered to New York's elite for almost a century. Birthdays, anniversaries, and other notable occasions were celebrated in its public and private dining rooms. Each event was duly recorded in massive ledgers that read like a social history of the city's upper classes. Below: Patrons enjoying lunch in 1902.

ample portion of roast beef, and an extravagant sampling of desserts. Dinner would follow suit. Indeed, Brady consumed such prodigious quantities of fine food that restaurateur George Rector was fond of describing him as "my twenty-five best customers."

Around the turn of the century, the countless numbers of immigrants arriving in New York created an ethnic restaurant culture that is unique in the United States. Indeed, there is almost no for-

eign cuisine that is not represented in the eateries of "the city." In the space of a day, a New Yorker with wanderlust can visit Chinatown for a dim sum (dumpling) breakfast, enjoy a Caribbean lunch in the West Indian section of Brooklyn, and sit down to Sicilian dinner in Little Italy.

Above: The homestyle diner and the train station lunch counter were among America's first fast-food establishments. Although there was nothing glamorous about them, both were inspired by the luxurious railroad dining cars that gave literal meaning to eating on the run.

Below left: Until the mid-nineteenth century, Americans who ate out had few choices. Fine dining was done privately, at home. A Pennsylvania stitcher created this cover, circa 1870, to dress up a table.

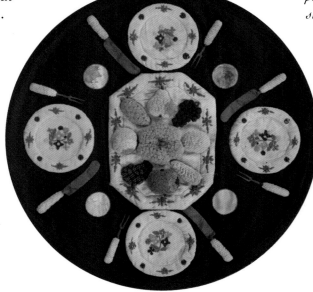

Philipsburg Manor, North Tarrytown, New York.

Celebrating Saint Nicholas Day

Each year on December 6, the old Dutch celebration of Saint Nicholas Day is brought back to life at Philipsburg Manor, a grand house situated along the east bank of the Hudson River, about an hour's drive north of New York City. The mansion's original owner, Frederick Philipse, was an enterprising Dutchman who made his fortune in milling and trading during the early eighteenth century. Since the Dutch considered Christmas Day a solemn time for churchgoing, Philipse and his fellow countrymen made merry a few weeks beforehand in honor of Saint Nicholas, who was as revered in New Amsterdam as he had been in Holland.

According to custom, the children who lived in Philipsburg Manor gathered on December 5, Saint Nicholas Eve, to decorate cakes with gold and silver leaf and to await the arrival of the saint, dressed in long flowing robes and holding a staff in his hand. Greeting them all, the kindly saint asked each child if he or she had been good, offered a few words of advice, and then left as quickly as he came. (Sound familiar?)

The children immediately rushed off to stuff hay into their wooden shoes and set them before the fireplace. This hay, plus a bucket of water, was left for Saint Nicholas's horse—the very horse who later that night carried the saint across the rooftops so he could hop down chimneys with gifts and toys. After the little ones had fallen asleep, the adults spread a white tablecloth on the table and sat down to enjoy some of the specially made gold and silver cakes with hot tea or punch and a dish of steaming hot chestnuts, dotted with butter and sprinkled with salt.

These age-old traditions are brought back to life in the 1680 stone house at Philipsburg Manor during the first few weeks of December each year. Guides wearing period garb bustle about the kitchen decorating the Saint Nicholas cakes and arranging tables decked with all of the special sweetmeats enjoyed by the Dutch during the holiday season: crystallized ginger from the Orient, flaked coconut from the West Indies, Madeira wine, marzipan, and glazed fruit.

In the front parlor, a lilac branch, forced into early bloom, stands in a jar of water, symbolic of the impending good fortune and renewed life of the coming year. The greener the leaf and the fuller the blossoms, the better the family fortune will be in the year to come—or so the Dutch believed.

Flavors from the Middle Atlantic

New York

BUFFALO CHICKEN WINGS

Since 1964 Buffalo's Anchor Bar & Restaurant has been famous for its deep-fried chicken wings, doused with hot sauce and cooled with blue cheese dressing. Buffalo is now firmly fixed on the culinary map as home to one of America's premier pub munchies. (Pictured on page 72)

12 chicken wings (2 pounds)
    Cooking oil *or* shortening for deep-fat frying
3 tablespoons margarine *or* butter
½ to 1 2-ounce bottle hot pepper sauce (2 tablespoons to ¼ cup)
    Bottled blue cheese salad dressing
    Celery sticks

Cut off and discard tips of chicken wings. Cut wings at joints to form 24 pieces. Fry a few wing pieces at a time in deep hot cooking oil or shortening (375°) for 8 to 10 minutes or till golden brown. Drain on paper towels.

In a small saucepan melt margarine or butter. Stir in hot pepper sauce. Pour mixture over wings, turning them to coat. Serve wings with blue cheese dressing and celery sticks. Makes 24 servings.

Nutrition information per serving: 139 calories, 7 g protein, 1 g carbohydrate, 12 g total fat (3 g saturated), 22 mg cholesterol, 145 mg sodium, 52 mg potassium

Hot Cross Buns with Hazelnut Icing (see recipe, page 81), Buckwheat Pecan Waffles, and Eggs Benedict with Easy Orange Hollandaise (see recipe, page 72)

New York

BUCKWHEAT PECAN WAFFLES

Waffle irons were among the important household goods carried in Dutch ships to New Amsterdam. Buckwheat flourished in the colonies.

1 cup all-purpose flour
¾ cup buckwheat flour
1 tablespoon baking powder
2 egg yolks
1¾ cups milk
1 tablespoon brown sugar
½ cup margarine *or* butter, melted
1 cup finely chopped pecans
2 egg whites
    Fresh fruit and powdered sugar *or* maple syrup (optional)

In a mixing bowl combine flours and baking powder. In another bowl beat egg yolks slightly. Beat in milk, brown sugar, and melted margarine or butter. Add egg yolk mixture and pecans to flour mixture all at once. Stir just till combined but still slightly lumpy.

In a bowl beat egg whites till stiff peaks form (tips stand straight). Gently fold beaten egg whites into flour mixture. *Do not overmix.* Pour about *1 cup* batter onto grids of a preheated, lightly greased waffle baker. Close lid quickly; do not open during baking. Bake according to manufacturer's directions. When done, lift waffle off grid. Repeat with remaining batter.

Serve warm; if desired, top with fresh fruit and powdered sugar or maple syrup. Makes 4 to 5 waffles.

Nutrition information per waffle: 680 calories, 14 g protein, 52 g carbohydrate, 48 g total fat (7 g saturated), 115 mg cholesterol, 515 mg sodium, 424 mg potassium

Three-Pepper Slaw (see recipe, page 81), and Scallops with Fresh Herb Tartar Sauce

New York

SCALLOPS WITH FRESH HERB TARTAR SAUCE

Long Island is known for the small, sweet, juicy bay scallops that grow in surrounding shallow waters. Homemade tartar sauce is altogether different—and so much better— than the sauce that comes in a jar.

12	ounces fresh *or* frozen sea scallops
2	tablespoons margarine *or* butter, melted
¼	teaspoon pepper
⅛	teaspoon paprika
⅔	cup mayonnaise *or* salad dressing
1	tablespoon finely chopped onion
½	teaspoon finely shredded lemon peel
2	teaspoons lemon juice
1½	teaspoons snipped fresh dill *or* ½ teaspoon dried dillweed
1½	teaspoons snipped fresh thyme *or* ½ teaspoon dried thyme, crushed
1½	teaspoons snipped fresh parsley *or* ½ teaspoon dried parsley, crushed
	Fresh lemon wedges (optional)

Thaw scallops, if frozen. Halve any large scallops. Thread scallops onto four 8- to 10-inch skewers, leaving a ¼-inch space between pieces. Place skewers on the greased unheated rack of a broiler pan.

In a small bowl stir together melted margarine or butter, pepper, and paprika. Brush *half* of the margarine mixture over scallops. Broil about 4 inches from the heat for 8 to 10 minutes or till scallops are opaque, turning and brushing often with the remaining melted margarine mixture. *Or*, place the kabobs on a greased grill rack. Grill, uncovered, directly over *medium* coals for 5 to 8 minutes; turn once. Brush frequently with remaining margarine mixture during the last 2 minutes of grilling.

For the tartar sauce, in a medium bowl stir together mayonnaise or salad dressing, onion, lemon peel, lemon juice, dill, thyme, and parsley. Serve with tartar sauce and, if desired, lemon wedges. Makes 4 servings.

Nutrition information per serving: 404 calories, 13 g protein, 4 g carbohydrate, 38 g total fat (6 g saturated), 47 mg cholesterol, 585 mg sodium, 279 mg potassium

New York

EGGS BENEDICT WITH EASY ORANGE HOLLANDAISE

Delmonico's restaurant catered to Manhattan's elite for almost a century, from 1831 to 1923. Many famous dishes were born in its kitchen, including this one, the result of a request by a Mr. and Mrs. LeGrand Benedict for something new for lunch.
(Pictured on page 71)

2	English muffins, split
8	slices Canadian-style bacon Cooking oil *or* shortening (optional) Water
2	teaspoons instant chicken bouillon granules (optional)

Buffalo Chicken Wings (see recipe, page 71)

4	eggs Easy Orange Hollandaise Orange wedges (optional)

Place muffins and bacon in a single layer on a baking sheet. Bake in a 350° oven 10 to 15 minutes or till muffins are toasted and bacon is hot. Keep warm. If desired, lightly grease a 2-quart saucepan. Add water to half-fill pan; if desired, stir in bouillon granules. Bring water to boiling. Reduce heat to simmering. Break *one* egg into a measuring cup. Carefully slide egg into simmering water. Repeat with remaining eggs. Simmer, uncovered, 3 to 5 minutes or to desired doneness. (*Or*, use an egg poaching pan.)

To serve, top each muffin half with 2 slices of bacon and an egg. Spoon Easy Orange Hollandaise over eggs. If desired, serve with orange wedges. Makes 4 servings.

Easy Orange Hollandaise: In a small saucepan combine ¼ cup dairy *sour cream*, ¼ cup *mayonnaise or salad dressing*, ½ to 1 teaspoon finely shredded *orange peel*, 1 to 2 table-spoons *orange juice*, and ½ teaspoon *Dijon-style mustard*. Cook and stir over low heat just till warm; do not boil. Makes about ½ cup.

Nutrition information per serving: 364 calories, 21 g protein, 16 g carbohydrate, 24 g total fat (6 g saturated), 256 mg cholesterol, 1,105 mg sodium, 268 mg potassium

Spicy Manhattan Clam Chowder

New York

SPICY MANHATTAN CLAM CHOWDER

Is New England's creamy white the only true clam chowder, or is tomato-rich Manhattan red equally worthy? It's an ongoing debate. In an attempt to settle the question, at least in Maine, a state legislator there once introduced a bill that made it illegal to mix clams and tomatoes!

1   pint shucked clams *or* two 6½-ounce cans minced clams
4   slices bacon
1   cup chopped onion
1   cup chopped celery
½   cup chopped green pepper
½   cup chopped red sweet pepper

¼   cup chopped carrots
2   tablespoons chopped shallots
1   16-ounce can tomatoes, cut up
2   cups finely chopped, peeled potatoes
1   cup chicken broth
½   teaspoon dried basil, crushed
⅛   to ¼ teaspoon ground red pepper
⅛   teaspoon ground black pepper
2   tablespoons snipped parsley

Chop shucked clams, reserving juice; set aside. Strain clam juice to remove bits of shell. (*Or*, drain canned clams, reserving juice.) If necessary, add water to reserved juice to equal 1½ cups. Set aside.

In a large saucepan cook bacon till crisp. Remove bacon, reserving *2 tablespoons* drippings. Drain bacon on paper towels; crumble. Set aside.

Cook onion, celery, green pepper, red sweet pepper, carrots, and shallots in reserved bacon drippings till tender. Stir in reserved clam juice, *undrained* tomatoes, potatoes, chicken broth, basil, ground red pepper, and ground black pepper. Bring to boiling; reduce heat. Cover and simmer for 20 to 25 minutes or till vegetables are tender.

Stir in clams. Return to boiling; reduce heat. Cook for 1 to 2 minutes more. Sprinkle each serving with cooked bacon and parsley. Makes 4 main-dish or 6 to 8 side-dish servings.

Nutrition information per main-dish serving: *360 calories, 36 g protein, 40 g carbohydrate, 6 g total fat (2 g saturated), 81 mg cholesterol, 647 mg sodium, 1,627 mg potassium*

Pennsylvania Pot Roast, and Buttery Homemade Noodles (see recipe, page 82)

Pennsylvania

PENNSYLVANIA POT ROAST

In the early days of the Pennsylvania Dutch settlements, pigs were left to forage in the woods. When they were slaughtered, they were tough. Slow-cooked dishes like pot roast tenderized the pork into something very satisfying.

1	2½- to 3-pound boneless pork shoulder roast
2	tablespoons cooking oil
1½	cups beef broth
2	medium leeks, trimmed and cut into 1-inch pieces
1	teaspoon dried basil, crushed
1	teaspoon dried marjoram, crushed
½	teaspoon salt
½	teaspoon pepper
1	bay leaf
1	medium acorn squash
8	small parsnips, quartered
3	medium carrots, sliced
8	ounces fresh mushrooms, sliced
½	cup cold water
¼	cup all-purpose flour

Trim fat from meat. In a 6-quart Dutch oven brown meat on all sides in hot oil. Drain fat. Add beef broth, leeks, basil, marjoram, the ½ teaspoon salt, the ½ teaspoon pepper, and bay leaf. Bring to boiling; reduce heat. Cover and simmer for 1¼ hours.

Cut squash in half lengthwise; discard seeds. Cut each half into 4 pieces. Add squash to meat mixture. Then add parsnips, carrots, and mushrooms. Return to boiling; reduce heat. Cover and simmer for 20 to 25 minutes more or till vegetables and meat are tender. Remove meat and vegetables from Dutch oven; keep warm. Discard bay leaf.

For sauce, skim fat from pan juices. Measure *1½ cups* juices. Stir cold water into flour; stir into reserved juices in Dutch oven. Cook and stir till thickened and bubbly. Cook and stir 1 minute more. Season to taste with salt and pepper. Serve sauce with meat and vegetables. Makes 8 servings.

Nutrition information per serving: 410 calories, 38 g protein, 27 g carbohydrate, 17 g total fat (5 g saturated), 122 mg cholesterol, 491 mg sodium, 1,055 mg potassium

Roast Beef with Peppered Yorkshire Pudding, and Sweet-and-Sour Beans and Carrots (see recipe, page 84)

(see recipe, page 84)

Delaware

ROAST BEEF WITH PEPPERED YORKSHIRE PUDDING

Benjamin Franklin's wife, Deborah, kept him well supplied with food from home during his travels, including roast beef. Like English cooks before them, colonists would roast meat over a dripping pan, then use the fat to make a savory batter pudding like Yorkshire.

1 **4- to 6-pound beef standing rib roast**
4 **eggs**
2 **cups milk**
2 **cups all-purpose flour**
½ **teaspoon coarsely ground pepper**
¼ **teaspoon salt**

Place meat, fat side up, in a 15 x 10½ x 2-inch roasting pan. Insert a meat thermometer. Roast in a 325° oven for 1¾ to 3 hours for rare (140°), 2¼ to 3¾ hours for medium (160°), or 2¾ to 4¼ hours for well-done (170°).

After removing meat from oven, increase oven temperature to 450°.

Transfer meat to a serving platter; cover to keep warm. Measure pan drippings. If necessary, add enough cooking oil to drippings to equal ¼ cup; return to pan.

In a medium mixing bowl combine eggs, milk, flour, pepper, and salt. Beat with an electric mixer or rotary beater till smooth. Stir into drippings in pan. Bake for 20 to 25 minutes or till puffy and golden brown. Cut into squares. Serve at once with roast beef. Makes 12 to 14 servings.

Nutrition information per serving: 328 calories, 29 g protein, 18 g carbohydrate, 15 g total fat (6 g saturated), 142 mg cholesterol, 147 mg sodium, 404 mg potassium

75

Schnitz un Knepp, Sweet-and-Sour Red Cabbage with Pears (see recipe, page 85), and Rhubarb Chutney (see recipe, page 84)

(see recipe, page 85)

(see recipe, page 84)

Pennsylvania

SCHNITZ UN KNEPP

Few dishes are so locally famous, yet so little known elsewhere, as
schnitz un knepp. *It combines two foods, ham and apples, that are staples of Pennsylvania Dutch cooking.*
Schnitz *means "sliced, dried apples," and* knepp *is "dumpling."*

1   **3-pound smoked pork picnic**
1   **6-ounce package (2 cups) dried apples**
¼   **cup packed brown sugar**
1½   **cups all-purpose flour**
2   **teaspoons baking powder**
¼   **teaspoon salt**
1   **beaten egg**
½   **cup milk**
2   **tablespoons margarine *or* butter, melted**

Remove skin and fat from outside of smoked pork. Place pork in a Dutch oven; add enough water to cover meat. Bring to boiling; reduce heat. Cover and simmer for 30 minutes. Stir in dried apples and brown sugar. Cover; simmer 1 hour more.

Meanwhile, for dumplings, in a bowl stir together flour, baking powder, and salt. In a small bowl combine egg, milk, and melted

76

margarine or butter. Add to flour mixture; stir with a fork just till combined. Drop dough by rounded tablespoonfuls in 10 mounds atop the simmering liquid. Cover; simmer for 20 minutes (do not lift the cover) or till a toothpick inserted into the dumplings comes out clean.

Serve pork on a platter with the dumplings and apples. Spoon a small amount of the remaining

liquid over the meat. Makes 8 to 10 servings.

Nutrition information per serving: 390 *calories, 32 g protein, 37 g carbohydrate, 12 g total fat (4 g saturated), 82 mg cholesterol, 1,601 mg sodium, 492 mg potassium*

Pennsylvania

CREAMY NAVY BEAN SOUP WITH PESTO

The Pennsylvania Dutch made the most of what they had. They enjoyed soups, but if only flour and milk were available, that's what they used. When the farms became more productive, the soup pot would reflect the bounty. The addition of pesto adds an Italian twist to this old favorite.

1	pound dry navy beans (2⅓ cups)
6	cups water
4	cups chicken broth
2	cups shredded cabbage
1	cup shredded carrot
1	cup chopped onion
2	cloves garlic, minced
1	teaspoon dried oregano, crushed
½	teaspoon dried marjoram, crushed
2	bay leaves
½	teaspoon salt
¼	teaspoon pepper
2	cups milk
2	tablespoons Homemade Pesto *or* purchased pesto

Rinse beans. In a 4½-quart Dutch oven combine beans and water. Bring to boiling; reduce heat. Simmer for 2 minutes. Remove from heat. Cover and let stand 1 hour. (*Or,* skip boiling the water and soak beans overnight in a covered pan.)

Drain and rinse beans. Return beans to Dutch oven. Add chicken broth, cabbage, carrot, onion, garlic, oregano, marjoram, bay leaves, salt, and pepper. Bring to boiling; reduce heat. Cover and simmer for 2½ to 3 hours or till beans are very tender, stirring occasionally.

Leek and Wild Mushroom Soup, top (see recipe, page 85), and Creamy Navy Bean Soup with Pesto

Discard bay leaves. Mash beans slightly. Stir in milk and heat through. Ladle into soup bowls. Dollop each serving with pesto. Makes 6 servings.

Homemade Pesto: In a blender container or food processor bowl combine 1 cup firmly packed fresh *basil leaves,* ½ cup firmly packed *parsley sprigs* with stems removed, ½ cup grated *Parmesan or Romano cheese,* ¼ cup *pine nuts, walnuts, or almonds,* 1 large clove *garlic,* and ¼ teaspoon *salt.* Cover and blend or process with several on-off turns till a paste forms, stopping machine several times and scraping the sides.

With the machine running slowly, gradually add ¼ cup *olive oil or cooking oil* and blend or process to the consistency of soft butter. Store in an airtight container. Refrigerate for 1 or 2 days or freeze up to 1 month. Makes about ⅔ cup.

Nutrition information per serving: 385 *calories, 24 g protein, 61 g carbohydrate, 6 g total fat (2 g saturated), 7 mg cholesterol, 786 mg sodium, 1,154 mg potassium*

Bake, uncovered, in a 425° oven about 15 minutes or till pastry is golden and meat is medium-rare. If desired, serve with Bordelaise Sauce. Makes 2 servings.

Note: If desired, insert a meat thermometer into pastry-wrapped meat and roast to 140°.

Bordelaise Sauce: In a small saucepan combine ¾ cup *water;* ⅓ cup *dry red wine;* 1 tablespoon finely chopped *shallot or onion;* ½ teaspoon *instant beef bouillon granules;* ¼ teaspoon *dried thyme,* crushed; and 1 *bay leaf.* Bring to boiling; reduce heat. Simmer, uncovered, for 5 to 7 minutes or till mixture is reduced to ¾ cup. Remove bay leaf.

Stir together 2 tablespoons softened *margarine or butter* and 1 tablespoon *all-purpose flour.* Add to wine mixture. Cook and stir till thickened and bubbly. Cook and stir for 1 minute more. Stir in 1½ teaspoons snipped *parsley.* Makes about ¾ cup.

Nutrition information per serving: 743 calories, 36 g protein, 46 g carbohydrate, 45 g total fat (4 g saturated), 122 mg cholesterol, 985 mg sodium, 396 mg potassium

Individual Beef Wellington, and Vegetables in Spicy Sour Cream (see recipe, page 85)

New Jersey

INDIVIDUAL BEEF WELLINGTON

The English have relished meat baked in pastry "coffins" since Shakespeare's day. It's a taste they carried with them to the American colonies. Amelia Simmons, in her American Cookery *of 1796, recommends Puff Paste No.8 as excellent for meat pies.*

½	of a 17½-ounce package (1 sheet) frozen puff pastry
¼	teaspoon salt
¼	teaspoon pepper
¼	teaspoon dried marjoram, crushed
2	beef tenderloin steaks (4 to 6 ounces each)
2	tablespoons deli *or* canned mushroom pâté *or* liver pâté
1	beaten egg white Bordelaise Sauce (optional)

Thaw pastry according to package directions; set aside. In a small bowl stir together salt, pepper, and marjoram. Rub salt mixture over steaks, coating all sides.

Cut thawed pastry into 2 portions. Spread *1 tablespoon* pâté over one side of each steak. Place a steak, pâté side down, on the center of each portion of pastry. Wrap pastry around meat. Trim excess pastry from ends; seal ends.

Place pastry-wrapped meat, seam sides down, in a greased, shallow baking pan. Brush pastry with beaten egg white. If desired, reroll trimmings to make cutouts. Place cutouts on pastry-wrapped meat. Brush with beaten egg white.

Pennsylvania

PHILADELPHIA CHEESE STEAK SANDWICH

How to make a Philadelphian homesick? Just say "cheese steak." This beef sandwich with cheese and onions on a long roll has been a favorite fast food in the City of Brotherly Love since at least the 1930s.

1	12-ounce boneless beef rib eye steak
2	tablespoons margarine *or* butter
2	medium onions, thinly sliced and separated into rings
1	medium red *or* green sweet pepper, cut into thin strips
4	French rolls *or* hoagie buns
4	ounces thinly sliced cheddar cheese

Philadelphia Cheese Steak Sandwich, and Philadelphia Soft Pretzels (see recipe, page 82)

Partially freeze beef. Thinly slice beef across the grain into bite-size strips. In a 10-inch skillet melt margarine or butter; add onions and pepper. Cover and cook over medium-low heat about 10 minutes or till tender, stirring occasionally.

Remove onion-pepper mixture from skillet with a slotted spoon. If necessary, add additional margarine to skillet. Add beef; cook and stir over medium-high heat for 2 to 3 minutes or till done.

To serve, spread rolls open face on a baking sheet. Divide beef and onion-pepper mixture among rolls. Top with cheese. Broil 4 to 5 inches from the heat for 1 to 2 minutes or till cheese is melted. Serve immediately. Makes 4 servings.

Nutrition information per serving: 484 calories, 30 g protein, 34 g carbohydrate, 25 g total fat (10 g saturated), 81 mg cholesterol, 615 mg sodium, 448 mg potassium

New York

CHICKEN À LA KING

Supposedly this creamed chicken dish, served over toast points, was the creation of chef George Greenwald of the Brighton Beach Hotel, who named it after hotel owner E. Clark King III. Other sources say the dish came out of Delmonico's kitchen and was originally "à la Keene," after Jim Keene, a Delmonico's regular. (Pictured on page 80)

1½ **cups loose-pack frozen mixed vegetables**
1   **cup water**
1   **tablespoon instant chicken bouillon granules**
1   **tablespoon white wine Worcestershire sauce, dry white wine, *or* Worcestershire sauce**
⅛   **teaspoon dried basil, crushed**
⅛   **teaspoon pepper**

2   **cups milk**
½   **cup all-purpose flour**
2   **cups chopped cooked chicken *or* turkey**
4   **frozen patty shells, baked according to package directions, with tops removed**

In a large saucepan combine the frozen vegetables, water, bouillon granules, Worcestershire sauce or wine, basil, and pepper. Bring mixture to boiling; reduce heat. Cover and simmer for 5 minutes.

Meanwhile, combine milk and flour. Stir into vegetable mixture. Cook and stir till thickened and bubbly. Cook and stir 1 minute more. Stir in chicken or turkey; heat through.

Serve the chicken mixture in the patty shells. Makes 4 servings.

Nutrition information per serving: 558 calories, 36 g protein, 51 g carbohydrate, 23 g total fat (4 g saturated), 81 mg cholesterol, 1,056 mg sodium, 691 mg potassium

THREE-PEPPER SLAW

Cabbage for coleslaw, or kool sla in Dutch, grew in New Amsterdam kitchen gardens. Small, tight heads were preferred for this salad, which was simply dressed with oil, vinegar, salt, and pepper. (Pictuerd on page 72)

1	medium red sweet pepper, cut into thin strips
1	medium yellow sweet pepper, cut into thin strips
1	medium orange *or* green sweet pepper, cut into thin strips
1	cup shredded cabbage
¼	cup currants *or* raisins
2	green onions, sliced
¼	cup white wine vinegar
3	tablespoons salad oil
2	to 3 tablespoons sugar
	Few dashes bottled hot pepper sauce (optional)

In a large mixing bowl combine red sweet pepper, yellow sweet pepper, orange or green sweet pepper, cabbage, currants or raisins, and green onions.

For dressing, in a screw-top jar combine wine vinegar, oil, sugar, and, if desired, hot pepper sauce. Cover and shake well. Pour the dressing over the pepper mixture, tossing to coat. Cover and chill for 2 to 24 hours. Stir before serving. Makes 4 servings.

Nutrition information per serving: 170 calories, 1 g protein, 20 g carbohydrate, 10 g total fat (1 g saturated), 0 mg cholesterol, 11 mg sodium, 306 mg potassium

Waldorf Salad, and Chicken à la King (see recipe, page 79)

HOT CROSS BUNS WITH HAZELNUT ICING

The recipe for this yeast roll, with its distinctive sugar-icing cross, emigrated to America with the English. It is associated with Easter, in particular Good Friday. (Pictured on page 70)

1½	cups all-purpose flour
1	package active dry yeast
1	teaspoon ground cinnamon
¾	cup milk
½	cup cooking oil
⅓	cup sugar
½	teaspoon salt
3	eggs
⅔	cup currants *or* raisins
½	cup chopped hazelnuts (filberts) (optional)
2¼	to 2¾ cups all-purpose flour
1	slightly beaten egg white
	Hazelnut Icing

In a large mixing bowl combine the 1½ cups flour, yeast, and cinnamon. In a small saucepan heat and stir milk, oil, sugar, and salt till warm (120° to 130°). Add to flour mixture along with eggs. Beat with an electric mixer on low speed for 30 seconds, scraping bowl. Beat on high speed for 3 minutes

Using a spoon, stir in currants or raisins, hazelnuts (if desired), and as much of the 2¼ to 2¾ cups flour as you can. Turn out onto a floured surface. Knead in enough remaining flour to make a moderately soft dough (3 to 5 minutes total). Shape into a ball. Place dough in a greased bowl; turn once to grease surface. Cover and let rise till nearly double (about 1½ hours).

Punch dough down. Turn out onto a floured surface. Cover and let rest 10 minutes. Divide dough into 20 portions; shape each portion into a smooth ball. Place balls 1½ inches apart on a greased baking sheet. Cover and let rise till nearly double (30 to 45 minutes). With a sharp knife, make a shallow crisscross slash across each bun. Brush with egg white. Bake in a 375° oven for 12 to 15 minutes or till golden brown. Cool slightly. Drizzle buns with Hazelnut Icing. Serve warm. Makes 20 buns.

Hazelnut Icing: In a mixing bowl combine 1 cup sifted *powdered sugar,* 1 tablespoon *hazelnut liqueur,* and ¼ teaspoon *vanilla.* Stir in *milk,* 1 teaspoon at a time, till it reaches drizzling consistency.

Nutrition information per bun: 201 calories, 4 g protein, 31 g carbohydrate, 7 g total fat (1 g saturated), 33 mg cholesterol, 71 mg sodium, 92 mg potassium

WALDORF SALAD

"Oscar of the Waldorf," Oscar Tschirky, was the imperious maître d' at New York's Waldorf-Astoria hotel at the turn of the century. This famous salad, originally a simple mixture of apples, celery, and walnuts in a mayonnaise dressing, was his creation. There have been many variations since.

2	cups chopped apples *or* pears (2 medium)
1½	teaspoons lemon juice
⅓	cup slivered almonds *or* chopped pecans, toasted
¼	cup celery
¼	cup dried red tart cherries *or* raisins
¼	cup seedless grapes, halved
⅓	cup whipping cream
¼	cup mayonnaise *or* salad dressing

In a medium mixing bowl toss chopped apples or pears with lemon juice. Stir in nuts, celery, cherries or raisins, and grapes.

For dressing, in a chilled, small mixing bowl whip the cream to soft peaks. Fold mayonnaise or salad dressing into the whipped cream. Fold dressing into fruit mixture. Cover and chill for 2 to 24 hours. Makes 4 to 6 servings.

Nutrition information per serving: 317 calories, 4 g protein, 24 g carbohydrate, 24 g total fat (7 g saturated), 35 mg cholesterol, 94 mg sodium, 247 mg potassium

Pennsylvania

BUTTERY HOMEMADE NOODLES

Noodles were a main starch on Pennsylvania Dutch tables. They were served boiled and buttered, fried, steamed, and even cooked with eggs like a frittata. (Pictured on page 74)

1   **egg**
¼   **teaspoon salt**
⅔   **cup all-purpose flour**
2   **14½-ounce cans chicken broth *or* 3½ cups water**
1   **tablespoon margarine *or* butter, cut up**
1   **tablespoon snipped parsley**

In a medium bowl combine egg and salt. Using a fork, stir in flour. Form the dough into a ball. On a lightly floured surface knead dough for 2 to 3 minutes or till smooth. Cover and let rest 10 minutes.

On a lightly floured surface roll dough into an 18x9-inch rectangle. It may be necessary to allow dough to rest a few minutes between rolls. Dust the top of the dough lightly with flour. Roll up dough, jelly-roll style, from one of the long sides to form an 18-inch roll. Slice the dough crosswise into ¼-inch slices.

Carefully shake out the rings to form noodles. Let stand on a baking sheet about 10 minutes.

In a large saucepan or Dutch oven bring chicken broth or water to boiling. Add noodles. Return to boiling; reduce heat. Simmer for 2 to 3 minutes or till tender; drain. Toss hot noodles with margarine or butter till melted. Sprinkle with parsley and season to taste with salt and pepper. Serve warm. Makes 4 servings.

Nutrition information per serving: 121 calories, 4 g protein, 16 g carbohydrate, 4 g total fat (1 g saturated), 55 mg cholesterol, 307 mg sodium, 29 mg potassium

Pennsylvania

PHILADELPHIA SOFT PRETZELS

Soft pretzels are sold from carts on street corners all over Philadelphia. The only way to eat them, according to locals, is squirted with yellow ballpark mustard. Pretzels are from the Pennsylvania Dutch settlers who learned the art in Germany. (Pictured on page 79)

4   **to 4½ cups all-purpose flour**
1   **package active dry yeast**
1½   **cups milk**
¼   **cup sugar**
2   **tablespoons cooking oil**
1   **teaspoon salt**
2   **tablespoons salt**
3   **quarts boiling water**
1   **slightly beaten egg white**
1   **tablespoon water**
     Sesame seed, poppy seed, *or* coarse salt
     Cheddar Sauce (optional)

In a mixer bowl combine *1½ cups* of the flour and the yeast. In a saucepan heat and stir milk, sugar, oil, and the 1 teaspoon salt *just till warm* (120° to 130°). Add to flour mixture. Beat with an electric mixer on low to medium speed 30 seconds, scraping the sides of the bowl. Then beat on high speed for 3 minutes. Using a wooden spoon, stir in as much remaining flour as you can.

Turn dough out onto a lightly floured surface. Knead in enough of remaining flour to make a moderately stiff dough that is smooth and elastic (6 to 8 minutes total). Shape into a ball. Place dough in a greased bowl, turning once to grease the surface. Cover; let rise in a warm place till double (about 1¼ hours).

Punch dough down. Turn out onto a lightly floured surface. Cover and let rest for 10 minutes. Meanwhile, grease 2 baking sheets. Roll dough into a 12x10-inch rectangle. Cut into twenty 12x½-inch strips. Gently pull each strip into a rope about 16 inches long. Shape into pretzels. Place pretzels ½ inch apart on the prepared baking sheets. Bake in a 475° oven for 4 minutes. Remove from oven. Reduce oven temperature to 350°.

Meanwhile, dissolve the 2 tablespoons salt in the boiling water. Reduce heat. Lower 4 or 5 pretzels at a time into simmering water. Simmer for 2 minutes, turning once. Remove with a slotted spoon and drain on paper towels. Leave pretzels on towels only a few seconds; if left too long, they will stick. Then place pretzels ½ inch apart on well-greased baking sheets.

Brush pretzels with a mixture of egg white and the 1 tablespoon water. Lightly sprinkle with sesame seed, poppy seed, or coarse salt. Bake in a 350° oven 20 to 25 minutes or till golden brown. Remove from baking sheet and cool on a wire rack. If desired, serve with Cheddar Sauce. Makes 20 pretzels.

Cheddar Sauce: In a small saucepan melt 1 tablespoon *margarine or butter.* Stir in 4 teaspoons *all-purpose flour* and dash ground *red pepper.* Add ½ cup *milk* all at once. Cook and stir over medium heat till thickened and bubbly. Cook and stir for 1 minute more. Stir in ½ cup shredded *cheddar cheese* till melted. Makes ⅔ cup.

Nutrition information per pretzel: 132 calories, 4 g protein, 23 g carbohydrate, 3 g total fat (0 g saturated), 1 mg cholesterol, 170 mg sodium, 68 mg potassium

Pennsylvania

CINNAMON ROLLS

Cinnamon is a favored spice in Pennsylvania regional recipes. It appears in all sorts of baked goods, a legacy perhaps from Germany or an influence of the far-reaching Dutch who settled in the Middle Atlantic states. These yeast-leavened cinnamon rolls are usually associated with Philadelphia.

6¼ to 6¾ cups all-purpose flour
2 packages active dry yeast
1½ cups milk
½ cup margarine *or* butter
½ cup sugar
1 teaspoon salt
3 eggs
¾ cup sugar
½ cup margarine *or* butter, softened
4 teaspoons ground cinnamon *or* finely shredded orange peel
2 teaspoons all-purpose flour
¾ cup chopped nuts, miniature semisweet chocolate pieces, *or* raisins (optional)
Powdered Sugar Glaze

In a large mixing bowl combine *3 cups* of the flour and the yeast.

In a saucepan heat milk, ½ cup margarine or butter, the ½ cup sugar, and salt just till warm (120° to 130°) and margarine is almost melted, stirring constantly. Add to flour mixture. Add eggs. Beat with an electric mixer on low speed for 30 seconds, scraping sides of bowl constantly. Beat on high speed for 3 minutes. Using a wooden spoon, stir in as much of the remaining flour as you can.

Turn dough out onto a lightly floured surface. Knead in enough of the remaining flour to make a moderately stiff dough that is smooth and elastic (6 to 8 minutes total). Shape into a ball. Place in a greased bowl, turning once to grease surface. Cover; let rise in a warm place till double (about 1 hour).

For filling, in a small bowl combine the ¾ cup sugar, the ½ cup margarine or butter, cinnamon or orange peel, and the 2 teaspoons flour; set aside.

Punch dough down; divide in half. Cover and let rest 10 minutes. On a lightly floured surface roll each half of the dough into a 12-inch square.

Spread *half* of the filling over each dough square. If desired, sprinkle with *half* of the nuts,

Cinnamon Rolls

chocolate pieces, or raisins. Roll each square up jelly-roll style; pinch edges to seal. Slice each roll into 8 pieces. Place pieces in two greased 13x9x2-inch baking pans, 12-inch pizza pans, or 9-inch round baking pans.

Cover loosely with clear plastic wrap, leaving room for rolls to rise. Refrigerate 2 to 24 hours. Uncover and let stand at room temperature for 30 minutes. (*Or*, don't chill dough. Instead, cover loosely; let rise in a warm place till nearly double, about 45 minutes). Break any surface bubbles with a greased toothpick.

Bake in a 375° oven for 20 to 25 minutes for 13x9x2-inch baking

pans or 12-inch pizza pans, or about 30 minutes for 9-inch round baking pans.If necessary, cover loosely with foil during the last 5 to 10 minutes of baking to prevent over-browning Remove from pans. Cool slightly. Spread with Powdered Sugar Glaze. Makes 16 rolls.

Powdered Sugar Glaze: In a bowl combine 2 cups sifted *powdered sugar* and ½ teaspoon *vanilla.* Add enough *milk* (2 to 3 tablespoons) to reach drizzling consistency.

Nutrition information per roll: 457 calories, 8 g protein, 69 g carbohydrate, 17 g total fat (3 g saturated), 42 mg cholesterol, 256 mg sodium, 146 mg potassium

Pennsylvania

SWEET-AND-SOUR BEANS AND CARROTS

*A German dish, this vegetable
mixture is more traditionally called
Blindehuhn, or "blind hen,"
by the Westphalian immigrants who
brought it to this country.
The original version is a casserole made
with green and white beans, carrots,
potatoes, onions, and apples.
(Pictured on page 75)*

1   cup chopped carrot
1   9-ounce package frozen
    cut green beans
2   slices bacon
1   medium onion, sliced
1   apple, peeled, cored, and
    sliced
2   tablespoons vinegar
1   tablespoon sugar
¼   teaspoon salt

In a saucepan cook the chopped
carrot, covered, in small amount
boiling salted water till nearly tender, about 10 minutes. Add cut
green beans and return to boiling.
Cover and cook till the vegetables
are tender, about 5 minutes more;
drain well.

Meanwhile, in a skillet cook
bacon till crisp; drain, reserving
1 tablespoon drippings. Crumble
bacon and set aside. Cook sliced
onion in reserved drippings over
medium heat till tender but not
brown. Add sliced apple, vinegar,
sugar, and salt. Cover and cook just
till apples are tender, 3 to 4 minutes. Add cooked beans and carrot;
heat through. Sprinkle with the
bacon. Makes 4 to 6 servings.

*Nutrition information per serving: 89
calories, 2 g protein, 17 g carbohydrate, 2 g total
fat (1 g saturated), 3 mg cholesterol, 219 mg
sodium, 248 mg potassium*

Baby Corn Relish

New York

BABY CORN RELISH

*As early as 1811, Shaker communities
were selling a variety of jellies,
relishes, sauces, and preserves to their
neighbors. Not only were the Shakers
superb cooks, but they also devised
ingenious inventions like a kernel cutter
for corn to lighten household work.*

1   cup small cauliflower
    flowerets
1   15-ounce can baby corn,
    drained
⅓   cup sugar
1   tablespoon cornstarch
½   cup vinegar
⅓   cup cold water
¼   cup chopped celery
¼   cup chopped green pepper
¼   cup chopped red sweet
    pepper
2   tablespoons finely chopped
    onion
1   teaspoon ground turmeric
½   teaspoon dry mustard
¼   teaspoon salt

Cook the cauliflower, covered, in a
small amount of boiling water for

6 to 8 minutes or till crisp-tender;
drain. Meanwhile, halve the baby
corn lengthwise and cut it into
1-inch pieces.

In a saucepan combine sugar and
cornstarch. Stir in vinegar and
water. Stir in the corn, cauliflower,
celery, green pepper, red sweet pepper, onion, turmeric, dry mustard,
and salt. Cook and stir till thickened and bubbly. Cook and stir for
2 minutes more; cool.

Cover and store in the refrigerator for up to 4 weeks. Serve with
beef, pork, or poultry. Makes about
2½ cups.

*Nutrition information per ¼ cup: 45 calo-
ries, 1 g protein, 11 g carbohydrate, 0 g total fat
(0 g saturated), 0 mg cholesterol, 61 mg sodium, 40 mg potassium*

Pennsylvania

RHUBARB CHUTNEY

*Although rhubarb is nicknamed
the "pie plant" because that is one
of its most popular uses, it
also makes a delicious condiment.
Pennsylvania Dutch housewives
put up vegetable relishes of all kinds
in sterilized jars for later use.
(Pictured on page 77)*

½   cup packed brown sugar
⅓   cup vinegar
¼   cup water
¼   teaspoon salt
¼   teaspoon dry mustard
⅛   teaspoon ground allspice
⅛   teaspoon ground cinnamon
    Dash ground cloves
½   cup chopped onion
¼   cup raisins
2   cups chopped rhubarb
¾   cup pitted whole dates,
    snipped
¼   cup toasted slivered
    almonds (optional)

In a large saucepan stir together the
brown sugar, vinegar, water, salt,
dry mustard, allspice, cinnamon,

and cloves. Bring to boiling, stirring till sugar dissolves. Boil gently, uncovered, for 5 minutes. Stir in the onion and raisins. Return to boiling; reduce heat. Simmer, covered, for 20 minutes. Add rhubarb and dates and simmer, uncovered, for 10 minutes more or till thick, stirring occasionally.

Cool; cover and store in the refrigerator up to 4 weeks. Before serving, if desired, stir in almonds. Serve with pork, poultry, or ham. Makes about 2 cups.

Nutrition information per 2 tablespoons: 108 calories, 0 g protein, 28 g carbohydrate, 0 g total fat (0 g saturated), 0 mg cholesterol, 72 mg sodium, 294 mg potassium

Pennsylvania

SWEET-AND-SOUR RED CABBAGE WITH PEARS

"Plant cabbage on Friday and lettuce in the dark of the moon." The Pennsylvania Dutch were excellent farmers, but according to their folklore, some precautions were necessary for a successful crop. (Pictured on page 76)

1 cup chopped onion
1 clove garlic, minced
1 tablespoon cooking oil
4 cups shredded red cabbage
2 medium pears, peeled and coarsely chopped
½ cup mixed dried fruit bits
½ cup dry red wine
⅓ cup red wine vinegar
2 tablespoons brown sugar
1 teaspoon caraway seed
¼ teaspoon salt
¼ teaspoon pepper

In a large skillet cook onion and garlic in oil till tender. Stir in cabbage, pears, mixed dried fruit bits,

red wine, wine vinegar, brown sugar, caraway seed, salt, and pepper. Bring to boiling; reduce heat.

Cover and simmer for 30 minutes, stirring occasionally and adding water, if necessary. Makes 6 servings.

Nutrition information per serving: 122 calories, 2 g protein, 22 g carbohydrate, 3 g total fat (0 g saturated), 0 mg cholesterol, 110 mg sodium, 314 mg potassium

Pennsylvania

VEGETABLES IN SPICY SOUR CREAM

Pennsyvania Dutch tradition insists that each meal include seven sweets and seven sours. The number and variety of these dishes was actually up to the cook, and depended on what else was being served. (Pictured on page 78)

½ cup dairy sour cream
1 tablespoon white wine vinegar *or* lemon juice
1 teaspoon sugar
½ teaspoon salt
⅛ teaspoon ground red pepper
1 small yellow summer squash *or* zucchini, sliced (1 cup)
½ of a small cucumber, halved lengthwise and thinly sliced (1 cup)
½ of a small red onion, thinly sliced and separated into rings
1 medium carrot, cut into thin strips
2 tablespoons diced pimiento *or* red sweet red pepper

In a medium bowl stir together sour cream, vinegar or lemon juice, sugar, salt, and ground red pepper. Add squash, cucumber, red onion, carrot, and pimiento or red sweet pepper; toss to coat. Cover and chill for 2 to 24 hours, stirring often.

Stir before serving. Serve with a slotted spoon. Makes 4 servings.

Nutrition information per serving: 78 calories, 2 g protein, 5 g carbohydrate, 6 g total fat (4 g saturated), 13 mg cholesterol, 288 mg sodium, 188 mg potassium

Pennsylvania

LEEK AND WILD MUSHROOM SOUP

Pennsylvania has been a leading mushroom producer since the 1920s. Most of the nation's mushroom crop is grown there in underground caves. (Pictured on page 77)

8 ounces Chanterelle mushrooms *or* Cremini mushrooms, sliced (3 cups)
½ cup sliced leeks
1 clove garlic, minced
2 tablespoons margarine *or* butter
1 tablespoon all-purpose flour
⅛ teaspoon pepper
2 cups chicken broth *or* beef broth
1 cup half-and-half, light cream, *or* whole milk
1 tablespoon dry sherry
Leek strips

In a large saucepan cook the mushrooms, leeks, and garlic in margarine or butter till leeks and mushrooms are tender. Stir in flour and pepper. Add chicken or beef broth and half-and-half all at once. Cook and stir till slightly thickened and bubbly. Cook and stir for 1 minute more. Stir in sherry; heat through. If desired, garnish with leek strips. Makes 4 to 6 servings.

Nutrition information per serving: 182 calories, 6 g protein, 9 g carbohydrate, 14 g total fat (5 g saturated), 22 mg cholesterol, 466 mg sodium, 427 mg potassium

NEW YORK CHEESECAKE

There's nothing "lite" about New York cheesecake. It is a dense, heavy dessert that consists of a lemon-accented cream cheese mixture in a thin pastry crust. (Today, it is commonly served in a graham cracker crust.) When properly made, as it was at Lindy's restaurant in New York City, it is creamy, smooth, and irresistible.

2	cups finely crushed graham cracker crumbs
½	cup margarine *or* butter, melted
5	8-ounce packages cream cheese, softened
1¾	cups sugar
2	tablespoons all-purpose flour
1½	teaspoons vanilla
5	eggs
2	egg yolks
⅓	cup whipping cream
1	teaspoon finely shredded lemon peel

For crust, combine graham cracker crumbs and melted margarine. Stir till well combined. Press onto bottom and about 2½ inches up the sides of a 9x3-inch springform pan.

Mix cream cheese, sugar, flour, and vanilla. Beat with an electric mixer till fluffy. Add eggs and egg yolks, beating on low speed just till combined. Stir in whipping cream and lemon peel. Pour into pan.

Place pan on a shallow baking pan in the oven. Bake in a 325° oven about 1½ hours or till center appears nearly set when shaken. Cool 15 minutes. Loosen crust from sides of pan. Cool 30 minutes more; remove sides of pan. Cool completely. Chill at least 4 hours. If desired, garnish with fresh berries. Makes 12 to 16 servings.

Nutrition information per serving: 664 calories, 12 g protein, 48 g carbohydrate, 48 g total fat (25 g saturated), 237 mg cholesterol, 494 mg sodium, 153 mg potassium

New York Cheesecake

JEWISH FRUIT KUGEL

Kugel is German for "pudding." Jews from Germany and eastern Europe often serve some type of kugel as part of a holiday meal. It could be sweet, like this one with fruit and noodles, or a savory mixture made with potatoes.

4	ounces wide noodles
2	beaten eggs
¼	cup sugar
2	tablespoons cooking oil
⅛	teaspoon ground cinnamon
1	medium apple, peeled, cored, and diced
¼	cup dried apricots, chopped
¼	cup raisins

Cook noodles according to package directions; drain well. In a large mixing bowl combine eggs, sugar, cooking oil, and cinnamon; beat well. Stir in apples, apricots, and raisins. Toss fruit mixture with drained noodles. Transfer to a greased 1-quart casserole. Cover and bake, stirring once, in a 350° oven for 30 minutes or till a knife inserted near center comes out clean. Serve hot. Makes 6 servings.

Nutrition information per serving: 212 calories, 5 g protein, 33 g carbohydrate, 7 g total fat (1 g saturated), 101 mg cholesterol, 31 mg sodium, 192 mg potassium

CRULLERS

The Dutch in New Amsterdam loved krulljes, crispy puffs of fried dough that we know as crullers. One shape, called tangled britches, was made by pulling one end of a strip of dough through a slit cut in the strip's center. (Pictured on page 90)

⅓	cup sugar
¼	cup margarine *or* butter
2	eggs
2	tablespoons milk
1¾	cups all-purpose flour
½	teaspoon ground mace *or* nutmeg
¼	teaspoon salt
	Cooking oil *or* shortening for deep-fat frying
	Powdered sugar *or* sugar

In a large mixing bowl beat sugar and margarine or butter with an electric mixer till light and fluffy. Add eggs, one at a time; beat well after each addition. Add milk (batter may appear slightly curdled). Stir together flour, mace or nutmeg, and salt. Stir into the egg mixture. Chill at least 1 hour.

On a well floured surface, gently roll *half* of the dough into a 12x6-inch rectangle. Cut into 2-inch squares (do not reroll). Repeat with remaining dough. Fry 3 or 4 squares at a time in deep hot fat (365°) about 1 minute on each side or till golden, turning once with a slotted spoon. Drain on paper towels. Repeat with remaining squares of dough. Gently shake warm crullers in a bag with powdered sugar or sugar; cool. Makes 36 crullers.

Nutrition information per cruller: 94 calories, 1 g protein, 9 g carbohydrate, 6 g total fat (1 g saturated), 12 mg cholesterol, 30 mg sodium, 9 mg potassium

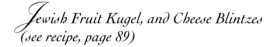

Jewish Fruit Kugel, and Cheese Blintzes (see recipe, page 89)

Dutch Apple Cake, top, Shoofly Pie, left, and Baked Apples in Phyllo Nests

BAKED APPLES IN PHYLLO NESTS

Apple orchards flourished in New York and New Jersey in the seventeenth century. The first commercial apple nursery was established on Long Island a hundred years later.

4　medium cooking apples
　　(about 1⅓ pounds)
½　cup raisins *or* mixed dried
　　fruit bits
2　tablespoons brown sugar
½　teaspoon ground cinnamon
¼　teaspoon ground nutmeg
⅓　cup apple juice *or* water
4　sheets frozen phyllo dough
　　(18x14-inch rectangles),
　　thawed
¼　cup margarine *or* butter,
　　melted
　　Half-and-half *or* light cream
　　(optional)

If desired, cut a slice off of the stem end of each apple. Then core apples; peel a strip from the top of each. Place apples in a 2-quart casserole. Combine raisins or dried fruit bits, brown sugar, cinnamon, and nutmeg. Spoon mixture into centers of apples. Replace apple slice, if using. Add apple juice or water to dish. Bake, uncovered, in a 350° oven for 45 to 50 minutes or till apples are tender, basting occasionally with the cooking liquid. Remove from oven. Cover with foil to keep warm. Increase oven temperature to 375°.

For nests, unfold phyllo dough; cover with a damp towel or clear plastic wrap. Lay 1 sheet of phyllo dough flat. Brush with some of the melted margarine or butter. Top with another sheet of phyllo dough. Brush with more melted margarine or butter. Add the remaining 2 sheets of dough, making a total of 4 sheets, brushing each sheet with margarine or butter. Cut stack in half lengthwise and crosswise to make 4 smaller stacks.

Place each stack of phyllo dough in a greased 10-ounce custard cup. Place the custard cups on a baking sheet. Bake in the 375° oven for 7 to 10 minutes or till phyllo dough is crisp and golden.

To serve, gently lift each phyllo nest out of custard cups and onto individual dessert plates. Set a baked apple in each nest, spooning apple liquid over apples. If desired, serve with half-and-half or light cream. Makes 4 servings.

Nutrition information per serving: 323 calories, 3 g protein, 55 g carbohydrate, 12 g total fat (2 g saturated), 0 mg cholesterol, 169 mg sodium, 359 mg potassium

New York

DUTCH APPLE CAKE

Both the New Amsterdam Dutch and the Pennsylvania Germans loved apple cakes. This one is probably from New York. A Pennsylvania recipe would use yeast as the leavener, which was kept in a crock above the stove.

2 cups all-purpose flour
1½ cups sugar
1 teaspoon baking powder
1 teaspoon baking soda
1 teaspoon ground cinnamon
¼ teaspoon ground nutmeg
¼ teaspoon ground cloves
¼ teaspoon ground ginger
1 cup applesauce
¼ cup buttermilk
¼ cup margarine *or* butter, softened
¼ cup shortening
½ teaspoon vanilla
3 eggs
2 cups chopped peeled apples
   Apple Brandy Glaze

In a large mixing bowl combine flour, sugar, baking powder, baking soda, cinnamon, nutmeg, cloves, and ginger. Add applesauce, buttermilk, margarine or butter, shortening, and vanilla. Beat with an electric mixer on low to medium speed till combined. Beat 2 minutes on medium to high speed. Add eggs and beat 2 minutes more. Fold in chopped apples.

Pour batter into a greased 13x9x2-inch baking pan. Bake in a 350° oven for 35 to 40 minutes or till a toothpick inserted near the center comes out clean. Cool on a wire rack. Drizzle with Apple Brandy Glaze. Makes 12 servings.

Apple Brandy Glaze: In a small bowl stir together 1 cup sifted *powdered sugar,* 1 tablespoon *apple brandy or apple juice,* and ¼ teaspoon *vanilla.* Stir in additional *apple brandy or apple juice,* 1 teaspoon at a time, till mixture is of drizzling consistency.

Nutrition information per serving: 321 calories, 4 g protein, 55 g carbohydrate, 10 g total fat (2 g saturated), 53 mg cholesterol, 149 mg sodium, 70 mg potassium

Pennsylvania

SHOOFLY PIE

Shoofly pie is perhaps the most famous Pennsylvania Dutch recipe. While there are no firm theories on how the pie got its name, one possibility is that the sweetness of the filling made flies a nuisance.

   Pastry for Single-Crust Pie (see recipe, page 55)
1½ cups all-purpose flour
½ cup sugar
6 tablespoons margarine *or* butter
½ cup molasses
½ cup water
½ teaspoon baking soda

Prepare and roll out pastry. Line a 9-inch pie plate. Line pastry with a double thickness of foil. Bake in a 450° oven for 8 minutes. Remove foil. Bake for 4 to 5 minutes more or till set and dry. Cool on a wire rack.

In a medium mixing bowl stir together flour and sugar. Cut in margarine or butter till the mixture resembles coarse crumbs. Set aside.

In another mixing bowl stir together the molasses, water, and baking soda. Pour *one-fourth* of the molasses mixture into pastry shell. Sprinkle with *one-fourth* of the flour mixture. Repeat layers, ending with the flour mixture. Cover edge of pie with foil.

Bake in a 375° oven 15 minutes; remove foil. Bake about 20 minutes more or till a knife inserted near the center comes out clean. Cool on a wire rack. Makes 8 servings.

Nutrition information per serving: 383 calories, 4 g protein, 55 g carbohydrate, 17 g total fat (3 g saturated), 0 mg cholesterol, 254 mg sodium, 345 mg potassium

New York

CHEESE BLINTZES

The traditional filling for a blintz, from the Yiddish blintseh, *is either sweetened, spiced farmer cheese and/or fruit. It commonly appears on the menu of Jewish dairy restaurants like Ratner's in New York. The wrapping is somewhat like a French crêpe or Russian blini.*
(Pictured on page 87)

¾ cup all-purpose flour
½ teaspoon salt
1 cup milk
2 eggs
1 12-ounce carton dry cottage cheese (1½ cups)
1 beaten egg
2 tablespoons sugar
½ teaspoon vanilla
   Dash ground cinnamon
2 tablespoons butter
   Sliced strawberries (optional)
   Dairy sour cream (optional)

In a bowl mix flour and salt. Combine milk and the 2 eggs; gradually add to the flour mixture, beating till batter is smooth. Pour about 2 tablespoons batter into a hot, lightly greased, 6-inch skillet; quickly swirl skillet to spread batter evenly. Cook over medium heat till pancakes are golden on bottom, 1½ to 2 minutes. Loosen; turn out onto paper towels. Repeat with remaining batter, making 12 pancakes.

In a bowl beat cottage cheese, the 1 egg, sugar, vanilla, and cinnamon with electric mixer till nearly smooth. Lay pancakes browned side up; spoon about 2 tablespoons of cheese mixture down centers. Fold in ends and overlap sides over filling. In a 12-inch skillet melt butter; add blintzes, seam side down. Cook over medium heat for 10 minutes, turning once halfway through cooking time. Serve hot; if desired, serve with strawberries and sour cream. Makes 6 servings.

Nutrition information per serving: 195 calories, 12 g protein, 19 g carbohydrate, 7 g total fat (4 g saturated), 122 mg cholesterol, 273 mg sodium, 92 mg potassium

Crullers, top (see recipe, page 86), and Funnel Cakes

(see recipe, page 86)

FUNNEL CAKES

Deep-fried funnel cakes drizzled with molasses fortified Pennsylvania Dutch farmers in the early morning so they could return to their chores. To create the distinctive spiral, the batter is channeled through a large metal funnel that is slowly swirled over a pan of bubbling hot fat.

2	beaten eggs
1½	cups milk
¼	cup packed brown sugar
2	cups all-purpose flour
1½	teaspoons baking powder
¼	teaspoon salt
2	cups cooking oil
	Powdered sugar *or* Caramel Sauce (optional)

For batter, in a large mixing bowl stir together eggs, milk, and brown sugar. In another bowl combine flour, baking powder, and salt. Add flour mixture to egg mixture. Beat with a rotary beater till smooth.

In an 8-inch skillet heat cooking oil to 360°. Hold a funnel with a ½-inch spout (inside diameter), covering the bottom of the spout with your finger. Pour about ½ cup of the batter into the funnel. Remove your finger, carefully releasing the batter into the hot oil; start at the center of the skillet and move the funnel in a circular motion to form a spiral. (*Or,* if a funnel is not available, use a small glass measuring cup to carefully pour batter into the hot oil.)

Cook batter about 2½ minutes or till golden brown. Using 2 wide metal spatulas, carefully turn the funnel cake. Cook about 1 minute more or till golden. Remove the funnel cake from the skillet and drain on paper towels. Repeat with the remaining batter.

If desired, sprinkle funnel cakes with powdered sugar or drizzle with Caramel Sauce. Serve warm. Makes 4 or 5 cakes.

Caramel Sauce: In a heavy small saucepan stir together ¼ cup packed *brown sugar* and 1½ teaspoons *corn-starch.* Stir in ¼ cup *milk, half-and-half,* or *light cream,* 2 tablespoons *water,* and 1 tablespoon *light corn syrup.* Cook and stir till bubbly (mixture may appear curdled). Cook and stir for 2 minutes more. Remove from the heat. Stir in 1 tablespoon *margarine or butter* and ½ teaspoon *vanilla.* Serve warm. Makes about ½ cup.

Nutrition information per cake: 476 calories, 13 g protein, 64 g carbohydrate, 18 g total fat (4 g saturated), 113 mg cholesterol, 334 mg sodium, 239 mg potassium

WHOLE WHEAT GINGERBREAD PEOPLE

Since the Middle Ages, European bakers—German, English, Dutch— have been masters at fashioning elaborate images out of flat, rich gingerbread dough. When these groups emigrated to America, the tradition of shaped spice cookies came with them.

1	cup margarine *or* butter
3	cups all-purpose flour
1	cup whole wheat flour
1	cup packed brown sugar
⅓	cup molasses
1	egg
1	tablespoon finely shredded orange peel
2	tablespoons orange juice
2	teaspoons ground cinnamon
1	teaspoon ground ginger
½	teaspoon baking soda
½	teaspoon ground cloves
¼	teaspoon salt
	Creamy Lemon Icing
	Decorative candies

In a large mixing bowl beat margarine or butter with an electric mixer on medium to high speed for

30 seconds. Add about *half* of the all-purpose flour, the whole wheat flour, brown sugar, molasses, egg, orange peel, orange juice, cinnamon, ginger, baking soda, cloves, and salt. Beat with an electric mixer on medium to high speed till thoroughly combined. Beat or stir in remaining all-purpose flour. Cover and chill for 1 to 2 hours or till firm enough to roll out.

Divide the chilled dough in half. On a lightly floured surface, roll *half* of the dough at a time to ¼-inch thickness. Cut into desired shapes with cookie cutters. Place the shapes 1 inch apart on an ungreased cookie sheet.

Bake in a 375° oven for 8 to 10 minutes or till edges are firm. Cool on cookie sheet for 1 minute. Remove cookies and cool on a wire rack. Decorate cookies with Creamy Lemon Icing and decorative candies. Makes 24 cookies.

Creamy Lemon Icing: In a small mixing bowl beat ¼ cup *shortening* and ¼ teaspoon *vanilla* with an electric mixer for 30 seconds or till softened. Gradually beat in 1¼ cups sifted *powdered sugar.* Beat in enough *lemon juice* (about 1 tablespoon) till icing is of spreading consistency. If desired, stir in several drops of *food coloring.*

Nutrition information per cookie: 220 calories, 3 g protein, 30 g carbohydrate, 10 g total fat (2 g saturated), 9 mg cholesterol, 111 mg sodium, 133 mg potassium

Pennsylvania

GINGERSNAP ICE CREAM COOKIES

Like American gingerbread, crinkle-top gingersnaps claim multi-national European ancestry. The Pennsylvania Dutch enjoy them both as a dessert and as a thickener for sauerbraten gravy. These cookies also appear in New England recipe collections.

Whole Wheat Gingerbread People and Gingersnap Ice Cream Cookies

2¼ cups all-purpose flour
1 cup packed brown sugar
¾ cup shortening *or* cooking oil
¼ cup molasses
1 egg
1 teaspoon baking soda
1 teaspoon ground ginger
½ teaspoon ground cloves
¼ cup sugar
½ cup whipping cream
1 quart vanilla ice cream *or* frozen yogurt
1 teaspoon shredded lemon peel

In a large mixing bowl combine about *half* of the flour, the brown sugar, shortening or oil, molasses, egg, baking soda, ginger, and cloves. Beat with an electric mixer on medium to high speed till thoroughly combined. Beat in the remaining flour.

Shape dough into 2-inch balls. Roll balls in sugar. Place 2 inches apart on an ungreased cookie sheet. Flatten slightly with the bottom of a glass dipped in sugar. Bake in a 375° oven for 10 to 12 minutes or till set and tops are crackled. Cool cookies completely on a wire rack.

For filling, beat the whipping cream with an electric mixer till soft peaks form. Stir the vanilla ice cream or yogurt just to soften; fold in the whipped cream and lemon peel. For each sandwich, quickly spread about ⅓ cup filling onto the bottom side of *one* cookie. Top with another cookie. Immediately place onto a baking sheet in the freezer (keep baking sheet in freezer to prevent sandwiches from softening while assembling the rest). Repeat with remaining cookies and filling. Cover and freeze for 12 to 24 hours. Let stand at room temperature for 10 minutes before serving. Makes 12 sandwiches.

Nutrition information per sandwich: 408 calories, 5 g protein, 49 g carbohydrate, 22 g total fat (9 g saturated), 51 mg cholesterol, 120 mg sodium, 263 mg potassium

FUNERAL PIE

*It was the custom among the
Pennsylvania Dutch to bake this lemony
raisin pie, also known as a rosina
(from the German word for raisin)
to serve at funerals. Other groups, like
the Welsh, Dutch, and English, also
reserved special cakes, breads, and
cookies for times of mourning.*

3	egg whites
⅔	cup sugar
2	tablespoons cornstarch
2	cups raisins
1⅓	cups cold water
1	teaspoon finely shredded lemon peel *or* orange peel
¼	cup lemon juice *or* orange juice
2	tablespoons margarine *or* butter
	Pastry for Single-Crust Pie (see recipe, page 55)
½	teaspoon vanilla
¼	teaspoon cream of tartar
6	tablespooms sugar

Allow egg whites to stand at room temperature for 30 minutes.

In a medium saucepan combine the ⅔ cup sugar and cornstarch. Stir in raisins, cold water, lemon or orange peel, and lemon or orange juice. Cook and stir till thickened and bubbly; cook and stir 2 minutes more. Stir in margarine or butter till margarine melts. Remove from heat. Pour hot filling into pastry shell

For meringue in a medium mixing bowl combine the egg whites, ½ teaspoon vanilla, and cream of tartar. Beat with an electric mixer on medium speed about 1 minute or till soft peaks form (tips curl). Gradually add the remaining sugar, 1 tablespoon at a time, beating on high speed about 4 minutes more or till mixture forms stiff, glossy peaks and sugar dissolves. Immediately spread over pie, carefully sealing to

Fish House Punch

edge of pastry to prevent shrinking. Bake in a 350° oven for 15 minutes or till golden. Cool on a wire rack for 1 hour; chill. Cover and chill to store. Makes 8 servings.

Nutrition information per serving: 385 calories, 4 g protein, 72 g carbohydrate, 11 g total fat (2 g saturated), 0 mg cholesterol, 177 mg sodium, 357 mg potassium

FISH HOUSE PUNCH

*The Fish House, formally known
as The State in Schuylkill, is
Philadelphia's oldest and most famous
private cooking and eating club.
It was chartered in 1732, when
America was still an English colony.
This punch, the house drink,
has been served from the same nine-
gallon Lowestoft bowl since 1812.*

2	cups water
½	cup sugar
2	cups rum
1	cup brandy
¾	cup lemon juice
½	cup peach brandy
	Lemon slices *or* Lemon Ice Ring

In a bowl or pitcher combine water and sugar; stir till sugar dissolves. Stir in rum, brandy, lemon juice, and peach brandy. Cover and chill till serving time. Serve in a large pitcher with lemon slices and ice cubes or in a punch bowl with Lemon Ice Ring. Makes 12 (4-ounce) servings.

Lemon Ice Ring: Line the bottom of a ring mold with sliced *lemons*. Add enough *water* to cover the fruit. Freeze till firm. Then fill the mold with more *water* and freeze till firm.

Nutrition information per serving: 194 calories, 0 g protein, 10 g carbohydrate, 0 g total fat (0 g saturated), 0 mg cholesterol, 1 mg sodium, 20 mg potassium

Funeral Pie

The South

From the kitchens of tidewater Maryland down to the bayous of Louisiana, southern cooks over the last three centuries have sent forth some of the finest regional dishes this country has to offer. The South is comprised of a large and varied geographical area that includes the Atlantic Coast states of Maryland, Virginia, the Carolinas, Georgia, and Florida as well as the Gulf Coast states of Alabama, Mississippi, and Louisiana, and the landlocked states of Tennessee, Arkansas, Kentucky, and West Virginia.

Although culinary distinctions can often be made from one state to the next, there is one characteristic for which all of this region's kitchens is famous, namely southern hospitality. Listen to the report of a mid–eighteenth century traveler passing through Virginia: "All over the Colony, a universal Hospitality reigns; full Tables and open Doors. . . . Their Dinner [includes] good Beef, Veal, Mutton, Venison, Turkies and Geese, wild and tame, Fowls, boil'd and roasted; and perhaps somewhat more, as Pies, Puddings, etc. for Dessert. . . . And this is the constant life they lead, and to this Fare every Comer is welcome."[1]

Due to the South's warm climate and long growing season, the bounty of the land was equal to the bounty of the sea. For the native Muskhogean tribe, sweet potatoes, squash, and melons were common fare along with the wild strawberries and blackberries that grew in profusion. The region also boasts a special variety of grape called scuppernong (after a river in North Carolina where it grew in abundance). Scuppernong wine was known to Virginia's Thomas Jefferson, and wines, jams, and jellies made from this regional grape are available in the South to this day.

Wild game abounded in the early South. Venison and bear meat were prized by the Indians, and small animals such as rabbit, squirrel, and opossum became the inspiration for one-pot hunter's stews, such as Kentucky's burgoo and Virginia's Brunswick stew (nowadays made more often with chicken).

But arguably the most memorable culinary legacy of the southern kitchen is the dishes featuring the region's prodigious range of seafood. Thoughts of Maryland bring to mind crab cakes and she-crab soup. There is Louisiana's crawfish étouffée, Mississippi's fried catfish, Virginia's Chesapeake oysters, South Carolina's shrimp pie, and Florida's stone crab. Sometimes the simplest preparation is the most fondly recalled: travelers visiting Maryland, for example, are in awe when a steaming pile of boiled crab is set before them, demanding nothing more than a keen appetite and the pounding of a wooden mallet.

As in New England, a staple of the colonial diet was corn, and the early settlers initially relied upon Native Americans to instruct them in the complexities of corn production and cookery. To this day, corn plays a significant role in the southern kitchen, and the cornmeal that results from grinding dried whole kernels is used

to create a prodigious variety of fritters, crumbly cracklin' breads, and moist spoon breads.

The colonists learned to prepare hominy in the Indian way by boiling dried white corn kernels in a lye solution until the hulls fell off. The poisonous lye was thoroughly rinsed away and the remaining "hearts" were cooked with small bits of meat or vegetables. As time went on, the settlers built mills to grind the hominy into grits. To the Indians' simple porridge, they began adding knobs of butter and replacing some or all of the water with milk. The result? The ultimate bowl of creamy grits that is the pride of many a southern cook.

Leftover grits are never put to waste. They are molded, sliced, and fried or mixed with eggs and milk to make puddinglike spoon bread known as Awendaw.

The Black Influence

Beginning as early as 1619, the availability of slave labor had a tremendous impact not only in the fields but in the kitchens of the South. Historians now believe that it was the rice-growing expertise of West African slaves that made it possible for novice planters of South Carolina to succeed in turning their marshes into Carolina Gold, as the famous strain of Carolina rice was called.

The burgeoning population of blacks, soon outnumbering the whites, made possible a socially stratified plantation culture and a master's table laden with labor-intensive foods. Wealthy southerners, for example, enjoyed a wide range of freshly baked breads daily,

Formal entertaining was an important part of plantation life in the antebellum South. Its public face was the elegant dining room of the main house (above). Behind the scenes, slaves labored in a bare-bones kitchen often situated in another building (right). Below: Enterprising oyster peddlers capitalized on the nineteenth-century frenzy for the shellfish that overtook the South and just about everywhere else in this country.

whether the sweet and yeasty Sally Lunn, or the puffy buttermilk or sweet potato biscuit. The crackerlike beaten biscuit has become a symbol of the old plantation South since it was so time-consuming to prepare. Tradition required that the dough be continuously folded over and clubbed with a heavy mallet or iron skillet hundreds of times until filled with tiny pockets of air so that the resultant biscuit would have just the right texture.

Unlike the New England kitchen—where the hearth served as the focal point of the home—the plantation kitchen was a separate outbuilding, both to diminish any fire hazards and to keep the cooking heat and aromas as far as possible from the main house. To this kitchen, the black slaves

brought their own ingredients and culinary traditions, introducing pilaus (rice pilafs), okra, black-eyed peas, and the sesame seeds they called benne.

In the big iron kettles in the slaves' quarters, these cooks prepared dishes based on ingredients that were cast off by the master. Pigs' intestines were soaked, cleaned, and cut up into tiny bits, dipped in cornmeal, and deep-fried in lard to create chitlins. The pot greens slow-cooked with a smoked ham bone, the shortnin' bread dotted with crackling (fried pork skin), and the collards simmered with black-eyed peas all contributed to the hearty repertoire we now think of as southern soul food.

Thomas Jefferson
America's First Gourmet

The kitchen garden at Monticello.

During his presidency, John F. Kennedy once remarked to a visiting group of Nobel laureates that they constituted the most extraordinary collection of talent ever gathered at the White House, "with the possible exception of when Thomas Jefferson dined alone."

Jefferson's curiosity knew no bounds, and he brought his brilliant mind to bear on the subjects of gardening and dining with as much enthusiasm as he approached architecture and politics.

In his kitchen garden at Monticello, Jefferson grew many exotic food plants from seeds he imported from all parts of the world. He carefully recorded the cultivation of vegetables in his Farm Book, where he lists broccoli, globe artichokes, asparagus, cabbage in great variety, beans, cauliflower, celery, eggplant, salsify, Jerusalem artichokes, potatoes, and pumpkins. He also included more than thirty varieties of peas!

But Jefferson's world of food grew even larger during a five-year stint based in Paris as minister to the court of Louis XVI. As he acquired new tastes, Jefferson made arrangements to have these specialty foods regularly shipped to his residences, either in Washington or in Monticello. Thus, we have surviving correspondence discussing the importation of vanilla beans, Parmesan cheese, figs from Marseilles, tarragon vinegar, and anchovies. After tasting macaroni for the first time, Jefferson describes in great length how it is properly made, and then puts great effort and energy into locating just the right mold for his home kitchen. No detail escaped his attention.

Jefferson's hospitality during his presidency was legendary, provoking John Adams to observe that while he hosted a large crowd once or twice a week, Jefferson's whole eight years was a party. He had become quite an oenophile during his time abroad, and fine wines flowed freely during his White House tenure. One New England clergyman described the menu for a dinner he was fortunate enough to share: rice soup, roast beef, mutton, ham, loin of veal, fried eggs, a "pie" called macaroni, ice cream, a great variety of fruit, plenty of wines and good ones.

Jefferson is often credited with introducing ice cream to this country, but there are records showing that even before his presidency, George Washington was in possession of an icecream maker. Probably, the confusion comes in because Jefferson first tasted French vanilla ice cream while in Paris and popularized the use of the vanilla bean here. During his White House years, Jefferson liked to surprise guests by serving ice cream enclosed in cases of warm pastry—an early form of baked Alaska.

Despite an unquenchable joy and curiosity about food, Jefferson himself was a modest eater. He often attributed his long life—he lived to be eighty-three (an especially ripe age for his time)—to a diet predominantly made up of fresh foods from the garden and a preference for wine over strong spirits.

Indeed, much of his passionate quest for fine foods abroad had a humanitarian end, for Jefferson strongly believed that the introduction of a useful plant was the greatest service that any man could render his country. His rich legacy on the subjects of food and gardening are living proof that Jefferson was a man who lived according to his beliefs.

Rice Is King

During the last decade of the seventeenth century, a strain of Madagascar rice was introduced to the South Carolina Low Country. This Carolina Gold was soon to change the face and kitchens of the South.

Over the next two hundred years, cooks argued in print about the proper way to boil rice, but what has become the most traditional southern method was described as early as 1756 in the manuscript cookbook of Eliza Pinckney. First the rice is picked over and cleaned, then boiled for approximately fifteen minutes in ample salted water. When tender, the rice is strained and then set back into a covered pot to steam "near the fire . . . and if the process is well observed it will be white, dry, and every grain Separate."[2]

An examination of Sarah Rutledge's *The Carolina Housewife*, published in 1847, reveals at a glance that rice by that time formed the basis for dozens of dishes, from breads, muffins, and griddle cakes to pilafs, soups, casseroles, and pies. Perhaps the most famous of rice dishes to come out of the southern kitchen is hoppin John, a flavorful pilaf made of rice and black-eyed peas cooked with bacon and seasoned with salt and pepper. Thought to bring good luck, it is traditionally eaten on New Year's Day.

Fancy Fare

When it came to elegant desserts, the southern plantation kitchen arguably had no peer. Drawing upon a long heritage of English tradition, Dixie cooks turned out fruitcakes, wines, jellies, trifles, and syllabubs and served them in their most elegant crystal and china.

The richness of these creations makes a contemporary calorie-counter gasp. Martha Washington's recipe for "Great Cake," for example, called for forty eggs, four pounds each of butter and sugar, and five pounds of fruit and flour. (Granted that this recipe produced a very large cake, indeed.)

As baking powder became more readily available, it replaced yeast to create the rich but crumbly cakes that are best known today. Every cook had her favorite basic pound cake recipe, and fine layer cakes like coconut cake, Robert E. Lee cake, Lane cake, and Lady Baltimore are still well known throughout the South today.

But "ask the average man what he prefers for dessert, and almost invariably he will answer 'pie,'" says Mrs. Henrietta Dull in her very popular *Southern Cooking*, first published in 1928. Given that fact, it's no wonder that pies figure prominently in the repertoire of southern cooks. In North Carolina, the category is divided into three types: covered, uncovered, and latticed (or "kivered, unkivered, and barred," as the locals put it). Among the most traditional are the custardy egg-and-butter-rich chess pies flavored with lemon, chocolate, or lots of

Before the era of the superhighway, the meandering waterways of the South, like this gentle Maryland stream, transported its people and its products.

Elegant, lacy cast-iron balconies grace historic New Orleans buildings (left). It's hard to believe that the city was once a steamy bog when it was founded in 1718. Above: In this 1870s depiction, a fisherman rests while his wife cooks up his catch of local prawns. The historic diet of southern blacks is a spicy mixture of ingredients—part African, part regional, part subsistence. When available, fish and seafood played an important role.

brown sugar. Or how about sweet potato, coconut cream, butterscotch, or pecan pie?

The southern sweet tooth is legendary, and certainly such elegant desserts provided the ideal grand finale to a meal filled with the generous kindness known as southern hospitality.

Louisiana Creole And Cajun

Louisiana is the very proud home of two highly sophisticated and somewhat distinct cuisines—Cajun and Creole. The rural Cajun cuisine was strongly influenced by the arrival of French Acadians exiled

from Nova Scotia. They brought with them a simple country style of cooking which was blended with the ingredients that grew wild in the state's southernmost bayous and swamplands where they settled.

The Creole cooking that developed in the bustling port of New Orleans represents a unique blend of many more culinary traditions. When the French founded that city in 1718, they brought the inspiration for such famous regional dishes as shrimp rémoulade, pompano *en papillote, pain perdue,* and beignets. France ceded the Louisiana territory to Spain in 1762, opening the kitchen doors to jambalaya (a close cousin to paella) and to the generous use of red peppers, tomatoes, and garlic.

The native Choctaw Indians contributed their filé powder made of ground sassafras leaves, which black slave cooks combined with their favorite spices into spicy soups and stews. So great was the influence of black cooks on the Creole kitchen that when the encyclopedic *Picayune Creole Cookbook* was published in 1900, it was dedicated to preserving the kitchen skills of "the Creole negro cooks of nearly two hundred years ago, carefully instructed and directed by their white Creole mistresses."

Both Cajun and Creole cooks make use of abundant local seafood —crawfish, oysters, shrimp—as well as chicken, smoked ham, and seasonal game. In addition to filé powder, common seasonings include bay leaves and a wide variety of hot peppers, including bird's-eye, cayenne, banana, and tabasco (which gave its name to the tomato-based hot sauce produced on Louisiana's Avery Island). Louisiana cooking reveals its strong connection to the southern tradition through its abundant use of rice and its love of grits and corn bread.

Perhaps the two best-known Louisiana dishes are *gumbo* and jambalaya. The word gumbo is derived from the African word for okra, a common ingredient used to thicken this stew, made of shrimp, crab, or chicken and smoked sausage simmered with green pepper, onions, and celery. The rice-based jambalaya can include bits of smoked ham, chicken, sausage, or seafood and is often flavored with tomatoes. The word itself comes from the French word *jambon*, meaning "ham," and the African *ya*, denoting "rice."

Visitors to New Orleans' restaurants are hard-pressed to decide what famous regional dish they might like to try. Perhaps some oysters Bienville (baked with a creamed shrimp topping) or crayfish étouffée, the tiny shellfish stewed under a "blanket" of finely minced onion, green pepper, celery, and garlic. Or perhaps the elegant pompano *en papillote*, the fish poached in an envelope of parchment—an invention of Antoine's restaurant to honor a visiting French balloonist in 1901.

For more casual dining, there's a choice of one of the city's famous sandwiches. The first choice of bivalve lovers, will surely be oyster loaves, for nowhere will they taste more succulent fried oysters, more generously stuffed into an individual white loaf. Others will opt for a taste of the Italian influence when

they try a *muffaletta*, a round loaf crowned with sesame seeds and stuffed with ham, salami, and mozzarella, topped with lettuce, tomato, and olives.

No matter what the choice of food, every visitor ends up at the Morning Call in the old French market along the banks of the Mississippi. It's here you have your taste of Creole coffee accompanied by a steaming hot beignet sprinkled with sugar, participating in a

centuries-old tradition that began when all of the local farmers and ships' merchants gathered there to sell their produce and wares. The coffee may taste peculiar, since it's blended with chicory. In the early days, this blending was an economic necessity. Now it's done because Creole coffee is just one of the many things that makes the Louisiana kitchen unique.

This ten-plate stove was probably made in Frederick County, Maryland, between 1815 and 1820. Ornamental scenes are cast in raised relief on its sides.

Florida Cookery

It's easy to forget that the first permanent settlement in the U.S. was not Jamestown, Virginia, but St. Augustine, Florida. It was here that the Spanish established a fort in 1565, but they were not the first to arrive. Ponce de Leon had landed on Easter Sunday in 1513 and named the area *Pascua florida*, Spanish for "flowery Easter."

The Spanish settlers in St. Augustine quickly began importing livestock as well as their preferred vegetables and fruits—including the now famous Florida oranges, lemons, and grapefruits. The tiny limes that are traditionally used for making the state's famous Key lime pie are actually wild fruits indigenous to the southern string of islands known as the Florida Keys.

When author Marjorie Kinnan Rawlings wrote her classic *Cross Creek Cookery* in 1942, she included many traditional southern recipes plus such local specialties as Florida soft-shell turtle soup, stone crabs, Spanish chicken fricassee, alligator-tail steak, fried plantains, and grapefruit marmalade. Stone crabs are still readily available in Miami, but alligator steak and turtle soup have gone the way of the hula-hoop.

In recent decades the large influx of Cubans to southern Florida has inundated the Florida kitchen with another strong wave of Spanish influence, this one doused with the foods and flavors of the Caribbean. The "fusion" cooking style that has emerged results in dishes like grilled pompano served with yucca chips and star fruit, or a spicy tomato-based taro stew flecked with fresh coriander—yet other examples of the ever-changing face of American regional cuisine.

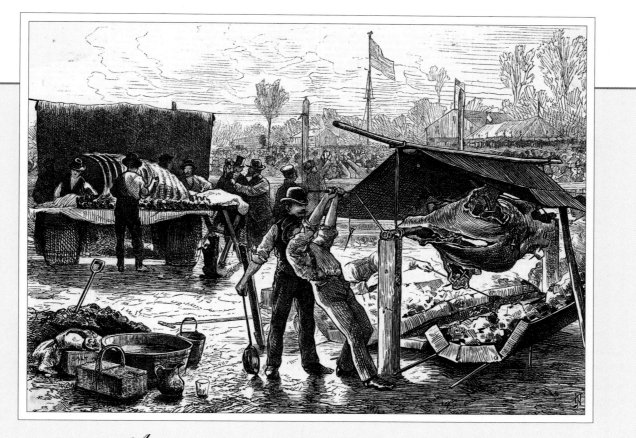

A southern barbecue often involved—and fed—the whole town.

Fire and Smoke

The long months of sultry heat in the South necessitated the preservation of food. That fact, combined with their great love of pork, inspired cooks to create two great southern specialties: country ham and barbecue.

In Smithfield, Virginia, this country's acknowledged source of the finest cured ham, tradition dates back to colonial times when pigs were fattened on peanuts before they were slaughtered, salt-cured, smoked over hardwood, and then aged for close to one year. In the words of one Virginian: "No self-respecting pig can imagine a higher distinction than becoming, in due course, a Virginia ham— spicy as a woman's tongue, sweet as her kiss, as tender as her love."[3]

Such properly prepared ham is hard to come by nowadays, but locals who've grown up on it will abide no other: "Let those who prefer Tennessee country ham backed with pickled peaches, Texas ham with corn-meal coating, Georgia country ham, glazed sugar-coated ham with champagne sauce, fried Kentucky ham with red gravy, Alabama ham loaf with mustard sauce, or Florida ham with cayenne pepper argue their cases. All one has to do to be completely won over to Virginia ham is to eat it."[4] And if you are lucky enough to taste proper Virginia ham, it is likely to be tucked into feather-light baking powder biscuits.

Southerners wax equally eloquent on the subject of barbecue. Let there be no mistake:

we are not talking about the kind of barbecue that involves grilling a steak or a hamburger over hot coals in the backyard. Along the barbecue belt—Alabama, Arkansas, Georgia, the Carolinas, Kentucky, and Tennessee—barbecue means one thing only: pork roasted in an open pit over hickory or oak. While cooking, it is basted with a tomato-and-vinegar-based sauce that's often spiked with hot peppers. When ready, the meat is either sliced, chopped, minced, pulled from, or served still attached to the ribs. And depending upon what state you're in, the pork will be sandwiched between white bread, corn bread, or the halves of a bun, then doused with hot sauce, and topped with coleslaw or pickles. Some purists eat it plain.

Most of all, barbecue means community, an occasion for people from all backgrounds and socioeconomic groups to gather and share a mutual passion. This was already true back at the turn of the century when the British traveler John Watkins observed: "No one who has had the good fortune to attend a barbecue will ever forget it. The smell of it all, the meat slowly roasting to a delicious brown over smoking fires, the hungry and happy crowds. . . . It is no exaggeration to say that many a gubernatorial election in Georgia has been carried by means of votes gained at barbecues, and no campaign for Governor is complete without a series of such popular feasts."[5]

Flavors from the South

Florida

HOT SPINACH AND OYSTER DIP

During the nineteenth century, Americans consumed oysters in amounts almost unimaginable today. Southerners succumbed to oyster fever as much as people anywhere else, perhaps because so many succulent varieties grew in local waters.
(Pictured on page 109)

¼   cup finely chopped onion
¼   cup chopped red sweet pepper
1   tablespoon margarine *or* butter
1   tablespoon all-purpose flour
¼   teaspoon garlic powder
¼   teaspoon pepper
¼   cup water
1½   cups chopped fresh spinach
1   8-ounce jar cheese spread with jalapeño peppers
1   8-ounce can oysters, drained Melba toast rounds, toasted French baguette bread slices, *or* crackers

In a saucepan cook onion and red sweet pepper in hot margarine or butter till tender. Stir in flour, garlic powder, and pepper. Add water. Cook and stir over medium heat till slightly thickened and bubbly. Cook and stir for 1 minute more. Stir in spinach and cheese. Cook and stir till well blended.

Rinse oysters and drain well; coarsely chop. Stir into cheese mixture; heat through. Transfer to a serving bowl or chafing dish. Serve warm with melba toast rounds, French baguette bread slices, or crackers. Makes 12 servings.

Nutrition information per serving: 78 calories, 5 g protein, 4 g carbohydrate, 5 g total fat (2 g saturated), 21 mg cholesterol, 323 mg sodium, 146 mg potassium

Georgia

SPICY PECANS

Georgia produces one-third of the nation's pecan crop, although the nut isn't native to that state. It did grow wild in other parts of the South and was prized by Native Americans for its flavor and nutrition. The word pecan comes from the Algonquian paccan and the Cree pakan.
(Pictured on page 108)

1   to 1½ teaspoons chili powder
1   teaspoon curry powder
1   teaspoon garlic salt
¼   teaspoon ground cumin
¼   teaspoon ground ginger
¼   teaspoon ground cinnamon
3   tablespoons olive oil
1   teaspoon Worcestershire sauce
¼   to ½ teaspoon bottled hot pepper sauce
3   cups pecan halves

In a skillet mix chili powder, curry powder, garlic salt, cumin, ginger, and cinnamon. Stir in olive oil, Worcestershire sauce, and hot pepper sauce. Cook and stir over low heat 5 minutes to mellow flavors.

Place pecan halves in a bowl; add the spice mixture. Toss to coat evenly. Spread pecan halves in a single layer on a 15x10x1-inch baking pan. Bake in a 325° oven for 15 minutes, shaking pan occasionally. Cool completely. Makes 3 cups.

Nutrition information per 1/4 cup: 212 calories, 2 g protein, 5 g carbohydrate, 22 g total fat (2 g saturated), 0 mg cholesterol, 153 mg sodium, 121 mg potassium

Maryland Crab Cakes, top (see recipe, page 110), and Panfried Soft-Shell Crabs (see recipe, page 109)

Louisiana

BOURBON-PECAN PÂTÉ

Although this pâté recipe is contemporary, its combination of French technique and southern tastes — bourbon and pecans — has its roots in Thomas Jefferson's day. Some credit Jefferson's love of French cooking, acquired while he served in Paris as the United States envoy, with adding a French accent to southern cooking.

½ cup finely chopped pecans
2 tablespoons margarine *or* butter
½ pound chicken livers, rinsed and drained
¼ cup finely chopped onion
1 clove garlic, minced
⅓ cup apple juice
½ teaspoon paprika
¼ teaspoon salt
⅛ teaspoon pepper
⅛ teaspoon ground allspice
⅓ cup chicken broth
1 teaspoon unflavored gelatin
2 tablespoons bourbon whiskey
   Parsley
   Toasted pecan halves
   Apple *and/or* pear wedges
   Assorted crackers *or* toasted breads

In a skillet cook the chopped pecans in margarine till golden. Remove pecans; set aside. Add chicken livers, onion, and garlic to skillet. Cook over medium heat till livers are brown and onion is tender. Stir in apple juice, paprika, salt, pepper, and allspice. Reduce heat. Cover; simmer for 3 minutes.

Combine chicken broth and gelatin; let stand for 5 minutes to soften. Stir broth mixture into hot mixture; stir to dissolve gelatin. Remove from heat; stir in bourbon and let mixture cool slightly.

In a blender container or food processor bowl carefully blend or process about half of the liver mixture at a time till smooth. Stir in chopped pecans. Pour into a lightly oiled 2½ to 3 cup mold. Cover and chill for 6 hours or till firm.

Bourbon-Pecan Pâté, and Spicy Pecans (see recipe, page 106)

Unmold onto platter; garnish with parsley and pecan halves.* Serve with apple and/or pear wedges and crackers or breads. Makes 16 appetizer servings.

*Note: To help unmold the pâté, place the mold in a bowl or sink of warm water just till the edges are loosened from the mold. Invert.

Nutrition information per serving: 70 calories, 3 g protein, 2 g carbohydrate, 5 g total fat (1 g saturated), 67 mg cholesterol, 68 mg sodium, 52 mg potassium

West Virginia

CHUTNEY DIP

Most likely, southern sea captains and spice traders carried home Indian recipes from England for curries and condiments like chutney as part of their exotic cargo.

1 8-ounce carton dairy sour cream *or* plain yogurt
¼ teaspoon onion powder
⅛ teaspoon garlic powder
1 teaspoon lemon juice
¼ cup chutney, finely snipped
   Snipped chutney (optional)

Combine all ingredients. Cover and chill for 1 to 2 hours before serving. If desired, garnish with additional chutney. Serve as a dip with crudités, fruit, melba toast rounds, or crackers. Makes about 1¼ cups.

Nutrition information per tablespoon: 35 calories, 0 g protein, 3 g carbohydrate, 2 g total fat (1 g saturated), 5 mg cholesterol, 39 mg sodium, 17 mg potassium

North Carolina

SPICY DOUBLE CHEESE STRAWS

According to North Carolina chef and cookbook author Bill Neal, cheese straws are the penultimate southern cocktail food. Even so, they aren't exclusive to the South. Many regional cookbooks offer recipes for similar paprika- or pepper-spiced pastries, including one that suggests serving them stacked "log-cabin fashion."
(Pictured on page 110)

1 cup all-purpose flour
¼ teaspoon ground red pepper
1 cup finely shredded cheddar cheese (4 ounces)
¼ cup margarine *or* butter
3 to 5 tablespoons cold water
1 beaten egg
2 tablespoons grated Parmesan cheese

In a large mixing bowl combine flour, red pepper, and ⅛ teaspoon *salt*. Cut in cheddar cheese and margarine or butter till pieces are the size of small peas. Sprinkle *1 tablespoon* of the water over part of the mixture. Gently toss with a fork. Push to side of bowl. Repeat till all of the flour mixture is moistened. Shape dough into a ball.

On a lightly floured surface, flatten dough with your hands. Roll out dough from center to edges, forming a 10-inch square. Brush with egg; sprinkle with Parmesan cheese. Cut dough into 5x½-inch strips. Place strips ½ inch apart on a lightly greased baking sheet. Bake in a 400° oven for 10 to 12 minutes or till golden brown. Makes 40 strips.

Nutrition information per strip: 36 calories, 1 g protein, 2 g carbohydrate, 2 g total fat (1 g saturated), 9 mg cholesterol, 41 mg sodium, 7 mg potassium

Chutney Dip, top, and Hot Spinach and Oyster Dip (see recipe, page 106)

CLAM FRITTERS

*Fritters are another of those well-loved
fried breads characteristic
of the region. A hallmark of many
southern fritter recipes is
the use of cornmeal in the batter.
(Pictured on page 111)*

1 6½-ounce can minced clams
    Milk
1 cup all-purpose flour
¼ cup blue cornmeal
2 teaspoons baking powder
¼ teaspoon salt
1 beaten egg
    Shortening *or* cooking oil
      for deep-fat frying
    Seafood cocktail sauce
      (optional)

Drain clams, reserving liquid. Add
milk to liquid to equal ⅔ cup. Mix
flour, cornmeal, baking powder,
and salt. Combine the milk mixture,
clams, and egg. Stir into the dry
ingredients just till moistened.

Carefully drop by tablespoon into
deep, hot fat (365°). Fry 5 or 6 fritters at a time about 2 minutes or till
golden brown. Serve immediately
with cocktail sauce, if desired
Makes 6 to 8 appetizer servings.

*Nutrition information per serving: 162
calories, 8 g protein, 23 g carbohydrate, 4 g total
fat (1 g saturated), 47 mg cholesterol, 453 mg
sodium, 218 mg potassium*

PANFRIED
SOFT-SHELL CRABS

*Chesapeake Bay blue crabs shed their
shells and grow new ones more
than 20 times during their life span.
During the brief stage right after
they molt and before their new shells
harden, they are completely edible.
(Pictured on page 107)*

4 large *or* 8 small soft-shell
    blue crabs, cleaned
    (10 to 12 ounces total)
1 beaten egg

¼ cup milk
¾ cup finely crushed rich
    round crackers
2 tablespoons all-purpose
    flour
2 tablespoons grated
    Parmesan cheese
¼ teaspoon pepper
7 tablespoons cooking oil
    Curly endive (optional)

Rinse crabs; pat dry with paper
towels. In a dish mix egg and milk.
In another dish mix crushed crackers, flour, Parmesan cheese, and
pepper. Dip crabs into egg mixture,
then roll them in cracker mixture.

In a 10-inch skillet heat *4 tablespoons* of the oil over medium heat.
Add *half* of the crabs, back side
down. Fry 3 to 5 minutes or till
golden. Turn carefully and fry 3 to 5
minutes more or till golden and
crisp. Drain on paper towels. Keep
warm in a 300° oven. Repeat. Serve
crabs on a platter lined with curly
endive, if desired. Makes 4 servings.

*Nutrition information per serving: 374
calories, 20 g protein, 8 g carbohydrate, 29 g total
fat (5 g saturated), 111 mg cholesterol, 400 mg
sodium, 330 mg potassium*

Spicy Double Cheese Straws (see recipe, page 108)

Cook over medium heat about 3 minutes on each side or till golden and heated through. Add additional oil, if necessary. Serve crab cakes hot with lemon wedges and, if desired, tartar sauce. Serves 4.

Nutrition information per serving: 230 calories, 11 g protein, 12 g carbohydrate, 15 g total fat (2 g saturated), 84 mg cholesterol, 380 mg sodium, 201 mg potassium

Maryland

MARYLAND CRAB CAKES

The blue crabs of Chesapeake Bay are delicate and sweet. A Maryland specialty is panfried patties of crabmeat, bound with breadcrumbs and flavored with lively seasonings. Recipes for crab cakes date back to the eighteenth century. (Pictured on page 107)

1   6-ounce package frozen, cooked crabmeat *or*
    1 6-ounce can crabmeat, drained and cartilege removed
1   egg, slightly beaten
2   tablespoons finely chopped green onion
2   tablespoons mayonnaise *or* salad dressing
1   tablespoon snipped parsley

2   teaspoons Dijon-style mustard *or* Creole mustard
2   teaspoons fresh thyme, snipped, *or* ½ teaspoon dried thyme, crushed
½   teaspoon white wine Worcestershire sauce
½   cup fine dry bread crumbs
¼   cup cornmeal
2   tablespoons cooking oil
    Lemon wedges
    Tartar sauce (optional)

Thaw crab, if frozen; drain. In a mixing bowl combine egg, green onion, mayonnaise, parsley, mustard, thyme, Worcestershire sauce, ⅛ teaspoon *salt*, and ¼ *cup* of the bread crumbs. Stir in crab; mix well. Shape into four patties about ¾ inch thick.

Combine the remaining bread crumbs and cornmeal. Coat patties with cornmeal mixture. In a large skillet heat oil. Add crab cakes.

Louisiana

CHICKEN, OYSTER, AND SAUSAGE GUMBO

Gumbo is from an African word for okra, one of the two thickeners used for this Cajun stew. The other is filé powder, the invention of Choctaw Indians, who ground it from dried sassafras leaves. Southern purists like Mississippian Craig Claiborne say to use one or the other, never both. (Pictured on page 112)

⅓   cup all-purpose flour
⅓   cup cooking oil
1   large onion, chopped
½   cup chopped green pepper
4   cloves garlic, minced
½   teaspoon ground black pepper
¼   teaspoon ground red pepper
4   cups hot water
1   pound skinless, boneless chicken thighs, cut into bite-size pieces
12   ounces andouille *or* smoked sausage, cut into ½-inch slices and halved
1   pint shucked oysters, drained
    Hot cooked rice
    Whole okra, split to stem (optional)
    Filé powder (optional)

In a heavy 4-quart Dutch oven stir together the flour and oil till smooth. Cook over medium-high heat for 5 minutes, stirring constantly. Reduce heat to medium. Cook and stir constantly about 15 minutes more or till a dark, reddish brown roux is formed.

Stir in the onion, green pepper, garlic, black pepper, and red pepper. Cook and stir over medium heat for 3 to 5 minutes or till vegetables are tender.

Gradually stir the hot water into the vegetable mixture. Stir in chicken. Bring mixture to boiling. Reduce heat. Cover and simmer for 40 minutes.

Stir in the sausage. Cover and simmer about 20 minutes more or till chicken is tender. Remove from heat. Skim off fat.

Rinse oysters and drain well; stir into gumbo. Cover and simmer for 5 to 10 minutes or till the oysters are done and mixture is hot.

Spoon over hot cooked rice and, if desired, garnish with okra. If desired, serve ¼ to ½ teaspoon filé powder to the side of each serving to stir into gumbo. Serves 6.

Nutrition information per serving: 572 calories, 32 g protein, 41 g carbohydrate, 30 g total fat (7 g saturated), 131 mg cholesterol, 549 mg sodium, 481 mg potassium

---

Louisiana

CHICKEN AND TASSO JAMBALAYA

Most sources say jambalaya is from jambon, *the French word for "ham," an appropriate heritage for a Creole dish, plus the African* ya, *meaning "rice." Others link it to Spanish paella, which is also appropriate. Creole cooking is a blend of all of these cultures.*
(Pictured on page 112)

1   **cup long-grain rice**
¾   **cup chopped onion**
½   **cup chopped celery**
½   **cup chopped green pepper**
2   **cloves garlic, minced**
¼   **cup margarine *or* butter**
1   **16-ounce can tomatoes, cut up**
½   **of a 6-ounce can (⅓ cup) tomato paste**
½   **cup chopped tasso *or* smoked sausage**
1   **teaspoon Creole seasoning *or* Three-Pepper Seasoning**

Clam Fritters (see recipe, page 109)

2   **whole chicken breasts (about 16 ounces each), skinned, boned, and cut into bite-size pieces**
¼   **teaspoon bottled hot pepper sauce**

Cook rice according to package directions. Set aside.

In a 3-quart saucepan cook onion, celery, green pepper, and garlic in margarine or butter till tender. Stir in the *undrained* tomatoes, tomato paste, tasso or sausage, and seasoning. Bring to boiling. Reduce heat. Cover and simmer 30 minutes.

Stir in chicken and hot pepper sauce. Simmer, covered, about 15 minutes more or till chicken is tender. Stir in rice. Cook, stirring occasionally, till heated through. Makes 6 servings.

Three-Pepper Seasoning: In a tightly covered container combine 2 tablespoons *salt,* 1 tablespoon ground *red pepper,* 1 teaspoon ground *white pepper,* 1 teaspoon *garlic powder,* and 1 teaspoon ground *black pepper.* Makes about ¼ cup seasoning.

Nutrition information per serving: 358 calories, 23 g protein, 34 g carbohydrate, 14 g total fat (3 g saturated), 57 mg cholesterol, 672 mg sodium, 579 mg potassium

---

Louisiana

CRAWFISH ÉTOUFFÉE

In Louisiana it's crawfish, not crayfish. The latter pronunciation just "won't do," according to famed Cajun chef Paul Prudhomme. In Cajun cooking, étouffée means "smothered in a sauce."
(Pictured on page 112)

1   **pound fresh *or* frozen peeled crawfish tails *or* shrimp**
2   **large onions, chopped (1½ cups)**
1   **cup chopped celery**
½   **cup chopped green pepper**
2   **cloves garlic, minced**
¼   **cup cooking oil, margarine, *or* butter**
2   **tablespoons crawfish fat*, margarine, *or* butter**
4   **teaspoons cornstarch**
1   **cup water**
½   **cup tomato sauce**
½   **teaspoon salt**
¼   **to ½ teaspoon ground red pepper**
¼   **teaspoon ground black pepper**
    Hot cooked rice

Thaw crawfish or shrimp, if frozen.

In a heavy, 3-quart saucepan cook onions, celery, green pepper, and garlic, covered, in oil, margarine, or butter about 10 minutes or till tender. Add crawfish fat, margarine, or butter, stirring till melted. Stir in cornstarch.

Stir in crawfish or shrimp, water, tomato sauce, salt, red pepper, and black pepper. Bring mixture to boiling. Reduce heat. Simmer, uncovered, about 5 minutes or till crawfish are tender or shrimp turn pink. Serve with hot cooked rice. Makes 4 servings.

*Note: The orange fat found in the heads of crawfish adds extra richness and flavor to dishes. Since it's difficult to find crawfish fat outside of southern Louisiana, margarine or butter is a good substitute.

Nutrition information per serving: 400 calories, 14 g protein, 41 g carbohydrate, 20 g total fat (3 g saturated), 83 mg cholesterol, 625 mg sodium, 442 mg potassium

Chicken, Oyster, and Sausage Gumbo, left (see recipe, page 110), Chicken and Tasso Jambalaya, top right (see recipe, page 111), and Crawfish Étouffée (see recipe, page 111)

Kentucky

KENTUCKY BURGOO

Many traditional recipes for this celebrated Kentucky stew make enough to feed a small town. It has long been standard fare in the South at political rallies and church suppers, and even on Derby Day.

4 cups water
1 16-ounce can tomatoes, cut up
¾ pound boneless beef chuck roast, cut into ¾-inch cubes
2 teaspoons instant chicken bouillon granules

1 pound meaty chicken pieces (breasts, thighs, drumsticks), skinned, if desired
2 cups cubed, peeled potatoes
1 10-ounce package frozen succotash
1 10-ounce package frozen cut okra
1 cup sliced carrots
½ cup chopped onion
2 teaspoons curry powder
1 teaspoon sugar

In a 4½-quart Dutch oven combine the water, *undrained* tomatoes, beef, and chicken bouillon granules. Bring to boiling; reduce heat. Cover and simmer for 30 minutes. Add chicken pieces. Return to boiling; reduce heat. Simmer, covered, about 45 minutes more or till beef and chicken are tender. Remove chicken pieces and set aside.

Stir potatoes, succotash, okra, carrots, onion, curry powder, and sugar into Dutch oven. Return to boiling; reduce heat. Simmer, covered, about 20 minutes or till vegetables are tender.

Meanwhile, when chicken is cool enough to handle, remove meat from bones; discard skin, if any, and bones. Cut the chicken into bite-size pieces. Add chicken pieces to Dutch oven. Cook about 5 minutes more or till the chicken is heated through. Makes 5 or 6 servings.

Nutrition information per serving: 419 calories, 33 g protein, 42 g carbohydrate, 14 g total fat (5 g saturated), 89 mg cholesterol, 629 mg sodium, 1,079 mg potassium

Kentucky Burgoo

Po' Boys, top left, Red Beans and Rice, top right (see recipe, page 120), and Creole Shrimp and Eggplant

(see recipe, page 120)

PO' BOYS

*Submarines, grinders, hoagies, heros —
every part of the country has a version of
a giant sandwich. In New Orleans,
it's the po' boy. Local legend says that
such an oyster-filled loaf was dubbed
la médiatrice (the peacemaker) because
it was used by errant husbands to
appease their angry spouses.*

1　**pint shucked oysters *or***
　　¾ pound fresh *or* frozen
　　peeled and deveined
　　shrimp
½　**cup all-purpose flour**
½　**teaspoon salt**
¼　**teaspoon pepper**
1　**beaten egg**
¼　**cup cooking oil *or***
　　shortening
2　**6- or 7-inch-long loaves**
　　French bread *or* four
　　4-inch-long French-style
　　rolls
¼　**cup Tartar Sauce,**
　　mayonnaise, *or* salad
　　dressing

1　**cup shredded lettuce**
1　**tomato, thinly sliced**
　　Bottled hot pepper sauce
　　(optional)
　　Lemon wedges (optional)

Drain oysters. (*Or,* thaw shrimp, if
frozen.) Rinse and pat dry with
paper towels. In a small bowl combine flour, salt, and pepper. Dip
oysters or shrimp into beaten egg,
then coat with flour mixture.

In a large skillet heat oil or shortening. Add *half* of the oysters or
shrimp in a single layer. Cook over
medium-high heat for 2 to 3 minutes per side or till golden. Drain on
paper towels. Transfer to a wire
rack on a baking sheet. Keep fried
fish warm in a 300° oven while you
cook remaining seafood and assemble sandwiches.

Slice French bread or rolls in half
horizontally. Place bread or roll
halves on a baking sheet in a 300°
oven about 3 minutes or till heated
through.

Spread cut sides of bread with
Tartar Sauce, mayonnaise, or salad
dressing. Arrange lettuce and tomato slices on bottoms of bread. Add

oysters or shrimp. If desired, sprinkle with hot pepper sauce and
squeeze lemon juice over oysters or
shrimp. Add bread tops. Makes 4
servings.

Tartar Sauce: In a small mixing
bowl stir together 1 cup *mayonnaise
or salad dressing,* ¼ cup *sweet dill pickle
relish,* 1 tablespoon chopped *green
onion,* 1 teaspoon finely shredded
lemon peel, and dash bottled *hot pepper sauce.* Cover and chill at least
2 hours to blend flavors. Makes
about 1⅓ cups.

*Nutrition information per serving: 590
calories, 19 g protein, 63 g carbohydrate, 29 g
total fat (5 g saturated), 123 mg cholesterol, 897
mg sodium, 476 mg potassium*

CREOLE SHRIMP
AND EGGPLANT

*This Creole dish gets a little heat from
bottled hot pepper sauce. One of the
best known of these sauces is Tabasco,
once available only to southern
Louisiana cooks. The McIlhenny family
has manufactured the product since
just after the Civil War.*

1 pound fresh *or* frozen peeled and deveined shrimp
1 medium eggplant (about 1 pound)
3 tablespoons all-purpose flour
½ teaspoon salt
¼ teaspoon pepper
2 to 3 tablespoons olive oil
2 cups sliced fresh mushrooms
2 cloves garlic, minced
1 tablespoon olive oil
1 14½-ounce can stewed tomatoes
1 tablespoon snipped fresh oregano *or* 1 teaspoon dried oregano, crushed
¼ teaspoon bottled hot pepper sauce
2 tablespoons cornstarch
2 tablespoons water
Fresh oregano (optional)

Thaw shrimp, if frozen. Peel eggplant, if desired. Cut lengthwise into 4 slices. Combine flour, salt, and pepper. Coat eggplant slices with flour mixture. In a 12-inch skillet heat 2 tablespoons olive oil. Cook eggplant slices in hot oil over medium heat for 4 minutes on each side or till tender. (Add remaining 1 tablespoon oil, if necessary.)

Meanwhile, in a medium saucepan cook the mushrooms and garlic in the 1 tablespoon olive oil till tender. Stir in the *undrained* tomatoes, oregano, and hot pepper sauce. Stir together the cornstarch and water; stir into tomato mixture. Add shrimp. Cook and stir till thickened and bubbly. Cook and stir for 2 minutes more or till shrimp are done. Serve tomato mixture over eggplant slices. If desired, garnish with fresh oregano. Serves 4.

Nutrition information per serving: 274 calories, 22 g protein, 22 g carbohydrate, 11 g total fat (2 g saturated), 166 mg cholesterol, 741 mg sodium, 512 mg potassium

 Baked Chicken Country Captain

Georgia

BAKED CHICKEN COUNTRY CAPTAIN

A recipe for this chicken curry appeared in Eliza Leslie's New Cookery Book *in 1857. Leslie traced its origins to East India and the British Army. It is also linked to Savannah, Georgia, a seaport where spices were readily available to local cooks.*

2 pounds meaty chicken pieces (breasts, thighs, and drumsticks)
1 large onion, cut into thin wedges
1 small green pepper, cut into 1-inch pieces
2 tablespoons raisins
2 cloves garlic, minced
1 tablespoon cooking oil
1 tablespoon curry powder
1 16-ounce can tomatoes, cut up
½ teaspoon sugar
½ teaspoon salt
½ teaspoon ground mace
¼ teaspoon dried thyme, crushed
2 tablespoons cornstarch
2 tablespoons cold water
3 cups hot cooked rice

If desired, skin chicken. Rinse chicken; pat dry with paper towels. Arrange chicken, onion wedges, green pepper pieces, and raisins in a 2-quart rectangular baking dish.

In a small saucepan cook garlic in hot oil for 1 minute. Add curry powder. Cook and stir for 1 minute more. Stir in the *undrained* tomatoes, sugar, salt, mace, thyme, and ¼ teaspoon *pepper.* Bring to boiling; pour over ingredients in dish.

Cover and bake in a 350° oven about 1 hour or till tender. Using a slotted spoon, transfer chicken, vegetables, and raisins to a platter.

For sauce, measure pan juices; if necessary, add enough water to equal 2 cups. Transfer to a saucepan. In a small bowl combine cornstarch and cold water; add to saucepan. Cook and stir till thickened and bubbly. Cook and stir 2 minutes more.

To serve, spoon chicken, vegetables, and raisins over hot cooked rice. Spoon some of the sauce atop chicken; pass remaining sauce when serving. Makes 4 servings.

Nutrition information per serving: 548 calories, 33 g protein, 62 g carbohydrate, 18 g total fat (4 g saturated), 87 mg cholesterol, 538 mg sodium, 677 mg potassium

Louisiana

GRILLADES AND GRITS

*Without grits, commented the
New Orleans Picayune, "no breakfast
in Louisiana is considered complete."
Grits served with grillades, meat pounded
thin and braised, is a morning
institution in that part of the South.*

1	pound veal round steak, cut ½ inch thick
2	tablespoons all-purpose flour
¼	teaspoon salt
¼	teaspoon ground black pepper
⅛	to ¼ teaspoon ground red pepper
1	tablespoon cooking oil
1	8-ounce can stewed tomatoes
¾	cup beef broth
1	cup chopped onion
1	green pepper, cut in strips
1	tablespoon water
1	teaspoon cornstarch
2	cups hot cooked grits Italian parsley (optional)

Cut meat into 4 serving-size pieces. Trim fat. Combine the flour, salt, black pepper, and red pepper. With a meat mallet, pound meat to ¼-inch thickness, pounding flour mixture into meat. Roll up from a short side. Secure with a wooden toothpick. Repeat with remaining pieces of meat.

In a large skillet brown veal rolls on all sides in hot oil just till nicely browned. Drain fat. Add stewed tomatoes, beef broth, onion, and pepper strips. Cover tightly and cook over low heat about 45 minutes or till meat is tender. Transfer meat to a platter; keep warm.

Combine water and cornstarch. Stir into tomato mixture. Cook and stir till slightly thickened and bubbly. Cook and stir for 1 minute more. Serve meat and sauce with hot grits. Garnish with Italian parsley, if desired. Makes 4 servings.

*Nutrition information per serving: 286
calories, 29 g protein, 28 g carbohydrate, 7 g total
fat (2 g saturated), 88 mg cholesterol, 492 mg
sodium, 488 mg potassium*

Grillades and Grits

Virginia

SOUTHERN FRIED CHICKEN AND GRAVY

*In her 1824 cookbook The Virginia
Housewife, Mary Randolph offered a
classically southern recipe for "fried
chickens:" Dredge pieces of chicken
in seasoned flour and fry in boiling lard
until crisp and brown. Randolph then
says to add "rich milk" to the drippings,
"stew it a little," and pour over the
chicken. Other traditional versions mix
fine cornmeal with the flour or even dip
the chicken in an egg batter.*

2	pounds meaty chicken pieces (breasts, thighs, and drumsticks)
¾	teaspoon poultry seasoning
½	teaspoon salt
⅛	teaspoon ground red pepper
⅛	teaspoon garlic powder (optional)
⅓	cup all-purpose flour*
2	tablespoons cooking oil
2	tablespoons all-purpose flour
¼	teaspoon salt
⅛	teaspoon ground black pepper
1¾	cups milk

If desired, skin chicken. Rinse chicken; pat dry with paper towels. For coating mixture, combine poul-

try seasoning, the ½ teaspoon salt, red pepper, and, if desired, garlic powder. Divide coating mixture in half. Rub *half* of the coating onto the chicken pieces.

In a plastic bag combine the ⅓ cup flour and remaining coating mixture. Add chicken pieces, a few at a time, shaking to coat.

In a large skillet heat cooking oil; add chicken pieces. Cook, uncovered, over medium heat for 15 minutes, turning pieces to brown evenly. Reduce heat to medium-low. Cook, uncovered, for 35 to 40 minutes more or till chicken is no longer pink, turning once.

Transfer the chicken pieces to a serving platter, reserving *2 tablespoons* drippings. Cover chicken and keep warm.

For gravy, stir the 2 tablespoons flour, the ¼ teaspoon salt, and black pepper into reserved drippings. Add milk all at once. Cook and stir till thickened and bubbly. Cook and stir for 1 to 2 minutes more. Serve gravy with chicken. Makes 4 to 6 servings.

*Note: If desired, substitute ¼ cup *all-purpose flour* and 2 tablespoons fine dry *bread crumbs or yellow cornmeal* for the ⅓ cup all-purpose flour.

*Nutrition information per serving: 403
calories, 32 g protein, 16 g carbohydrate, 22 g
total fat (6 g saturated), 95 mg cholesterol, 554
mg sodium, 403 mg potassium*

Tennessee

HAM WITH RED-EYE GRAVY

*Coffee is the surprise ingredient
that deepens the color of this
whimsically named southern
ham gravy to a rich reddish brown.
(Pictured on page 120)*

2	8-ounce slices country-style ham, cut ¼ inch thick
2	tablespoons brown sugar
½	cup strong black coffee

Southern Fried Chicken and Gravy, and Peppers and Grits (see recipe, page 121)

In the refrigerator, soak ham in water for several hours or overnight. Drain; pat dry with paper towels.

Trim fat from the ham slices. In a large skillet cook fat trimmings over medium-low heat for 6 to 8 minutes or till crisp. Discard trimmings; reserve *2 tablespoons* drippings in the skillet. Add ham slices to the skillet. Cook over medium heat for 9 to 12 minutes on each side or till brown. Remove ham slices from the skillet, reserving drippings in the skillet. Cover to keep ham warm.

For gravy, stir brown sugar into drippings. Cook over medium heat till sugar dissolves, stirring constantly. Stir in coffee. Boil for 2 to 3 minutes or till gravy is slightly thickened and a rich, reddish brown color, scraping the skillet to loosen any crusty bits. Serve gravy over ham slices. Makes 4 servings.

Nutrition information per serving: 293 calories, 24 g protein, 5 g carbohydrate, 19 g total fat (7 g saturated), 70 mg cholesterol, 1,347 mg sodium, 356 mg potassium

Mississippi

CATFISH PECAN

"His meat's as white as snow and makes a good fry," Huck Finn said with relish about the catfish. But until recently, its sweet, firm flesh was appreciated only in the South and Midwest. Now, however, catfish appears on the menus of the trendiest restaurants across the country.
(Pictured on page 118)

1 to 1¼ pounds catfish fillets
     (½ to ¾ inch thick)
¼ **cup fine dry bread crumbs**
2 **tablespoons cornmeal**
2 **tablespoons grated**
     Parmesan cheese

2 **tablespoons ground pecans**
¼ **teaspoon salt**
¼ **cup all-purpose flour**
¼ **cup milk**
2 **to 3 tablespoons cooking oil**
⅓ **cup chopped pecans**

Cut fish into 4 portions. Set aside. In a bowl mix bread crumbs, cornmeal, Parmesan cheese, ground pecans, salt, and ¼ teaspoon *pepper.* Coat each portion of fish with flour, then dip in milk, then coat evenly with crumb mixture.

In a large skillet fry fish in hot oil 4 to 6 minutes on each side or till golden and fish flakes easily with a fork; keep warm.

Remove excess crumbs from skillet. Add additional oil, if necessary. Add pecans. Cook and stir about 2 minutes or till toasted; sprinkle pecans over catfish. Serves 4.

Nutrition information per serving: 353 calories, 24 g protein, 15 g carbohydrate, 22 g total fat (4 g saturated), 65 mg cholesterol, 313 mg sodium, 420 mg potassium

Virginia

BRUNSWICK STEW

Brunswick County, Virginia or Brunswick County, North Carolina? The debate still rages over which state gave this country stew its name, although Virginia usually gets more votes. Originally, squirrel was the meat of choice. Today, chicken or rabbit is considered equally authentic.

2   pounds meaty chicken *or* rabbit pieces, skinned

1½ cups onion, cut in small wedges

4   cloves garlic, minced

1   16-ounce can tomatoes, cut up

1   10-ounce package frozen sliced okra

½   cup chicken broth

1   teaspoon prepared mustard

1   teaspoon Worcestershire sauce

½   teaspoon dried thyme, crushed

¼   teaspoon bottled hot pepper sauce

1   8-ounce can whole kernel corn, drained

1   8-ounce can baby lima beans, drained

½   cup cubed ham

1   12-ounce jar brown gravy

In a 4½ quart Dutch oven combine chicken or rabbit, onion, garlic, tomatoes, okra, chicken broth, mustard, Worcestershire sauce, thyme, ¼ teaspoon *pepper,* and hot pepper sauce. Bring to boiling; reduce heat. Cover and simmer for 30 to 40 minutes or till chicken or rabbit is tender. Add corn, lima beans, and ham. Stir in gravy. Return to boiling; reduce heat. Simmer 5 minutes. Serves 6.

Nutrition information per serving: 359 calories, 40 g protein, 28 g carbohydrate, 10 g total fat (2 g saturated), 100 mg cholesterol, 876 mg sodium, 811 mg potassium

Fried Green Tomatoes, and Catfish Pecan (see recipe, page 117)

Brunswick Stew

Kentucky

FRIED GREEN TOMATOES

Early settlers devised many ways to use all the food available to them. In the South, the last tomatoes of the season were picked green, then thickly sliced, dipped in white cornmeal, and fried until golden brown. It's still a popular side dish.

1   pound green tomatoes (about 4 tomatoes)

½   cup white cornmeal

¼   cup all-purpose flour

2   tablespoons sesame seed

¼   teaspoon onion salt

⅛   teaspoon pepper

1   beaten egg

2   tablespoons milk

    Cooking oil for frying

Slice tomatoes into ¼-inch-thick slices. In a pie plate or baking dish combine cornmeal, flour, sesame seed, onion salt, and pepper. In a small mixing bowl combine egg and milk. Dip tomato slices into egg mixture, then coat both sides of tomato slices with the cornmeal mixture.

In a heavy large skillet heat about ¼ inch of cooking oil over medium heat. Fry tomato slices in a single layer about 2 minutes on each side or till golden brown. Drain on paper towels. Keep slices warm in a 300° oven while frying remaining tomatoes. Serve immediately. Makes 4 to 6 servings.

Nutrition information per serving: 202 calories, 6 g protein, 16 g carbohydrate, 13 g total fat (2 g saturated), 54 mg cholesterol, 136 mg sodium, 276 mg potassium

South Carolina

CHEESY CORN AND GRITS

As southern as we may think grits are, they are really a Native American food. It was the Indians who taught settlers to make hominy out of dried kernels of corn, then to grind the hominy into grits. Southern cooks proceeded to devise dozens of ways to enjoy them. (Pictured on page 120)

1½ cups water

1   teaspoon instant chicken bouillon granules

½   cup quick-cooking grits

¼   cup finely chopped green onion *or* chives

½   cup shredded cheddar cheese (2 ounces)

2   eggs, slightly beaten

½   cup milk

1   8-ounce can cream-style corn

¼   cup shredded cheddar cheese (1 ounce)

In a medium saucepan bring water and chicken granules to boiling. Gradually stir in grits. Remove from heat. Cover and let stand 5 minutes. Stir in onion and the ½ cup cheese. Stir in eggs, milk, and corn. Transfer to a lightly greased 1-quart casserole.

Bake, uncovered, in a 350° oven for 45 to 50 minutes or till set in center. Sprinkle with the remaining cheese. Let stand 1 to 2 minutes before serving to melt cheese. Makes 4 servings.

Nutrition information per serving: 255 calories, 12 g protein, 28 g carbohydrate, 11 g total fat (6 g saturated), 131 mg cholesterol, 566 mg sodium, 188 mg potassium

Cheesy Corn and Grits (see recipe, page 119), Lemony Moravian Sugar Bread (see recipe, page 127), and Ham with Red-Eye Gravy (see recipe, page 116)

Virginia

BAKED COUNTRY HAM

Good home-cured hams could be found in every colony, but those of Smithfield, Virginia, made from peanut-fattened pigs, were considered perhaps the finest. Their reputation remains stellar today. By law, to be a Smithfield ham, the meat must be cured, smoked, and aged for one year within Smithfield city limits.

1 12- to 14-pound country ham *or* country-style ham
2 teaspoons whole cloves
8 cups apple cider *or* apple juice
½ cup packed brown sugar
2 teaspoons ground cloves

Dry sherry *or* red wine vinegar
Small apples (optional)
Lemon leaves (optional)

Place ham in a large container. Cover with cold water and soak for 16 hours in the refrigerator, changing water once. Pour off water. Scrub ham in warm water with a stiff brush and rinse well. Cut skin from ham and trim off fat. Insert cloves into ham.

Place ham, fat side up, in a large roasting pan. Insert a meat thermometer into the thickest portion of the ham, making sure it doesn't touch fat or bone. Pour apple cider or apple juice over ham.

Bake ham, covered, in a 325° oven for 4 to 4½ hours or till the meat thermometer registers 160°. Drain off pan juices.

For glaze, in a small bowl combine brown sugar and ground cloves. Add just enough sherry or wine vinegar to make a paste. Spread glaze over fat side of ham.

Bake ham, uncovered, about 30 minutes more or till the meat thermometer registers 170°. Let stand for 15 to 20 minutes before slicing. Transfer to a large platter and garnish with apples and lemon leaves, if desired. Makes 25 to 30 servings.

Nutrition information per serving: 427 calories, 35 g protein, 7 g carbohydrate, 27 g total fat (10 g saturated), 101 mg cholesterol, 1,939 mg sodium, 525 mg potassium

Louisiana

RED BEANS AND RICE

Beans and rice are a famous pair in the South. In New Orleans, the beans are red kidneys, and the dish is traditionally served on Mondays. Louis Armstrong, a New Orleans native son, always signed his letters, "Red beans and ricely yours." (Pictured on page 114)

1 cup dry red beans (about 8 ounces)
6½ cups cold water
1 pound meaty smoked pork hocks
2 cups sliced carrots (about 4 carrots)
1 cup sliced celery (about 2 stalks)
½ cup chopped onion
2 cloves garlic, minced
2 bay leaves
1½ teaspoons snipped fresh thyme *or* ½ teaspoon dried thyme, crushed
½ teaspoon bottled hot pepper sauce
4 ounces smoked sausage, chopped (about ¾ cup)
3 cups hot cooked rice
Bottled hot pepper sauce (optional)
Celery leaves (optional)

Rinse beans. In a Dutch oven or large kettle combine beans and *4 cups* of the water. Bring to boiling; reduce heat. Simmer for 2 minutes.

Peach Chutney (see recipe, page 124), Beaten Biscuits (see recipe, page 126), and Baked Country Ham

Remove from the heat. Cover; let stand for 1 hour. (Or, soak beans in water overnight in a covered pan.) Drain beans and rinse.

In the same Dutch oven or kettle combine beans, *2½ cups* of the water, pork hocks, carrots, celery, onion, garlic, bay leaves, thyme, and the *½* teaspoon hot pepper sauce. Bring to boiling; reduce heat. Cover and simmer about 2 hours or till beans are tender, stirring occasionally. (Add additional water during cooking, if necessary.)

Discard bay leaves. Remove pork hocks. When pork hocks are cool enough to handle, remove meat from the bones. Cut meat into bite-size pieces. Discard bones. Return meat to bean mixture; add sausage.

Simmer beans and meat, uncovered, about 15 minutes or till a thick gravy forms. (Add water, if

necessary, so beans are saucy but not soupy.) Serve over rice. If desired, garnish with celery leaves and pass bottled hot pepper sauce when serving. Makes 5 servings.

Nutrition information per serving: 428 calories, 18 g protein, 67 g carbohydrate, 10 g total fat (3 g saturated), 23 mg cholesterol, 421 mg sodium, 859 mg potassium

Louisiana

PEPPERS AND GRITS

Grits soak up the good flavors of this classic Creole/Cajun mixture of sweet peppers, tomatoes, and onions.
(Pictured on page 117)

4	slices bacon
¾	cup chopped green pepper
½	cup chopped red sweet pepper
½	cup chopped onion
1	cup quick-cooking grits
¼	teaspoon pepper
¼	teaspoon paprika
⅔	cup chopped, peeled, and seeded tomato

In a large skillet cook bacon till crisp. Drain bacon on paper towels, reserving *2 tablespoons* drippings in skillet. Crumble bacon and set aside. Add green pepper, red sweet pepper, and onion to drippings. Cook about 2 minutes or till vegetables are crisp-tender.

Meanwhile, cook grits according to package directions, adding the salt; keep hot. Sprinkle pepper and paprika over vegetable mixture. Stir in hot grits. Add chopped tomato and bacon; toss to mix. Makes 6 servings.

Nutrition information per serving: 136 calories, 4 g protein, 24 g carbohydrate, 3 g total fat (1 g saturated), 4 mg cholesterol, 70 mg sodium, 160 mg potassium

Maryland

CORN AND CRAB CHOWDER

"Milking" young green ears of corn by scraping the cob was a Native American technique adopted by southern cooks, who used both the whole kernel and its liquid to thicken and flavor chowders and puddings.

2 ears fresh sweet corn *or* 1 cup loose-pack frozen whole kernel corn
2 cups chicken broth
⅓ cup sliced green onion
⅓ cup chopped green pepper
1 teaspoon fines herbes, crushed, *or* ½ teaspoon dried basil, crushed
¼ teaspoon ground white pepper
2 cups milk
2 tablespoons cornstarch
4 ounces process Swiss cheese *or* process Gruyère cheese, shredded (1 cup)
1 6- to 7-ounce can crabmeat, drained, flaked, and cartilage removed, *or* meat from 1 pound cooked crab legs
Snipped fresh chives (optional)

Cut kernels from ears of corn, scraping ears to remove milky portion also (you should have about 1 cup corn). In a large saucepan combine the fresh or frozen corn, broth, green onion, green pepper, fines herbes, and white pepper. Bring to boiling. Reduce heat. Cover and simmer for 5 minutes.

Stir together the milk and cornstarch. Stir into hot mixture. Cook and stir till thickened and bubbly. Stir in cheese and crab; heat and stir till cheese is melted. Garnish with chives, if desired. Makes 4 main-dish or 8 side-dish servings.

Nutrition information per main-dish serving: 252 calories, 24 g protein, 20 g carbohydrate, 9 g total fat (5 g saturated), 64 mg cholesterol, 985 mg sodium, 627 mg potassium

Corn and Crab Chowder, top, and Black Bean Soup

Corn and Ham Chowder: Prepare as above, *except* use 1 cup chopped *ham* in place of the crabmeat. Makes 4 main-dish or 8 side-dish servings.

Nutrition information per main-dish serving: 277 calories, 26 g protein, 20 g carbohydrate, 10 g total fat (6 g saturated), 50 mg cholesterol, 1,407 mg sodium, 602 mg potassium

Florida

BLACK BEAN SOUP

Black beans reached the American South by traveling north. They were brought to Florida by conquistadores from Spanish settlements in the Caribbean.

1 15-ounce can black beans, drained, *or* ½ cup dry black beans (4 ounces)
2½ cups beef broth
½ cup chopped onion
½ cup chopped celery
½ cup chopped carrot
2 cloves garlic, minced, *or* 1 teaspoon bottled minced garlic
¼ teaspoon dried thyme, crushed
⅛ teaspoon crushed red pepper
⅛ teaspoon ground black pepper

1 tablespoon balsamic vinegar *or* red wine vinegar
½ cup finely chopped ham
3 tablespoons coarsely chopped red onion
3 lemon wedges

In a large saucepan combine beans, broth, onion, celery, carrot, garlic, thyme, red pepper, black pepper, and balsamic vinegar. Bring to boiling; reduce heat. Cover and simmer 20 minutes. Remove about *half* of the hot mixture.

In a blender or food processor carefully blend or process a small amount at a time till nearly smooth. Transfer the entire mixture to saucepan. Stir in ham. Cover and simmer for 5 minutes. Garnish with red onion and serve with lemon wedges. Makes 4 to 6 servings.

Nutrition information per serving: 157 calories, 13 g protein, 23 g carbohydrate, 2 g total fat (1 g saturated), 10 mg cholesterol, 750 mg sodium, 532 mg potassium

South Carolina

HOPPIN JOHN

"Collards for luck, hoppin John for money." Served together, these foods are a New Year's tradition in the Deep South. Hoppin John combines rice, the premier crop of South Carolina's Low Country, and some type of pea, with black-eyed peas the best known.

4 slices bacon
¾ cup chopped onion
½ cup finely chopped green pepper
⅓ cup chopped celery
2 cloves garlic, minced
1 15-ounce can black-eyed peas, drained
½ cup beef broth
½ teaspoon dried thyme, crushed
½ teaspoon dried marjoram, crushed
⅛ teaspoon ground red pepper
2 cups cooked rice
1 medium tomato, cut in wedges, *or* 6 cherry tomatoes, halved

Hoppin John, top, and Black-Eyed Pea Salad

2　tablespoons thinly sliced
　　green onion
　　Fresh thyme (optional)
1　bay leaf (optional)

In a large skillet, cook bacon slices till crisp. Drain bacon on paper towels, reserving *2 tablespoons* drippings in skillet. Crumble bacon and set aside. Add onion, green pepper, celery, and garlic to reserved drippings. Cook till nearly tender. Stir in black-eyed peas, beef broth, thyme, marjoram, and red pepper. Stir in cooked rice; heat through.

Garnish with bacon, tomato, green onion and, if desired, the fresh thyme and the bay leaf. Makes 6 servings.

Nutrition information per serving: *188 calories, 8 g protein, 33 g carbohydrate, 3 g total fat (1 g saturated), 4 mg cholesterol, 233 mg sodium, 310 mg potassium*

Alabama

BLACK-EYED PEA SALAD

African ingredients and flavors permeate southern cooking. Black-eyed peas, which actually are beans, arrived in the South with the slaves.

2　cups cooked black-eyed peas
　　or one 15-ounce can black-
　　eyed peas, rinsed and
　　drained
1½　cups chopped, peeled
　　tomatoes
　　(about 2 tomatoes)
1　cup cooked corn
¼　cup thinly sliced green onion
1　medium jalapeño pepper,
　　seeded and finely chopped
⅓　cup salad oil
2　tablespoons red wine
　　vinegar
2　tablespoons lemon juice

1　tablespoon snipped fresh
　　thyme *or* 1 teaspoon dried
　　thyme, crushed
1　tablespoon Dijon-style
　　mustard
¼　teaspoon pepper
　　Collard greens (optional)

In a large mixing bowl stir together black-eyed peas, tomatoes, corn, green onion, and jalapeño pepper. Cover and chill for several hours.

For dressing, in a screw-top jar combine salad oil, red wine vinegar, lemon juice, thyme, mustard, and pepper. Cover and shake well. Chill dressing for several hours.

Just before serving, shake dressing well; pour dressing over the vegetable mixture. Toss gently to coat. If desired, garnish with collard greens. Makes 6 servings.

Nutrition information per serving: *236 calories, 7 g protein, 24 g carbohydrate, 13 g total fat (2 g saturated), 0 mg cholesterol, 368 mg sodium, 182 mg potassium*

123

Okra Mix, top, and Fried Okra

FRIED OKRA

A number of influences are at work in this recipe: the cornmeal is definitely New World, but okra is African, as is the generous dose of pepper in the batter.

1   **pound fresh okra (about 45 small to medium)**
½   **cup all-purpose flour**
½   **cup yellow cornmeal**
½   **teaspoon salt**
¼   **teaspoon ground red pepper**
¼   **teaspoon ground black pepper**
1   **egg**
2   **tablespoons milk**
    Cooking oil for deep-fat frying

Wash okra; trim ends. Slice okra into bite-size pieces; set aside. In a medium bowl combine flour, cornmeal, salt, red pepper, and black pepper; mix well.

In a shallow bowl beat together egg and milk. Dip okra into milk mixture, then into cornmeal mixture; coat well. Fry about *one-third* of the okra at a time in deep, hot fat (365°) for 3 to 4 minutes or till tender. Remove with a slotted spoon. Drain on paper towels. Keep warm in a 300° oven while frying remaining okra. Makes 6 servings.

Nutrition information per serving: 208 calories, 4 g protein, 16 g carbohydrate, 15 g total fat (2 g saturated), 36 mg cholesterol, 195 mg sodium, 267 mg potassium

OKRA MIX

Black slaves carried okra seeds from West Africa to the American South. The vegetable took root in southern soil and in the southern diet, appearing in vegetable casseroles like this one. These mixtures were never bland. Pepper sauce was used to turn up the heat.

1   **10-ounce package frozen cut okra**
1   **8-ounce can stewed tomatoes**
1   **8¾-ounce can whole kernel corn, drained**
½   **cup finely chopped onion**
¼   **teaspoon garlic powder**
⅛   **teaspoon pepper**
    Dash bottled hot pepper sauce

In a medium saucepan combine okra, tomatoes, corn, onion, garlic powder, pepper, and hot pepper sauce. Bring to boiling. Reduce heat; cover and simmer for 6 to 8 minutes or till tender. Makes 4 to 6 servings.

Nutrition information per serving: 83 calories, 3 g protein, 19 g carbohydrate, 1 g total fat (0 g saturated), 0 mg cholesterol, 288 m sodium, 279 mg potassium

PEACH CHUTNEY

Condiments have appeared on southern tables since colonial days. Their piquancy woke up dull winter meals. Pickles and preserves were put up from a cornucopia of fruits, nuts, and vegetables. (Pictured on page 121)

½   **cup chopped onion**
1   **to 2 teaspoons grated gingerroot**

2 cloves garlic, minced
1 tablespoon cooking oil
⅓ cup sugar
2 teaspoons cornstarch
¼ cup balsamic vinegar *or*
  red wine vinegar
1 tablespoon lemon juice
¼ teaspoon dry mustard
¼ teaspoon ground allspice
  Dash ground cloves
1½ cups chopped, peeled
  peaches
½ cup dried tart red cherries
  or raisins
⅓ cup toasted chopped
  almonds (optional)

In a medium saucepan cook onion, gingerroot, and garlic in hot oil till tender but not brown.

Stir together the sugar and cornstarch. Stir into saucepan. Stir in vinegar, lemon juice, mustard, allspice, and cloves till well blended. Stir in the peaches and cherries. Cook and stir till slightly thickened and heated through. If desired, stir in almonds. Serve warm as a meat or fish accompaniment. Makes about 2 cups.

Nutrition information per tablespoon: 24 calories, 0 g protein, 5 g carbohydrate, 0 g total fat (0 g saturated), 0 mg cholesterol, 1 mg sodium, 23 mg potassium

South Carolina

SPOON BREAD

A well-known 1847 Carolina recipe for soufflélike spoon bread from The Carolina Housewife, *by Sara Rutledge, described it this way: "It has the appearance when cooked, of a baked batter pudding, and when rich, and well mixed, it has almost the delicacy of a baked custard." A serving spoon was required tableware for this dish.*

4 slices bacon
1 cup water
½ cup yellow cornmeal
1 cup shredded cheddar
  cheese (4 ounces)
1 8¾-ounce can cream-style
  corn

Spoon Bread, top, and Candied Sweet Potatoes with Apples

2 tablespoons margarine *or*
  butter
¼ teaspoon onion powder
  Dash garlic powder
¾ cup milk
3 egg yolks
1 teaspoon baking powder
3 egg whites

Cook bacon till crisp; drain and crumble. Set bacon aside. In a medium saucepan combine water and cornmeal; bring to boiling. Reduce heat; cook and stir till very thick, about 1 minute. Remove from heat. Stir in cheese, corn, margarine, onion powder, and garlic powder. Stir till cheese melts and mixture is smooth. Stir in milk.

In a small mixing bowl beat egg yolks and baking powder till well blended. Stir into cornmeal mixture along with bacon.

In a medium mixing bowl beat egg whites till stiff peaks form. Fold beaten egg whites into cornmeal mixture. Pour into a lightly greased 1½-quart casserole. Bake in a 325° oven for 50 to 60 minutes or till a knife inserted near the center comes out clean. Serve immediately. Makes 6 servings.

Nutrition information per serving: 227 calories, 11 g protein, 12 g carbohydrate, 15 g total fat (6 g saturated), 132 mg cholesterol, 431 mg sodium, 178 mg potassium

Mississippi

CANDIED SWEET POTATOES WITH APPLES

In his 1952 novel, Invisible Man, *Ralph Ellison evokes memories of favorite sweet potato dishes: "Yes, and we'd loved them candied, or baked in a cobbler, deep-fat fried in a packet of dough, or roasted with pork and glazed with the well-browned fat. . . ."*

3 medium sweet potatoes
  (about 1 pound)
1 large cooking apple
⅓ cup packed brown sugar
1 tablespoon water
1 tablespoon margarine *or*
  butter
  Dash ground cloves
¼ cup chopped pecans *or*
  walnuts, toasted

Wash and peel sweet potatoes. Cut off woody portions and ends. Cut potatoes diagonally into ½-inch-thick slices. Place a steamer basket in a saucepan. Add water to just below the bottom of the steamer basket. Bring to boiling. Add potato slices. Cover and reduce heat. Steam for 10 to 15 minutes or till just tender; cool.

Meanwhile, core the unpeeled apple and cut into 12 wedges. In a greased, two-quart casserole combine potato slices and apple wedges.

In a small saucepan bring the brown sugar, water, margarine or butter, and cloves to boiling. Drizzle the mixture evenly over potatoes and apples.

Bake, uncovered, in a 350° oven for 30 to 35 minutes or till potatoes and apples are glazed, stirring twice. Sprinkle potatoes and apples with toasted pecans or walnuts. Makes 4 servings.

Nutrition information per serving: 255 calories, 2 g protein, 47 g carbohydrate, 8 g total fat (1 g saturated), 0 mg cholesterol, 48 mg sodium, 448 mg potassium

Arkansas

CORN BREAD

*In the South cornmeal is white, and
yellow meal is dismissed as inferior. One
nineteenth-century woman complained
that in the corn bread she encountered on
her travels outside the south, yellow corn
was used and the meal was too fine,
which made clammy bread!*

1¼   **cups cornmeal**
¾   **cup all-purpose flour**
1   **tablespoon baking powder**
¼   **teaspoon baking soda**
¼   **teaspoon salt**
2   **eggs**
1   **cup buttermilk *or* sour milk**
¼   **cup honey *or* maple-flavored
syrup**
2   **tablespoons margarine *or*
butter, melted, *or*
cooking oil**

In a mixing bowl stir together cornmeal, flour, baking powder, baking
soda, and salt.

In another bowl beat together
eggs, buttermilk, honey or syrup,
and melted margarine or butter or
cooking oil. Add to cornmeal mixture and stir just till combined. *Do
not overbeat.*

Pour into a greased 9x9x2-inch
baking pan. Bake in a 425° oven
about 20 minutes or till golden
brown. Makes 9 servings.

***Nutrition information per serving:** 187
calories, 5 g protein, 32 g carbohydrate, 4 g total
fat (1 g saturated), 48 mg cholesterol, 256 mg
sodium, 101 mg potassium*

Virginia

BEATEN BISCUITS

*Beaten biscuits were a true test of the
fabled southern hospitality. If the biscuits were for family, it was acceptable to
stop working the dough after 300 whacks
with an ax handle. However, biscuits for
company demanded twice as many.
(Pictured on page 121)*

Sally Lunn, top, and Corn Bread

2   **cups all-purpose flour**
1   **teaspoon sugar**
½   **teaspoon salt**
⅛   **teaspoon baking powder**
¼   **cup shortening *or* lard**
⅓   **cup ice water**
⅓   **cup cold milk**

In a medium mixing bowl stir
together flour, sugar, salt, and baking powder. Using a pastry blender
or two knives, cut in shortening or
lard till mixture resembles coarse
crumbs. Make a well in the center
of the dry ingredients. Add ice
water and milk all at once. Using a
fork, stir just till moistened. If necessary, stir in enough additional ice
water to make dough cling together.
(Dough will be very stiff.)

Turn dough out onto a lightly
floured surface. Using the flat side
of a wooden spoon or a metal meat
mallet, beat dough vigorously for 15
minutes, folding dough over and
giving it a quarter turn frequently.
Dip spoon or mallet into flour as
necessary to prevent sticking.

Lightly roll or pat dough to
⅜-inch thickness. Cut dough with a
floured 2-inch biscuit cutter, dipping the cutter into flour between
cuts. Place biscuits 1 inch apart on
an ungreased baking sheet. Using
the tines of a fork, prick biscuits
several times. Bake in a 400° oven
about 20 minutes or till light brown.
Serve warm. Makes 24 biscuits.

***Nutrition information per serving:** 59
calories, 1 g protein, 8 g carbohydrate, 2 g total
fat (1 g saturated), 0 mg cholesterol, 48 mg
sodium, 16 mg potassium*

Alabama

SALLY LUNN

*Did an English baker, Sally Lunn,
sell these rich, briochelike tea cakes in
the streets of eighteenth-century Bath?
Or is the name a mispronunciation
of the French* soleil lune, *meaning "sun
and moon"? No one knows for sure. The
recipe is probably French, but it was the
English who brought it with them to
America. It has always been a particular
favorite in the South.*

3   **cups all-purpose flour**
1   **package active dry yeast**
1   **cup milk**
3   **tablespoons sugar**
3   **tablespoons margarine *or*
butter**
½   **teaspoon salt**
2   **eggs**

In a bowl stir together *1½ cups* of the
flour and the yeast; set aside. In a
medium saucepan heat and stir the
milk, sugar, margarine or butter,
and salt just till warm (120° to
130°) and margarine almost melts.
Add to the flour mixture. Then add
eggs. Beat with an electric mixer on
low to medium speed for 30 seconds, scraping sides of bowl. Beat
on high speed for 3 minutes.

Using a spoon, stir in enough of
the remaining flour to make a stiff
batter. Cover; let rise in a warm
place till double (about 1 hour).

Stir down batter; spoon into a
well-greased Turk's head mold or 7-
cup tube mold. Cover; let rise in a
warm place till nearly double
(about 45 minutes). Bake in a 375°
oven about 40 minutes or till bread
sounds hollow when tapped.
Remove from pan. Serve warm or
cool. Makes 1 loaf (24 servings).

***Nutrition information per serving:** 88
calories, 3 g protein, 14 g carbohydrate, 2 g total
fat (0 g saturated), 18 mgcholesterol, 67 mg
sodium, 39 mg potassium*

Lord Baltimore Cake, left (see recipe, page 129), and Blondies

North Carolina

LEMONY MORAVIAN SUGAR BREAD

The Moravians, a religious sect from Bohemia, established settlements in the mid-1800s in Pennsylvania, Georgia, and North Carolina. They were famous bakers and served this flat, sweet bread during the Christmas holidays and at their religious love feasts, a ritualized sharing of food and drink.
(Pictured on page 120)

1	cup Sourdough Starter (see recipe, page 244)
3½	cups all-purpose flour
1	package active dry yeast
½	cup sugar
½	cup milk
¼	cup margarine *or* butter
½	teaspoon salt
2	slightly beaten eggs
2	tablespoons lemon juice
2	teaspoons finely shredded lemon peel
¾	cup packed brown sugar
⅓	cup margarine *or* butter
1	teaspoon ground cinnamon

Bring the Sourdough Starter to room temperature. In a large mixing bowl stir together *1½ cups* of the flour and the yeast.

In a small saucepan heat and stir sugar, milk, the ¼ cup margarine or butter, and salt till warm (120° to 130°) and margarine almost melts. Add to the flour mixture. Add Sourdough Starter, eggs, and lemon juice. Beat with an electric mixer on low speed for 30 seconds, scraping the sides of the bowl constantly. Beat on high speed about 2 minutes. Using a spoon, stir in lemon peel and remaining flour.

Lightly grease a 13x9x2-inch baking pan. Transfer dough to the prepared baking pan and pat dough evenly into the pan with your floured hands. Cover and let rise in a warm place till nearly double (about 60 minutes).

In a small saucepan combine brown sugar, the ⅓ cup margarine or butter, and cinnamon. Heat and stir till melted and smooth. Poke holes in dough with the handle of a wooden spoon. Pour brown sugar mixture over dough. Bake in a 375° oven for 20 to 25 minutes or till done. Serve warm. Serves 12.

Nutrition information per serving: 339 calories, 7 g protein, 55 g carbohydrate, 10 g total fat (2 g saturated), 36 mg cholesterol, 184 mg sodium, 123 mg potassium

South Carolina

BLONDIES

These butterscotch bar cookies are an example of the South's partiality for brown sugar in baked goods. Short'nin' bread, a Scottish shortbread made with brown sugar rather than white, is another.

2	cups packed brown sugar
⅔	cup margarine *or* butter
2	eggs
2	teaspoons vanilla
2	cups all-purpose flour
1	teaspoon baking powder
¼	teaspoon baking soda
1	cup semisweet chocolate pieces
1	cup chopped nuts

Heat sugar and margarine, stirring till sugar dissolves. Cool slightly. Stir in eggs, one at a time, and vanilla. Stir in flour, baking powder, and soda. Spread in a greased 13x9x2-inch baking pan. Sprinkle with chocolate and nuts. Bake in a 350° oven 25 to 30 minutes or till done. Cut while warm. Makes 36.

Nutrition information per bar: 134 calories, 2 g protein, 17 g carbohydrate, 7 g total fat (2 g saturated), 12 mg cholesterol, 51 mg sodium, 71 mg potassium

South Carolina

LORD BALTIMORE CAKE

This recipe is a variation of one of the South's most famous desserts. Writer Owen Wister was so taken with an elaborate cake created by a Charleston, South Carolina, woman that he popularized it in his 1906 novel, Lady Baltimore.
(Pictured on page 127)

2¼ cups all-purpose flour
1¼ cups sugar
1 tablespoon baking powder
½ teaspoon salt
¾ cup margarine *or* butter
¾ cup milk
1 tablespoon rum
½ teaspoon lemon extract
8 egg yolks
Fluffy Frosting
Lord Baltimore Filling

Grease and lightly flour two 9x1½-inch round baking pans; set aside. In a large mixing bowl combine flour, sugar, baking powder, and salt. Add margarine or butter, milk, rum, and lemon extract. Beat with an electric mixer on low speed till combined. Beat on high speed for 2 minutes. Add egg yolks and beat 1 minute more or till combined. Pour into prepared pans.

Bake in a 350° oven for 25 to 30 minutes or till a toothpick inserted near the center comes out clean. Cool 10 minutes on wire racks. Remove from pans; cool.

Meanwhile, prepare Fluffy Frosting and Lord Baltimore Filling. Spread filling between cake layers. Frost the top and sides of the cake with the remaining frosting. Makes 12 servings.

Fluffy Frosting: In a medium saucepan combine 1½ cups packed *brown sugar*, ⅓ cup *water*, and ¼ teaspoon *cream of tartar*. Cook and stir till bubbly and sugar dissolves.

In a large mixing bowl combine 2 *egg whites* and 1 teaspoon *vanilla*. Add hot sugar mixture very slowly to egg white mixture, beating constantly with an electric mixer on high speed about 7 minutes or till stiff peaks form (tips stand up).

Lord Baltimore Filling: Combine *1 cup* of the *Fluffy Frosting*, ½ cup crumbled *soft macaroons*, ½ cup chopped *pecans*, and 12 *candied cherries*, chopped (about ¼ cup).

Nutrition information per serving: 496 calories, 6 g protein, 69 g carbohydrate, 22 g total fat (5 g saturated), 143 mg cholesterol, 319 mg sodium, 189 mg potassium

Louisiana

BANANAS FOSTER

Created in the 1950s at Brennan's in New Orleans, the dish was originally part of the breakfast menu. It was named after Richard Foster, a Brennan's regular.

⅓ cup butter
⅓ cup brown sugar
3 ripe bananas, bias-sliced (2 cups)
¼ teaspoon ground cinnamon
2 tablespoons crème de cocoa *or* banana liqueur
¼ cup rum
Rich vanilla ice cream (about 2 cups)

In a skillet melt butter; stir in brown sugar till melted. Add bananas; cook and gently stir over medium heat about 2 minutes or till heated through. Sprinkle with cinnamon. Stir in crème de cocoa or banana liqueur.

In a small saucepan, heat rum till it almost simmers. Carefully ignite rum and pour over bananas, coating evenly. Serve immediately with ice cream. Makes 4 servings.

Nutrition information per serving: 490 calories, 4 g protein, 50 g carbohydrate, 28 g total fat (17 g saturated), 86 mg cholesterol, 50 mg sodium, 465 mg potassium

Florida

KEY LIME PIE

This pie was perhaps created to showcase sweetened condensed milk, a new product developed by Gail Borden in 1858, as much as to feature the extra tart Key lime of south Florida.
(Pictured on page 131)

3 eggs
1 14½-ounce can (1¼ cups) sweetened condensed milk
½ to ¾ teaspoon finely shredded Key lime peel *or* 1½ teaspoons finely shredded Persian lime peel
⅓ cup lime juice (8 to 10 Key limes *or* 2 to 3 Persian limes)
½ cup water
Few drops green food coloring (optional)
Pastry for Single-Crust Pie (see recipe, page 55)
½ teaspoon vanilla
¼ teaspoon cream of tartar
⅓ cup sugar

Separate egg yolks from whites; set whites aside for meringue. In a bowl beat yolks well with a fork or whisk. Gradually stir in sweetened condensed milk and lime peel. Add lime juice, water, and, if desired, food coloring; mix well. (Mixture will thicken.) Spoon into pastry shell. Bake in a 325° oven for 30 minutes. Remove from oven. Increase oven temperature to 350°.

Meanwhile, for meringue, in a mixing bowl combine egg whites, vanilla, and cream of tartar. Beat with an electric mixer on medium speed about 1 minute or till soft peaks form (tips curl). Gradually add sugar, 1 tablespoon at a time, beating on high speed about 4 minutes more or till mixture forms stiff, glossy peaks and sugar dissolves. Immediately spread meringue over hot pie filling; seal to edge of pastry. Bake in a 350° oven 15 minutes; cool 1 hour. Chill to store. Serves 8.

Nutrition information per serving: 351 calories, 8 g protein, 49 g carbohydrate, 14 g total fat (5 g saturated), 97 mg cholesterol, 218 mg sodium, 221 mg potassium

Bananas Foster

Louisiana

RAISIN BREAD PUDDING WITH WHISKEY SAUCE

Another New Orleans classic, bread pudding most likely developed as a way to recycle what was left of yesterday's loaf. The result is truly sublime, as is the rich sauce that blankets every serving. It's an indulgence well worth the calories.

3	cups French bread cubes
⅔	cup sugar
¼	cup margarine *or* butter
2	eggs
1	cup whipping cream
3	tablespoons raisins
2	teaspoons vanilla
¾	cup sugar
2	teaspoons cornstarch
	Dash cinnamon *or* nutmeg
¾	cup whipping cream
1	to 2 tablespoons bourbon whiskey

Arrange bread cubes in a single layer in a 2-quart square baking dish or 10-inch round baking dish.

Beat the ⅔ cup sugar and margarine or butter till creamy. Add eggs; beat till fluffy. Stir in the 1 cup whipping cream, raisins, and vanilla. Pour over bread cubes.

Place baking dish in a larger baking pan on the oven rack. Pour boiling water into larger pan around dish to a depth of 1 inch. Bake in a 325° oven for 40 to 50 minutes or till a knife inserted near the center comes out clean. Remove dish from hot water. Cool slightly.

Meanwhile, for sauce, in a small saucepan combine the remaining sugar, cornstarch, and cinnamon. Stir in the remaining whipping cream. Cook and stir over medium heat till thickened and bubbly. Cook and stir for 1 minute more. Remove from heat; stir in bourbon.

Serve warm bread pudding with the whiskey sauce. Store any remaining sauce in a covered container in refrigerator. Reheat over low heat, stirring occasionally. Makes 6 servings.

Triple Peanut Bars, and Raisin Bread Pudding with Whiskey Sauce

Nutrition information per serving: 605 calories, 6 g protein, 67 g carbohydrate, 36 g total fat (18 g saturated), 166 mg cholesterol, 256 mg sodium, 123 mg potassium

South Carolina

TRIPLE PEANUT BARS

"Goodness how delicious, eating goober peas." The old Southern ditty is really about peanuts, not peas. Goober is derived from the African nguba. Southerners enjoy peanuts raw, baked, roasted, and boiled, and in peanut butter, peanut soup, peanut gravy, and peanut brittle.

¾	cup peanut butter
¼	cup cooking oil
1½	cups all-purpose flour
½	cup packed brown sugar
½	cup sugar
2	eggs
¾	cup milk
1	teaspoon vanilla
½	teaspoon baking powder
¼	teaspoon baking soda
⅔	cup chopped peanuts
1½	cups semisweet chocolate pieces
	Peanut Butter Icing

In a bowl beat peanut butter and oil with an electric mixer on low to medium speed about 30 seconds or till combined. Add about *half* of the flour, the brown sugar, sugar, eggs, about *half* of the milk, the vanilla, baking powder, and baking soda. Beat till combined. Stir in remaining flour and milk. Stir in peanuts.

Spread batter in a greased 15x10x1-inch baking pan. Bake in a 350° oven about 20 minutes or till a toothpick inserted near the center comes out clean. Place pan on a wire rack. Sprinkle with chocolate pieces; let stand 5 minutes. Spread chocolate over surface. Cool completely. Drizzle with Peanut Butter Icing. Cut into bars. Makes 48 bars.

Peanut Butter Icing: Beat together ¾ cup sifted *powdered sugar*, ¼ cup *creamy peanut butter*, and enough *milk* (2 to 3 tablespoons) to make icing of drizzling consistency.

Nutrition information per bar: 118 calories, 3 g protein, 13 g carbohydrate, 7 g total fat (2 g saturated), 9 mg cholesterol, 58 mg sodium, 90 mg potassium

Tennessee

LEMON CHESS PIE

Chess is another example of a word that likely evolved from one that sounded similar, in this case cheese (as in cheesecake). The heritage of the pie is British, the inclusion of lemon particularly southern. Basically, it is a lemon custard pie.

	Pastry for Single-Crust Pie (see recipe, page 55)
4	slightly beaten eggs
1½	cups sugar
¼	cup margarine *or* butter, melted
2	teaspoons finely shredded lemon peel
2	tablespoons lemon juice
1	tablespoon cornmeal
1½	teaspoons vanilla
½	cup light raisins

Line pastry-lined 9-inch pie plate with a double thickness of foil. Bake in a 450° oven 5 minutes; remove foil. Bake 5 minutes more.

For filling, in a mixing bowl stir together the eggs, sugar, margarine or butter, lemon peel, lemon juice,

Key Lime Pie, top left (see recipe, page 129), Lemon Chess Pie, right, and Sweet Potato Pie with Hazelnut Streusel Topping

cornmeal, and vanilla. Mix well. Stir in raisins. Place the prepared pastry shell on the oven rack. Pour filling into the pastry shell.

To prevent overbrowning, cover edge of pie with foil. Reduce oven temperature to 350° and bake for 20 minutes. Remove foil. Bake for 20 to 25 minutes more or till a knife inserted near the center comes out clean. Cool pie on a wire rack. Cover and chill to store. Serves 8.

Nutrition information per serving: 457 calories, 6 g protein, 64 g carbohydrate, 21 g total fat (5 g saturated), 107 mg cholesterol, 274 mg sodium, 111 mg potassium

Mississippi

SWEET POTATO PIE WITH HAZELNUT STREUSEL TOPPING

The American version of sweet potato pie may have English roots, but more likely it was the creation of black slaves. They prepared sweet potatoes in dozens of ways, a legacy of African cooking, which used similar tubers.

1	**pound sweet potatoes**
¼	**cup margarine *or* butter**
	Cornmeal Pastry
½	**cup packed brown sugar**
1	**tablespoon finely shredded orange peel**
1	**teaspoon ground cinnamon**
½	**teaspoon ground nutmeg**
½	**teaspoon ground ginger**
3	**slightly beaten eggs**
1	**cup half-and-half *or* light cream**
	Hazelnut Streusel Topping

Peel sweet potatoes. Cut off woody portions and ends. Cut into quarters. Cook, covered, in enough boiling salted water to cover for 25 to 35 minutes or till tender; drain and mash. (You should have 1½ cups.) Cut up margarine; add to hot potatoes, stirring till melted.

Meanwhile, prepare Cornmeal Pastry. Roll dough into a 12-inch circle; ease into a 9-inch pie plate. Trim pastry to ½ inch beyond edge of plate. Fold under extra pastry; crimp edge high. *Do not prick pastry.*

For filling, add brown sugar, orange peel, cinnamon, nutmeg, and ginger to potatoes. Stir in eggs and half-and-half. Place pastry shell on the oven rack; pour in filling. Cover edge of pie with foil. Bake in a 375° oven 30 minutes. Remove foil. Sprinkle with Hazelnut Streusel Topping. Bake 20 to 25 minutes more or till knife inserted near center comes out clean, cool. Serves 8.

Cornmeal Pastry: Mix ¾ cup *all-purpose flour*, ½ cup *yellow cornmeal*, 1 tablespoon *sugar*, and ¼ teaspoon *salt*. Cut in ⅓ cup *shortening or lard* till pieces are the size of small peas. Sprinkle 3 to 5 tablespoons cold *water*, 1 tablespoon at a time, over mixture, tossing with a fork after each addition till all is moistened. Form into a ball.

Hazelnut Streusel Topping: Mix ¼ cup *all-purpose flour*, ¼ cup packed *brown sugar*, ⅛ teaspoon ground *cinnamon*, and ⅛ teaspoon ground *nutmeg*. Cut in 2 tablespoons *margarine or butter* till mixture resembles coarse crumbs. Stir in ¼ cup chopped, toasted *hazelnuts (filberts)* or *almonds*.

Nutrition information per serving: 456 calories, 7 g protein, 52 g carbohydrate, 25 g total fat (6 g saturated), 91 mg cholesterol, 214 mg sodium, 341 mg potassium

and vanilla. Cover and blend or process till smooth. Add the 2½ cups pecans. Blend or process about 1 minute or till nearly smooth. Add flour mixture; blend or process just till combined. Spread batter evenly into 2 greased and floured 8x1½-inch round baking pans. Bake in a 350° oven for 20 to 25 minutes or till lightly browned. Cool on wire racks for 10 minutes. Remove from pans; cool thoroughly on racks.

Meanwhile, in a skillet heat water and lemon juice to boiling. Add apple slices. Reduce heat. Cover; simmer 2 to 3 minutes or just till tender. Drain apple slices.

In a medium bowl beat whipping cream and sugar till soft peaks form. Place a torte layer on a cake plate. Spread about *half* of the whipped cream evenly over layer. Arrange apple slices in a single layer on whipped cream, using as many as needed to cover surface and reserving remaining for top. Top with second torte layer. Spread remaining whipped cream on top of second torte layer. Arrange remaining apple slices and, if desired, pecan halves on top. Chill 1 to 2 hours. Makes 12 servings.

Nutrition information per serving: 331 calories, 5 g protein, 24 g carbohydrate, 26 g total fat (6 g saturated), 98 mg cholesterol, 55 mg sodium, 136 mg potassium

Pralines, top left, Huguenot Apple-Pecan Torte, top right, and Southern Pecan Pie

South Carolina

HUGUENOT APPLE-PECAN TORTE

Close to half of the Europeans who settled in South Carolina in the seventeenth century were French Huguenots fleeing Catholic persecution. The food of Charleston and all of South Carolina reflects their influence.

2   tablespoons all-purpose
    flour
1   teaspoon baking powder
1   teaspoon finely shredded
    lemon peel
4   eggs
¾   cup sugar
1   teaspoon vanilla
2½ cups pecans
1   cup water
1   tablespoon lemon juice
2   cups sliced, peeled apple
1   cup whipping cream
2   tablespoons sugar
    Toasted pecan halves
    (optional)

Stir together flour, baking powder, and lemon peel; set aside.

In a blender container or food processor bowl place eggs, sugar,

Lousiana

PRALINES

New Orleans satisfies its sweet tooth with pralines, a confection made from caramel and nuts. Like many dishes linked with this city, its origins are French. It was named after a seventeenth-century French aristocrat, Cesar du Plessis-Pralin.

1½ cups sugar
1½ cups packed brown sugar
1   cup half-and-half *or* light
    cream

3 tablespoons margarine *or* butter
2 cups pecan halves

Butter the sides of a heavy 2-quart saucepan. In the saucepan combine sugar, brown sugar, and half-and-half. Cook over medium-high heat to boiling, stirring constantly with a wooden spoon to dissolve sugars. (This should take 6 to 8 minutes.) Avoid splashing the mixture on sides of the pan.

Carefully clip a candy thermometer to pan. Cook over medium-low heat, stirring occasionally, till thermometer registers 234° (soft-ball stage). Mixture should boil at a moderate, steady rate over entire surface. Reaching soft-ball stage should take 18 to 20 minutes.

Remove pan from heat. Add margarine but *do not stir.* Cool, without stirring, to 150°. (This should take about 30 minutes.) Remove thermometer, then stir in pecans. Beat vigorously with a wooden spoon till candy is just beginning to thicken but is still glossy. This should take 2 to 3 minutes.

Drop about *2 tablespoons* candy from a large serving spoon onto baking sheets lined with waxed paper, forming 3-inch pralines. If candy becomes too stiff to drop, stir in a few drops of hot water. Store in a tightly covered container. Makes 15 large pralines.

Nutrition information per praline: 269 calories, 2 g protein, 37 g carbohydrate, 14 g total fat (2 g saturated), 6 mg cholesterol, 32 mg sodium, 129 mg potassium

Georgia

SOUTHERN PECAN PIE

Depending on which part of the South the recipe came from, a pecan pie might be made with corn syrup or molasses or brown sugar, or even sweet potatoes.

1¼ cups all-purpose flour
¼ teaspoon salt
⅓ cup shortening

Peach Pie (see recipe, page 134)

¼ cup finely chopped pecans
3 to 4 tablespoons cold water
3 eggs
1 cup corn syrup
⅔ cup sugar
⅓ cup margarine *or* butter, melted
1 tablespoon all-purpose flour
2 tablespoons bourbon whiskey
1 teaspoon vanilla
1½ cups pecan halves
Whipped cream

For pastry, in a bowl stir together the 1¼ cups flour and salt. Cut in shortening till pieces are the size of small peas. Stir in finely chopped pecans. Sprinkle *1 tablespoon* of the water over part of the mixture; gently toss with a fork. Push to side of bowl. Repeat till all is moistened. Form dough into a ball.

On a lightly floured surface, flatten dough with your hands. Roll dough from center to edges, forming a circle about 12 inches in diameter. Wrap pastry around a rolling pin. Unroll pastry onto a 9-inch pie plate. Ease pastry into pie plate, being careful not to stretch pastry. Trim to ½ inch beyond edge of pie plate; fold under extra pastry. Make a fluted edge. *Do not prick pastry.*

For filling, in a mixing bowl beat eggs lightly with a rotary beater till combined. Stir in corn syrup, sugar, margarine, the 1 tablespoon flour, the bourbon, and vanilla. Mix well. Stir in the pecan halves.

Place pastry-lined pie plate on the oven rack. Pour the filling into the pastry-lined pie plate. Cover edge of pie with foil. Bake in a 350° oven for 25 minutes. Remove foil; bake for 20 to 25 minutes more or till a knife inserted near the center comes out clean. Cool.

Serve with whipped cream. Cover and chill to store. Makes 8 servings.

Nutrition information per serving: 608 calories, 7 g protein, 69 g carbohydrate, 36 g total fat (5 g saturated), 80 mg cholesterol, 204 mg sodium, 130 mg potassium

Lousiana

CAFÉ BRÛLOT

Brûlot means "burnt brandy" in French. Special fireproof brûlot bowls were important tableware in fine New Orleans homes during the 1800s. For a dramatic effect, the lights were dimmed before the mixture was flamed and the coffee added to it. (Pictured on page 135)

3 inches stick cinnamon, broken
6 whole cloves
4 sugar cubes
1 3x¼-inch strip orange peel, membrane removed
1 3x¼-inch strip lemon peel, membrane removed
½ cup brandy
2 cups hot, double-strength coffee

In the blazer pan of a chafing dish combine cinnamon, cloves, sugar cubes, orange peel, and lemon peel.

In a small saucepan heat brandy till it almost simmers. Remove from heat and ignite. Pour over mixture in blazer pan. Place blazer pan over chafing dish burner. Spoon brandy over sugar till cubes melt. Stir in coffee. Makes 4 (4-ounce) servings.

Nutrition information per serving: 87 calories, 0 g protein, 6 g carbohydrate, 0 g total fat (0 g saturated), 0 mg cholesterol, 5 mg sodium, 133 mg potassium

Café au Lait, and Beignets

Georgia

PEACH PIE

When the first settlers arrived in the Piedmont area of Georgia, peach trees were already flourishing. They were planted from seed by Native Americans who quickly took to the fruit after it was brought to America by the Spanish in the sixteenth century.
(Pictured on page 133)

½ to ¾ cup sugar
3 tablespoons all-purpose flour
½ teaspoon ground cinnamon
Dash ground nutmeg
6 cups thinly sliced, peeled peaches *or* frozen, unsweetened peach slices
Pastry for Double-Crust Pie (see recipe, page 274)
1 teaspoon sugar
Dash ground cinnamon
Milk

In a large mixing bowl stir together the ½ to ¾ cup sugar, the flour, the ½ teaspoon cinnamon, and nutmeg. Add fresh or frozen peaches. Gently toss till the peaches are coated. If using frozen peaches, let stand for 15 to 30 minutes or till peaches are partially thawed but still icy.

Prepare and roll out the pastry as directed. Line a 9-inch pie plate with *half* of the pastry. Stir peach mixture, then transfer to the pastry-lined pie plate. Trim the bottom pastry to the edge of the pie plate.

Cut slits in the top crust. Place top crust on filling. Seal and crimp edge. In a small bowl stir together the 1 teaspoon sugar and the dash cinnamon. Brush top crust with milk and sprinkle with sugar-cinnamon mixture.

To prevent overbrowning, cover edge of pie with foil. Bake in a 375° oven for 25 minutes for fresh peaches (50 minutes for frozen peaches). Remove foil. Bake for 20 to 25 minutes more for fresh peaches (20 to 30 minutes more for frozen peaches) or till top is golden. Cool pie on a wire rack. Makes 8 servings.

Nutrition information per serving: 382 calories, 4 g protein, 55 g carbohydrate, 18 g total fat (4 g saturated), 0 mg cholesterol, 134 mg sodium, 289 mg potassium

Lousiana

BEIGNETS

The New Orleans version of a doughnut and cup of joe is the sugar-dusted, deep-fried beignet (French for fritter) and strong, chicory-laced Creole coffee. Together they've been a French Quarter tradition for generations of Big Easy residents and visitors.

2¾ to 3¼ cups all-purpose flour
1 package active dry yeast
½ teaspoon ground nutmeg (optional)
1 cup milk
¼ cup sugar
2 tablespoons shortening
½ teaspoon salt
1 egg
Shortening *or* cooking oil for deep-fat frying
Powdered sugar

Mint Julep

In a bowl stir together *1¼ cups* of the flour, yeast, and, if desired, nutmeg. In a saucepan heat milk, sugar, the 2 tablespoons shortening, and salt just till warm (120° to 130°) and the shortening is almost melted, stirring the mixture constantly.

Add the heated mixture to the flour mixture. Add egg. Beat with an electric mixer on low speed for 30 seconds, scraping sides of bowl. Beat for 3 minutes on high speed. Using a wooden spoon, stir in enough of the remaining flour to make a soft dough. Place dough in a greased bowl; turn once to grease the surface. Cover bowl and refrigerate the dough overnight or till well chilled.

Turn the dough out onto a lightly floured surface. Cover and let rest for 10 minutes. Roll into an 18x12-inch rectangle. Cut into thirty-six 3x2-inch rectangles. Cover and let rest for 30 minutes (dough will not be doubled).

In a large, deep saucepan or deep-fat fryer heat 2 inches of shortening or cooking oil to 375°. Fry 2 or 3 of the dough rectangles at a time about 1 minute or till golden, turning once. Drain on paper towels. Sift powdered sugar atop. Makes 36 beignets.

Nutrition information per beignet: 101 calories, 1 g protein, 11 g carbohydrate, 6 g total fat (1 g saturated), 6 mg cholesterol, 5 mg sodium, 25 mg potassium

Alabama

CAPPUCCINO EGGNOG

Along with hoppin John and collard greens, eggnog is part of Christmas and New Year's celebrations in the South. It is closely related to syllabub, a recipe that appears in many early southern cookbooks, except that it uses hard liquor, while the latter requires wine.

6   beaten eggs
2   cups milk
⅓   cup sugar
1   tablespoon instant espresso powder *or* 4 teaspoons instant coffee crystals
¼   cup light rum *or* milk
1   teaspoon vanilla
1   cup whipping cream
2   tablespoons sugar
3   tablespoons finely shredded orange peel
10   long cinnamon sticks

In a large, heavy saucepan mix eggs, milk, the ⅓ cup sugar, and espresso or coffee. Cook and stir over medium heat about 8 minutes or till mixture coats a metal spoon. Remove from heat. Cool quickly by placing pan in a sink or bowl of *ice water* and stirring for 1 to 2 minutes. Stir in rum or milk and vanilla. Cover surface with plastic wrap. Chill 4 to 24 hours.

At serving time, in a medium mixing bowl beat whipping cream and the 2 tablespoons sugar with an electric mixer on medium speed till soft peaks form. Transfer chilled egg mixture to a punch bowl. Fold in whipped cream mixture. Serve at once. Sprinkle each serving with shredded orange peel and serve with cinnamon sticks. Makes ten 4-ounce servings.

Nutrition information per serving: 203 calories, 6 g protein, 13 g carbohydrate, 13 g total fat (7 g saturated), 164 mg cholesterol, 71 mg sodium, 110 mg potassium

Café Brûlot, left (see recipe, page 133), and Cappuccino Eggnog

Kentucky

MINT JULEP

On eighteenth-century plantations, juleps were sipped in the morning before breakfast. They were thought to have medicinal properties. According to Kentucky tradition, a proper julep can be mixed only in a silver goblet.

1   cup water
½   cup sugar
1   cup fresh mint sprigs
9   ounces bourbon whiskey *or* rum
6   cups crushed ice
    Fresh mint (optional)

In a small saucepan combine water and sugar; bring to boiling. Add the 1 cup mint. Reduce heat; cover and simmer 10 minutes. Remove from heat; cool. Cover and chill mint mixture several hours or overnight. Strain syrup; discard mint leaves.

For *each* drink, place about *1 cup* crushed ice in a mug. Pour *1½ ounces* bourbon or rum and *3 tablespoons* mint syrup over ice. If desired, garnish with fresh mint. Serves 6.

Nutrition information per serving: 174 calories, 0 g protein, 17 g carbohydrate, 0 g total fat (0 g saturated), 0 mg cholesterol, 6 mg sodium, 56 mg potassium

Louisiana

CAFÉ AU LAIT

Creole coffee, from New Orleans, gets its distinctive bitter flavor from the addition of chicory to the grind. Adding milk or cream softens its bite. Chicory was first used as an extender for coffee during the hard times of the Civil War. Now it's used because locals demand it.

1   cup ground coffee with chicory
3   cups water
3   cups half-and-half, light cream, *or* milk

Using coffee with chicory and water, prepare coffee in a coffee maker according to manufacturer's directions.

Meanwhile, heat the half-and-half, light cream, or milk over low heat. Beat with a rotary beater till foamy. Transfer cream to a warmed serving container.

Stir coffee. Pour coffee and cream in equal amounts into serving cups. Makes twelve 4-ounce servings.

Nutrition information per serving: 81 calories, 2 g protein, 3 g carbohydrate, 7 g total fat (4 g saturated), 22 mg cholesterol, 27 mg sodium, 139 mg potassium

The Midwest

*I*f ever there was a melting pot, it can be found in the kitchens of the Midwest, where history and geography have conspired to make dinner-plate companions of wild rice, Cornish pasties, and Swiss cheese.

The theme of heartland cooking is the practical, no-nonsense sustenance required by hard toil on the farm. It is the kind of hale-and-hearty fare that relies upon high-quality ingredients proudly set forth without the blandishments of fuss and exotic seasonings. It is the kind of robust cooking that has made church suppers an American institution.

Unlike the Native Americans in many other parts of the country, the early inhabitants of the northern states in this region developed a dependency on wild rice rather than on corn. Actually an aquatic grass (and therefore not technically a grain), wild rice is indigenous to the Great Lakes area. It grows in the backwaters to a height of eight feet, and some wild rice is still harvested by the Minnesota Ojibway Indians in the same way described by a traveler back in 1820: "It is now gathered by two of the women passing around in a canoe, one sitting in the stern and pushing it along, while the other, with two small pointed sticks about three feet long, collects it in by running one of the sticks into the rice, and bending it into the canoe, while with the other she threshes out the grain. This she does on both sides of the canoe alternately, and while it is moving."[1]

As the tall grass is released and resumes its upright position, a few kernels naturally fall into the water to become seeds of the next year's harvest—a beautiful completion to the natural rhythm and beauty of this native technique.

For the earliest inhabitants of the midwestern Great Lakes states—Minnesota, Wisconsin, Illinois, Indiana, and Michigan—herring, perch, trout, and whitefish were staple foods. In some pockets of the

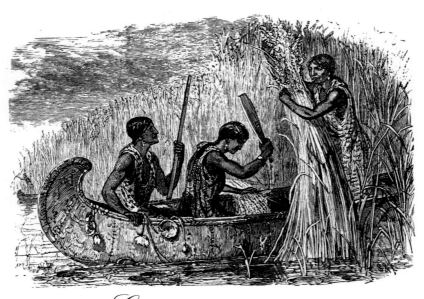

Gathering wild rice in Wisconsin.

region, you can still taste "planked" fish prepared in the old Indian way: First the cleaned and split fish is placed skin side down on a thick oak or maple plank that has been heated. Then the fish is brushed with butter (the Indians would have used animal fat), seasoned

with salt and pepper, and baked in a hot oven until done. For a dramatic presentation, it is served right on the plank, which has imbued the fish with a subtle but distinctive flavor.

The area was also very rich in game birds, including wild ducks, geese, partridge, and turkey. Larger game such as elk, deer, and moose roamed the woods, and Michigan hunters developed a technique of mixing the tough meat with vegetables and simmering it over a slow fire. They called the stew *booyaw*, using the French-Canadian dialect word for "bouillon."

The woods were also abundant in mushrooms and berries. Michigan is still famous for its wild morels, considered king of mush-

Previous pages: One glimpse of the heartland's rich, tillable soil convinced many pioneers that they needn't travel any farther west to find the good life. Corn fields shimmer in the fading light of a midsummer evening in Dane County, Wisconsin. Below: Like a mirror, this pond in Michigan's Tahquamenon Falls State Park reflects passing clouds. The region has countless miles of freshwater shoreline. Right: Fish from the Great Lakes—including Lake Superior, site of Wisconsin's Apostle Islands—sustained Native American and settler alike.

rooms by many connoisseurs. When they're in season, locals drop everything to forage for them. What's not used fresh in sauces, omelettes, and soufflés is carefully dried for year-round use. And it is also customary to put up jams with such tasty regional fruits as blackberries, thimbleberries, and wild red cherries.

With such natural bounty, it's no wonder that pioneers en route to the West were literally stopped in their tracks. The most dominant draws of this region were the westernmost Great Lakes—Superior, Huron, and Michigan—and the endless miles of fertile plain that eventually became America's breadbasket. The flow of immigrants grew dramatically after the Erie Canal opened in 1825, making the northern route across country a viable alternative. Over the ensuing decades, the brave pioneers added their particular variations of ethnic

styles, flavors, and textures to the hale-and-hearty culinary theme.

The pasty of northern Michigan is a good example. Cornish miners who arrived in the mid–nineteenth century brought this convenient meat-wrapped-in-dough lunch with them. Reminded of their waterlocked home countries, many Scandinavian settlers were also drawn to the region, particularly the Finns. Before long, Finnish bakeries in the area were specializing in pasties, which they called their own.

Because of the significant Scandinavian influence in Minnesota and Wisconsin, cookbooks of the area read like smorgasbords, replete with Swedish meatballs, herring salads, rye bread, Finnish cardamom-scented cakes, and Danish pastries.

But the largest single immigrant group was German, a fact nowhere more obvious than in Milwaukee,

A pioneer family's first job after choosing a homestead was to build a shelter. A location close to a creek and wooded area was considered best. Often a season passed before sufficient land was cleared and the soil tilled to plant a crop. Corn, a staple, was usually planted first. Next in priority were wheat and oats. Inventions like the steel plowshare by John Deere of Illinois in 1847 sped up the transformation of wilderness into cultivated farmland.

Cook's Library:
The Way to a Man's Heart

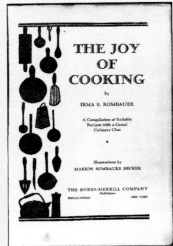

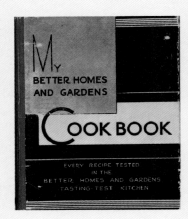

Three of America's best-selling basic cookbooks were born in the Midwest: *The Settlement Cookbook*, with its famous subtitle "The Way to a Man's Heart," *The Joy of Cooking*, and *My Better Homes and Gardens Cook Book*.

The Settlement Cookbook was written by Mrs. Simon Kander. Kander was deeply involved in the Milwaukee Settlement House, established at the turn of the century to help new immigrants become accustomed to the ways of their adopted country. Kander felt that copying recipes from the blackboard during cooking classes wasn't a good use of her students' time, so she requested eighteen dollars from the Settlement House board to have the recipes printed. The request was denied!

Undaunted, Kander and her committee sought advertisements from local merchants to defray costs, and published the first *Settlement Cookbook* in 1903. This kitchen standby includes recipes for such contemporary classics as cream of tomato soup, roast chicken with chestnut stuffing, lobster à la Newburg, scalloped potatoes, sponge cake, and pumpkin pie. Of special interest are the recipes contributed by the German-Jewish immigrants of the area, including matzoh balls, potato pancakes, and apple strudel. There is also a whole chapter on the yeast pastries known as kuchen.

Three decades after *The Settlement Cookbook* was published, Mrs. Irma Rombauer of St. Louis, Missouri, saw the need to wield that "mighty weapon, the cooking spoon." As a result, *The Joy of Cooking* first appeared in the midst of the Great Depression in 1931. Written by a recently widowed Rombauer in response to the fancy fare presented in so many contemporary cookbooks, the book set out to offer practical recipes more suitable to limited budgets. She published the first edition—a personal collection of her own recipes—at her own expense. Before long, the little book came to the attention of an Indianapolis publishing house, the Bobbs-Merrill Company, which brought out the first trade edition in 1936.

To Rombauer, the ultimate joy of cooking lay in the shifting but perpetual challenge "to make palatable dishes with simple means and to lift everyday cooking out of the commonplace." Her daughter, Marion Rombauer Becker, joined forces with her to create later editions.

My Better Homes and Gardens Cook Book, later titled *Better Homes and Gardens® New Cook Book*, was first published in 1930 as a premium to boost subscriptions to *Better Homes and Gardens®* magazine. Readers could receive the cookbook for two two-year subscriptions at one dollar, or it could also be purchased by direct sale for one dollar plus twenty cents handling.

The book was a new kind of cookbook for a new kind of homemaker. The difference—it was designed for the woman interested in bringing the same efficiency of a well-run business into the home. Modern appliances and improved equipment for food storage and meal preparation were necessary tools. The book championed level measurements and the listing of ingredients in order of use. In fact, homemakers who wished to submit their own recipes to the magazine's test kitchen, were requested to follow these same techniques. A chart of equivalents inside the front cover came to the aid of the homemaker unfamiliar with standard measurements.

Wisconsin. There, restaurant menus feature such specialties as sauerbraten, *rouladen* (rolled steak), and schnitzel. But nowhere in the United States is sausage making brought to such a high art. Reflecting the combined influences of German, Polish, and other eastern European immigrants, butcher shops opened up all over the state and became known for their individual specialties.

Depending upon the type and combination of meats as well as the special blends of spices, sausage making developed more branches than a complicated family tree. There was bratwurst, bologna, cervelat, kielbasa, wiener, and *bockwurst*, to name but a few. And let's not forget the good old frankfurter, a food that most people consider so all-American that few people are even aware of its European ancestry.

And what do the locals use to wash down all this goodness? Beer, of course, lager style, in the old Bavarian tradition. Indeed, it's the beer that made Milwaukee famous!

America's Dairyland

In the rolling green hills of western Wisconsin, license plates still read "America's Dairyland"—a reasonable appellation since this state has for decades been the major producer of milk, butter, and cheese for this country. Although the industry was set into motion by early Swiss settlers who made cheese in their home-farm dairies, production had moved from cottage industry to factory by the 1860s. The Badger State has broadened its cheese-making skills far beyond Swiss and now makes a wide variety of cheese including cheddar, Limburger, mozzarella, Muenster, and blue.

But when it comes to blue cheese, Wisconsin has stiff competition from Iowa Maytag. Unlike some of its European look-alikes, Maytag was created more by design

Even if just one corner of a room, the pioneer kitchen was the heart of the house. Family members were drawn to the warmth of its wood-fired stove.

than by accident when an heir to the Maytag washing machine industry became interested in raising Holstein cows. The cows' milk was so rich and delicious that the Maytag family sought a way to put it to good use. They eventually linked up with an Iowa State University dairy scientist named Dr. Verner Nielsen who had developed a technology for creating an American blue cheese. The company made its first Iowa Maytag in 1941 and now produces over three hundred thousand pounds annually.

Locals brag that the taste and texture of their local blue-veined cheese rivals the best Stiltons, Roqueforts, and Gorgonzolas. This judgment may reflect a serious local

The Legacy of Johnny Appleseed

*A*lthough born in Boston, John Chapman became a legend in the Midwest during the first half of the nineteenth century. A disciple of the Swedish mystic Emanuel Swedenborg, Chapman spent forty years walking barefoot, preaching the gospel, and planting apple seeds in the wilderness of Indiana, Ohio, and Illinois. He tended young saplings on return visits, and the prolific fruits they eventually bore turn up on many regional dishes in the form of apple pie, dried apples, and apple butter. This American folk hero is buried in Johnny Appleseed Park in Fort Wayne, Indiana.

bias, but even the objective cheese connoisseur would agree that Iowa Maytag is a serious cheese worthy of respect.

Preserving Tradition

In addition to the keen German influence felt in the kitchens of Wisconsin, three religious groups from that country brought their old-world cooking traditions to parts of the Midwest. These groups now form the Amish and Men-

nonite communities of northern Indiana and the Amana Colonies in eastern Iowa. Due to the isolation created by the groups' strong religious convictions and life-styles, the foods still retain a strong flavor of the mother country and have been a major influence on the cooks in surrounding areas.

The Amish and Mennonite sects grew out of the Church of the Brethren, a religious group that began in the 1700s in Germany and had its roots in the Swiss Anabaptist movement. The Mennonites are named for the

Dutch priest Menno Simons and the Amish for Joseph Ammann, a Mennonite elder who formed his own sect. Both groups believed in dressing and living simply and in rejecting worldly goods. After a period of settlement in eastern Pennsylvania, some members of these groups moved to the Midwest.

In the kitchens of the Amish and Mennonites, the predominance of German, Swiss, and Alsatian cooking is only slightly tempered by midwestern influences. Although prepared foods have made some inroads in recent decades, in many old-fashioned kitchens, you are still likely to taste homemade noodles, hot cabbage salad, onion tarts, dumplings, and potato doughnuts.

In traditional farm families, the day begins early with a hearty breakfast of locally cured ham or sausages and eggs or fried cornmeal mush with tomato gravy. The dinner meal is still eaten at midday and is likely to start with soup, then move to pot roast or meat loaf, vegetables, noodles, mashed potatoes, and "whoopie pie" for dessert.

The Amana Colonies were founded along the Iowa River in 1859 by a group of German Lutherans who sought religious freedom. They built sixteen communal kitchens to serve their seven clustered colonies. Like the Amish and Mennonites, they enjoyed huge meals that relied heavily on such items as meat, potatoes, sauerkraut, homegrown vegetables, hearty breads, cakes, and pies. In *Amana Recipes*, a cookbook compiled by the Ladies Auxiliary of Homestead Iowa in 1948, the recipe titles are all in German and include such specialties as *Kartofel Suppe* (potato soup), *Herring Salat* (herring salad), *Krummen Kuchen* (crumb cake), and *Lebkuchen* (honey cookies). You can still visit the Amana Colonies today and try some of their locally prepared smoked pork and homemade breads and desserts. And you may have even once owned an Amana refrigerator, produced by the business that developed in the colonies during World War II.

In the Corn Belt states of the Midwest, planting became more efficient with the invention of devices like the one shown in this 1896 painting by Olof Krans (above). They were not reserved solely for female use, however. Below: Life on the Great Plains was particularly rugged and barren. There was little but the tough prairie sod to build with, so houses—called soddies—were constructed from blocks of this turf. A Nebraska family has their portrait taken, circa 1890.

The Rugged Pioneer Cooking of Nebraska

On those plains where the buffalo roamed, the earliest settlers encountered Indians living on wild game, fruits, and vegetables plus whatever they cultivated in the way of corn, beans, and squash. Like the Indians on the East Coast, the Plains Indians preserved their meat in the form of pemmican, and the first pioneers followed suit.

About forty years after Meriwether Lewis and William Clark reported back from the Nebraska territory in 1804, pioneers began heading west along the Platte River. Many of them gave up their dreams of panning for gold, and settled in Nebraska.

145

No kitchen was more compact than the chuck wagon. Yet it was able to serve the needs of a team of hungry cowboys as they drove their huge herds north from Texas to the stockyards of Oklahoma and Kansas.

Until the housewife had established her kitchen garden and the family had acquired some cows, meals might consist of a simple and hearty cornmeal mush three times a day, plus wild game when it was available. Perhaps an even bigger challenge was the fact that the barren plains offered little wood for fuel, and the pioneer cook had to make do with cow chips and corncobs in her stove.

In 1863, the first land claim was made in Nebraska under the auspices of the Homestead Act. The offer of free land attracted thousands of settlers, many of them coming from Germany, Scandinavia, and Bohemia (later part of Czechoslovakia). Bringing with them the foods of home, these European pioneers slowly refined the rugged fare of those who came before them.

Home on the Range: Chuck Wagon Cooking

The invention of the chuck wagon is credited to Col. Charles Goodnight, a Texas cattleman who wanted to keep his cowboys well fed on the cattle drive from Texas north through Oklahoma to Kansas, where the steer were loaded onto freight cars and shipped to Chicago for slaughter. The chuck wagon was little more than an ordinary Conestoga wagon that had a dropped door and built-in pantry in the back. When it came time to eat, the door was let down to create a working surface for the cowboy cook—also known as "cookie" or "pot wrangler" (or perhaps something worse if the hungry crowd didn't like the dinner menu).

The five pillars of cowboy fare are coffee, beans, meat, sourdoughs, and stew according to cowboy historian Ramon Adams. These basic staples were supplemented by dried fruit, rice, and perhaps canned vegetables such as corn and tomatoes.[2] This was rough-and-ready fare, prepared over open fires in black iron Dutch ovens.

The goal of the cowboy cook was to produce an edible, sustaining meal in as little time as possible while dirtying the minimum number of dishes. Such a goal produced the following technique for making biscuits: "I'd just open up the flour sack. . . . Make a hole in the flour, right in the sack; put in some baking powder, salt, and warm lard; and pour in some water. When I had enough flour mixed in with the other stuff to make a dough, I lifted the wad out of the sack and shaped up my biscuits. Quick and easy."[3]

One of "cookie's" most prized possessions was his sourdough starter, the fermented mixture of flour, water, salt, and boiled potatoes that was mixed into bread dough and caused the loaf to rise. He handled it with great care as extremes of temperature could destroy the natural yeast and render bread baking impossible.

Like all pragmatic use-what's-available cooks, the chuck-wagon chef threw every edible part of the cow into his beef stew. This included the heart, spleen, liver, tongue, sweetbreads, and brains. Seasoning was no fancier than a sprinkling of salt and pepper, but the cowboys were always hungry after a hard day on the range, and it's often been said that hunger makes the tastiest sauce.

Kansas City Barbecue

To a real southerner, Kansas City barbecue is not at all the authentic item, but to those born and bred in Kansas City, Missouri, there is no reason to travel since the best is available right in their own hometown. Indeed, by all accounts Kansas City is a serious contender for the title of "Barbecue Capital of the United States."

Barbecue evolved during the 1920s and 1930s along with blues and jazz in the urban ghettos of town. The black influence is undeniable, and the unquestioned king of Kansas City barbecue is Arthur Bryant. Born the son of poor east Texas farmers, Bryant left his home in 1931. He stopped in Kansas City to visit his brother Charlie, then working for a barbecue outfit. Arthur joined the team, soon perfected his own tomato-based sauce, and thereby created a memorable chapter in local gastronomic history.

Here's what typical Kansas City barbecue looks like: "Take fresh, thin slices of slowly smoked barbecued beef brisket, pile high on a cushion of plain, white bread and slather with thick, brick-red Kansas City barbecue sauce. Top with another slice of bread and hickory-smoked ham, and crown with more spice sauce, dill pickles and another slice of bread. . . At least four inches high, the triple delight is a party for your mouth."[4]

Barbecue scholars consider Kansas City's the most eclectic style of barbecue, making use as it does of a variety of meats, sauces, and woods for smoking (although hickory and oak are the most consistently used). The inspiration for sauces came primarily from Texas, and the open-pit style of cooking was transported from the Deep South. Meats selected for undergoing the KC treatment run the gamut from beef brisket to lamb and chicken to ribs.

Want the recipe for Arthur's barbecue sauce? Sorry, to this day it's a trusted family secret. If you want to taste it, you'll just have to go there.

Chicago's Deep Dish Pizza

Chicago is a vibrant city which, much like New York, offers an extraordinary variety of ethnic cuisine. But by a quirk of fate, more than any other town in America, Chicago is famous for its pizza. But if this statement leads you to believe that you can pop down to the Loop and grab a slice at the corner parlor, you are in for a surprise. For pizza-by-the-slice is not to be had in Chicago, a city that is known for a unique type of pizza and takes its specialty very seriously. As one resident put it, "For us, eating pizza is a communal experience."

The man who started the special ethos of the Chicago deep-dish pizza was a Texan named Ike Sewell, who arrived in the windy city, after the Depression, at age twenty with nineteen dollars in his pocket. Before long, he ran into an Italian restaurateur named Ric Riccardo and the two decided to join forces and open a pizza parlor—quite a revolutionary idea for World War II America.

Sewell wasn't convinced that such a restaurant could succeed since this newfangled thing called pizza wasn't substantial enough to make into a meal. That's where the toppings came in, and in 1943 Pizzeria Uno opened, featuring a deep-dish pizza that virtually overflowed with sausage, cheese, peppers, and onions. The public was so wary at first that the owners had to give away small portions at the bar, but soon journalists wrote about this new phenomenon and soldiers returning from the war in Italy made Pizzeria Uno a great success.

In 1980 Pizzeria Uno was franchised, and you may even have a branch in your town. But just as New Yorkers believe that the only real bagels can be had in the Big Apple, Chicagoans contend that you have to go the original Uno to get truly authentic deep-dish pizza.

Flavors from the Midwest

Wisconsin

WISCONSIN CHEDDAR-BACON PUFFS

An abundance of milk led to Wisconsin's first cottage-industry cheese factory. In 1841, Mrs. Anne Pickett began manufacturing cheese at her home using milk from a neighbor's cows. A few decades later, another Wisconsin cheesemaker, John Smith, was successful enough to market his product outside of the state. (Pictured on page 150)

⅓ cup margarine *or* butter
1 cup all-purpose flour
4 eggs
½ cup shredded sharp cheddar cheese (2 ounces)
4 slices bacon, crisp-cooked, drained, and crumbled
2 tablespoons grated Parmesan cheese

In a medium saucepan combine margarine and 1 cup *water.* Bring to boiling, stirring till margarine melts. Add flour all at once, stirring vigorously. Cook and stir till mixture forms a ball that doesn't separate. Remove from heat; cool 10 minutes.

Add eggs, one at a time, beating after each addition about 1 minute or till smooth. Beat in cheddar cheese and crumbled bacon.

On a well-greased extra-large baking sheet drop dough by well-rounded tablespoons into 2 rings of 10 mounds per ring with mounds spaced about ½ inch apart. Sprinkle rings with Parmesan cheese. Bake in a 400° oven about 30 minutes or till golden brown and puffed. Remove from baking sheet; cool slightly. Serve warm. Serves 20.

Nutrition information per serving: 86 calories, 3 g protein, 5 g carbohydrate, 6 g total fat (2 g saturated), 47 mg cholesterol, 87 mg sodium, 18 mg potassium

Michigan

CHERRY-SWISS CHEESE SPREAD

French colonists from Normandy planted cherry trees in the Great Lakes area of the Midwest. They carried pits with them from France to ensure a ready supply of this well-loved fruit. Michigan's first cherry orchards were the work of a Presbyterian minister, Peter Dougherty, in 1852. Today, the state is the nation's leading producer of tart cherries. (Pictured on page 150)

3 cups shredded Swiss cheese
¼ cup margarine *or* butter
½ cup dried tart red cherries
½ cup mayonnaise *or* salad dressing
2 teaspoons Dijon-style mustard
½ cup finely chopped green onion

Bring cheese and margarine to room temperature. Meanwhile, pour boiling water over cherries to cover; let stand 10 minutes. Drain well; pat with paper towels; set aside. In a food processor bowl, process cheese, margarine, mayonnaise, and mustard till combined. Stir in cherries and onion. Serve in a bowl or on a serving plate with crackers. Makes 12 to 16 servings.

Nutrition information per serving: 226 calories, 9 g protein, 6 g carbohydrate, 19 g total fat (7 g saturated), 31 mg cholesterol, 184 mg sodium, 49 mg potassium

Beef Pot Roast, left (see recipe, page 150), Cream of Chicken and Wild Rice Soup, right (see recipe, page 153), and Black Walnut-Wild Raspberry Bread (see recipe, page 169)

Cherry-Swiss Cheese Spread, and Wisconsin Cheddar-Bacon Puffs (see recipes, page 148)

Wisconsin

BEEF POT ROAST

Pot roast was the first recipe in the meat chapter of the 1903 Settlement Cookbook, written by Mrs. Simon Kander. It was a favorite of the Germans who settled in Wisconsin and all over the Midwest. (Pictured on page 149)

1 1½- to 2-pound beef chuck pot roast
1 teaspoon lemon-pepper seasoning *or* ½ teaspoon cracked black pepper
1 tablespoon cooking oil
½ cup water
¼ cup tomato juice
¼ cup dry white wine, beef broth, *or* water
1 teaspoon instant beef bouillon granules
½ teaspoon dried thyme, crushed
4 medium carrots, cut into 1½-inch pieces
2 medium potatoes, peeled and quartered
1 medium onion, cut into wedges
⅓ cup cold water
3 tablespoons all-purpose flour

Trim separable fat from roast. Rub 1 side with lemon-pepper seasoning. In a Dutch oven brown roast on all sides in hot oil. Drain off fat.

Combine the ½ cup water; tomato juice; wine, beef broth, or water; bouillon granules; and thyme. Pour around roast in Dutch oven. Bring to boiling; reduce heat. Cover and simmer 1 hour. (*Or,* bake, covered, in a 325° oven 1 hour.)

Add carrots, potatoes, and onion to meat. Cover; simmer or bake 45 to 60 minutes more or till tender, adding additional water, if necessary. Use a slotted spoon to remove meat and vegetables; keep warm.

For gravy, pour pan juices into a large measuring cup. Skim off fat; discard. If necessary, add water to pan juices to equal 1¼ cups. Return liquid to Dutch oven. Combine cold water and flour. Stir into juices in Dutch oven. Cook and stir till thickened and bubbly. Cook and stir 1 minute more. Serve with meat and vegetables. Serves 4 to 6.

Nutrition information per serving: 452 calories, 34 g protein, 28 g carbohydrate, 19 g total fat (7 g saturated), 105 mg cholesterol, 587 mg sodium, 796 mg potassium

Illinois

WINE-AND-HERB-MARINATED RIB EYE ROAST

Chicago has been a center for the meat industry in the United States since before the Civil War. At first its stockyards were a rest stop for cattle destined for slaughter in the East. With the development of refrigerated railcars, cattle was processed in Chicago slaughterhouses and then shipped by rail to retail markets.

1 4-pound beef rib eye roast
¾ cup dry red wine
¼ cup lemon juice
2 tablespoons olive oil *or* cooking oil
1 tablespoon coarsely ground black pepper
1 tablespoon snipped fresh rosemary *or* 1 teaspoon dried rosemary, crushed

Wine-and-Herb-Marinated Rib Eye Roast

1 tablespoon snipped fresh marjoram *or* 1 teaspoon dried marjoram, crushed
1 tablespoon Worcestershire sauce
1 tablespoon Dijon-style mustard
¼ teaspoon garlic salt

Place roast in a plastic bag set in a deep bowl. For marinade, in a mixing bowl combine wine, lemon juice, olive oil or cooking oil, pepper, rosemary, marjoram, Worcestershire sauce, mustard, and garlic salt. Pour marinade over roast. Seal bag. Marinate in the refrigerator for 6 to 24 hours, turning bag occasionally.

Remove roast from bag, reserving marinade. Place roast, fat side up, on a rack in a shallow roasting pan. Insert a meat thermometer. Roast in a 350° oven for 1¼ to 2 hours for rare (140°), 1¼ to 2¼ hours for medium (160°), or 1½ to 2½ hours for well-done (170°), brushing with marinade occasionally. (Do not brush with marinade during the last 5 minutes of roasting.) Cover with foil and let stand 15 minutes before carving. Makes 8 to 10 servings.

Nutrition information per serving: 441 calories, 44 g protein, 2 g carbohydrate, 26 g total fat (9 g saturated), 128 mg cholesterol, 247 mg sodium, 665 mg potassium

Chicken-Fried Steak with Gravy, top, and Pierogis (see recipe, page 166)

(see recipe, page 166)

Iowa

CHICKEN-FRIED STEAK WITH GRAVY

In some areas of the Midwest, chicken was such a favorite that it was considered food for company. Perhaps this dish came about as way to satisfy appetites that would rather be eating a piece of crumb-coated, gravy-smothered hen than a tough slice of meat.

1   **pound beef top round steak, cut ½ inch thick**
¾   **cup fine dry bread crumbs**
1½   **teaspoons snipped fresh basil *or* oregano *or* ½ teaspoon dried basil *or* oregano, crushed**
½   **teaspoon salt**
¼   **teaspoon pepper**
1   **beaten egg**
1   **tablespoon milk**
2   **tablespoons cooking oil**
1   **small onion, sliced and separated into rings**
2   **tablespoons all-purpose flour**
1⅓   **cups milk**

Cut steak into 4 serving-size pieces. Trim fat. Place meat pieces between 2 pieces of plastic wrap. Pound meat with a meat mallet to ¼-inch thickness.

In a dish or on a piece of waxed paper combine bread crumbs, basil or oregano, salt, and pepper. In another shallow dish stir together egg and the 1 tablespoon milk. Dip meat pieces in egg mixture, then coat with bread crumb mixture.

In a 12-inch skillet brown meat pieces in hot oil over medium heat about 3 minutes on each side. Reduce heat to low. Cover and cook for 45 to 60 minutes more or till tender. Transfer meat pieces to a platter. Cover to keep warm.

For gravy, cook onion in pan drippings till tender but not brown. (Add more oil, if necessary.) Stir in flour. Add the 1⅓ cups milk all at once. Cook and stir till thickened and bubbly. Cook and stir for 1 minute more. Season to taste with salt and pepper. Serve gravy with meat. Makes 4 servings.

Nutrition information per serving: 363 calories, 32 g protein, 22 g carbohydrate, 16 g total fat (4 g saturated), 118 mg cholesterol, 539 mg sodium, 558 mg potassium

151

Fresh Tomato Scallop with Horseradish Sauce, left (see recipe, page 168), and Beer-Marinated Peppered T-Bones

(see recipe, page 168)

Oklahoma

BEER-MARINATED PEPPERED T-BONES

The Oklahoma Territory was the last area of the plains to be opened to homesteaders. The date? High noon, April 22, 1889. Oklahoma has always had ties to both the Midwest and the Southwest, a split that is reflected in the slightly spicy flavor of its down-home cooking.

1   cup chopped onion
½   of a 12-ounce can (¾ cup) beer
¾   cup chili sauce
¼   cup parsley
3   tablespoons Dijon-style mustard
1   tablespoon Worcestershire sauce
2   teaspoons brown sugar
½   teaspoon paprika

½   teaspoon ground black pepper
3   beef T-bone steaks, cut 1 inch thick (about 1 pound each), *or* 6 beef top loin steaks, cut 1 inch thick (about 1¾ pounds total)
1   to 1½ teaspoons cracked black pepper
    Fresh herbs (optional)

In a large glass baking dish combine onion, beer, chili sauce, parsley, mustard, Worcestershire sauce, brown sugar, paprika, and the ½ teaspoon pepper. Place steaks in marinade. Cover and refrigerate 4 to 6 hours or overnight, turning steaks over occasionally.

Remove steaks from marinade; discard marinade. Sprinkle both sides of steaks with the cracked black pepper.

Grill steaks on an uncovered grill directly over *medium-hot* coals for 5 minutes. Turn and grill to desired doneness, allowing 3 to 7 minutes more for rare or 7 to 10 minutes more for medium. If desired, garnish with fresh herbs. Serves 6.

Nutrition information per serving: 231 calories, 27 g protein, 7 g carbohydrate, 10 g total fat (4 g saturated), 73 mg cholesterol, 390 mg sodium, 486 mg potassium

Michigan

CORNISH BEEF PASTIES

Cornishmen came to the United States to work in the iron and copper mines in Michigan's Upper Peninsula. Their lunch in the new country was the same as it was in the old: this meat-and-potato turnover, which they carried to the mines in a cotton pouch called a crib bag.

3   cups all-purpose flour
1   cup shortening
7   to 8 tablespoons cold water
1½ cups chopped peeled potatoes
1   pound beef round steak, cut in ¼-inch cubes

¾ cup peeled turnip cut in
   ¼-inch cubes
½ cup finely chopped onion
½ cup catsup (optional)

Combine flour and 1½ teaspoons
salt. Cut in shortening till mixture
resembles coarse crumbs. Gradually
add the 7 to 8 tablespoons cold
water, *1 tablespoon at a time*, tossing
with a fork till all is moistened.
Form dough into a ball. If desired,
cover and chill the dough 1 hour.

Meanwhile, for filling, combine
potato, beef, turnip, onion, 1½ teaspoons *salt*, and ¼ teaspoon *pepper*.
Set aside. Divide dough into 6
equal pieces. Roll each piece into a
9-inch circle. Place about *1 cup* filling on *half* of *each* circle; fold other
half of dough over filling. Seal edge;
cut slits in top for steam to escape.
Place on an ungreased baking sheet.
If desired, brush with milk. Bake in
a 400° oven about 45 minutes or till
golden. If desired, mix catsup and ¼
cup *water*; heat through. Serve with
pasties. Makes 6 servings.

*Nutrition information per serving: 824
calories, 29 g protein, 73 g carbohydrate, 46 g
total fat (12 g saturated), 47 mg cholesterol,
1,126 mg sodium, 632 mg potassium*

Kansas

BIEROCKS

Like Cornish pasties, German Bierocks
(also called Runzas*) are hand-held
dinner pies. They were popular in wheat-
growing areas of the Midwest.*

1 16-ounce package hot roll
   mix
1 pound ground beef
1 cup finely chopped onion
3 cups shredded cabbage
   Milk

Make roll mix according to package
directions for basic recipe through
kneading step. Cover; let rest.

Meanwhile, for filling, cook beef
and onion till meat is brown. Drain
fat. Stir in cabbage and ¼ cup *water*.
Cook 5 minutes or till cabbage is
tender; drain. Stir in ¼ teaspoon *salt*
and ¼ to ½ teaspoon *pepper*.

Bierocks, top, and Cornish Beef Pasties

Divide dough into 6 pieces. Roll
each piece to a 7x5-inch rectangle.
Spoon filling lengthwise down center of rectangles. Bring long edges
of dough together over filling; pinch
edges and ends to seal. Place bundles, seam sides down, on a greased
baking sheet. Let stand in a warm
place 20 minutes; brush with milk.
Bake in a 350° oven for 25 to 30
minutes or till golden. Serves 6.

*Nutrition information per serving: 438
calories, 25 g protein, 60 g carbohydrate, 10 g
total fat (4 g saturated), 56 mg cholesterol, 663
mg sodium, 445 mg potassium*

Minnesota

CREAM OF CHICKEN
AND WILD RICE SOUP

*Wild rice is rich in nutrients
and was a dietary staple of the Native
Americans, who would collect it
by hand from the waterways of the
Great Lakes region. The wild crop is
still gathered that way. A recent
innovation, begun in Minnesota
in the mid-1960s, is machine-
harvested cultivated wild rice.*
(Pictured on page 149)

2 14½-ounce cans chicken
   broth (3½ cups)
1 cup sliced carrots
½ cup sliced celery
⅓ cup wild rice
⅓ cup sliced leek *or* green
   onion
½ teaspoon dried thyme,
   crushed
2 tablespoons margarine *or*
   butter
3 tablespoons all-purpose
   flour
1 cup half-and-half *or* milk
1½ cups chopped cooked
   chicken
2 tablespoons dry sherry

In a saucepan mix broth, carrots,
celery, *uncooked* rice, leek, thyme,
and ¼ teaspoon *pepper*. Bring to boiling; reduce heat. Cover; simmer 50
minutes or till rice is tender.

Meanwhile, melt margarine. Stir
in flour, then stir in half-and-half.
Cook and stir till bubbly. Cook and
stir 1 minute more. Slowly add half-
and-half mixture to rice mixture,
stirring constantly. Stir in chicken
and sherry; heat through. Serves 4.

*Nutrition information per serving: 342
calories, 25 g protein, 23 g carbohydrate, 16 g
total fat (6 g saturated), 67 mg cholesterol, 809
mg sodium, 585 mg potassium*

Minnesota

SWEDISH MEATBALLS

The great Swedish immigration to America began in the 1850s. Minnesota was the destination of the majority of the immigrants. Most became farmers, while others found jobs as railroaders and carpenters, or in similar trades requiring skilled labor.

1½ cups soft bread crumbs
⅔ cup half-and-half, light cream, *or* milk
1 slightly beaten egg
½ cup finely chopped onion
¼ cup finely snipped parsley
½ teaspoon salt
⅛ teaspoon ground ginger
⅛ teaspoon ground nutmeg
¾ pound lean ground beef
½ pound ground veal
¼ pound ground pork
2 tablespoons margarine *or* butter
2 tablespoons all-purpose flour
⅔ cup half-and-half, light cream, *or* milk
1¼ cups water
1 teaspoon instant beef bouillon granules
½ teaspoon instant coffee crystals

In a mixing bowl soak the bread crumbs in ⅔ cup half-and-half for 5 minutes. Add egg, onion, parsley, salt, ginger, and nutmeg. Add ground meats; mix well. Shape into 1- to 1¼-inch-thick meatballs.

In an ungreased shallow baking pan bake meatballs in a 350° oven 15 to 20 minutes or till no longer pink. Drain well on paper towels.

Meanwhile, melt margarine or butter in a large skillet. Stir in flour. Stir in the remaining half-and-half, the water, bouillon granules, and coffee crystals. Cook and stir till thickened and bubbly. Add meatballs to skillet and heat through, about 1 minute. Makes 8 servings.

Nutrition information per serving: 270 calories, 21 g protein, 9 g carbohydrate, 16 g total fat (7 g saturated), 110 mg cholesterol, 399 mg sodium, 324 mg potassium

Swedish Limpa Bread (see recipe, page 164), and Swedish Meatballs

Ohio

PORK TENDERLOIN SANDWICHES

Although cattle drives are more famous, hogs were taken to market the same way, by foot. Before the Civil War, hog drovers moved their large herds hundreds of miles at a time to eastern markets from Ohio, the center of the pork industry at the time. It was slow going, averaging five to eight miles a day.

¾ pound pork tenderloin
¼ cup all-purpose flour
¼ teaspoon onion powder *or* garlic powder
¼ teaspoon pepper
1 beaten egg
1 tablespoon milk *or* water
1 cup finely crushed rich round crackers (about 24) *or* ¾ cup fine dry bread crumbs
1 tablespoon cooking oil
4 hamburger buns *or* kaiser rolls, split and toasted
Mustard, catsup, onion slices, dill pickle slices, *and/or* roasted red sweet peppers (optional)

Cut pork crosswise into 4 slices. With a meat mallet, pound each pork slice between plastic wrap to ¼-inch thickness.

In a shallow bowl combine flour, onion or garlic powder, and pepper. In another shallow bowl combine egg and milk or water. In a third bowl place crushed crackers or bread crumbs. Dip each pork slice into the flour mixture, coating well, then into the egg mixture, and then into the crumbs to coat.

In a large skillet cook 2 pork slices in hot oil over medium heat for 6 to 8 minutes or till pork is no longer pink, turning once. Remove from skillet; keep warm. Repeat with remaining slices, adding more oil, if necessary.

Place on buns. If desired, serve with mustard, catsup, onion, pickle, and/or peppers. Serves 4.

Nutrition information per serving: 405 calories, 26 g protein, 40 g carbohydrate, 15 g total fat (4 g saturated), 114 mg cholesterol, 477 mg sodium, 460 mg potassium

Missouri

HAMBURGERS

Despite attempts to dress it up with fancy buns and special sauces, the hamburger has always been food for the masses. It became popular at the St. Louis Exposition of 1904 and probably was named after the German city of Hamburg.

1 pound ground beef, ground pork, *or* ground turkey
2 tablespoons catsup
1 teaspoon prepared mustard
1 teaspoon Worcestershire sauce
½ teaspoon onion salt *or* garlic salt
¼ teaspoon pepper
4 slices American, Swiss, cheddar, *or* brick cheese (optional)

Pork Tenderloin Sandwiches, top, Cincinnati Chili, center, and Hamburgers

4   hamburger buns, split and
      toasted
      Catsup, mustard, *and/or*
      pickle slices (optional)

In a mixing bowl stir together the ground beef, pork, or turkey; catsup; mustard; Worcestershire sauce; onion salt or garlic salt; and pepper.

Shape meat mixture into four ½- or ¾-inch-thick patties. Place patties on the unheated rack of a broiler pan. Broil 3 to 4 inches from the heat till no pink remains, turning once. Allow 10 to 12 minutes for ½-inch-thick patties or 15 to 18 minutes for ¾-inch-thick patties.

If desired, top burgers with a slice of cheese. Broil just till cheese melts. Place burgers on toasted buns. If desired, serve with catsup, mustard, and/or pickle slices. Makes 4 servings.

Nutrition information per serving: 351 calories, 23 g protein, 25 g carbohydrate, 17 g total fat (6 g saturated), 68 mg cholesterol, 652 mg sodium, 338 mg potassium

Ohio

CINCINNATI CHILI

Texas "chili heads" probably wouldn't eat it, but Cincinnatians love chili their way, or actually three-way, four-way, or five-way. Three-way means chili, spaghetti, and grated yellow cheese. Four-way is three-way plus beans or onions. With five-way, you get it all: chili, spaghetti, cheese, beans, and onions.

2   pounds ground beef
3   large onions, chopped
      (3 cups)
3   cloves garlic, minced
1   15-ounce can tomato sauce
1   cup beef broth
2   tablespoons chili powder
2   tablespoons semisweet
      chocolate pieces
2   tablespoons vinegar
2   tablespoons honey
1   tablespoon pumpkin pie
      spice
1   teaspoon ground cumin
½   teaspoon ground cardamom
¼   teaspoon ground cloves

16   ounces fettuccine, broken
       into 4-inch lengths
2   15½-ounce cans kidney
       beans
3   cups shredded American
       cheese (12 ounces)

In a 4½-quart Dutch oven cook beef, *2 cups* of the onions, and garlic till beef is brown and onion is tender. Drain fat. Stir in remaining ingredients *except* fettuccine, kidney beans, cheese, and remaining onion. Bring to boiling; reduce heat. Cover and simmer over low heat for 1 hour. Skim off fat.

Cook fettuccine; drain. Keep warm. In a 2-quart saucepan heat kidney beans; drain. Keep warm. To serve, divide fettuccine among 8 plates. Make an indentation in center of each fettuccine portion. Top with meat sauce, beans, remaining onions, and cheese. Makes 8 servings.

Nutrition information per serving: 768 calories, 49 g protein, 77 g carbohydrate, 30 g total fat (14 g saturated), 136 mg cholesterol, 1,123 mg sodium, 1,151 mg potassium

Hot German Potato and Pea Salad, top (see recipe, page 166), Corn on the Cob, left (see recipe, page 168), and KC Barbecued Ribs

Missouri

KC BARBECUED RIBS

Kansas City barbecue boosters aren't shy about promoting their own. Natives of this Missouri city, including writer Calvin Trillin, insist that the smoky, wood-infused barbecue of their hometown is the best.

1   cup water
1   cup catsup
3   tablespoons vinegar
1   tablespoon sugar

1   tablespoon Worcestershire
     sauce
1   teaspoon celery seed
¼   teaspoon bottled hot pepper
     sauce
4   pounds pork loin back ribs
     or meaty spareribs
     (2 strips)

For barbecue sauce, in a saucepan combine water, catsup, vinegar, sugar, Worcestershire sauce, celery seed, and bottled hot pepper sauce. Heat to boiling; reduce heat. Simmer, uncovered, for 30 minutes, stirring occasionally.

Sprinkle ribs with salt and pepper. Lace ribs, accordion style, onto a spit rod, securing with holding forks. Test balance. Arrange *medium-hot* coals around a drip pan; test for *medium* heat where meat will be.

Attach spit, turn on the motor, and lower grill hood. Let ribs rotate over drip pan for 1¼ to 1½ hours or till well-done, brushing ribs with sauce the last 15 minutes of cooking. To serve, remove the meat from the spit. Makes 4 servings.

156

Michigan

HAM BALLS WITH CURRANT GLAZE

Red currants grew across northern Europe and were a favorite of the Dutch and the Scandinavians, who would use the fruit in sauces, soups, jellies, and desserts. When they immigrated to the Midwest, these groups cultivated the berry.
(Pictured on page 158)

2   beaten eggs
¾   cup finely crushed graham crackers (11 or 12 squares)
½   cup chopped onion
¼   cup milk
1   tablespoon Dijon-style mustard
¼   teaspoon pepper
1   pound ground fully cooked ham
8   ounces ground pork
    Currant Glaze
    Kumquats (optional)

In a large mixing bowl combine eggs, crushed crackers, onion, milk, mustard, and pepper. Add ground ham and ground pork; mix well. Shape into 12 balls, using about *⅓ cup* mixture for each ball. Place ham balls in a lightly greased 2-quart rectangular baking dish.

Bake ham balls, uncovered, in a 350° oven about 45 minutes or till juices run clear. Remove balls from baking dish; spoon Currant Glaze over ham balls. If desired garnish with kumquats. Makes 6 servings.

Currant Glaze: In a small saucepan combine ½ cup *currant jelly*, 1 tablespoon *prepared horseradish*, 1 teaspoon finely shredded *orange peel*, and 1 tablespoon *orange juice*. Cook and stir till jelly melts and mixture is smooth.

Nutrition information per serving: 356 calories, 30 g protein, 31 g carbohydrate, 12 g total fat (4 g saturated), 141 mg cholesterol, 1,227 mg sodium, 428 mg potassium

Minnesota

SPINACH-TOPPED PIKE WITH CHEESE SAUCE

Along the upper reaches of the Midwest, hardy fishermen bait their lines and go for pike during the cold winter. The white-fleshed fish lives in lakes and streams in the northern United States and Canada. The Shakers of northern Ohio would fish for pike in the waters of Lake Erie.
(Pictured on page 159)

6   fresh *or* frozen northern pike *or* whitefish fillets (about 1½ pounds)
2   tablespoons margarine *or* butter
2   tablespoons all-purpose flour
1¼ cups milk
1   cup shredded cheddar cheese (4 ounces)
1   10-ounce package frozen, chopped spinach, thawed and well drained
1   beaten egg
1   cup corn-bread stuffing mix
¼   cup grated Parmesan cheese *or* Romano cheese
¼   cup dairy sour cream
4   slices bacon, crisp-cooked, drained, and crumbled

Thaw fish, if frozen. For sauce, in a saucepan melt margarine. Stir in flour. Add milk all at once. Cook and stir till bubbly. Cook and stir 1 minute more. Add cheddar cheese; stir till cheese melts. Set aside.

For stuffing, mix spinach, egg, stuffing mix, Parmesan cheese, sour cream, and crumbled bacon. Stir ⅓ cup of the sauce into the stuffing.

Place fillets lengthwise in a 3-quart rectangular baking dish. Spoon *one-sixth* of the stuffing over each fillet in dish. Bake, covered, in a 350° oven for 25 to 30 minutes or till fish flakes easily with a fork.

To serve, reheat sauce and serve over each fillet and stuffing. Pass remaining sauce. Makes 6 servings.

Nutrition information per serving: 555 calories, 53 g protein, 23 g carbohydrate, 28 g total fat (13 g saturated), 172 mg cholesterol, 790 mg sodium, 862 mg potassium

Indirect grilling: Prepare sauce and ribs as directed. In a covered grill arrange *medium-hot* coals around a drip pan. Test for *medium* heat above the drip pan. Place ribs, fat side up, on the grill rack over the drip pan but not over the coals. Lower grill hood. Grill ribs for 1¼ to 1½ hours or till well-done, brushing often with sauce the last 15 minutes of cooking.

Nutrition information per serving: 498 calories, 49 g protein, 21 g carbohydrate, 24 g total fat (8 g saturated), 134 mg cholesterol, 849 mg sodium, 1,066 mg potassium

Ham Balls with Currant Glaze, top (see recipe, page 157), and Sausage-and-Apple-Stuffed Iowa Chops

Bake chops, uncovered, in a 375° oven for 20 minutes. Brush again with glaze. Place covered casserole of stuffing in oven beside pork chops. Bake about 20 minutes more or till no pink remains in chops and stuffing is heated through. If desired, garnish with apple wedges. Makes 4 servings.

Nutrition information per serving: 569 calories, 45 g protein, 48 g carbohydrate, 23 g total fat (8 g saturated), 118 mg cholesterol, 998 mg sodium, 735 mg potassium

Iowa

SAUSAGE-AND-APPLE-STUFFED IOWA CHOPS

After the Civil War, the introduction of refrigerated railroad cars allowed the center of the pork industry to shift from the Ohio Valley (Cincinnati was once known as Porkopolis) to a handful of states farther to the west. Iowa is now the country's top pork producer.

4   pork loin rib chops,
         cut 1¼ inches thick
         (about 2 pounds total)
½   pound bulk pork sausage
1   cup chopped onion
1   cup corn-bread stuffing mix
⅔   cup shredded apple
2   teaspoons snipped fresh
         thyme *or* ½ teaspoon
         dried thyme, crushed
¼   teaspoon pepper
⅓   cup apple cider *or* apple
         juice

⅓   cup apple jelly
1   tablespoon lemon juice
         Apple wedges (optional)

Trim fat from chops. Cut a pocket in each chop by cutting a slit the length of the fat side almost to the bone. Set chops aside.

For stuffing, in a large skillet cook sausage and onion till sausage is brown and onion is tender; drain well. Stir in stuffing mix, shredded apple, thyme, and pepper. Drizzle with *2 tablespoons* of the apple cider to moisten, tossing lightly.

Spoon about *2 tablespoons* of the stuffing into each pork chop pocket. Secure pockets with wooden toothpicks. Stir remaining apple cider into remaining stuffing.

Place stuffed pork chops on a rack in a shallow roasting pan. Place remaining stuffing in a greased 1-quart casserole. Cover and refrigerate till ready to bake.

For glaze, in a small saucepan, combine apple jelly and lemon juice. Cook and stir till jelly melts; brush chops with some of the glaze.

CHICKEN WITH MAYTAG BLUE CHEESE SAUCE

Across the top of the stationery of the Maytag Dairy Farms in Newton, Iowa, is written "Famous Blue Cheese." For over fifty years, the small dairy, located about an hour from Des Moines and owned by the family that developed the Maytag washing machine, has been producing a quality product from its herd of prize Holsteins.

4   medium skinless, boneless,
         chicken breast halves
         (12 ounces total)
1   tablespoon olive oil *or*
         cooking oil
⅓   cup finely chopped green
         onion
1   clove garlic, minced
2   tablespoons margarine *or*
         butter
3   tablespoons all-purpose
         flour
¼   teaspoon pepper
¾   cup chicken broth
½   cup whipping cream
1½ teaspoons white wine
         Worcestershire sauce
1   beaten egg yolk
¼   cup crumbled Maytag blue
         cheese *or* other blue
         cheese

In a large skillet cook chicken in hot oil over medium heat for 8 to 10 minutes or till chicken is tender and no pink remains, turning often to brown evenly.

Chicken with Maytag Blue Cheese Sauce, top, and Spinach-Topped Pike with Cheese Sauce (see recipe, page 157)

Meanwhile, in a medium saucepan cook green onion and garlic in margarine or butter till tender. Stir in flour and pepper. Add chicken broth, whipping cream, and white wine Worcestershire sauce all at once. Cook and stir over medium heat till thickened and bubbly. Reduce heat. Gradually stir about *half* of the hot mixture into the beaten egg yolk. Transfer entire egg mixture to saucepan. Bring to a gentle boil. Cook and stir 2 minutes more. Stir in blue cheese. Serve sauce over chicken. Serves 4.

Nutrition information per serving: 372 calories, 25 g protein, 7 g carbohydrate, 27 g total fat (11 g saturated), 155 mg cholesterol, 395 mg sodium, 298 mg potassium

Wisconsin

SAUSAGE AND KRAUT

The Germans are master wurst-makers. They also know how to ferment sliced cabbage in a caraway-seasoned brine to make a crunchy sauerkraut accompaniment. Sauerkraut is so popular in the Midwest that one regional cookbook offers a recipe for a sauerkraut sandwich: kraut, mustard dressing, and radishes!

4   fully cooked smoked bratwurst, knockwurst, *or* Polish sausage (about 12 ounces total)
6   cups shredded cabbage
1   cup water
½   cup chopped onion
½   cup shredded carrot
1   teaspoon caraway seed
¼   teaspoon pepper
⅛   teaspoon salt
4   slices process Swiss cheese, torn (4 ounces)

Make slits in bratwurst at 1-inch intervals, cutting to, but not through, opposite side. Set aside.

In a 12-inch skillet combine cabbage, water, onion, carrot, caraway seed, pepper, and salt. Arrange bratwurst atop cabbage mixture. Bring to boiling; reduce heat. Cover and simmer for 10 to 15 minutes or till cabbage is tender and bratwurst in heated through.

Remove bratwurst from skillet; keep warm. Drain cabbage mixture. Add Swiss cheese to cabbage. Stir over low heat till cheese is melted. Serve cabbage with bratwurst. Makes 4 servings.

Nutrition information per serving: 344 calories, 17 g protein, 11 g carbohydrate, 26 g total fat (12 g saturated), 63 mg cholesterol, 1,164 mg sodium, 540 mg potassium

Wisconsin

BRATS AND BEER

Milwaukee, on the Wisconsin side of Lake Michigan, attracted a large number of Germans immigrating to this country after 1850. It's not surprising that a brewery opened in that city early in the next decade. Bottled beer is a Milwaukee invention of the 1870s. Beer and bratwurst are the usual fare at local events wherever Germans have settled.

4   fresh bratwursts (about 12 ounces total)
1   12-ounce can beer
10   whole black peppercorns
1   large onion, sliced and separated into rings

Sausage and Kraut, top, Brats and Beer, lower left, and Apple Strudel (see recipe, page 165)

1   tablespoon margarine *or* butter
1½   teaspoons caraway seed
2   tablespoons white wine vinegar
1   teaspoon Worcestershire sauce
4   frankfurter buns, split and toasted
    Coarse-grain brown mustard

Use a fork to prick several holes in the skin of each bratwurst. In a saucepan combine bratwursts, beer, and peppercorns. Bring to boiling; reduce heat. Cover and simmer about 20 minutes or till bratwursts are no longer pink. Drain.

Meanwhile, in a small skillet cook onion in hot margarine till tender but not brown. Add caraway seed and cook 5 minutes more. Stir in vinegar and Worcestershire sauce.

Grill bratwursts on an uncovered grill directly over *medium-hot* coals for 7 to 8 minutes or till skins are golden, turning frequently. Serve bratwursts on buns with mustard. Spoon onion mixture over bratwursts. Makes 4 servings.

Nutrition information per serving: 362 calories, 12 g protein, 28 g carbohydrate, 20 g total fat (6 g saturated), 34 mg cholesterol, 585 mg sodium, 273 mg potassium

South Dakota

PHEASANT MARSALA

Pheasant was not one of the wild game birds available to the pioneers. It was introduced at the turn of the century. The ring-necked pheasant continues to be a favorite of Midwest hunters.

2   to 2½ pounds cut-up pheasant *or* broiler-fryer chicken
2   tablespoons cooking oil
2   tablespoons margarine *or* butter
3   cups sliced fresh mushrooms
1   cup small onion wedges
2   garlic cloves, minced
½   cup chicken broth
¼   cup marsala wine
½   teaspoon finely shredded orange peel
¼   teaspoon juniper berries
1   8-ounce carton dairy sour cream
2   tablespoons all-purpose flour

Rinse pheasant breasts and remove skin. In a large skillet, heat oil and margarine or butter. Brown pheasant in hot oil mixture till golden. Place in a 2-quart rectangular baking dish or a 2-quart casserole. Sprinkle with salt and pepper. Add mushrooms, onion, and garlic to skillet. Cook till onion is tender. Stir in broth, wine, orange peel, and juniper berries. Pour over breasts. Cover; bake in a 325° oven for 45 to 60 minutes or till meat is tender.

Using a slotted spoon, transfer meat and vegetables to a serving platter; keep warm.

Pour juices into a saucepan. Stir together sour cream and flour. Add to juices; cook and stir till bubbly. Cook and stir 1 minute more. Pour some sour cream sauce over meat and vegetables; pass remaining sauce when serving. Serves 4.

Nutrition information per serving: 595 calories, 60 g protein, 12 g carbohydrate, 32 g total fat (12 g saturated), 156 mg cholesterol, 388 mg sodium, 944 mg potassium

Wisconsin

WISCONSIN BEER-CHEESE CHOWDER

This recipe is a showcase for Wisconsin fine foods. The state is one of the nation's largest cheese producers, manufacturing about one-third of the entire domestic supply, while Milwaukee is famous for its beer and sausage.

1½   cups small broccoli flowerets
¾   cup shredded carrot
¾   cup chicken broth *or* water
¼   cup chopped onion
¼   cup margarine *or* butter
¼   cup all-purpose flour
½   teaspoon dry mustard
¼   teaspoon pepper
2   cups milk
1   3-ounce package cream cheese, cut into cubes and softened
8   ounces fully cooked Polish sausage, cut into thin slices
1½   cups shredded sharp cheddar cheese *or* American cheese (6 ounces)
¾   cup beer

In a medium saucepan combine broccoli, carrot, chicken broth or water, and onion. Bring to boiling. Reduce heat and simmer, covered, for 8 to 10 minutes or till tender. *Do not drain;* set aside.

Meanwhile, in a large saucepan melt margarine or butter. Stir in flour, dry mustard, and pepper. Add milk all at once. Cook and stir till thickened and bubbly. Cook and stir 1 minute more. In a mixing bowl stir about *½ cup* of the hot milk mixture into the cream cheese; stir till well combined. Stir cream cheese mixture into remaining milk mixture in saucepan. Stir sausage, cheddar or American cheese, and beer into thickened mixture. Cook and stir over low heat till cheese melts and sausage is heated through. Stir in *undrained* vegetables; heat through. Ladle into soup bowls. Makes 4 servings.

Nutrition information per serving: 669 calories, 28 g protein, 21 g carbohydrate, 52 g total fat (23 g saturated), 117 mg cholesterol, 1,142 mg sodium, 648 mg potassium

Illinois

BIGOS

A majority of the Polish immigrants who arrived in the United States after 1900 chose city life over rural and became factory workers. Chicago's Polish population rivals that of Warsaw. This hunter's stew is an old-world recipe originally prepared with bear or other game. (Pictured on page 166)

6   slices bacon, cut in 1-inch pieces
1   large onion, chopped (1 cup)
8   ounces boneless beef, cut in 1-inch cubes
8   ounces boneless pork, cut in 1-inch cubes
8   ounces fully cooked Polish sausage, sliced
2   cups sliced fresh mushrooms
2   cups beef broth
½   cup dry white wine
1   teaspoon paprika
1   bay leaf
2   16-ounce cans sauerkraut, drained and snipped

Cook bacon and onion till bacon is cooked and onion is tender. Drain, reserving *2 tablespoons* drippings. Set aside. Brown beef and pork cubes in reserved drippings; drain.

Stir in bacon-onion mixture, sausage, mushrooms, broth, wine, paprika, and bay leaf. Simmer till meat is tender, about 1½ to 2 hours. Stir in sauerkraut. Heat through. Remove bay leaf. Makes 6 servings.

Nutrition information per serving: 272 calories, 20 g protein, 7 g carbohydrate, 17 g total fat (6 g saturated), 68 mg cholesterol, 943 mg sodium, 545 mg potassium

Wisconsin Beer-Cheese Chowder, top, and Pheasant Marsala

 Turkey with Creamy Morel Sauce, and Fruity Wild Rice Pilaf (see recipe, page 168)

(see recipe, page 168)

Michigan

TURKEY WITH CREAMY MOREL SAUCE

In the spring, mushroom hunters throughout the Midwest thrill to the chase: it's time to stalk that most special fungus, the wild morel. Michigan is particularly well known for this woodland delicacy.

4   turkey breast steaks *or* 4 medium skinless, boneless, chicken breast halves (12 ounces total)
3   tablespoons all-purpose flour
¼   teaspoon salt
¼   teaspoon lemon-pepper seasoning
3   tablespoons margarine *or* butter
2   ounces fresh morels *or* ½ ounce dried morels, rehydrated*
2   tablespoons sliced green onion
1   clove garlic, minced
1¼ cups half-and-half, light cream, *or* milk
1   tablespoon all-purpose flour
1   tablespoon dry sherry
    Fresh herbs (optional)

Rinse turkey; pat dry. Combine the 3 tablespoons flour, salt, and lemon-pepper seasoning; coat turkey with flour mixture.

In a large skillet cook turkey in *2 tablespoons* of the margarine or butter over medium heat for 8 to 10 minutes or till tender and no pink remains, turning once. Transfer turkey to individual plates; cover to keep warm.

Cut any large morels into bite-size strips. For sauce, in the same skillet cook morels, green onion, and garlic in the remaining margarine or butter for 3 to 4 minutes or till tender.

Combine half-and-half and the 1 tablespoon flour; add to vegetables in skillet. Cook and stir till thickened and bubbly; add sherry. Cook and stir for 1 minute more. Season to taste with salt and pepper.

Spoon some of the sauce over turkey; pass remainder when serving. If desired, garnish with fresh herbs. Makes 4 servings.

*Note: To rehydrate dried morels, cover them with warm water. Let stand for 30 to 45 minutes; drain. You should have ¾ cup.

Nutrition information per serving: 301 calories, 23 g protein, 11 g carbohydrate, 18 g total fat (7 g saturated), 83 mg cholesterol, 324 mg sodium, 353 mg potassium

Illinois

CHICAGO-STYLE DEEP-DISH SPINACH PIZZA

When Chicagoans Ike Sewell and Ric Riccardo decided to open Pizzeria Uno in 1943, they concluded that the traditional thin-crusted pizza so popular in the East just wouldn't make it in the Windy City. They developed a substantial two-crust version that became wildly successful and widely imitated.

Chicago-Style Deep-Dish Spinach Pizza

¾   pound bulk Italian sausage
1   cup chopped onion
1   8-ounce can pizza sauce
1   4-ounce can sliced mushrooms, drained
1   3-ounce package sliced pepperoni
2   tablespoons snipped fresh basil *or* 2 teaspoons dried basil, crushed
1   tablespoon snipped fresh oregano *or* 1 teaspoon dried oregano, crushed
¼   teaspoon crushed red pepper
1   16-ounce loaf frozen whole wheat bread dough *or* white bread dough, thawed
1½ cups shredded mozzarella cheese (6 ounces)
1   10-ounce package frozen chopped spinach, thawed and well drained
1   slightly beaten egg
1   tablespoon margarine *or* butter, melted
2   tablespoons grated Parmesan cheese *or* Romano cheese

For meat filling, in a large skillet cook Italian sausage and onion till meat is brown and onion is tender. Drain fat. Pat with paper towels to remove additional fat. Stir in pizza sauce, mushrooms, pepperoni, basil, oregano, and red pepper.

For crust, on a lightly floured surface roll *two-thirds* of the bread dough into a 12-inch circle. (If necessary, let dough rest once or twice during rolling.) Carefully place the circle in a greased 9-inch spring-form pan, pressing the dough 1½-inches up the sides. Sprinkle bottom of the dough with *½ cup* of the mozzarella cheese. Spoon meat filling over cheese.

Pat spinach dry with paper towels. Mix spinach, egg, and remaining mozzarella cheese. Spread spinach mixture over meat filling.

Roll remaining dough into a 10-inch circle on a lightly floured surface.

Cut circle into 10 to 12 wedges. Arrange wedges atop spinach mixture, slightly overlapping edges and sealing ends to bottom crust along edge of pan. Brush top with melted margarine or butter and sprinkle with Parmesan or Romano cheese.

Bake in a 375° oven for 40 to 45 minutes or till filling is hot and bread is done. If necessary, cover with foil the last 10 minutes of baking to prevent overbrowning. Cool on a wire rack for 10 minutes. Remove sides of springform pan. Cut into wedges. Makes 8 servings.

Nutrition information per serving: 392 calories, 22 g protein, 32 g carbohydrate, 20 g total fat (17 g saturated), 71 mg cholesterol, 1,078 mg sodium, 293 mg potassium

Nebraska

PORK ROAST WITH APPLES AND MUSHROOMS

Pork was the meat most available to plains homesteaders. It appeared on the table with unfailing regularity, as well as in the household's soap and shortening (in the form of lard). One Nebraska cook even made her fruitcake with chopped pork, probably in an attempt to create something new with the same tiresome ingredients.

Pork Roast with Apples and Mushrooms

2	tablespoons snipped fresh thyme *or* 2 teaspoons dried thyme, crushed
½	teaspoon salt
¼	teaspoon pepper
1	3 to 4-pound boneless pork loin roast (double loin, tied)
⅓	cup apple cider *or* apple juice
2	cups whipping cream
1	cup chicken broth
¼	cup dry sherry
2	tablespoons margarine *or* butter
3	or 4 small cooking apples, peeled, cored, and cut into wedges
2	cups sliced fresh mushrooms

Combine thyme, salt, and pepper; rub pork roast with thyme mixture. Place roast on a rack in a shallow roasting pan. Insert meat thermometer. Roast in a 325° oven for 1½ to 2½ hours or till meat thermometer registers 160°. Transfer meat to a platter; keep warm.

For sauce, skim fat from pan juices. Place roasting pan over medium heat; add apple cider or apple juice, stirring to scrape up any browned bits. Pour into a large saucepan. Stir in whipping cream, chicken broth, and dry sherry. Bring to boiling. Cook over medium-high heat about 20 minutes or till reduced to 1½ cups, stirring occasionally.

Meanwhile, in a large skillet melt the margarine or butter; add apple wedges and cook and stir till golden. Remove apple wedges from skillet with slotted spoon, reserving drippings; keep warm.

In the same skillet; add mushrooms to reserved drippings and cook till tender. Stir into thickened cream mixture.

To serve, place slices of pork roast and apples wedges on individual plates. Spoon sauce over meat. Makes 12 to 14 servings.

Nutrition information per serving: 344 calories, 26 g protein, 6 g carbohydrate, 25 g total fat (13 g saturated), 122 mg cholesterol, 225 mg sodium, 489 mg potassium

Wild Rice Muffins (see recipe, page 168), and Norwegian Fruit Soup

NORWEGIAN FRUIT SOUP

Of all the Scandinavians to settle in the United States, the Norwegians were firstcomers, beginning in earnest in the 1840s and reaching a total of three-quarters of a million by World War I. Cold fruit soups are a Scandinavian specialty.

1   **8-ounce package mixed dried fruit**
3½ **cups water**
¼   **cup packed brown sugar**
4   **teaspoons quick-cooking tapioca**
¼   **teaspoon ground nutmeg**
1   **16-ounce can pitted light sweet cherries**
¼   **cup orange liqueur *or* cream sherry**

Pit prunes (from mixed dried fruit), if necessary, and cut fruit into bite-size pieces. In a large saucepan stir together the water, brown sugar, quick-cooking tapioca, and nutmeg. Let stand for 5 minutes. Stir in dried fruit. Bring to boiling. Reduce heat and simmer, covered, for 8 to 10 minutes or till fruit is tender. Mixture should be slightly thickened and tapioca should be clear.

Stir in *undrained* cherries and orange liqueur or sherry. Heat through. Serve warm or chilled in bowls. Makes 8 servings.

Nutrition information per serving: 164 calories, 1 g protein, 38 g carbohydrate, 1 g total fat (1 g saturated), 1 mg cholesterol, 16 mg sodium, 326 mg potassium

SWEDISH LIMPA BREAD

In Swedish, limpa *means "loaf of bread," usually one made with rye flour. To Swedes in this country, it is specifically a type of free-form rye bread flavored with grated orange peel. (Pictured on page 154)*

3¼ **to 3¾ cups all-purpose flour**
2   **packages active dry yeast**
2   **teaspoons caraway seed**
½   **teaspoon fennel seed (optional)**
2   **cups milk**
½   **cup packed brown sugar**
2   **tablespoons molasses**
2   **tablespoons margarine *or* butter**
1   **teaspoon salt**
2   **tablespoons grated orange peel**
2½ **cups rye flour**

In a large mixing bowl combine 2½ cups of the all-purpose flour, the yeast, caraway seed, and, if desired, fennel seed.

In a saucepan combine the milk, brown sugar, molasses, margarine or butter, and salt; heat just till warm (120° to130°), stirring constantly. Add to dry mixture in mixing bowl; add orange peel. Beat with an electric mixer on low speed for 30 seconds, scraping sides of bowl. Beat 3 minutes at high speed. Use a wooden spoon to stir in as much of the rye flour as you can.

Turn dough out onto a floured surface. Knead in enough of the remaining all-purpose flour to make a moderately stiff dough that is smooth and elastic (6 to 8 minutes). Shape dough into a ball. Place in a greased bowl; turn once to grease surface. Cover; let rise in a warm place till double (about 1 hour).

Punch dough down; divide in half. Cover and let rest 10 minutes. Shape into 2 round loaves; place loaves on a greased baking sheet. Cover and let rise in a warm place till nearly double (about 30 minutes). Bake in a 375° oven about 35 minutes. Remove from pans; cool on a wire rack. Makes 2 loaves (32 servings).

Nutrition information per serving: 102 calories, 3 g protein, 20 g carbohydrate, 1 g total fat (0 g saturated), 1 mg cholesterol, 82 mg sodium, 102 mg potassium

Wisconsin

APPLE STRUDEL

According to the famous Settlement Cookbook *of 1903 by Mrs. Simon Kander, a proper strudel dough must be worked "until it is as large as the table and as thin as paper." Frozen phyllo dough lends modern convenience to an otherwise lengthy task.*
(Pictured on page 159)

½ **cup packed brown sugar**
¾ **teaspoon ground cinnamon**
½ **teaspoon finely shredded orange peel**

3 **cups thinly sliced, peeled tart apples *or* pears**
⅓ **cup raisins**
10 **to 12 sheets frozen phyllo dough, thawed**
⅓ **cup margarine *or* butter, melted**
2 **tablespoons margarine *or* butter, melted**
2 **tablespoons finely crushed vanilla wafers (optional)**
2 **cups whipped cream**

For filling, in a bowl stir together brown sugar, cinnamon, and orange peel. Add apples or pears and raisins, then gently toss till coated. Set filling aside. Lightly grease a 15x10x1-inch baking pan; set aside.

Cover a large surface with a cloth; flour cloth. Stack 2 sheets of phyllo on the floured cloth. *(Do not brush margarine or butter between sheets.)* Arrange another stack of 2 sheets on the cloth, overlapping the stacks 2 inches. Add 3 or 4 more stacks, forming a rectangle about 40x20 inches (stagger stacks so all seams are not down the middle). Trim to a 40x20-inch rectangle. Brush with the *⅓ cup* melted margarine or butter

Beginning 4 inches from a short side of dough, spoon the filling in a 4-inch-wide band across dough. Using the cloth underneath dough as a guide, gently lift the 4-inch piece of dough and lay it over the filling. Slowly and evenly lift the cloth and roll the dough and filling, jelly-roll style, into a tight roll. If necessary, cut excess dough from ends to within 1 inch of filling. Fold ends under to seal.

Carefully transfer strudel roll to the prepared baking pan. Curve ends together to form an 8-inch ring. Brush top of strudel with the 2 tablespoons melted margarine. If desired, sprinkle with vanilla wafer crumbs. Bake in a 350° oven for 35 to 40 minutes or till golden. Carefully remove from pan; cool.

Serve whipped cream with strudel. Makes 12 to 16 servings.

Nutrition information per serving: 272 calories, 3 g protein, 27 g carbohydrate, 18 g total fat (6 g saturated), 45 mg cholesterol, 95 mg sodium, 126 mg potassium

Ohio

BLACK WALNUT AND DATE PUDDING CAKE

Cakewalks were social events that afforded isolated homesteaders the opportunity to show off their baking skills. For a fee, a participant was allowed to walk to music around a circle of numbers marked on the floor. When the music stopped, a number would be called. Whoever was standing on that number won a cake donated by one of the guests.
(Pictured on page 169)

1¼ **cups all-purpose flour**
⅓ **cup packed brown sugar**
¾ **teaspoon baking soda**
½ **teaspoon baking powder**
⅛ **teaspoon ground nutmeg**
Dash ground cloves
1 **cup pitted whole dates, snipped**
3 **tablespoons margarine *or* butter, cut up**
1 **cup boiling water**
1 **teaspoon vanilla**
½ **cup chopped black walnuts**
1½ **cups boiling water**
1 **cup packed brown sugar**
Whipped cream (optional)

Combine the flour, the ⅓ cup brown sugar, the baking soda, baking powder, nutmeg, cloves, and ¼ teaspoon *salt*. Set flour mixture aside.

Combine dates and margarine. Add the 1 cup boiling water. Stir till margarine melts. Stir in vanilla. Stir date mixture and black walnuts into the flour mixture just till smooth. Spread in an ungreased 2-quart square baking dish.

Stir together the 1½ cups boiling water and the 1 cup brown sugar. Pour evenly over batter in pan. Bake in a 350° oven about 45 minutes or till cake tests done. Serve cake warm. If desired, serve with whipped cream. Makes 9 servings.

Nutrition information per servings: 275 calories, 4 g protein, 50 g carbohydrate, 8 g total fat (1 g saturated), 0 mg cholesterol, 187 mg sodium, 260 mg potassium

Illinois

PIEROGIS

Polish-Americans maintain strong cultural ties to the old country, especially when it comes to food. Pierogis are a Christmas tradition. These little cheese-filled pouches are an important part of the Festival of the Star, a dinner to commemorate the birth of Christ.
(Pictured on page 151)

1	beaten egg yolk
½	cup water
¼	teaspoon salt
1½	cups all-purpose flour
¾	cup cream-style cottage cheese, drained
1	slightly beaten egg white
1	tablespoon sugar
⅛	teaspoon salt
1	cup chopped onion
3	tablespoons margarine *or* butter

In a bowl combine the egg yolk, water, and salt. Stir in flour to make a stiff dough. On floured surface knead till smooth. Divide dough in half. Roll *half* the dough to less than ⅛ inch thick. Cut into twenty-eight 3-inch circles.

For filling, combine cottage cheese, egg white, sugar, and salt. To make pierogi, place *1 teaspoon* cottage cheese filling on half of each circle. Fold dough over the filling to form a half-circle; seal edge with the tines of a fork. Set aside. Repeat with remaining dough and filling.

Cook onion in margarine or butter over low heat about 20 minutes or till very tender. Keep warm.

Meanwhile, in a large kettle bring 12 cups *salted water* to boiling. Add 10 to 12 pierogis; cook 8 to 10 minutes. Drain on paper towels. Transfer to a serving dish; keep warm. Repeat till all are cooked. Serve pierogis topped with cooked onions. Makes 7 servings.

Nutrition information per serving: 149 calories, 7 g protein, 25 g carbohydrate, 2 g total fat (1 g saturated), 34 mg cholesterol, 221 mg sodium, 93 mg potassium

Kansas Whole Wheat-Honey Bread, and Bigos (see recipe, page 160)

North Dakota

HOT GERMAN POTATO AND PEA SALAD

Potato salad made an appearance at just about every church supper and family reunion in the Midwest. If the salad was German style, the potatoes were tossed while still warm in a vinegar-based dressing.
(Pictured on page 156)

4	medium potatoes (about 1¼ pounds)
4	slices bacon
½	cup chopped onion
1	tablespoon all-purpose flour
1	tablespoon sugar
¾	teaspoon salt
½	teaspoon celery seed
⅛	teaspoon pepper
⅔	cup water
¼	cup balsamic vinegar *or* white wine vinegar
1	cup frozen peas
¼	cup snipped fresh basil, oregano, *or* parsley

In a covered saucepan cook potatoes in boiling salted water for 20 to 25 minutes or till potatoes are just tender; drain well. Cool slightly. Peel and slice potatoes. Set potatoes aside while preparing dressing.

For dressing, in a large skillet cook bacon till crisp. Drain bacon on paper towels, reserving *2 tablespoons* drippings in skillet. Crumble

bacon and set aside. Cook onion in reserved drippings till tender.

Stir in flour, sugar, salt, celery seed, and pepper. Stir in water and vinegar. Cook and stir till thickened and bubbly. Stir in potatoes, bacon, and peas. Cook for 2 to 3 minutes more or till heated through, stirring gently. Fold in basil, oregano, or parsley. Transfer to a serving bowl. Serve warm. Makes 4 servings.

Nutrition information per serving: 276 calories, 7 g protein, 39 g carbohydrate, 10 g total fat (4 g saturated), 13 mg cholesterol, 591 mg sodium, 659 mg potassium

Kansas

KANSAS WHOLE WHEAT-HONEY BREAD

One problem in opening up the prairie was that wheat did not grow well there. Then in the early 1870s, members of the German religious sect called Mennonites immigrated to Kansas. Each family brought along carefully selected seed wheat which had come originally from Turkey. This hard winter wheat, known as Turkey red, thrived where other varieties failed.

3	to 3½ cups all-purpose flour
1	package active dry yeast
1½	cups water
⅓	cup honey
3	tablespoons shortening, margarine, *or* butter
1	teaspoon salt
2	cups whole wheat flour
1	slightly beaten egg white
1	tablespoon water
2	tablespoons roasted sunflower nuts *or* chopped toasted pine nuts

In a large mixing bowl combine *2 cups* of the all-purpose flour and the yeast; set aside. In a medium saucepan heat and stir water, honey, shortening, and salt just till warm (120° to 130°) and shortening almost melts. Add to flour mixture. Beat with an electric mixer on low speed for 30 seconds, scraping bowl constantly. Beat on high speed for 3 minutes. Using a wooden spoon, stir in the whole wheat flour and as much of the remaining all-purpose flour as you can.

Turn out onto a lightly floured surface. Knead in enough remaining all-purpose flour to make a moderately stiff dough that is smooth and elastic (6 to 8 minutes total). Shape into a ball. Place in a lightly greased bowl; turn once to grease surface. Cover and let rise in a warm place till double (1 to 1½ hours).

Punch dough down. Turn out onto a lightly floured surface. Divide dough into 4 equal portions. Cover and let rest 10 minutes.

Roll each portion into an evenly thick 14-inch-long rope. Loosely twist 2 ropes together; press ends together to seal. Repeat with remaining 2 ropes. Place bread twists on a greased baking sheet. Cover; let rise in a warm place till nearly double (30 to 35 minutes).

Mix egg white and water; brush tops of loaves. Sprinkle loaves with sunflower nuts or pine nuts. Bake in a 375° oven about 35 minutes or till bread sounds hollow when tapped. If necessary, cover loosely with foil the last 10 to 15 minutes to prevent overbrowning. Cool. Makes 2 loaves (32 servings).

Nutrition information per serving: 94 calories, 3 g protein, 17 g carbohydrate, 2 g total fat (0 g saturated), 0 mg cholesterol, 69 mg sodium, 54 mg potassium

Ohio

WALNUT POTICA

The Slovenes are a central European group from the area that was known until recently as northwestern Yugoslavia. This rich nut roll is a Slovenian favorite.

2   to 2½ cups all-purpose flour
1   package active dry yeast
⅓   cup milk
¼   cup margarine *or* butter
2   tablespoons sugar
2   eggs

Walnut Potica

3   cups ground walnuts
¾   cup sugar
¼   cup margarine *or* butter,
¼   cup honey
1   slightly beaten egg
3   tablespoons milk
½   teaspoon vanilla

In a bowl combine *1 cup* of the flour and the yeast; set aside. In a saucepan heat the ⅓ cup milk, ¼ cup margarine, the 2 tablespoons sugar, and ½ teaspoon *salt* just till warm (120° to 130°) and margarine almost melts. Add to flour mixture. Then add 2 eggs. Beat with an electric mixer on low to medium speed for 30 seconds, scraping bowl. Beat on high speed for 3 minutes. Using a wooden spoon, stir in as much of the remaining flour as you can.

On a lightly floured surface, knead in enough of the remaining flour to make a moderately soft dough that is smooth and elastic (3 to 5 minutes total). Shape into a ball. Place dough in a greased bowl, turning once to grease surface. Cover and let rise in a warm place till double (1 to 1¼ hours).

Meanwhile, for filling, mix walnuts, the ¾ cup sugar, ¼ cup mar-

garine, honey, remaining egg and milk, and the vanilla. Set aside.

Punch dough down. Cover and let rest 10 minutes. Meanwhile, lightly grease two 7½x3½x2- or 8x4x2-inch loaf pans. Cover with a floured cloth. On the cloth, roll dough into a 15-inch square. Cover and let rest 10 minutes. Then roll dough into a 30x20-inch rectangle.

To assemble, cut dough lengthwise in half to form two 30x10-inch sheets. Spread filling evenly over surface of both dough rectangles, keeping to within 1 inch of the edges. Using the cloth as a guide, roll each rectangle up jelly-roll style, starting from a short side. Pinch seams and ends to seal. Place loaves, seam sides down, in the prepared loaf pans. Cover; let rise till nearly double (45 to 60 minutes).

Bake in a 325° oven 45 to 50 minutes or till golden brown. If necessary, cover with foil the last 15 minutes of baking to prevent overbrowning. Remove from pans; cool. Makes 2 loaves (32 servings).

Nutrition information per serving: 165 calories, 3 g protein, 16 g carbohydrate, 10 g total fat (1 g saturated), 20 mg cholesterol, 67 mg sodium, 78 mg potassium

Missouri

FRESH TOMATO SCALLOP WITH HORSERADISH SAUCE

Missouri was populated with immigrants from Europe and also with New Englanders and southerners who wanted to move west. Mary Randolph's 1824 cookbook, The Virginia Housewife, *included a recipe for "scol-loped" tomatoes that is very similar to ones that appear in Missouri collections.*
(Pictured on page 152)

3	**large tomatoes**
3	**tablespoons fine dry bread crumbs**
2	**tablespoons finely chopped toasted pecans**
1	**tablespoon grated Parmesan cheese** *or* **Romano cheese**
1	**tablespoon snipped fresh marjoram, basil,** *or* **rosemary** *or* ½ **teaspoon dried marjoram, basil,** *or* **rosemary, crushed**
1	**tablespoon snipped fresh chives**
1	**tablespoon margarine** *or* **butter, melted**
⅛	**teaspoon pepper** **Dash garlic salt** **Horseradish Sauce**

Cut each tomato crosswise into 4 slices. Arrange tomato slices in a 2-quart square baking dish, over-lapping as necessary.

For topping, combine bread crumbs, pecans, Parmesan cheese, herb, chives, melted margarine, pepper, and garlic salt. Sprinkle topping over tomato slices.

Bake in a 375° oven for 10 to 15 minutes or till hot. Serve with Horseradish Sauce. Serves 4.

Horseradish Sauce: Beat ⅓ cup *whipping cream* till soft peaks form. Fold in 1 to 2 tablespoons *prepared horseradish.* (Or, stir 1 to 2 tablespoons *prepared horseradish* into one 8-ounce container *dairy sour cream.*)

Nutrition information per serving: 172 calories, 3 g protein, 11 g carbohydrate, 14 g total fat (5 g saturated), 28 mg cholesterol, 142 mg sodium, 336 mg potassium

Indiana

CORN ON THE COB

Corn was one of the first crops planted on the frontier, and it was the food most likely on hand when everything else was gone. As a service to its readers, one Nebraska farm paper of 1862 came up with thirty-three different uses for this vegetable.
(Pictured on page 156)

4	**medium ears of fresh corn**
¼	**cup butter**
1 ½	**teaspoons snipped fresh savory** *or* **thyme** *or* ½ **teaspoon dried savory** *or* **thyme, crushed**
½	**teaspoon finely shredded lime peel**

Remove husks from corn; scrub with a stiff brush to remove silks. Rinse corn. Cook, uncovered, in enough boiling water to cover for 5 to 7 minutes or till tender.

Meanwhile, mix butter, savory or thyme, and lime peel. Serve with hot corn. Makes 4 servings.

Nutrition information per serving: 183 calories, 3 g protein, 19 g carbohydrate, 12 g total fat (7 g saturated), 31 mg cholesterol, 129 mg sodium, 197 mg potassium

Minnesota

FRUITY WILD RICE PILAF

French and English explorers called the wild water grass enjoyed by Native Americans by a number of names: wild oats, fool's oats, Indian rice, and wild rice.
(Pictured on page 162)

½	**cup chopped onion**
½	**cup chopped celery**
2	**tablespoons margarine** *or* **butter**
1½	**cups water**
¾	**cup wild rice, rinsed**
1½	**teaspoons instant chicken bouillon granules**
1	**small apple, cored and chopped (1 cup)**
2	**tablespoons chopped toasted almonds** *or* **pecans**
½	**teaspoon finely shredded lemon** *or* **orange peel**

Cook the onion and celery in hot margarine or butter till the vegetables are tender but not brown.

Stir in the water, wild rice, and chicken bouillon granules. Bring to boiling; reduce heat. Cover and simmer for 45 to 50 minutes or till the rice is tender and the liquid is absorbed. Remove from heat.

Gently fold in the apple, almonds or pecans, and lemon or orange peel. Makes 4 to 6 servings.

Nutrition information per serving: 191 calories, 5 g protein, 27 g carbohydrate, 8 g total fat (1 g saturated), 0 mg cholesterol, 402 mg sodium, 224 mg potassium

Minnesota

WILD RICE MUFFINS

The Ojibwas (also called Chippewas) of Minnesota still gather the wild grass that they call manomin *(good berry) the traditional way: from canoes that they pole through the rice beds that form in local lakes.*
(Pictured on page 164)

1¾	**cups all-purpose flour**
½	**cup shredded cheddar cheese (2 ounces)**
2	**tablespoons sugar**
2	**teaspoons baking powder**
1	**beaten egg**
1	**cup cooked wild rice**
¾	**cup milk**
¼	**cup cooking oil**

Mix flour, cheese, sugar, baking powder, and ¼ teaspoon *salt.* Make a well in center of dry ingredients.

In another bowl mix egg, cooked rice, milk, and oil; add all at once to dry ingredients. Stir just till moistened (batter should be lumpy).

Lightly grease muffin cups or line them with paper bake cups; fill each cup ⅔ full. Bake in a 400° oven about 20 minutes or till golden. Remove muffins from pans; serve warm. Makes 10 to 12 muffins.

Missouri

BLACK WALNUT-WILD RASPBERRY BREAD

Black walnuts appear in many old-time midwestern recipes. They are a favorite not only in the Midwest, but in the South and the eastern heartland of Pennsylvania Dutch country. (Pictured on page 149)

3	cups all-purpose flour
1	cup sugar
1	tablespoon baking powder
2	teaspoons finely shredded orange peel
¼	teaspoon baking soda
1	beaten egg
1	cup milk
⅔	cup orange juice
¼	cup cooking oil
1	cup fresh *or* frozen wild raspberries *or* raspberries
¾	cup chopped black walnuts
½	cup sifted powdered sugar
2	to 3 teaspoons orange juice

Combine flour, sugar, baking powder, orange peel, baking soda, and ½ teaspoon *salt*. Combine egg, milk, the ⅔ cup orange juice, and oil. Add to flour mixture, stirring just till combined. Stir in raspberries and walnuts.

Pour batter into a greased 9x5x3-inch loaf pan, two 7½x3½x2-inch loaf pans, or six 4½x2½x1½-inch loaf pans. Bake in a 350° oven about 1¼ hours for the 9x5x3-inch loaf (40 to 45 minutes for the 7½x3½x2-inch loaves and 30 to 35 minutes for the 4½x2½x1½-inch loaves)or till a toothpick inserted near the center comes out clean.

Cool in pan(s) for 10 minutes; remove from pan(s). Combine powdered sugar and enough of the 2 to 3 teaspoons orange juice to make an icing of drizzling consistency. Drizzle over warm bread.

Black Walnut and Date Pudding Cake, top (see recipe, page 165), and Whole Wheat-Rhubarb Pudding Cake

Cool bread thoroughly; wrap and store overnight before serving. Makes 1 large loaf, 2 small loaves, or 6 mini loaves (18 servings).

Nutrition information per serving: 207 calories, 4 g protein, 33 g carbohydrate, 7 g total fat (1 g saturated), 13 mg cholesterol, 135 mg sodium, 101 mg potassium

Nebraska

WHOLE WHEAT-RHUBARB PUDDING CAKE

Early settlers were starved for fresh fruits and vegetables. Planting a garden and orchard was among the first tasks of the homesteaders. Rhubarb thrived on the plains. As it appeared in early spring, it was a symbol of the fresh bounty to come after a long winter of eating dried and preserved foods.

5	cups sliced rhubarb
¼	cup sugar
1¼	cups all-purpose flour
1	cup sugar
½	cup whole wheat flour
½	cup chopped pecans
1¼	teaspoons baking powder
½	teaspoon ground cinnamon
⅛	teaspoon ground nutmeg
¾	cup milk
¼	cup margarine *or* butter, melted
1¼	cups sugar
1	tablespoon cornstarch Whipped cream (optional)

In a 3-quart rectangular baking dish mix rhubarb and ¼ cup sugar.

Mix the all-purpose flour, the 1 cup sugar, the whole wheat flour, pecans, baking powder, cinnamon, nutmeg and ¼ teaspoon *salt*. Stir in milk and melted margarine. Spread batter evenly over rhubarb.

Mix 1¼ cups sugar and cornstarch. Add 1¼ cups *boiling water;* stir till sugar dissolves. Slowly pour over batter. Bake in a 375° oven about 45 minutes or till top tests done. If necessary, cover the last 10 minutes to prevent overbrowning. Serve warm. If desired, serve with whipped cream. Serves 8 to 10.

Nutrition information per serving: 445 calories, 5 g protein, 86 g carbohydrate, 11 g fat (2 g saturated), 2 mg cholesterol, 195 mg sodium, 313 mg potassium

WHOOPIE PIES

*These sandwich cookies are real
farmhouse treats: a pair of chocolate
wafers filled with rich vanilla
buttercream and iced with chocolate
butter frosting.*

½   cup shortening
2   cups all-purpose flour
1¼ cups buttermilk *or* sour milk
1   cup sugar
⅔   cup unsweetened cocoa
      powder
1   egg
1   teaspoon baking soda
1   teaspoon vanilla
¾   cup milk
¼   cup all-purpose flour
¾   cup margarine *or* butter
2   cups sifted powdered sugar
1   teaspoon vanilla
      Chocolate Butter Frosting

For cookies, beat shortening with
an electric mixer on medium to high
speed for 30 seconds. Add about
1 cup of the flour, *half* the buttermilk, sugar, cocoa, egg, baking soda,
1 teaspoon vanilla, and ⅛ teaspoon
salt. Beat till thoroughly combined.
Beat in remaining 1 cup flour and
remaining buttermilk. Drop by
rounded tablespoons 2 inches apart
onto ungreased cookie sheets. Bake
in a 350° oven for 8 to 10 minutes
or till edges are firm; cool.

For filling, in a saucepan combine milk and the ¼ cup flour. Cook
and stir till thickened and bubbly.
Cook and stir 2 minutes more.
Remove from heat; cool.

In a mixing bowl beat margarine
or butter with an electric mixer on
medium to high speed for 30 seconds. Add powdered sugar; beat till
fluffy. Add 1 teaspoon vanilla. Beat
cooled milk mixture, 1 large spoonful at a time, into margarine mixture. Beat on high for 1 minute or
till filling is smooth and fluffy.
Spread about *2 tablespoons* filling on
the flat side of *half* the cooled cookies. Top with remaining cookies, flat
side down. Frost with Chocolate
Butter Frosting. Store in refrigerator. Makes 14 filled cookies.

*Whoopie Pies, left, Cream-and-Lingonberry-Filled Pastry Cones, top right, and
Kringle (see recipe, page 172)*

Chocolate Butter Frosting: Beat
together ¼ cup *unsweetened cocoa powder* and 3 tablespoons *butter or margarine*. Gradually beat in 1 cup sifted *powdered sugar*. Slowly beat in 2
tablespoons *milk* and ½ teaspoon
vanilla. Gradually beat in another 1
cup sifted *powdered sugar*. Beat in
additional *milk*, if needed, to reach
spreading consistency.

*Nutrition information per serving: 421
calories, 5 g protein, 56 g carbohydrate, 21 g total
fat (6 g saturated), 24 mg cholesterol, 222 mg
sodium, 171 mg potassium*

CREAM-AND-
LINGONBERRY-FILLED
PASTRY CONES

*Swedes immigrating to the Midwest
didn't have to forgo at least one
of their favorite foods. The lingonberries
that grew wild in Scandinavia
also flourished in the bogs of northern
Wisconsin and Minnesota.*

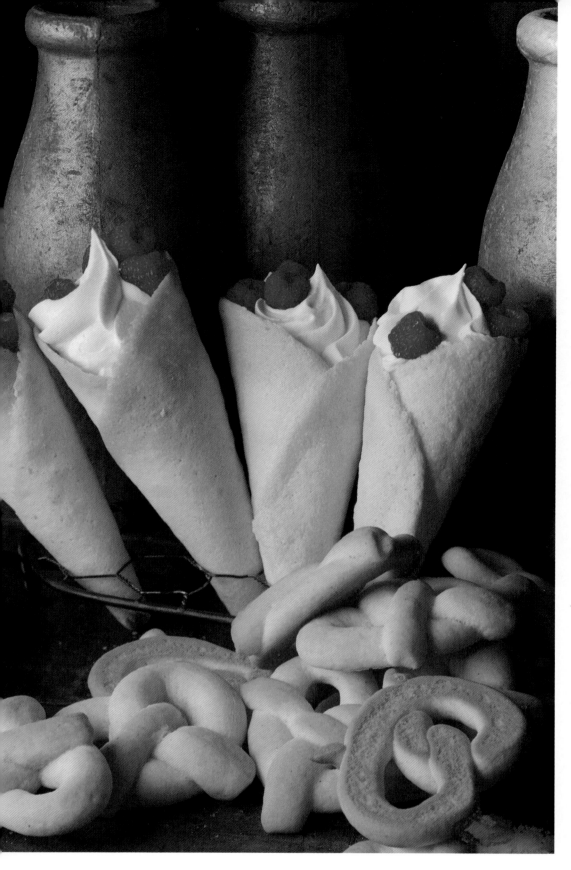

soft peaks form (tips curl). Gradually add the sugar, 1 tablespoon at a time, beating on medium to high speed till stiff peaks form (tips stand straight). Fold about *half* of the flour into the egg white mixture. Gently stir in the butter. Fold in the remaining flour till thoroughly combined.

Drop batter from a *heaping tablespoon* about 3 inches apart on the prepared cookie sheet. (Bake only 3 cookies at a time.) Using a knife or narrow metal spatula, spread batter into 4-inch circles. Bake in a 375° oven for 5 to 6 minutes or till edges of cookies begin to brown.

Immediately remove cookies from cookie sheet, one at a time. Roll each cookie, bottom side in, around a metal cone. *Or,* to form cookie cups, place each cookie over an inverted glass, then gently fold edges down to form ruffles or pleats. (If cookies harden before you can shape them, reheat them in the oven about 1 minute or till softened.) When cookie is firm, slide cookie off cone or remove from glass and cool on a wire rack.

Just before serving, spoon the Sweetened Whipped Cream into a decorating bag fitted with a medium star or round tip (about a ¼-inch opening). Pipe some of the whipped cream into each cookie cone or cup. Sprinkle with lingonberries or raspberries. Makes 14 cones.

Sweetened Whipped Cream: Chill a mixing bowl and the beaters of an electric mixer in the refrigerator. In the chilled bowl combine 1 cup *whipping cream,* 2 tablespoons *powdered sugar,* and ½ teaspoon *vanilla.* Beat with the chilled beaters on low speed till soft peaks form.

Nutrition information per cone: 142 calories, 1 g protein, 13 g carbohydrate, 10 g total fat (6 g saturated), 32 mg cholesterol, 47 mg sodium, 38 mg potassium

2	egg whites
¼	cup butter
½	cup sugar
½	cup all-purpose flour
2	cups Sweetened Whipped Cream
1	14½-ounce can lingonberries, drained, *or* 1 cup fresh raspberries

In a medium mixing bowl let egg whites stand at room temperature for 30 minutes. Meanwhile, generously grease a cookie sheet. (Repeat greasing the cookie sheet for each batch.) Set the cookie sheet aside.

In a small saucepan heat butter over low heat *just till melted.* Set aside to cool.

Beat egg whites with an electric mixer on medium to high speed till

lackberry Jam Cake with Lemon-Buttercream Frosting, top, Danish
Peppernuts, right, and Swedish Torte

Ohio

BLACKBERRY JAM CAKE WITH LEMON-BUTTERCREAM FROSTING

Some of the berries that grew wild around early frontier homesteads were made into jellies and jams. They were usually served with bread, but sometimes they were used as cake filling for the fresh flavor they would impart.

3   cups all-purpose flour
2   cups sugar
1   tablespoon baking powder
1   teaspoon finely shredded
     lemon peel
1½ cups milk
½   cup margarine *or* butter,
     softened
1½ teaspoons vanilla
2   eggs
¾   cup seedless blackberry *or*
     raspberry jam
     Lemon-Buttercream
     Frosting
     Lemon peel (optional)

In a medium mixing bowl combine flour, sugar, baking powder, and lemon peel. Add milk, margarine or butter, and vanilla. Beat with an electric mixer on low speed till combined. Beat on medium to high speed for 2 minutes. Add eggs and beat 2 minutes more. Pour into 2 greased and floured 9x1½-inch round baking pans.

Bake in a 375° oven for 25 to 30 minutes or till a wooden toothpick inserted near the center comes out clean. Cool on wire racks for 10 minutes. Remove from pans. Cool thoroughly on racks.

Split cakes in half horizontally to form 4 layers. Place 1 cake layer on a serving plate. Spread with *¼ cup* of the jam. Top with a second cake layer and spread with another *¼ cup* of the jam. Top with a third cake layer and spread with the remaining jam. Top with remaining cake layer. Frost top and sides of cake with Lemon-Buttercream Frosting. If desired, garnish with long, thin pieces of lemon peel. Lightly cover and refrigerate to store. Makes 12 servings.

Lemon-Buttercream Frosting: In a small heavy saucepan combine ⅔ cup *sugar,* 2 tablespoons *water,* and 2 tablespoons *lemon juice.* Bring to boiling. Remove from heat. Gradually stir about *half* of the sugar mixture into 4 slightly beaten *egg yolks.* Transfer all of the egg yolk mixture to saucepan. Bring to a gentle boil; reduce heat. Cook and stir for 2 minutes. Remove from heat. Stir in 1 teaspoon *vanilla.* Cover surface and cool to room temperature.

In a large mixing bowl beat 1 cup softened *butter* and ½ teaspoon finely shredded *lemon peel* with an electric mixer on medium to high speed till fluffy. Add cooled sugar mixture, beating till combined. If necessary, chill till easy to spread.

Nutrition information per serving: 592 *calories, 7 g protein, 84 g carbohydrate, 26 g total fat (12 g saturated), 150 mg cholesterol, 332 mg sodium, 117 mg potassium*

Minnesota

KRINGLE

Most of the Norwegians who settled in the United States before the Civil War moved to the newly opened territories of the upper Mississippi Valley. Later on, many more homesteaded in the Dakotas, Utah, and Washington. (Pictured on page 171)

3   cups all-purpose flour
2½   teaspoons baking powder
1   teaspoon baking soda
¼   teaspoon ground nutmeg *or*
      cardamom
½   cup butter
1   cup sugar
1   egg
1   teaspoon vanilla
¾   cup buttermilk

Combine flour, baking powder, soda, and nutmeg or cardamom. In a mixing bowl beat butter till softened. Add sugar and beat till fluffy. Add egg and vanilla and beat well. Alternately add flour mixture and buttermilk, beating till well mixed. Chill about 4 hours or overnight.

Divide dough in half. On a floured surface, roll each half into a 10x5-inch rectangle. With a sharp knife, cut each rectangle into twenty 5x½-inch strips. Roll each strip into a 10-inch-long rope. Shape each rope into a loop, crossing 1½ inches from ends. Twist rope at crossing point. Lift loop over to touch ends and seal, forming a pretzel shape. Place on an ungreased cookie sheet.

Bake in a 425° oven about 5 minutes or till cookie bottoms are lightly brown (tops will be pale). Remove from cookie sheet and cool on a wire rack. Makes 40 cookies.

Nutrition information per cookie: 78 calories, 1 g protein, 12 g carbohydrate, 3 g total fat (1 g saturated), 12 mg cholesterol, 57 mg sodium, 18 mg potassium

Minnesota

DANISH PEPPERNUTS

Despite its name, this rich Danish cookie doesn't use pepper, unlike the similar German Pfeffernusse, which does. It is seasoned with cardamom, a very traditional Scandinavian spice.

¾ **cup sugar**
⅔ **cup dark corn syrup**
¼ **cup milk**
¼ **cup shortening**
1 **teaspoon anise extract**
½ **teaspoon baking powder**
½ **teaspoon vanilla**
¼ **teaspoon salt**
¼ **teaspoon ground cinnamon**
¼ **teaspoon ground cardamom**
¼ **teaspoon ground cloves**
3⅓ **cups all-purpose flour**
Sifted powdered sugar

In a large saucepan combine sugar, corn syrup, milk, and shortening. Bring to boiling. Remove from heat and cool about 15 minutes. Stir in anise extract, baking powder, vanilla, salt, cinnamon, cardamom, and cloves. Stir in the flour till well mixed. Cover and chill about 2 hours or till easy to handle.

Divide dough into 24 equal portions. On a surface dusted lightly with sifted powdered sugar, roll each portion of the dough into a ¼-inch-thick rope. Cut into pieces about ⅜ inch long. Place 1 inch apart on a greased cookie sheet.

Bake in a 375° oven about 10 minutes or till lightly browned on bottom. Immediately remove and cool on paper towels. Makes 8 cups of cookies.

Nutrition information per ¼-cup serving: 100 calories, 1 g protein, 20 g carbohydrate, 2 g total fat (0 g saturated), 0 mg cholesterol, 33 mg sodium, 20 mg potassium

Illinois

SWEDISH TORTE

The town of Bishop Hill was founded in 1840 by Eric Janson, a Swede who sought an austere way of life, free from the corruption of the church in Sweden. As time passed, the restrictions were eased, and the tables at Bishop Hill eventually reflected the bounty of the surrounding Illinois farmland.

4 **egg whites**
1⅓ **cups all-purpose flour**
⅔ **cup sugar**
2 **teaspoons baking powder**
⅔ **cup milk**
¼ **cup butter *or* margarine**
1 **egg**
½ **teaspoon finely shredded lemon peel**
¼ **teaspoon almond extract**
¼ **teaspoon cream of tartar**
Dash salt
1 **cup sugar**
¼ **cup sliced almonds**
⅓ **cup sugar**
1 **tablespoon all-purpose flour**
1 **tablespoon cornstarch**
Dash salt
¾ **cup milk**
1 **slightly beaten egg yolk**
1 **tablespoon butter *or* margarine**
1 **teaspoon vanilla**
2 **cups whipped cream (optional)**

Place egg whites in a large mixing bowl; set aside. For cake layer, in a bowl combine the 1⅓ cups flour, the ⅔ cup sugar, and baking powder. Add the ⅔ cup milk, the ¼ cup butter or margarine, egg, lemon peel, and almond extract. Beat with an electric mixer on low speed till combined. Beat on medium speed for 1 minute. Divide batter between two greased and floured 8x1½-inch round baking pans. The batter will be in a thin layer. Set aside.

For meringue layer, add cream of tartar and dash salt to the egg whites. Beat with an electric mixer on medium speed till soft peaks form (tips curl). Add the 1 cup sugar, 1 tablespoon at a time, beating on high speed till very stiff peaks form (tips stand straight) and sugar is almost dissolved. Divide meringue mixture between the two cake pans, spreading evenly over the cake batter. Sprinkle sliced almonds on top of meringue.

Bake in a 350° oven for 25 to 35 minutes or till golden brown. Cool in pans on a wire rack for 10 minutes. Carefully remove from pans and cool completely on wire rack, meringue side up. (Meringues will puff while baking but will sink again while cooling.)

For custard filling, in a saucepan combine the ⅓ cup sugar, the 1 tablespoon flour, cornstarch, and dash salt. Stir in the ¾ cup milk. Cook and stir till thickened and bubbly. Reduce heat; cook and stir 2 minutes more. Stir about ½ cup of the hot mixture into the beaten egg yolk; transfer entire mixture to saucepan. Cook and stir 2 minutes more, but *do not boil*. Remove from heat. Stir in the 1 tablespoon butter and vanilla. Cover surface with plastic wrap; cool completely.

To assemble, place a torte layer on a cake plate, meringue side up. Spread custard filling evenly over meringue. Top with second layer, meringue side up. Cover and chill for 2 to 6 hours. If desired, serve with whipped cream. Makes 8 to 10 servings.

Nutrition information per serving: 404 calories, 7 g protein, 70 g carbohydrate, 11 g total fat (6 g saturated), 76 mg cholesterol, 248 mg sodium, 143 mg potassium

Finnish Viipuri Twist, left, and Finnish Spice Cake

Michigan

FINNISH SPICE CAKE

Mining families from Finland populated the northern sections of Michigan and Wisconsin. Like the Cornish who arrived in the 1850s some fifty years earlier, the Finns brought their food customs with them. They even had their own version of a pasty, the famous savory turnover most commonly linked with Cornwall, England.

3	tablespoons ground almonds
1¼	cups all-purpose flour
1½	teaspoons ground cardamom
1	teaspoon ground cinnamon
1	teaspoon baking powder
½	teaspoon baking soda
¼	teaspoon ground cloves
⅛	teaspoon salt
2	eggs
1	cup packed brown sugar
1	teaspoon vanilla
½	cup margarine *or* butter, melted
¾	cup dairy sour cream
⅔	cup chopped raisins *or* currants
½	cup sifted powdered sugar

1	tablespoon brown sugar
1	to 2 tablespoons whipping cream *or* milk
2	tablespoons toasted sliced almonds

Generously grease an 8-inch fluted tube pan. Sprinkle pan with ground almonds; set aside. In a bowl stir together the flour, cardamom, cinnamon, baking powder, baking soda, cloves, and salt; set aside.

In a large bowl beat the eggs, the 1 cup brown sugar, and the vanilla on medium-high speed for 4 minutes or till thick. Pour in melted margarine or butter; mix well. Alternately add flour mixture and sour cream, beating on low speed after each addition just till combined. Stir in raisins or currants. Pour into prepared pan. Bake in a 350° oven for 45 to 55 minutes or till a wooden toothpick inserted in the center of cake comes out clean. Cool in pan on a wire rack for 10 minutes. Remove from pan; cool. Combine powdered sugar and the 1 tablespoon brown sugar. Stir in enough cream or milk to reach drizzling consistency. Drizzle over cooled cake; garnish with sliced almonds. Makes 12 servings.

Nutrition information per serving: 275 calories, 4 g protein, 36 g carbohydrate, 14 g total fat (4 g saturated), 44 mg cholesterol, 173 mg sodium, 179 mg potassium

Michigan

FINNISH VIIPURI TWIST

This Finnish Christmas pastry looks like a huge pretzel. The two loops created by its shape are traditionally filled with all sorts of cookies.

5¾	to 6¼ cups all-purpose flour
2	packages active dry yeast
½	teaspoon ground cardamom
½	teaspoon ground nutmeg
2	cups milk
¾	cup sugar
¼	cup margarine *or* butter
1	teaspoon salt
2	eggs
1	tablespoon water

In a bowl combine *2½ cups* of flour, the yeast, and spices. Set aside.

In a saucepan heat and stir milk, sugar, margarine, and salt just till warm (120° to 130°) and margarine is almost melted. Add to flour mixture; add *one* egg. Beat with an electric mixer on low speed 30 seconds, scraping bowl constantly. Beat on high speed for 3 minutes. Using a wooden spoon, stir in as much of the remaining flour as you can.

Turn dough out onto a lightly floured surface. Knead in enough of the remaining flour to make a moderately soft dough that is smooth and elastic (3 to 5 minutes). Place in a lightly greased bowl; turn once to grease surface. Cover and let rise in a warm place till double (about 1 hour). Punch dough down. Turn dough out onto a lightly floured surface. Divide dough into 3 equal portions. Cover; let rest 10 minutes.

Shape each portion into a 42-inch-long rope. Form 1 dough rope into a circle, leaving both ends extended 6 inches at the bottom of the circle. Holding ends of dough rope toward center of circle, twist together. Pull rope ends to top of circle and tuck ends under, forming a pretzel-shaped roll. Place on a greased baking sheet. Repeat with remaining dough ropes.

Cover; let rise till nearly double (about 30 minutes). Brush with a mixture of the remaining egg and the water. Bake in a 375° oven about 20 minutes or till bread tests done. Makes 3 loaves (36 servings).

Nutrition information per serving: 112 calories, 3 g protein, 20 g carbohydrate, 2 g total fat (0 g saturated), 13 mg cholesterol, 81 mg sodium, 51 mg potassium

Nebraska

PINK RHUBARB PUNCH

The rhubarb plant was as hardy and versatile as the pioneers who depended on it. Not only was it used as a pie filling, but it was cooked down for jams, or boiled until very soft and then strained to make a refreshing syrupy beverage.

Pink Rhubarb Punch

6 cups fresh rhubarb, cut in ½-inch pieces, *or* 6 cups frozen unsweetened, sliced rhubarb (24 ounces)

3 cups water

1 cup sugar

1 6-ounce can frozen pink lemonade concentrate

¼ cup lemon juice

1 1-liter bottle lemon-lime carbonated beverage, chilled

   Fresh mint leaves *and/or* lemon slices (optional)

In a large saucepan, combine the rhubarb and water. Bring to boiling; reduce heat. Cover and simmer for 5 minutes. Remove from heat; cool slightly. Strain rhubarb mixture, pressing to remove all juices. Discard pulp. Add sugar, lemonade concentrate, and lemon juice to rhubarb juice, stirring to dissolve sugar. Cover and chill.

To serve, combine rhubarb mixture with chilled lemon-lime beverage in a punch bowl or large pitcher. Serve with crushed ice. If desired, garnish with fresh mint and/or lemon slices. Makes ten 8-ounce servings.

Nutrition information per serving: 168 calories, 1 g protein, 42 g carbohydrate, 1 g total fat (0 g saturated), 0 mg cholesterol, 7 mg sodium, 238 mg potassium

The Southwest

It is an irony of America's culinary history that the parched lands of Texas, Arizona, and New Mexico should give birth to one of this country's most irresistible cooking styles. Those who think of southwestern fare as synonymous with Tex-Mex specialties have probably been missing out on the variety and subtlety of the region's cuisine.

Spanish influence in this region was profound. Shortly after Hernando Cortés conquered the Aztecs of Mexico, other Spanish explorers were sent farther north. His compatriot Coronado reached what is now New Mexico in 1540, and La Villa Real de la Santa Fe (the Royal City of the Holy Faith) was founded in 1609. Over the next 250 years, Spanish priests founded missions throughout the Southwest while wealthy Spaniards established vast domains and imported their favorite foods via Mexico. Indeed, until the United States won the Mexican War that ended in 1848, Texas, New Mexico, and Arizona were all part of Mexico.

In addition to the Spanish, indigenous peoples from different parts of Mexico came north to settle, bringing with them their own regional variations and cooking styles. From the sixteenth through nineteenth centuries,

Previous pages: The Spanish explorers came to what is now the American Southwest looking for gold. They didn't find it, but stayed anyway, perhaps awed by the vast and varied landscape. Monument Valley in Arizona is one magnificent example. Above: The missionaries arrived soon after the conquistadores to teach Catholicism to the native population. This adobe mission in Santa Fe, New Mexico, dates from the 1600s. Right: Instead of the Seven Golden Cities of Cíbola, Coronado's expedition stumbled upon the Grand Canyon in 1540. Winter snow blankets Hope Point, at the canyon's South Rim.

Spanish and Mexican dishes blended with native Indian cooking techniques and ingredients. When a dollop of Anglo influence was added during the latter half of the nineteenth century, what evolved was not only Tex-Mex, but distinguishable regional cooking styles like Arizona-Mex and New Mex.

In Arizona, for example, you'll be served tortillas so large—about a foot in diameter—that they are often folded and set beside your plate like a napkin. And the fried burritos known as chimichangas are said to have originated here. In Texas, chili con carne reigns supreme, while in New Mexico enchiladas are stacked rather than rolled. And so it goes, each state reflecting the particular preferences of its immigrants.

In recent years, many chefs all over the United States have become fascinated by the unique flavors of the Southwest. Indeed, if the tradition of grilling over mesquite can be taken as proof of this trend, it's safe to say the southwestern influence has spread like an out-of-control forest fire into kitchens from sea to shining sea.

Desert Fare

To the average traveler, the deserts of Arizona and New Mexico would not appear habitable, but the early Pueblo, Zuni, Hopi, and Navajo Indians were masters at discovering its hidden wealth. The Pueblo of New Mexico settled along the mighty Rio Grande, using the river's regular flooding as a form of natural irrigation. Along the banks they grew corn, beans, and squash in numerous varieties, supplementing their diets with bear, deer, and jackrabbits. Cactus fruits were squeezed for juice or made into preserves, while the prickly pads were scraped clean of their thorns, cooked, and eaten as a vegetable. The Indians also gathered wild tumbleweed, purslane, cattails, mustard, and peppergrass.

To the sacred triad of corn, beans, and squash, early cooks of the Southwest added a memorable fourth: the chili pepper. From fiery to mild, from bright green to tomato red, from tiny orbs to fist-sized bells, these varied members of the capsicum family stamp their unique

flavor signature on the regional dishes of the Southwest to this day.

In this land of blazing sun, drying food was the most common means of preservation, and the technique was taken to a fine art. Venison and pumpkin were air-dried in long strips for storage and then reconstituted in hearty winter soups and stews. Ripe red chilies strung into huge wreaths called *ristras* were hung to dry near the oven, never more than an arm's length away from the cook. *Ristras* are still prominently displayed in Southwest kitchens today.

The World of Chilies

The climate and soil of the Southwest, plus the knowledgeable devotion of this region's farmers, conspired to produce what aficionados consider the finest chilies in the world. Those grown in New Mexico are the most prized.

To the uninitiated, the world of chilies is indeed a confusing one. First, the name itself requires some explanation. Although chili peppers

Red chili wreaths known as ristras *(above) hang out to dry in the late fall sun. The sun was the best preservative for many southwestern foods, including meat, pumpkins, melons, and squash (below). Right: Thirteenth-century Anasazi Indians built seemingly inaccessible dwellings in the Arizona cliffs, like those preserved at Navajo National Monument.*

don't resemble the black pepper Columbus so avidly sought—nor are they botanically related—Columbus's contemporaries back in Europe assumed that the specimen he brought home was indeed a Calcutta pepper. So we ended up calling these members of the nightshade family *peppers* even though they are as different from black pepper as potatoes are from allspice.

Second, there's the spelling to contend with. To the Spanish, it's *chiles*. To Americans, it's *chilies*. To further complicate things, *chili* is also shorthand for the dish called *chili con carne* and for a spice blend of oregano, cumin, garlic, and ground chilies. This blend was actually created in the late nineteenth century by a German marketing genius who operated a restaurant in Texas. Before long, the spicy blend became popular among convenience-oriented cooks throughout America, but serious cooks in Arizona and New Mexico wouldn't ever dream of using it, favoring instead their own homemade blends of fresh and dried chilies.

Although there are close to two hundred varieties of chili peppers, only about a dozen are commonly used in southwestern kitchens. Most immature or young peppers are green; they turn red as they ripen. Often a particular pepper has one name in its fresh form and is called something else when it has been smoked or dried. For example, when the green jalapeño is smoked and dried, it is called a chipotle. And the long, thin fresh poblano (commonly used for making the stuffed peppers called *chiles rellenos*) in its dried form is known as the ancho chili.

The tongue-lashing heat of chilies varies a great deal, depending upon type, maturity, and the whimsy of each specimen. The central vein and clinging seeds within each pod contain a volatile oil that gives the chili this heat—but it also burns the skin, especially the eyes. So it's best to wear rubber gloves when you are working with fresh or dried chilies.

The two signature sauces made with chilies are conveniently labeled red and green. They are typically offered as toppings for such standard fare as enchiladas and burritos. Red sauce is prepared

Like the Pueblo Indians who came before them, the Navajos of the Southwest developed a reverence for corn. A Navajo Reservation petroglyph depicts a corn plant ready for harvesting (above). Below: According to Native American legend, corn is a sacred gift from the Great Spirit. Part of the harvest celebration was a ritual Corn Dance, which gave thanks for a good yield and asked that next year's crop be as plentiful.

from matured chili peppers that have been dried and then processed into flakes or powder. The chili is blended with a liquid (usually water) to form a paste. The paste is briefly cooked with sautéed garlic, onions, and seasonings such as oregano or cumin. The mixture is then blended to create a smooth purée. Taste will vary according to the seasonings and the type of red chilies used, but red sauce is characteristically thick and very full flavored.

Green sauce, on the other hand, is prepared with fresh green (unripened) chilies that have been roasted to remove their outer skins and impart a characteristic smoky taste. The chilies are chopped and mixed with garlic, green onions, and minced fresh cilantro. There are as many variations as there are cooks: sometimes oregano is used instead of cilantro; often chopped tomatoes are added.

Sacred Corn

At the very heart and soul of the Southwest kitchen is corn in its myriad guises. Sacred to Native Americans of this region, corn was

Mysterious monoliths of red sandstone thrust upward from the stark floor of Monument Valley. The valley lies within Navajo lands in Arizona and Utah.

traditionally planted and harvested with ceremonies and ritual dances. An elaborate mythology developed within each tribe. The Zunis, for example, spoke of the corn harvest as follows:

"The breaths of the Corn Maidens blew rain-clouds from their homes in Summer-land, and when the rains had passed away green corn plants grew everywhere the grains had been planted. And when the plants had grown tall and blossomed, they were laden with ears of corn: yellow, blue, red, white, speckled, and black. Thus to this day grows the corn, always eightfold more than is planted, and of six colors, which our women preserve separately during the moons of the sacred fire . . . ."[1]

With close care and the expertise of generations, Indians of the Southwest bred numerous types of corn, each type having its preferred use. The only variety commonly eaten fresh, right off the cob, is sweet corn. Some Native Americans roast and eat the green, unripened corn of other varieties, but most are left to mature on the stalk until their natural sugars convert to starch. They are then dried for storage or further processing.

The Indians used great ingenuity in their preparation of corn, and once the Spanish introduced pork, numerous dishes evolved that are still eaten with regularity throughout the Southwest. To make hominy, they cooked the dried kernels in a solution of slaked lime until the tough hulls separated from the starchy hearts. The hearts were ground on a stone metate into a moist meal called masa, which was shaped into patties, stuffed with bits of chili or roasted pork and steamed in cornhusk packets known as tamales. Hominy that had been dried for storage was slow-cooked with pork and heavily scented with garlic and oregano to create the famous regional dish known as posole. (Posole is also the Mexican name for dried hominy kernels.)

Corn was—and still is—processed in various other ways. To prepare parched corn, ripe kernels are either toasted or roasted and eaten as a snack. For making *chicos,* young (often sweet) corn is partially husked and then set into a very hot oven overnight. The next morning, the ears of corn are stripped of all husk and set on racks to dry for a few weeks. The kernels are sliced off and stored until needed. *Chicos* are traditionally used in long-cooking soups and stews, adding a delicate sweetness and a delightfully chewy texture.

Preserving the Art of Hopi Cookery

*S*oon after she arrived to teach grade school in Keams Canyon, Arizona, Juanita Tiger Kavena realized that traditional Hopi cooking was a dying art. For centuries, the traditional recipes had been handed down orally from one generation to the next, so nothing had ever been written down.

After marrying a Hopi and settling into life on the reservation, Kavena began interviewing the tribal elders and getting their recipes down on paper. This was not an easy task since these skilled cooks worked by eye and feel rather than by exact measurements. But she persevered, knowing that as the elders died, so would their knowledge of Hopi foodways.[2]

Kavena soon discovered that traditional Hopi dishes required great skill and were both labor-intensive and time-consuming to prepare. The ceremonial *piki* bread is a case in point. Traditionally made of blue cornmeal, *piki* is a tissue-paper-thin and crackly bread that is rolled into a tube while still hot.

Before a young Hopi woman was considered eligible for marriage, she had to develop the consummate skill needed to prepare *piki* bread. First she had to prepare the smooth surface of a sandstone slab with cottonseed oil. The slab was mounted on low supports and heated by a fire underneath. When very hot, the stone was covered with crushed watermelon seed, to fill any remaining surface pores.

Then the *piki* batter was made by combining ground blue cornmeal with boiling water and a few tablespoons of chamizo shrub ashes (which held fast the blue-gray color of the cornmeal and added valuable minerals). The thin batter was then spread across the *piki* stone with the deft sweep of a curved palm. When the edges began to curl, the *piki* was rolled up as it was removed from the stone and set on a large, rectangular, woven *piki* tray.

The Hopis were traditionally referred to as the "people of the blue corn," for it is this variety that they prefer for making *piki* and other specialties, whether it be greens boiled with blue-corn dumplings or blue-corn pancakes known as Hopi hush puppies.

Second to corn—which the Hopi grow in eight varieties—beans have long been the most important food in the Hopi diet. Pintos are a staple, but Hopis also favor limas and white and black teparies. The Hopis allow the beans to mature before harvesting them, and it is only when the vines have become dry and brittle that they are uprooted. Traditionally, Hopi women held a work party to shell the beans, which were then spread out on clean cloths and left until completely dried for storage. In this waste-not, want-not approach to desert cooking, the vines and pods were then burned, and the residue collected for use as culinary ashes.

Breads and Related Specialties of the Southwest

Tortillas made of the moist hominy called masa were the staple bread of the Indians of this region. When someone got the idea of rolling these thin, flat disks around beans, enchiladas were born. In New Mexico, cooks created the "stacked" enchilada by alternating layers of tortillas with red and green chili sauces, finely chopped onion, and grated cheese.

In her frugal desert kitchen, some ingenious cook tried deep-frying leftover tortillas until crisp and created tostados. When she folded the tortillas over before frying them, she invented the taco. Even broken bits of fried tortilla found a use as nachos, topped with cheese, beans, and a dollop of chili sauce.

Because cornmeal has no gluten, a cook cannot produce a leavened bread by using yeast. But Native Americans developed techniques for lightening their tortillas and other breads through the use of culinary ash, which was similar to the pearlash used by East Coast Indians. Indigenous southwestern cooks burned juniper and other woods to create an alkaline ash. When this ash came into contact with the natural acids in corn, it produced carbon dioxide.

Once the Spanish introduced wheat to the Native Americans, a whole new family of European-style leavened breads was brought to the New World. The beehive-shaped ovens called *hornos* that dot the countryside are a testimony to this long-standing tradition. Each oven is three to four feet high and made of stone plastered with adobe. Round adobe breads with their golden, crunchy crusts are still baked by the Pueblo Indians today.

The Southwestern Sweet Tooth

Before the Spanish introduced cane sugar, the Native Americans of this region relied upon natural sweeteners like berries, cactus fruit, and the sweetness in corn. To produce an early form of corn sweetener, young girls had the task of chewing some finely ground cornmeal until enzymes in their saliva reacted with the cornstarch to produce sugar. This cornmeal mash was mixed into batters to add an edge of sweetness.

In addition to sugar, the Spanish brought apricots, peaches, eggs, and a variety of cooking techniques from the Old World. What resulted is a panoply of very interesting desserts that are still very popular.

Baked fruit pasties called *pastelitos* are made by stuffing

Artisans of every culture have created beautiful containers to use as serving and storage vessels. This Acoma Pueblo jar (above right), 1890-1910, is a fine example. Right: An oven like this horno *from New Mexico's Taos Pueblo is heated by burning wood to an ash on the oven floor. The ash is swept away through the front opening.*

rounds of dough with dried fruit pastes, folding them in half, and crimping the edges. Crisp little cookies flecked with aniseed are called *biscochitos*, and a rich custard scented with cinnamon is known as *natilla*. Little molded cakes are made of ground pine nuts, gathered from the fallen cones of piñon pines and roasted.

Perhaps the Southwest's most unusual dessert is *panocha*, a rich pudding made of sprouted wheat berries which are dried and then ground into flour. The flour is mixed with sugar, butter, and spices, and boiled over low heat until very thick.

What's Cookin' In Texas

Over sixty percent of the population of Texas can trace its ancestors back to Mexico, so it comes as no surprise that Tex-Mex food is what this state is most famous for. However, Texas is the largest state in the continental United States, and more than one distinct regional cuisine developed within the Lone Star State.

On the Gulf Coast in and around Galveston, for example, southern cooking—particularly Creole and Cajun styles—still reflects the proximity to Louisiana and the influence of early settlers who came to Texas from the South. In western Texas, kitchens reflect the culinary character of New Mexico, with its vast range of chilies and its strong Native American influence.

The plains of the Texas Panhandle, where cattle have long roamed, is characterized by a

The Cowboy, painted by Frederic Remington in 1902, chararcterized the tough way of life on the range.

rough-and-ready style of cowboy cooking where beef (and lots of it) reigns supreme. It was here that dishes like son-of-a-bitch stew evolved, a reminder of the days when home was on the range, the kitchen was a chuck wagon, and every last edible part of the animal was thrown into the stew pot.

Anyone seeking out Tex-Mex food would do best to travel deep into the heart of south-central Texas, visiting towns like Austin and San Antonio. That's where you're likely to find the most authentic refried beans and chicken-fried steak and that's where you're most likely to find people arguing about whether or not you should add beans to chili con carne.

This is a subject that seems to spice up the lives of many Texans. Entire books have been written about chili, and the first chapter of

Frank Tolbert's *A Bowl of Red* begins by quoting a man named Harry James: "Congress should pass a law making it mandatory for all restaurants serving chili to follow a Texas recipe."[3] Never let it be said that Texans aren't chauvinistic when it comes to chili.

All that is well and good, but the trouble is that no one in Texas quite agrees on how an authentic chili should be made. This point becomes quite clear at the World Championship Chili Cookoff held every year in the desert town of Terlingua in the Rio Grande Valley of southwestern Texas. Here, every impassioned "chili head" has a personal blend of herbs and spices, a certainty about the right proportion of beef to beans (or no beans at all!), and an inner knowing about just how incendiary the final product should be. Whatever the recipe, a good chili con carne is indisputably the quintessential Tex-Mex dish.

No wonder that Kit Carson's dying words were reputed to be "Wish I had time for just one more bowl of chili."[4]

The Curious Case Of Chocolate

In the southwestern kitchen, chocolate appears in a most unusual guise. The cacao bean (from which chocolate is made) is indigenous to Mexico and was used by the Aztecs in a bitter drink they called *xocolatl* (the origin of our word *chocolate*).

During their sojourn in Mexico, the Spanish created a very flavorful paste by mixing a bit of the powdered cacao bean with black chilies, garlic, saffron, and spices. The cacao was added to deepen both the flavor and the color of this mole paste, which the Spanish cooked with wild turkey. Although it is usually reserved for special occasions in home kitchens, the lucky traveler may still spot turkey mole on restaurant menus through the Southwest.

Flavors from the Southwest

New Mexico

CHORIZO CON QUESO DIP

Early southwestern cooks learned how to make cheese and sausage from Spanish colonists, who brought the basic ingredients —cows and pigs —with them. (Pictured on page 190)

½   **pound chorizo *or* bulk pork sausage**
½   **cup chopped onion**
2   **cups chopped fresh mushrooms**
½   **cup tomato juice**
2   **cups shredded Monterey Jack cheese (8 ounces)**
2   **cups shredded American cheese (8 ounces)**
2   **tablespoons chopped jalapeño pepper**
    Tortilla chips *or* corn chips

In a large skillet cook chorizo and onion till no pink remains and onion is tender. Drain well. Add mushrooms; cook till tender. Stir in tomato juice, cheeses, and jalapeño pepper. Cook and stir just till cheese is melted and mixture is blended. Serve hot with chips. Makes 12 to 14 appetizer servings.

Nutrition information per serving: 213 calories, 13 g protein, 2 g carbohydrate, 17 g total fat (9 g saturated), 47 mg cholesterol, 604 mg sodium, 180 mg potassium

New Mexico

PINE NUT-CHEESE BITES

In September, the pine trees indigenous to the southwestern Rocky Mountains drop their cones, releasing the rich flavorful nuts known as piñons. (Pictured on page 190)

4   **ounces process Swiss cheese, shredded**
¼   **cup margarine *or* butter**
¼   **teaspoon dry mustard**
⅛   **teaspoon pepper**
½   **cup all-purpose flour**
2   **tablespoons pine nuts**

Bring cheese and margarine to room temperature. In a mixing bowl combine cheese, margarine, mustard, and pepper. Beat with an electric mixer till combined. Add flour to cheese mixture. Beat on low speed till well blended. Transfer to a lightly floured surface and knead about 30 seconds.

Using *1 teaspoon* for each, form into ¾-inch balls; place on baking sheet. Flatten slightly with bottom of a glass that has been dipped in flour. Sprinkle a few pine nuts on top of each flattened ball; press nuts into dough with the glass.

Bake in a 400° oven for 6 to 8 minutes or till set and edges start to turn golden. Cool on a wire rack. Makes about 48 appetizers.

Nutrition information per appetizer: 25 calories, 1 g protein, 1 g carbohydrate, 2 g total fat (1 g saturated), 2 mg cholesterol, 14 mg sodium, 8 mg potassium

Sangrita (see recipe, page 210), and Chimichangas (see recipe, page 198)

Chorizo Con Queso Dip, top left (see recipe, page 189), Pine Nut-Cheese Bites, top right (see recipe, page 189), Guacamole, lower left, and Green Chili Cheese Spread

Arizona

VEGETABLE-TOPPED CHEESE QUESADILLA

In the Southwest, a quesadilla is a turnover. At its simplest, it's a quick snack made with a corn or flour tortilla topped with cheese, then folded and browned. Another approach, like that for an empanada, uses a masa (corn) dough to completely enclose the filling. Once assembled, it is either deep-fried or baked.

4   7-inch flour tortillas
      (see recipe, page 204, *or*
      use purchased)
1   cup shredded Monterey
      Jack cheese with peppers
      (4 ounces)
1   cup shredded sharp cheddar
      cheese (4 ounces)
2   tablespoons snipped cilantro
½   cup shredded jicama
¼   cup chopped tomato

¼   **cup chopped green onion**
¼   **cup dairy sour cream**
2   **tablespoons chopped ripe
      olives**

On a large baking sheet place *two* of the tortillas. Combine Monterey Jack cheese, cheddar cheese, and cilantro. Sprinkle *half* of the cheese mixture evenly on each tortilla. Top with second tortilla, pressing slightly. Bake in a 400° oven for 10 to 15 minutes or till cheese starts to melt. Transfer to a wire rack.

In a small bowl stir together the jicama, tomato, and green onion. Spread sour cream on top of hot quesadillas. Top with jicama mixture; sprinkle with olives. Cut each quesadilla into 6 wedges and serve warm. Makes 6 appetizer servings.

Nutrition information per serving: *245 calories, 12 g protein, 14 g carbohydrate, 16 g total fat (9 g saturated), 41 mg cholesterol, 346 mg sodium, 130 mg potassium*

New Mexico

GUACAMOLE

Guacamole is a combination of two Aztec words: ahuacatl, *meaning "avocado," and* molli, *"mixture." While it is sometimes used as a sauce in Mexican cooking, in the Southwest it is served as an* antojito (appetizer), *as a salad with lettuce, and as a garnish for tacos, burritos, and tostadas.*

2   **medium avocados, seeded,
      peeled, and cut up**
1   **medium tomato, peeled,
      seeded, and coarsely
      chopped**
½   **of a small onion, cut up**
1   **tablespoon chopped serrano
      pepper** *or* **jalapeño pepper**
1   **tablespoon snipped cilantro**
      or **parsley**
1   **tablespoon lemon juice** *or*
      lime juice
¼   **teaspoon salt**
      Chopped tomato (optional)
      Chopped onion (optional)

In a blender container or food processor bowl combine the avocados, tomato, onion, serrano or jalapeño pepper, cilantro or parsley, lemon or lime juice, and salt.

Cover and blend or process till well combined, stopping machine occasionally to scrape down sides. Transfer mixture to a serving bowl. Cover and chill up to 4 hours. If desired, garnish with additional chopped tomato and onion. Use as a dip for chips or as a topping for main dishes. Makes about 1¾ cups.

Nutrition information per tablespoon: 24 calories, 0 g protein, 1 g carbohydrate, 2 g total fat (0 g saturated), 0 mg cholesterol, 21 mg sodium, 93 mg potassium

New Mexico

GREEN CHILI CHEESE SPREAD

In rural New Mexico, cheesemaking is still done at home. Sometimes cheese is prepared with cow's milk, sometimes with milk from the family's goats. Chile verde con queso, "green chili with cheese," is a popular combination.

½ **of an 8-ounce package cream cheese**
¼ **cup dairy sour cream**
2 **tablespoons margarine *or* butter**
1 **4-ounce can chopped green chilies, drained**
1 **tablespoon finely chopped serrano pepper *or* jalapeño pepper**
1 **tablespoon snipped fresh cilantro *or* parsley**
1 **tablespoon finely chopped onion**
1 **teaspoon snipped fresh oregano *or* ¼ teaspoon dried oregano, crushed**
¼ **teaspoon seasoned salt
Snipped fresh cilantro (optional)**

Allow cream cheese, sour cream, and margarine to stand at room temperature for 30 minutes. Beat with an electric mixer till combined. Stir in chilies, serrano pepper,

Shrimp with Cilantro-Lime Cocktail Sauce, top, and Vegetable-Topped Cheese Quesadilla

cilantro, onion, oregano, and seasoned salt. Cover and chill for 4 to 24 hours. If desired, sprinkle with additional cilantro. Serve with crackers, toasted tortilla wedges, corn chips, or raw vegetables. Makes 10 to 12 appetizer servings.

Nutrition information per serving: 76 calories, 1 g protein, 1 g carbohydrate, 7 g total fat (4 g saturated), 15 mg cholesterol, 232 mg sodium, 48 mg potassium

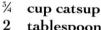

Texas

SHRIMP WITH CILANTRO-LIME COCKTAIL SAUCE

Limes, brought to the New World by Spanish conquistadores, add a fresh citrus note to seafood dishes. Perhaps the best known is seviche, a cold salad that uses citric acid to "cook" raw fish. Cilantro, which looks like flat-leaf parsley, appears in Mexican-American cooking as a flavoring and garnish, and in table condiments like this sauce.

¾ **cup catsup**
2 **tablespoons snipped fresh cilantro**
1 **tablespoon lime juice**
1 **tablespoon prepared horseradish
Several dashes bottled hot pepper sauce**
1 **pound fresh *or* frozen peeled, large shrimp, cooked, deveined, and chilled
Cracked ice
Lime wedges *or* lime slices**

For sauce, in a small mixing bowl combine catsup, cilantro, lime juice, horseradish, and hot pepper sauce. Cover and store in the refrigerator for at least 3 hours.

Serve shrimp on a bed of cracked ice. Garnish with lime wedges and serve with sauce. Makes 4 appetizer servings.

Nutrition information per serving: 134 calories, 19 g protein, 13 g carbohydrate, 1 g total fat (0 g saturated), 166 mg cholesterol, 738 mg sodium, 393 mg potassium

PICADILLO

Savory meat dishes sweetened with spices and dried fruits are a legacy from Spain. This is a favorite filling for tortillas, tacos, and empanadas. Its name is Spanish for hash, *probably because it looks like a jumble of chopped-up ingredients.* (Pictured on page 194)

1	pound lean ground beef
½	cup chopped onion
2	cloves garlic, minced
2	medium tomatoes
1	medium apple
⅓	cup raisins
2	tablespoons thinly sliced, pimiento-stuffed olives
1	tablespoon chopped, pickled jalapeño pepper
1	tablespoon vinegar
1	teaspoon sugar
½	teaspoon salt
½	teaspoon ground cinnamon
½	teaspoon ground cumin
⅛	teaspoon ground cloves
¼	cup toasted slivered almonds

In a large skillet cook ground beef, onion, and garlic till meat is brown and onion is tender. Drain off fat.

Meanwhile, peel and chop tomatoes. Peel, core, and chop apple. Stir tomatoes, apple, raisins, olives, jalapeño pepper, vinegar, sugar, salt, cinnamon, cumin, and cloves into the beef mixture. Cook, covered, over low heat for 20 minutes. Stir in the toasted almonds. Cook, uncovered, for 2 minutes more. Serve it with large corn chips or tortilla chips or in taco shells or flour tortillas. Makes about 3 cups.

Nutrition information per tablespoon: 25 calories, 2 g protein, 2 g carbohydrate, 1 g total fat (0 g saturated), 5 mg cholesterol, 16 mg sodium, 62 mg potassium

Texas-Style Beef Brisket with Five-Alarm Sauce, and Texas Coleslaw (see recipe, page 203)

EMPANADITAS

Like their cousins, the savory Cornish pasties of the Midwest and the fried fruit pies so relished in the South, these southwestern turnovers are beloved regional treats. At Christmas, they are filled with dried fruits preserved from the fall harvest. (Pictured on page 196)

1	cup chopped cooked beef *or* pork
¼	cup chopped green chilies
2	tablespoons raisins
1	tablespoon finely chopped onion
1	teaspoon garlic salt
⅛	teaspoon cumin
⅛	teaspoon ground red pepper
	Pastry for Double-Crust Pie (see recipe, page 274)
	Milk
	Salsa (optional)
	Dairy sour cream (optional)

For filling, in a mixing bowl combine the meat, chilies, raisins, onion, garlic salt, cumin, and red pepper. Set aside.

Divide pastry in half. On a lightly floured surface, roll half of the pastry into a circle about 12 inches in diameter. With a 3½-inch round cutter, cut pastry into ten circles, rerolling scraps as necessary.

Place a scant *1 tablespoon* filling on each circle. Moisten edges with water; fold each circle of dough in half, pressing edges with a fork to seal. Prick once or twice with fork to allow steam to escape.

Place on a baking sheet. Repeat with remaining dough and filling. Brush with milk. Bake in a 400° oven about 15 minutes or till golden. Serve warm. If desired, top with salsa and sour cream. Makes about 20 empanaditas.

Nutrition information per empanadita: 122 calories, 3 g protein, 10 g carbohydrate, 7 g total fat (2 g saturated), 5 mg cholesterol, 163 mg sodium, 55 mg potassium

TEXAS-STYLE BEEF BRISKET WITH FIVE-ALARM SAUCE

While the Spanish contributed the main ingredient to Texas barbecue, beef cattle, and gave it a name, barbacoa, *Native Americans developed the technique of roasting over a pit filled with coals. Typically, the meat gets a double dousing with sauce, one as it cooks (the mop), the other when it's served (the sop).*

4	to 6 cups mesquite wood chips
1	2- to 3-pound fresh beef brisket
2	teaspoons seasoned salt
1	teaspoon paprika
1	teaspoon pepper
	Brushing Sauce
	Five-Alarm Sauce

At least 1 hour before grilling, soak wood chips in enough water to cover. Trim excess fat from the beef. In a small mixing bowl stir together the seasoned salt, paprika, and pepper; rub onto brisket. Drain the wood chips.

In a covered grill arrange *medium-slow* coals around a drip pan. Pour 1 inch of water into the drip pan. Sprinkle some of the wood

Chili Rellenos Casserole, left (see recipe, page 196), and Chorizo-Stuffed Chayote

chips onto the coals. Test for *slow heat* above the pan. Place brisket, fat side up, on the grill rack over the drip pan but not over the coals. Lower the grill hood. Grill for 2 to 2½ hours or till meat is very tender. Every 30 minutes or as needed, brush meat with Brushing Sauce, and add more coals, drained wood chips, and water.

For serving, thinly slice the meat across the grain; arrange on plates. Top with some of the Five-Alarm Sauce; pass remaining sauce. Makes 12 servings.

Brushing Sauce: In a small bowl stir together ¼ cup *dry red wine*, 4 teaspoons *Worcestershire sauce*, 1 tablespoon *cooking oil*, 1 tablespoon *red wine vinegar or cider vinegar*, 1 clove minced *garlic*, ½ teaspoon crushed *coriander seed*, ½ teaspoon *hot-style mustard*, and a dash ground *red pepper.* Makes ⅔ cup.

Five-Alarm Sauce: In a small saucepan stir together 1 cup *catsup*; ¾ cup peeled, seeded, and chopped *tomato*; ½ cup chopped *green pepper*; 2 tablespoons chopped *onion*; 2 tablespoons *brown sugar*; 1 to 2 tablespoons *steak sauce*; 1 to 2 tablespoons *Worcestershire sauce*; ½ teaspoon *garlic powder*;

¼ teaspoon ground *nutmeg*; ¼ teaspoon ground *cinnamon*; ¼ teaspoon ground *cloves*; ⅛ teaspoon ground *ginger*; and ⅛ teaspoon *pepper.* Bring to boiling; reduce heat. Cover; simmer about 5 minutes or till green pepper is crisp-tender. Serve warm or at room temperature. Makes about 2½ cups.

Nutrition information per serving: 188 calories, 17 g protein, 10 g carbohydrate, 9 g total fat (3 g saturated), 53 mg cholesterol, 547 mg sodium, 345 mg potassium

---

New Mexico

CHORIZO-STUFFED CHAYOTE

The mild flavor of chayote (it tastes something like a cucumber) makes it a good foil for spicy foods like chorizo. The Aztecs named it chayotli *in their Nahuatl language. The Southwest isn't alone in pairing the two foods. Louisiana Cajuns call chayote* mirliton, *and chorizo,* chaurice.

3   **medium chayote squash (about 8 ounces each)**
4   **ounces chorizo**

1   **12-ounce can whole kernel corn with red and green sweet peppers, drained**
½   **cup salsa**
1   **tablespoon snipped fresh cilantro *or* parsley**
¾   **cup shredded Monterey Jack cheese *or* mild cheddar cheese (3 ounces)**

Cut chayotes in half lengthwise. Cook in boiling water about 15 minutes or till tender. *Do not overcook.* Drain and cool chayotes. Scoop out the flesh and seeds, leaving a shell about ⅛ to ¼ inch thick. Discard seeds; set shells aside. Chop flesh; set aside.

In a skillet cook chorizo till no pink remains; drain well. Stir in corn, salsa, cilantro, and chopped chayote. Fill the chayote halves with meat mixture. Place in a 2-quart rectangular baking dish.

Cover; bake in a 375° oven for 25 to 30 minutes or till heated through. Sprinkle with cheese. Bake for 2 minutes more to melt cheese. Makes 6 side-dish servings.

Nutrition information per serving: 194 calories, 9 g protein, 18 g carbohydrate, 10 g total fat (5 g saturated), 25 mg cholesterol, 580 mg sodium, 367 mg potassium

Picadillo, top (see recipe, page 192), and Swordfish and Salsa Verde

New Mexico

SWORDFISH AND SALSA VERDE

In New Mexico, salsa verde — "green sauce" — gets its color from chilies picked before they ripen to a rich, deep red. The addition of tart, lemony tomatillos, or husk tomatoes, is a Mexican touch.

5   or 6 fresh tomatillos (6 ounces), husks removed and finely chopped, *or* one 13-ounce can tomatillos, drained, rinsed, and finely chopped
2   tablespoons finely chopped onion
2   serrano peppers *or* jalapeño peppers, seeded and finely chopped
1   tablespoon snipped fresh cilantro *or* parsley
1   teaspoon finely shredded lime peel *or* grapefruit peel
½   teaspoon sugar
¼   teaspoon salt
¼   teaspoon ground cumin
¼   teaspoon pepper
4   swordfish steaks *or* tuna steaks, ¾ to 1 inch thick (1¼ pounds total)

1   tablespoon lime juice *or* grapefruit juice
½   of an avocado, seeded, peeled, and chopped
      Tomato slices (optional)
      Lime wedges (optional)
      Fresh tomatillos (optional)
      Fresh cilantro *or* green onion tops (optional)

For salsa verde, in a mixing bowl stir together tomatillos, onion, serrano or jalapeño peppers, cilantro or parsley, lime or grapefruit peel, and sugar; set aside. (To make ahead, cover and chill for up to 2 days.)

Combine salt, cumin, and pepper. Place fish in a 3-quart rectangular baking dish. Brush fish with lime juice. Sprinkle with cumin mixture. Stir avocado into salsa verde. Spoon salsa verde atop fish.

Bake fish, uncovered, in a 450° oven till fish flakes easily when tested with a fork, allowing 5 to 7 minutes per ½-inch thickness of fish. If desired, garnish with tomato slices, lime wedges, tomatillos, and cilantro. Makes 4 servings.

Nutrition information per serving: 221 calories, 29 g protein, 6 g carbohydrate, 10 g total fat (2 g saturated), 53 mg cholesterol, 260 mg sodium, 678 mg potassium

Arizona

CHICKEN ENCHILADAS

In Spanish, enchilada means "spiced with chili," a requisite step in preparing this casserole. Sometimes the tortillas are dipped in a chili sauce; sometimes they're covered with it. In New Mexico, tortillas made with blue corn are preferred for enchiladas (and just about everything else), but tortillas made of yellow or white cornmeal will do.

¼   cup chopped pecans
¼   cup chopped onion
1   tablespoon margarine *or* butter
1   3-ounce package cream cheese, softened
1   tablespoon milk
¼   teaspoon ground cumin
2   cups chopped cooked chicken
6   8-inch flour tortillas (see recipe, page 204, *or* use purchased)
1   10¾-ounce can condensed cream of chicken soup
1   8-ounce carton dairy sour cream
1   cup milk
5   or 6 chopped pickled jalapeño peppers, rinsed, seeded, and chopped
1   cup shredded cheddar cheese *and/or* Monterey Jack Cheese (4 ounces)
2   tablespoons chopped pecans

In a medium skillet cook the ¼ cup pecans and onion in margarine or butter till onion is tender and pecans are lightly toasted. Remove from heat.

In a bowl combine the softened cream cheese, the 1 tablespoon milk, and cumin. Add nut mixture and chicken. Stir together till well combined.

Spoon about *⅓ cup* chicken mixture onto each tortilla near one edge; roll up. Place filled tortillas, seam side down, in a greased 2-quart square baking dish.

In a bowl combine soup, sour cream, the 1 cup milk, and the pickled jalapeño peppers. Pour the soup

Chicken Enchiladas, top, Turkey and Chorizo Mole, and Refried Beans (see recipe, page 205)

mixture evenly over the tortillas in the baking dish. Cover with foil; bake in a 350° oven about 45 minutes or till heated through.

Remove foil. Sprinkle enchiladas with cheese and the 2 tablespoons pecans. Bake for 4 to 5 minutes more or till cheese is melted. Makes 6 servings.

Nutrition information per serving: 541 calories, 28 g protein, 30 g carbohydrate, 35 g total fat (15 g saturated), 99 mg cholesterol, 924 mg sodium, 405 mg potassium

---

Texas

TURKEY AND CHORIZO MOLE

Turkey and chocolate were enjoyed by Aztec nobility, so it's not surprising that both appear in a dish supposedly invented in honor of an archbishop's visit to a Mexican convent. Chocolate traveled north in the packs of Spanish traders, but southwestern Native Americans already knew about turkey, which they valued for its feathers.

4 ounces chorizo *or* bulk pork sausage, crumbled *or* sliced (optional)
1 tablespoon cooking oil (optional)
¾ cup whole almonds
1 small onion, chopped (¼ cup)
1 6-inch flour tortilla, torn, *or* 1 slice dry bread, torn
1 clove garlic, minced
¼ teaspoon ground cinnamon
⅛ teaspoon ground cloves
1 10-ounce can tomatoes with green chili peppers
¾ cup chicken broth
1 square (1 ounce) unsweetened chocolate, chopped
6 turkey breast tenderloin steaks (1 to 1½ pounds total)
½ cup shredded Monterey Jack cheese (2 ounces)
   Red sweet pepper strips (optional)
   Fresh herbs (optional)

If using sausage, in a 12-inch skillet cook chorizo or bulk pork sausage till brown. Remove with a slotted spoon, reserving *1 tablespoon* drippings in skillet; set sausage aside. If not using sausage, heat cooking oil in skillet.

Add the almonds, onion, tortilla or bread, garlic, cinnamon, and cloves to the skillet. Cook, uncovered, over medium heat, stirring frequently, about 5 minutes.

In a blender container or food processor bowl place almond mixture, *undrained* tomatoes, broth, chocolate, and ⅛ teaspoon *salt*. Cover and blend or process till nearly smooth.

Pour tomato mixture into the skillet. Bring to boiling; reduce heat. Add cooked sausage (if using) and turkey steaks. Return to boiling; reduce heat. Cover; simmer for 15 to 20 minutes or till turkey is no longer pink, stirring once or twice.

To serve, transfer sauce and turkey to dinner plates. Sprinkle with cheese. If desired, garnish with red sweet pepper strips and fresh herbs. Makes 6 servings.

Nutrition information per serving: 271 calories, 25 g protein, 10 g carbohydrate, 16 g total fat (4 g saturated), 56 mg cholesterol, 390 mg sodium, 438 mg potassium

CHILI RELLENOS CASSEROLE

When fresh chilies are available in the Southwest, cooks prefer them over canned for this classic stuffed-pepper dish, even though they require extra effort. As a subtle clue to guests that they are getting the real McCoy, the stems are left on. Canned peppers come stemmed, peeled, and seeded —no additional prep required. (Pictured on page 195)

2   **large poblano peppers *or* green sweet peppers (8 ounces)**
1   **cup shredded Monterey Jack cheese with jalapeño peppers (4 ounces)**
3   **beaten eggs**
¼   **cup milk**
⅓   **cup all-purpose flour**
½   **teaspoon baking powder**
¼   **teaspoon ground red pepper**
⅛   **teaspoon salt**
¾   **cup shredded cheddar cheese (3 ounces)**
1   **cup picante sauce**
¼   **cup dairy sour cream**

Halve or quarter the peppers and remove seeds and veins. Remove stems, if desired. Immerse peppers into boiling water for 3 minutes; drain. Invert peppers on paper towels to drain well. Place the peppers in a well-greased 1½-quart casserole. Top with shredded Monterey Jack cheese.

In a medium mixing bowl combine eggs and milk. Add flour, baking powder, red pepper, and salt. Beat till smooth. Pour egg mixture over peppers. Bake, uncovered, in a 450° oven for 15 minutes or till set. Sprinkle with the shredded cheddar cheese. Let stand about 5 minutes or till cheese melts. Serve with picante sauce and sour cream. Makes 4 servings.

Nutrition information per serving: *352 calories, 20 g protein, 17 g carbohydrate, 24 g total fat (13 g saturated), 215 mg cholesterol, 891 mg sodium, 382 mg potassium*

Pork Tenderloin in Corn Bread, left, Empanaditas, center (see recipe, page 192), and Flautas

PORK TENDERLOIN IN CORN BREAD

This dish is an emapanada gone uptown, or perhaps a southwestern version of beef Wellington. It is a fine example of how new dishes evolve out of traditional recipes and ingredients.

1¼   **cups all-purpose flour**
¼   **cup cornmeal**
1   **teaspoon sugar**
¾   **teaspoon baking powder**
¼   **cup cooking oil**
1   **beaten egg**
3   **tablespoons water**
2   **to 3 tablespoons snipped fresh cilantro *or* parsley**
1   **teaspoon chili powder**
1   **12 to 14-ounce pork tenderloin**
¾   **cup salsa *or* picante sauce**

Mix the flour, cornmeal, sugar, baking powder, and ¼ teaspoon *salt*. Combine oil, egg, and water. Stir liquid mixture into dry mixture till well blended, forming a ball.

On a lightly floured piece of waxed paper, roll or pat dough into an 8-inch square. Combine cilantro, chili powder, ¼ teaspoon *salt* and ¼ teaspoon *pepper*. Rub cilantro mixture on surface of pork, coating

196

½ cup chopped onion

2 garlic cloves, minced

1 tablespoon snipped fresh oregano *or* 1 teaspoon dried oregano, crushed

½ teaspoon ground cumin

¼ teaspoon salt

Dash ground cinnamon

Dash ground cloves

8 8-inch flour tortillas (see recipe, page 204, *or* use purchased)

Cooking oil for frying

Shredded lettuce

Salsa

Dairy sour cream

1 ripe avocado, seeded, peeled and sliced

For filling, in a medium skillet cook meat, pepper, onion, and garlic till no pink remains. Drain fat. Stir in oregano, cumin, salt, cinnamon, and cloves. Cover; cook over low heat for 3 minutes to blend flavors, stirring occasionally. Remove from heat; set aside. Meanwhile, stack tortillas and wrap tightly in foil. Heat in a 350° oven for 10 minutes to soften.

For each flauta, spoon about *2 tablespoons* of the meat filling lengthwise down the center of tortilla. Roll up lightly; secure with a wooden toothpick.

In a large skillet heat about ½ inch of oil over medium-high heat till a small piece of tortilla or bread sizzles when dropped into oil. Fry 3 or 4 flautas at a time, about 3 minutes or till crisp and golden, turning once. Use tongs to lift flautas from oil; tip carefully to allow fat to drain out of each end.

Drain on paper towels. Keep warm in a 300° oven while frying remaining flautas. To serve, remove toothpicks. Serve on shredded lettuce with salsa, sour cream, and avocado slices. Makes 4 servings.

Nutrition information per serving: 929 calories, 27 g protein, 47 g carbohydrate, 72 g total fat (12 g saturated), 56 mg cholesterol, 718 mg sodium, 683 mg potassium

evenly. Place tenderloin across center of dough, folding under narrow end of tenderloin to make an even thickness. With aid of the waxed paper, roll dough around tenderloin. Seal edge and ends. Place seam side down on a lightly greased baking sheet. Bake in a 425° oven 20 minutes. Cover loosely with foil; bake 15 to 20 minutes more or till a meat thermometer inserted in center of meat registers 155° to 160°. Serve with salsa. If desired, garnish with lemon leaves. Serves 4.

Nutrition information per serving: 434 calories, 25 g protein, 42 g carbohydrate, 19 g total fat (3 g saturated), 104 mg cholesterol, 674 mg sodium, 509 mg potassium

Texas

FLAUTAS

Another of the seemingly endless variations of the basic filled tortilla, these are poetically named "little flutes" because of their tubular shape. They are stuffed and rolled like enchiladas, and finished by frying like chimichangas. The inclusion of cinnamon and cloves hints at their Spanish heritage.

12 ounces lean ground beef *or* pork

¼ cup chopped fresh poblano pepper *or* Anaheim pepper

In a deep skillet or saucepan heat about ½ inch of oil till a small piece of tortilla or bread sizzles when dropped into oil. Place the chimichangas seam side down in oil. Fry 2 or 3 at a time about 1 minute on each side or till crisp and golden. Drain on paper towels.

Keep warm in a 300° oven while frying remaining Chimichangas. If desired, serve with cheese and salsa. Makes 4 servings.

Nutrition information per serving: 1,005 calories, 37 g protein, 76 g carbohydrate, 62 g total fat (14 g saturated), 74 mg cholesterol, 1,376 mg sodium, 764 mg potassium

Taco Salad, left, and Avocado Salsa (see recipe, page 207)

Arizona

CHIMICHANGAS

These fried burritos are considered border food, a unique culinary subcategory that developed in the southernmost areas of Arizona, Texas, and New Mexico. Oversize flour tortillas are typically Arizona-Mex. (Pictured on page 188)

4   dried tomato halves
     (not oil-packed)
12 ounces boneless beef round
     or chuck, cut into ½-inch
     cubes
½   cup chopped onion
2   garlic cloves, minced
1   tablespoon cooking oil
¾   cup beef broth
1   tablespoon finely chopped
     jalapeño pepper
1   teaspoon dried oregano,
     crushed
½   teaspoon salt
¼   teaspoon ground cumin
¼   teaspoon pepper
1   medium potato, peeled and
     cut in ½-inch cubes
     (1 cup)

8   10-inch flour tortillas
     (see recipe, page 204, *or*
     use purchased)
     Cooking oil for frying
1   cup shredded cheddar
     cheese *or* Monterey Jack
     cheese (4 ounces)
     (optional)
     Avocado Salsa (see recipe,
     page 207) *or* purchased
     salsa (optional)

In a small bowl, cover dried tomato halves with hot water. Let stand for 10 minutes or till softened; drain. Snip and set aside.

For filling, in a large saucepan brown meat, onion, and garlic in hot oil. Drain well. Add tomato, broth, jalapeño pepper, oregano, salt, cumin, and pepper. Bring to boiling. Reduce heat. Cover and simmer for 30 minutes. Stir in potatoes; simmer about 30 minutes or till meat and potatoes are tender. If necessary, add additional broth during cooking. Mixture should be slightly moist but not soupy.

Meanwhile, stack tortillas and wrap tightly in foil. Heat in a 350° oven for 10 minutes to soften. Spoon about *¼ cup* filling in center of each tortilla. Fold one edge over filling just till filling is covered. Fold in the 2 opposite sides, then the remaining side.

Arizona

TACO SALAD

Salads are not a traditional course in Mexican cooking. This contemporary southwestern buffet favorite is an Anglo invention that incorporates all the components of a tortilla-based main dish: meat, beans, vegetables, salsa, and fried tortillas.

1   pound ground beef *or*
     ground raw turkey
3   cloves garlic, minced
1   16-ounce can dark red
     kidney beans
1   8-ounce jar taco sauce
1   tablespoon chili powder
2   cups chopped tomatoes
2   cups shredded cheddar
     cheese (8 ounces)
1   cup chopped green pepper
½   cup sliced pitted ripe olives
¼   cup sliced green onion
     Lettuce leaves
1   medium avocado, seeded,
     peeled, and sliced
     (optional)
     Lime wedges (optional)
     Dairy sour cream (optional)
     Salsa *or* taco sauce
     (optional)

Texas Chili, left, and Blue Cornmeal Muffins (see recipe, page 202)

For meat mixture, in a large skillet cook beef or turkey and garlic till meat is no longer pink. Drain off fat. Stir in *undrained* kidney beans, taco sauce, and chili powder. Bring to boiling; reduce heat. Cover and simmer for 10 minutes.

Meanwhile, in a large mixing bowl combine tomatoes, cheddar cheese, green pepper, olives, and green onion; add hot meat mixture. Toss lightly to mix. Line 6 salad plates with lettuce leaves. Divide salad mixture among plates. If desired, garnish with avocado slices and, lime wedges, and serve with sour cream and salsa or additional taco sauce. Serves 6.

Nutrition information per serving: 407 calories, 30 g protein, 22 g carbohydrate, 23 g total fat (12 g saturated), 87 mg cholesterol, 800 mg sodium, 737 mg potassium

Texas

TEXAS CHILI

According to Frank Tolbert, who immortalized Texas chili in A Bowl of Red, *the authentic, original recipe included beef, hot peppers, oregano, cumin, and garlic—no beans. Beans are now considered acceptable, but "chili heads" are a contentious bunch. Their current controversy: beans in the chili or served alongside?*

1½   **pounds boneless beef top round steak**
1   **tablespoon cooking oil**
1   **cup chopped onion**
2   **cloves garlic, minced**
2   **16-ounce cans tomatoes, cut up**
1   **cup beef broth**
1   **4-ounce can diced green chilies *or* ⅓ cup chopped, pickled jalapeño peppers**
2   **tablespoons chili powder**
1   **tablespoon brown sugar**
2   **teaspoons dried oregano, crushed**
1   **teaspoon ground cumin**
½   **teaspoon salt**
3   **cups hot cooked rice *or* pinto beans**

Dairy sour cream *or* shredded cheddar cheese (optional)

Partially freeze meat. Thinly slice across the grain into bite-size strips or cut into ½-inch cubes. In a Dutch oven brown *half* of the meat in hot oil. Remove from pan. Brown remaining meat with the onion and garlic, adding more oil, if necessary. Drain off fat. Return all meat, onion, and garlic to pan.

Stir in the *undrained* tomatoes, the beef broth, green chili peppers or jalapeño peppers, chili powder, brown sugar, oregano, cumin, and salt. Bring mixture to boiling; reduce heat. Cover and simmer for 1 hour or till meat is tender.

Serve with rice or beans. If desired, top with sour cream or cheddar cheese. Makes 6 servings.

Nutrition information per serving: 366 calories, 30 g protein, 42 g carbohydrate, 8 g total fat (2 g saturated), 59 mg cholesterol, 856 mg sodium, 865 mg potassium

Black Bean and Chayote Burritos, left, Shredded Beef Burrito, center, and Flour Tortillas (see recipe, page 204)

New Mexico

BLACK BEAN AND CHAYOTE BURRITOS

Beans and squash, along with corn, were the three staple foods of southwestern Native Americans. The chayote, or vegetable pear, is in the squash family, but wasn't used by the Indians until it was introduced from Mexico. Burrito means "little donkey."

4 medium skinless, boneless chicken breast halves (12 ounces total)
1 cup chicken broth *or* water
1 bay leaf
½ teaspoon ground cumin
8 10-inch flour tortillas (see recipe, page 204, *or* use purchased)

½ cup chopped onion
1 tablespoon cooking oil
1 15-ounce can black beans *or* pinto beans, rinsed and drained
1 or 2 jalapeño peppers *or* serrano peppers, seeded and finely chopped, *or* one 4-ounce can diced green chilies, drained
1 ripe medium chayote squash, thinly sliced, *or* 2 oranges, peeled and sectioned
1 cup shredded Monterey Jack cheese *or* mozzarella cheese (4 ounces)
¼ cup snipped fresh cilantro *or* parsley
1 cup salsa (optional)

In a medium skillet place chicken breasts, chicken broth or water, bay leaf, and cumin. Bring to boiling; reduce heat. Simmer, covered, for 15 to 20 minutes or till chicken is tender and no longer pink. Drain, reserving broth. Let chicken stand till cool. Use a fork to pull chicken apart into long, thin shreds. Set aside. Remove bay leaf from broth.

Stack tortillas and wrap tightly in foil. Heat in a 350° oven for 10 minutes to soften.

Meanwhile, in a large skillet cook the chopped onion in hot oil till tender but not brown. Carefully add beans; jalapeño, serrano, or green chilies; and ¼ *cup* of the reserved broth. With a wooden spoon or potato masher, mash beans in skillet (mixture should be thick). Remove from heat.

Spread *2 to 3 tablespoons* of the bean mixture down the middle of each tortilla. Top each with some of the shredded chicken, chayote or orange, cheese, and cilantro or parsley. Fold the sides of each tortilla over the filling, overlapping the sides and forming a cone shape. Fasten each burrito with a wooden toothpick.

Arrange the burritos on a baking sheet. Cover lightly with foil. Bake in a 350° oven for 15 to 20 minutes or till the burritos are heated through. If desired, serve with salsa and garnish with cherry tomatoes and thyme sprigs. Makes 4 to 6 servings.

Nutrition information per serving: 723 calories, 44 g protein, 82 g carbohydrate, 23 g total fat (8 g saturated), 80 mg cholesterol, 909 mg sodium, 775 mg potassium

Texas

SHREDDED BEEF BURRITO

This burrito filling has all the flavors of a typical Texas chili: oregano, cumin, garlic, chili powder, and beef. The tortilla is another link to the Lone Star State.

1 **pound boneless beef chuck, 1 inch thick**
1 **4-ounce can diced green chilies**
¼ **cup salsa**
¼ **cup chopped onion**
2 **cloves garlic, minced**
½ **teaspoon chili powder**
½ **teaspoon dried oregano, crushed**
½ **teaspoon ground cumin**
¼ **teaspoon salt**
¼ **teaspoon crushed red pepper**
8 **7-inch flour tortillas (see recipe, page 204, *or* use purchased)**

Chicken with Peppers and Cilantro Pesto

1 **medium green *or* red sweet pepper, cut into thin strips (optional)**
½ **cup chopped tomato (optional)**
1 **6-ounce container frozen avocado dip, thawed, *or* ½ cup dairy sour cream (optional)**

Trim fat from meat. Cut meat into 1-inch cubes. In a medium saucepan combine beef, *undrained* chilies, salsa, onion, garlic, chili powder, oregano, cumin, salt, and red pepper. Add ½ cup *water.* Bring to boiling; reduce heat. Cover and simmer about 2 hours or till meat is very tender, stirring occasionally to break cubes of meat into shreds. Cook, uncovered, for 15 to 20 minutes or till excess liquid is evaporated and mixture is desired consistency.

Stack tortillas and wrap tightly in foil. Heat in a 350° oven for 10 minutes to soften.

For serving, immediately fill each warm tortilla with about *⅓ cup* beef mixture. If desired, top with pepper strips, chopped tomato, and avocado dip or sour cream. Fold in bottom and sides. Makes 4 servings.

Note: This meat mixture can be used for tacos, chimichangas, or on a hamburger bun.

Nutrition information per serving: 428 calories, 31 g protein, 39 g carbohydrate, 16 g total fat (6 g saturated), 71 mg cholesterol, 796 mg sodium, 552 mg potassium

Arizona

CHICKEN WITH PEPPERS AND CILANTRO PESTO

Before the advent of canned foods, some of the pepper crop was preserved to ensure a supply during the barren southwestern winter. So they could be peeled and frozen, peppers were roasted indoors on a stove-top comal (griddle) or outdoors in a horno, (a beehive-shaped mud oven).

1 **large red sweet pepper**
4 **large skinless, boneless chicken breast halves (1 pound total)**
¼ **cup Cilantro Pesto (see recipe, page 207)**
2 **teaspoons cooking oil**
¼ **teaspoon paprika**
½ **cup dairy sour cream (optional)**

To roast the pepper, halve it; remove stem, seeds, and membranes. Place the pepper halves, cut sides down, on a foil-lined baking sheet. Bake in a 425° oven 20 to 25 minutes or till skin is bubbly and browned. Place pepper in a new brown paper bag. Seal; let stand 20 to 30 minutes or till cool. Peel skin from pepper. Cut lengthwise into ½-inch strips. Set aside.

Place each chicken breast half between 2 pieces of clear plastic wrap. Pound lightly to ¼-inch thickness. Remove plastic wrap. Spread *1 tablespoon* Cilantro Pesto on boned side of each breast half. Place several pepper strips crosswise on one end of each breast half. Roll up chicken, jelly-roll style, starting from end near pepper strips. Secure rolls with wooden toothpicks.

Place chicken rolls in a shallow baking dish or pan. Brush lightly with oil; sprinkle with paprika. Bake in a 375° oven for 25 to 30 minutes or till no longer pink. If desired, serve with sour cream and additional Cilantro Pesto. Serves 4.

Nutrition information per serving: 245 calories, 28 g protein, 3 g carbohydrate, 13 g total fat (1 g saturated), 74 mg cholesterol, 143 mg sodium, 334 mg potassium

Posole, and Piñon Pine Muffins

New Mexico

POSOLE

Corn is a sacred food to Native Americans. They've developed hundreds of uses for it, including this stew of meat, chili, and the dried, hulled kernels known as hominy. It's a dish for celebrations, served on feast days and on New Year's Day for good luck.

1½	pounds lean, boneless pork, cut into 1-inch cubes
2	tablespoons cooking oil
1	medium onion, chopped (½ cup)
2	cloves garlic, minced
4	cups chicken broth
1½	teaspoons dried oregano, crushed
¼	teaspoon ground cumin
2	14½-ounce cans hominy, drained
1	4-ounce can chopped green chilies
	Sliced radishes (optional)
	Shredded cabbage (optional)
	Sliced green onion (optional)

In a large saucepan or Dutch oven brown *half* of the pork cubes in hot oil; remove meat and set aside. Brown the remaining meat with the onion and garlic; cook till meat is brown. Return all of the meat to saucepan. Stir in the chicken broth, oregano, and cumin. Bring to boiling; reduce heat. Cover and simmer for 40 minutes.

Stir in the hominy and green chilies. Cover and simmer for 30 minutes more. Skim off fat. Ladle into bowls. If desired, serve with sliced radishes, shredded cabbage, and sliced green onion. Makes 6 to 8 servings.

Nutrition information per serving: 306 calories, 31 g protein, 18 g carbohydrate, 12 g total fat (3 g saturated), 66 mg cholesterol, 798 mg sodium, 540 mg potassium

New Mexico

PIÑON PINE MUFFINS

Southwestern Native Americans have been eating pine nuts for centuries. They roast them as a snack, use them whole in cooking, or grind them into meal for baking.

1¼	cups all-purpose flour
⅓	cup whole wheat flour
2	tablespoons sugar
2	teaspoons baking powder
¼	teaspoon salt
1	beaten egg
¾	cup milk
¼	cup cooking oil
½	cup toasted chopped pine nuts *or* almonds
½	cup shredded Swiss cheese *or* cheddar cheese (2 ounces)
¼	cup sliced green onion

In a large mixing bowl stir together all-purpose flour, whole wheat flour, sugar, baking powder, and salt. Make a well in the center of the flour mixture. In a medium bowl combine egg, milk, and cooking oil. Stir in pine nuts, cheese, and green onion. Add all at once to flour mixture. Stir just till moistened (batter should be lumpy).

Lightly grease muffin cups; fill ¾ full. Bake in a 400° oven about 20 minutes or till golden. Remove from pans; serve warm. Makes 10 to 12 muffins.

Nutrition information per serving: 195 calories, 6 g protein, 19 g carbohydrate, 11 g total fat (2 g saturated), 28 mg cholesterol, 92 mg sodium, 108 mg potassium

New Mexico

BLUE CORNMEAL MUFFINS

Corn was so important to Native Americans in the Southwest that each color was associated with special qualities. In ceremonies, blue corn was the western direction. The color blue was also thought to have medicinal properties. A paste of blue cornmeal was prescribed as a balm for aching joints. (Pictured on page 199)

2	cups all-purpose flour
¾	cup yellow cornmeal
⅔	cup sugar
4	teaspoons baking powder
½	teaspoon salt
¾	cup blue cornmeal
2	beaten eggs
1	8¾-ounce can cream-style corn
¾	cup milk
½	cup oil

Using two mixing bowls, place *1 cup* of the flour in each bowl. In the first bowl, stir in the yellow cornmeal, *⅓ cup* sugar, *2 teaspoons* baking powder, and *¼ teaspoon* salt. In the second bowl, stir in the blue cornmeal, the remaining sugar, remaining baking powder, and remaining salt.

Combine eggs, corn, milk, and oil; mix well. Divide in half. Stir *half* of the liquid mixture into each bowl. Stir just till moistened (batter should be lumpy).

Lightly grease muffin cups or line with paper bake cups. Fill muffin cups ⅔ full using half blue cornmeal batter and half yellow cornmeal batter (spoon the batters side by side into the muffin cups). Bake in a 400° oven for 15 to 20 minutes or till golden. Remove from pans; serve warm. Makes about 18 muffins.

Nutrition information per muffin: 199 calories, 4 g protein, 30 g carbohydrate, 7 g total fat (1 g saturated), 24 mg cholesterol, 182 mg sodium, 68 mg potassium

Arizona

NAVAJO FRY BREAD

If you visit a Navajo reservation, you will have the opportunity to try this puffy fried bread. However, other Native Americans besides the Navajo prepare it, so it's also generically referred to as Indian fry bread. Topped with ground beef, shredded lettuce, and the like, it's called an Indian taco.

1½   **cups all-purpose flour**
1   **package active dry yeast**
1   **5-ounce can evaporated milk**
½   **cup sugar**
¼   **cup water**
¼   **cup shortening**
1   **teaspoon salt**
2   **eggs**
2½   **to 3 cups all-purpose flour Cooking oil for frying Powdered sugar**

Navajo Fry Bread

Combine *1½ cups* of the flour and the yeast. In a saucepan heat and stir milk, sugar, water, shortening, and salt till warm (120° to 130°) and shortening almost melts. Add to the flour mixture along with the eggs. Beat with an electric mixer on low speed for 30 seconds, scraping bowl constantly. Beat on high speed for 3 minutes. Stir in as much of the remaining flour as you can.

Turn out onto a lightly floured surface. Knead in enough of the remaining flour to make a moderately stiff dough that is smooth and elastic (6 to 8 minutes total). Shape into a ball. Place in a lightly greased bowl, turn once to grease surface. Cover and refrigerate several hours or overnight. (Dough can be refrigerated up to 3 days and fried as needed, but is best the first day.)

Remove dough from refrigerator; let stand at room temperature for 30 minutes. Punch dough down. Turn out onto a lightly floured surface. Cover and let rest for 10 minutes. Roll dough to ⅛- to ¼-inch thickness. Cut into 3x4-inch rectangles.

Heat cooking oil to 365°. Carefully fry 2 rectangles at a time about 1½ to 2 minutes or till golden, turning once. Drain on paper towels. Sprinkle with powdered sugar while still warm; serve immediately. Makes about 20 rectangles.

Nutrition information per rectangle: 184 calories, 4 g protein, 27 g carbohydrate, 7 g total fat (2 g saturated), 23 mg cholesterol, 122 mg sodium, 57 mg potassium

Texas

TEXAS COLESLAW

Yes, like almost everything on a Texas menu, this salad is hot. It has to be to stand up to true five-alarm barbecue, which it accompanies as a side dish. (Pictured on page 192)

2   **cups finely shredded green cabbage**
2   **cups finely shredded red cabbage**
1   **cup shredded jicama**
½   **cup chopped yellow sweet pepper**
½   **cup chopped green pepper**
½   **cup raisins**
½   **cup dairy sour cream *or* plain yogurt**
½   **cup mayonnaise *or* salad dressing**
1   **tablespoon finely chopped jalapeño pepper**
1   **teaspoon sugar**
½   **teaspoon ground cumin**
¼   **teaspoon salt**
¼   **teaspoon pepper**
½   **of a medium avocado, seeded, peeled, and chopped**

In a large mixing bowl stir together the green cabbage, red cabbage, jicama, yellow pepper, green pepper, and raisins.

For dressing, stir together the sour cream, mayonnaise, jalapeño pepper, sugar, cumin, salt, and pepper. Pour dressing over cabbage mixture; toss to coat. Cover and chill for 1 to 24 hours. Gently stir chopped avocado into coleslaw. Makes 6 servings.

Nutrition information per serving: 296 calories, 3 g protein, 21 g carbohydrate, 24 g total fat (5 g saturated), 19 mg cholesterol, 238 mg sodium, 514 mg potassium

Corn Tortillas

CORN TORTILLAS

While the corn tortilla is considered the sandwich bread of Mexico, in fact southwestern Native Americans were making a similar flat cake when the Spanish explorers arrived.

2   **cups Masa Harina tortilla flour**
1¼   **cups warm water**

In a medium mixing bowl combine tortilla flour and water. Stir mixture together with your hands till dough is firm but moist (if necessary, add more water, 1 tablespoon at a time). Let dough rest for 15 minutes.

Divide dough into 12 equal portions; shape each portion into a ball.

Using a tortilla press or rolling pin, flatten each ball between 2 pieces of waxed paper into a 6-inch circle.

Carefully peel off top sheet of waxed paper. Place tortilla, paper side up, on a medium-hot, ungreased skillet or griddle. As tortilla begins to heat, carefully peel off remaining sheet of waxed paper. Cook, turning occasionally, for 2 to 2½ minutes or till tortilla is dry and light brown (tortilla should still be soft). Wrap tortillas in foil if using immediately.* Makes twelve 6-inch tortillas.

*__Note:__ To freeze tortillas, stack them, alternating each tortilla with 2 layers of waxed paper. Wrap the stack in a moisture- and vaporproof bag, foil, or freezer wrap. Seal tightly and freeze. Thaw completely before using.

__Nutrition information per tortilla:__ 69 calories, 2 g protein, 14 g carbohydrate, 1 g total fat (0 g saturated), 0 mg cholesterol, 1 mg sodium, 56 mg potassium

FLOUR TORTILLAS

In the wheat-growing Mexican state of Sonora, the preference is to make tortillas out of wheat flour rather than ground corn. As Arizona is just over the border to the north, it too is partial to flour. Arizona tortillas tend to be very large, a foot in diameter or even more.
(Pictured on page 200)

2   **cups all-purpose flour**
1   **teaspoon salt**
1   **teaspoon baking powder**
2   **tablespoons shortening *or* lard**
½   **cup warm water**

In a medium mixing bowl combine flour, salt, and baking powder. Cut in shortening or lard till thoroughly combined. Gradually add water and toss together till dough can be gathered into a ball (if necessary, add more water, 1 tablespoon at a time). Knead dough 15 to 20 times. Let dough rest 15 minutes.

For 8-inch tortillas, divide dough into 12 equal portions; shape each portion into a ball. (For 10-inch tortillas, divide dough into 8 equal portions; shape each into a ball.)

On a lightly floured surface, use a rolling pin to flatten each ball into an 8-inch (or 10-inch) circle. Stack rolled-out tortillas between pieces of waxed paper.*

Carefully peel off top sheet of waxed paper. Place tortilla, paper side up, on a medium-hot, ungreased skillet or griddle. As tortilla begins to heat, carefully peel off remaining sheet of waxed paper. Cook tortilla about 30 seconds or till puffy. Turn and cook about 30 seconds more or till edges curl up slightly. Wrap tortillas in foil if using immediately.* Makes twelve 8-inch or eight 10-inch tortillas.

*__Note:__ To freeze tortillas, stack them, alternating each tortilla with 2 layers of waxed paper. Wrap the stack in a moisture- and vaporproof bag, foil, or freezer wrap. Seal tightly and freeze. Thaw completely before using.

__Nutrition information per 8-inch tortilla:__ 95 calories, 2 g protein, 16 g carbohydrate, 2 g total fat (0 g saturated), 0 mg cholesterol, 205 mg sodium, 22 mg potassium

Blue Cornmeal Pancakes with Fresh Berries

BLUE CORNMEAL PANCAKES WITH FRESH BERRIES

The Hopis made pancakes out of blue cornmeal on sandstone slabs, which they heated from below. To retain the revered blue color, the corn received a special alkali treatment.

1	cup all-purpose flour
⅓	cup blue cornmeal *or* yellow cornmeal
2	tablespoons sugar
1½	teaspoons baking powder
½	teaspoon baking soda
¼	teaspoon salt
1	beaten egg
1⅓	cups buttermilk
2	tablespoons cooking oil
¾	cup fresh blueberries
	Margarine *or* butter
	Maple syrup *or* maple-flavored syrup
	Fresh raspberries (optional)

In a mixing bowl stir together flour, cornmeal, sugar, baking powder, baking soda, and salt. In another bowl combine egg, buttermilk, and oil. Add to flour mixture all at once. Stir mixture just till blended but still lumpy. Fold in blueberries.

Pour about ¼ *cup* of the batter onto a hot, lightly greased griddle or heavy skillet. Cook till pancakes are golden brown, turning to cook second side when pancakes have bubbly surfaces and slightly dry edges. Serve warm with margarine and syrup and, if desired, fresh raspberries. Makes 12 pancakes.

Nutrition information per pancake: 189 calories, 3 g protein, 29 g carbohydrate, 7 g total fat (1 g saturated), 19 mg cholesterol, 143 mg sodium, 109 mg potassium

REFRIED BEANS

Along with the chili pepper, the speckled pinto bean is New Mexico's number one vegetable by action of the state legislature. In Spanish, beans are frijoles. *When cooked beans are pan-fried, then mashed, they are the famous* frijoles refritos. *(Pictured on page 195)*

1	pound dry pinto beans
2	tablespoons bacon drippings *or* cooking oil
1½	teaspoons salt
2	cloves garlic, minced

In a Dutch oven combine pinto beans and 6 cups *water.* Bring to boiling; reduce heat. Simmer for 2 minutes; remove from heat. Cover and let stand for 1 hour. (*Or,* soak beans in water overnight in a covered pan.) Drain beans.

In the same Dutch oven combine drained beans and 4 cups additional *water.* Bring to boiling. Cover and simmer for 2 hours or till beans are very tender. *Do not drain.*

Add bacon drippings or cooking oil, salt, and garlic. Using a potato masher, mash bean mixture completely. Cook, uncovered, for 10 to 15 minutes or till thick, stirring often. Makes 8 to 10 servings.

Nutrition information per serving: 208 calories, 10 g protein, 33 g carbohydrate, 4 g total fat (2 g saturated), 4 mg cholesterol, 421 mg sodium, 603 mg potassium

Spicy Corn Soufflé, left, Layered Black Bean Salad, center, and Pico de Gallo Salsa

Arizona

SPICY CORN SOUFFLÉ

Southerners who moved west brought their regional dishes with them. This corn soufflé is actually like a traditional spoon bread fired up with local seasonings like cumin, oregano, cinnamon, and hot pepper.

¼   **cup chopped onion**
¼   **cup finely chopped red *or* green sweet pepper**
1   **clove garlic, minced**
3   **tablespoons margarine *or* butter**
3   **tablespoons all-purpose flour**
½   **teaspoon oregano, crushed**
¼   **teaspoon ground cumin**
¼   **teaspoon ground cinnamon**
⅛   **teaspoon ground red pepper**
⅛   **teaspoon ground coriander**
¼   **teaspoon salt**
½   **cup milk**
1   **cup shredded cheddar cheese (4 ounces)**
1   **8¾-ounce can cream-style corn**
3   **egg yolks**
3   **egg whites**

In a medium saucepan cook onion, red or green pepper, and garlic in margarine till tender. Stir in flour, oregano, spices, and salt. Add milk all at once. Cook and stir till thickened and bubbly. Remove from heat. Add cheese and stir till melted. Stir in corn. In a medium bowl beat egg yolks with a fork till combined. Gradually add corn mixture, stirring constantly. Set aside.

In a large bowl beat egg whites till stiff peaks form (tips stand straight). Gently fold about *1 cup* of the beaten egg whites into the corn mixture to lighten it. Gradually pour corn mixture over remaining beaten egg whites, folding to combine. Pour into an ungreased 1½-quart soufflé dish. Bake in a 350° oven about 40 minutes or till a knife inserted near center comes out clean. Serve immediately. Makes 4 servings.

Nutrition information per serving: *335 calories, 15 g protein, 20 g carbohydrate, 23 g total fat (9 g saturated), 192 mg cholesterol, 616 mg sodium, 249 mg potassium*

Texas

LAYERED BLACK BEAN SALAD

While black beans are more popular in southern Mexico than in the American Southwest, they do appear in many of the region's dishes, including soups and salads.

2½   **cups shredded lettuce**
1   **15-ounce can black beans, rinsed and drained**
1   **to 2 tablespoons snipped fresh cilantro**
½   **cup chopped red onion**
½   **cup chopped green pepper**
½   **cup chopped red sweet pepper**
2   **to 4 tablespoons chopped fresh *or* canned green chilies**
¾   **cup dairy sour cream**
1   **tablespoon lime juice**
1   **clove garlic, minced**
¼   **teaspoon salt**
¾   **cup chopped tomato**
1   **small avocado, seeded, peeled, and chopped**

In a deep 2-quart bowl, place *1½ cups* of the lettuce. Layer black beans, cilantro, onion, green pepper, red pepper, and green chilies. Top with remaining lettuce.

For dressing, stir together sour cream, lime juice, garlic, and salt. Spread dressing over top of salad, sealing to edge of bowl. Cover and chill for 2 to 24 hours.

Before serving, sprinkle chopped tomato and chopped avocado over salad. Toss to coat the vegetables. Makes 4 to 6 servings.

Nutrition information per serving: 277 calories, 10 g protein, 28 g carbohydrate, 16 g total fat (7 g saturated), 19 mg cholesterol, 218 mg sodium, 759 mg potassium

Texas

PICO DE GALLO SALSA

It's not clear why this salsa, or the well-known jicama salad of the same name, is called "rooster's beak." Perhaps because a rooster pecks his food into little pieces, the size of ingredients used for both.

2   medium tomatoes, peeled and finely chopped
2   tablespoons finely chopped onion
2   tablespoons snipped fresh cilantro *or* parsley
1   serrano pepper, finely chopped
     Dash sugar

In a medium mixing bowl stir together the chopped tomatoes, onion, cilantro or parsley, serrano pepper, and sugar. Cover and chill for several hours or overnight, stirring occasionally.

Store, tightly covered, in the refrigerator up to 3 days. Use as a dip for chips or as a topping for main dishes. Makes 1¼ cups.

Nutrition information per tablespoon: 4 calories, 0 g protein, 1 g carbohydrate, 0 g total fat (0 g saturated), 0 mg cholesterol, 1 mg sodium, 33 mg potassium

Caramel Flan with Mangoes (see recipe, page 208)

Texas

CILANTRO PESTO

The musky, smoky character of cilantro can be an acquired taste for palates unfamiliar with it. In the Southwest, though, it's as common an ingredient as parsley is everywhere else. (Pictured on page 201)

1½   cups firmly packed, fresh cilantro leaves
½   cup firmly packed parsley sprigs with stems removed
½   cup grated Parmesan cheese *or* asiago cheese
¼   cup pine nuts *or* slivered almonds
2   cloves garlic, quartered
¼   teaspoon salt
¼   cup olive oil *or* cooking oil

In a blender container or food processor bowl combine cilantro, parsley, Parmesan or asiago cheese, pine nuts or almonds, garlic, and salt. Cover and blend or process with several on-off turns till a paste forms, stopping the machine several times and scraping the sides. With the machine running, gradually add the oil and blend or process to the consistency of soft butter.

Divide into 4 portions (about ¼ cup each) and place in small airtight containers. Refrigerate for 1 or 2 days or freeze up to 1 month. Bring to room temperature for serving. Use as directed in recipe. Makes about 1 cup.

Nutrition information per tablespoon: 55 calories, 2 g protein, 1 g carbohydrate, 5 g total fat (1 g saturated), 2 mg cholesterol, 93 mg sodium, 34 mg potassium

Arizona

AVOCADO SALSA

Avocados were served by Montezuma to the Spanish explorers. They were so plentiful that an old name for them was poor man's butter. This is like a chunky guacamole. (Pictured on page 198)

½   cup chopped avocado
1   tablespoon lime juice
1   teaspoon olive oil
¼   teaspoon salt
⅛   teaspoon pepper
½   cup chopped, peeled, and seeded tomato
⅓   cup finely chopped red onion
2   to 3 tablespoons finely chopped fresh *or* pickled jalapeño peppers
2   tablespoons finely chopped fresh cilantro

In a mixing bowl combine avocado and lime juice; toss to coat well. Stir in oil, salt, and pepper. Add tomato, onion, jalapeño pepper, and cilantro. Mix well.

Cover and chill for 2 to 24 hours before serving. Serve with tortilla chips or as a meat accompaniment. Makes 6 servings.

Nutrition information per serving: 48 calories, 1 g protein, 3 g carbohydrate, 4 g total fat (1 g saturated), 0 mg cholesterol, 134 mg sodium, 178 mg potassium

Texas | *New Mexico* | *New Mexico*

CARAMEL FLAN WITH MANGOES

In New Mexico and Texas, it isn't unusual to see this Spanish baked custard made with sweetened condensed milk rather than regular milk and eggs. There was a time when these dairy foods were hard to come by in rural areas. Even though they are now widely available, the recipe has yet to catch up. (Pictured on page 207)

⅓ cup sugar
3   beaten eggs
1½ cups milk
⅓   cup sugar
1   teaspoon vanilla
    Fresh mango slices *or* other
    fresh fruit

In a heavy, medium skillet place ⅓ cup sugar. Cook over medium-high heat till sugar begins to melt *(do not stir)*; shake skillet occasionally to heat sugar evenly. Reduce heat to low and cook till sugar is melted and golden brown; stir as necessary after sugar begins to melt. Pour caramelized sugar into an 8-inch quiche dish. Tilt dish to coat bottom. Let stand for 10 minutes.

Combine eggs, milk, ⅓ cup sugar, and vanilla. Beat till well combined. Place quiche dish in a 13x9x2-inch baking pan on the oven rack. Pour egg mixture into prepared quiche dish. Pour boiling water into the baking pan around quiche dish to a depth of ¾ inch. Bake in a 325° oven for 20 to 25 minutes or till a knife inserted near the center comes out clean.

Serve warm or chilled. Loosen edge of dish with a spatula or knife, slipping point of spatula down sides to let air in. Invert onto a serving plate. Garnish with mango slices. Makes 6 servings.

Nutrition information per serving: *171 calories, 5 g protein, 30 g carbohydrate, 4 g total fat (2 g saturated), 111 mg cholesterol, 63 mg sodium, 137 mg potassium*

BIZCOCHITOS

When children return from church on Christmas day in New Mexico, these anise-flavored sugar cookies, shaped like fleurs-de-lis (stylized irises), are given to them as a special holiday treat.

1   cup margarine *or* butter
2¼   cup all-purpose flour
1   teaspoon anise seed, finely
     crushed, *or* several drops
     anise flavoring
1   egg
1   cup sugar
1   tablespoon brandy *or* milk
1   teaspoon baking powder
1   teaspoon vanilla
¼   teaspoon salt
2   tablespoons sugar
1   teaspoon ground cinnamon
     (optional)

Beat margarine or butter with an electric mixer on high speed for 30 seconds. Add about *half* of the flour, the aniseed, egg, sugar, brandy or milk, baking powder, vanilla, and salt. Beat till thoroughly combined. Beat in remaining flour. Divide dough in half. Cover and chill for 3 hours.

On a lightly floured surface, roll half of the dough at a time to ⅛-inch thickness. Cut with a fleur-de-lis-shape cookie cutter (or other desired shape). Place on an ungreased cookie sheet.

If desired, combine the 2 tablespoons sugar with the cinnamon. Sprinkle sugar or sugar-cinnamon mixture lightly onto cookies. Bake in a 375° oven for 6 to 8 minutes or till edges are firm and bottoms are very lightly browned. Cool cookies on a wire rack. Makes 36 to 48 cookies.

Nutrition information per cookie: *101 calories, 1 g protein, 12 g carbohydrate, 5 g total fat (1 g saturated), 6 mg cholesterol, 68 mg sodium, 12 mg potassium*

MEXICAN HOT CHOCOLATE

The Aztecs thought that chocolate was an aphrodisiac. Viewed as very macho, it was reserved for men of the noble classes. Happily, hot chocolate is now an equal opportunity beverage in Mexico and throughout the Southwest.

6   cups milk
½   cup sugar
3   squares (3 ounces)
     unsweetened chocolate,
     chopped
1   teaspoon ground cinnamon
2   beaten eggs
2   teaspoons vanilla
     Whipped cream

In a large saucepan combine *1 cup* of the milk, the sugar, chocolate, and cinnamon. Cook and stir over medium-low heat till chocolate is melted. Gradually stir in remaining milk. Cook and stir till milk is very hot, almost boiling. *Do not boil.*

Gradually stir *1 cup* of the hot milk mixture into eggs, then transfer entire mixture to saucepan. Cook and stir for 2 minutes over low heat. Remove from heat and stir in vanilla. Beat with a rotary beater till very frothy.

Pour hot chocolate into mugs and dollop with whipped cream. Makes six 8-ounce servings.

Nutrition information per serving: *286 calories, 12 g protein, 33 g carbohydrate, 14 g total fat (8 g saturated), 89 mg cholesterol, 144 mg sodium, 496 mg potassium*

Mexican Hot Chocolate and Bizcochitos

Buñuelos

Nutrition information per buñuelos: 112 calories, 2 g protein, 12 g carbohydrate, 6 g total fat (1 g saturated), 18 mg cholesterol, 67 mg sodium, 18 mg potassium

Arizona

SANGRITA

The proper way to enjoy this southwestern Bloody Mary is as follows: alternate sips of Sangrita and tequila, then bite a lime wedge to cleanse the palate. The drink is aptly named, given its deep red color —from the Spanish word for blood. (Pictured on page 188)

6　medium tomatoes
　　(about 2 pounds), peeled,
　　seeded, and coarsely
　　cut up, *or* one 28-ounce
　　can tomatoes
⅓　cup lime juice
1　slice of a medium onion
1　jalapeño pepper, seeded
　　and cut up
1　teaspoon sugar
　　Several dashes bottled
　　hot pepper sauce
1　cup orange juice
⅓　cup tequila
　　Ice cubes
　　Celery stalks (optional)
　　Lime wedges (optional)

In a blender container place fresh tomatoes or *undrained* canned tomatoes, lime juice, onion, jalapeño pepper, sugar, and hot pepper sauce. Cover and blend till smooth.

Strain mixture through a sieve lined with cheesecloth. Transfer to a serving pitcher. Stir in orange juice and tequila. Serve over ice cubes. If desired, garnish with celery stalks and lime wedges. Makes seven to nine 4-ounce servings.

Nutrition information per serving: 69 calories, 1 g protein, 10 g carbohydrate, 0 g total fat (0 g saturated), 0 mg cholesterol, 12 mg sodium, 324 mg potassium

New Mexico

BUÑUELOS

These fritters belong to the greater family of southwestern breads that include tortillas, Indian fry bread, and sopapillas (deep-fried dough "pillows"). Along with cups of steaming hot chocolate, they are a winter favorite, particularly on Christmas Eve when they are served dipped in a wine syrup.

2　cups all-purpose flour
1　teaspoon baking powder
½　teaspoon salt
¼　teaspoon cream of tartar
2　tablespoons shortening
2　beaten eggs
⅓　cup milk
　　Cooking oil for frying
　　Sugar, Cinnamon Sugar, *or*
　　Cinnamon-Sugar Syrup

In a mixing bowl stir together flour, baking powder, salt, and cream of tartar. Cut in shortening till thoroughly combined. Make a well in the center of the flour mixture.

In a small mixing bowl combine eggs and milk. Add to flour mixture all at once. Stir just till dough clings together.

On a lightly floured surface knead dough about 2 minutes or till smooth. Divide dough into 24 equal portions; shape each portion into a ball. Cover dough and let rest for 15 to 20 minutes.

In a heavy 10-inch skillet heat ¾ inch oil to 375°. Meanwhile, on a lightly floured surface, roll each ball into a 4-inch circle.

Fry 1 circle at a time in hot oil for 1 to 1½ minutes on each side or till golden. Drain on paper towels. Sprinkle with sugar or Cinnamon Sugar, or drizzle with Cinnamon-Sugar Syrup. Make and serve the same day. Makes 24 buñuelos.

Cinnamon Sugar: In a mixing bowl stir together ½ cup *sugar* and 1 teaspoon ground *cinnamon.*

Cinnamon-Sugar Syrup: In a small saucepan combine ½ cup *sugar,* ¼ cup packed *brown sugar,* ¼ cup *water,* 1 tablespoon *corn syrup,* and 3 inches *stick cinnamon* or dash ground *cinnamon.* Bring to boiling. Reduce heat and boil gently, with-

Tortilla Torte

New Mexico

TORTILLA TORTE

In New Mexico, enchiladas are stacked like a torte, with filling in between each layer, rather than filled and rolled. While this recipe is new, the procedure is classic.

1 **12-ounce package (2 cups) semisweet chocolate pieces**

2 **8-ounce cartons dairy sour cream**

10 **8-inch flour tortillas (see recipe, page 204, *or* use purchased)**

½ **cup dairy sour cream**

2 **tablespoons powdered sugar**

In a medium saucepan melt chocolate over low heat, stirring constantly. Stir in the 2 cartons sour cream. Remove from heat; cool.

Place 1 tortilla on a serving plate. Spread a scant *⅓ cup* of the chocolate mixture atop. Repeat with remaining tortillas and chocolate mixture. Cover and chill for several hours or overnight.

Before serving, in a small mixing bowl stir together the ½ cup sour cream and the powdered sugar. Garnish torte with sour cream mixture. Makes 8 to 10 servings.

***Nutrition information per serving:** 505 calories, 8 g protein, 56 g carbohydrate, 31 g total fat (17 g saturated), 31 mg cholesterol, 254 mg sodium, 316 mg potassium*

211

The West

The discovery and settlement of the American West is the stuff of myth and legend. Beyond the vast herds of roaming buffalo on the eastern plains of Wyoming and Montana, travelers were awed by the mighty Rocky Mountains sprawling south through Colorado to New Mexico. The reward for crossing those perilous cliffs was the arid desserts of southern Utah, Nevada, and California. It was only the addiction to wide-open spaces and the lure of gold that drew men irresistibly beyond them.

The cooking of the earliest settlers was the rough-and-ready kind. What wasn't roasted directly on an open fire was cooked in large cast-iron Dutch ovens, used for both slow-cooked stews and sourdough breads. Cowboys responded to the call of "come and git it," eating whatever emerged from the back of the chuck wagon.

Among the earliest explorers of the wild and woolly west were Meriwether Lewis and William Clark, who arrived in the northern Rockies in 1805 at the behest of President Thomas Jefferson just after the acquisition of this territory as part of the Louisiana Purchase. For almost two years, these intrepid men lived off the land, surviving mostly on the wild game they saw in abundance—deer, buffalo, elk, bear, antelope, and fowl. Sacajawea, their Native American guide, also introduced Lewis and Clark to the wild roots, tubers, greens, and berries gathered and prepared by the Shoshone, Crow, Cheyenne, and other Indian tribes of the region.

When Lewis and Clark reported that beavers were to be found in abundance in the Rocky Mountains, fur trappers stampeded the area. Indeed, around mid-century the legendary Kit Carson is said to have stood on a ridge that overlooked Montana's Gallatin Valley and proclaimed: "Boys, this is the country I have been looking for, and I'll assure you if we can get in there and are not molested [by the natives], we can catch beaver by the hundred."[1] Such enthusiasm had a sad payoff, for within a few decades both buffalo and beaver were on the way to becoming extinct.

Beaver trappers were soon joined by gold prospectors in 1849 and then by cattle and sheep ranchers in the final decades of the century. The settlers were a diverse group, including the Chinese, who played a significant role in building the transcontinental railroad; the English; Scandinavians; Italians, who were drawn to mining; and the French and Spanish Basques, who developed a fine reputation as sheepherders.

Towns and eateries sprang up to meet the needs of these new settlers, but this sprawling and mountainous region never developed any single regional cuisine. The most

Previous pages: Pioneers trekking west had to overcome enormous physical obstacles like high-altitude mountain passes and little or no available water. The uppermost peaks of the San Juan Mountains in Colorado's Uncompahgre National Forest soar to 13,000 feet. Above: Food was scarce at first in the western wilderness. With the completion of the railroad, ingredients like flour for this woodsman's flapjacks became more available.

authentic meals are still likely to be the simplest: an outdoor barbecue featuring grilled, just-caught Rocky Mountain trout or—for the more adventurous—a stew containing Rocky Mountain oysters (a euphemism for lamb testicles). Accompaniments might be some crusty sourdough bread and a potato salad made of Idaho Russets.

Cook's Library: Early Montana Recipes

Women traveling across country in covered wagons rarely had time to write down their recipes, but once settled many kept a record of favorite dishes. In 1978, the Bridger Canyon Women's Club did a fine job of collecting local recipes of the Bozeman, Montana, area by interviewing local Native Americans and old-timers, and by scouring old newspapers.[2]

In this homespun and fascinating volume, Joy Yellowtail Toineeta, a member of the Crow tribe, describes how before the days of granulated sugar, her forefathers gathered natural sweeteners such as honey, box elder and cottonwood sap, and honeysuckle. Dried deer or buffalo meat and berries in the form of pemmican were reliable winter and travelers' fare, and tea was brewed from wild huckleberries, pine needles, and wild rose root.

As a glance at the recipes reveals, during the first half of the nineteenth century, Montana explorers ate camp-fire biscuits, salt pork, pasties, preserved eggs, dandelion salad, oxtail soup, and lots of corn mush. When coffee was unavailable, "and the old grounds which had been carefully saved, had been reboiled many times," they relied on various substitutes, such as dried potatoes, rye flour, toasted bread, dandelion roots, and burnt sugar.

The homesteaders who arrived during the last quarter of the century enjoyed considerably more variety as well as more sophisticated fare. Recipes published in the *Bozeman Avant Courier* during the 1870s include potato soup, dried beef frizzled in cream, chicken cheese, cream cheese, pickled onions, sour milk waffles, chocolate candy, angel food cake, apple pudding, and squash pie.

Right: Both farming and ranching flourished in Gunnison, Colorado, and in other fertile river valleys of the Rocky Mountain states.

The Mormons of Utah

Among the most industrious farmers to settle the West were the Mormons. The Church of Jesus Christ of Latter-day Saints, to which they belonged, had originated in western New York under Joseph Smith. Moving west to find religious freedom, they were constantly persecuted while attempting to set up communities in Ohio, Missouri, and Illinois—where Smith was actually slain.

Under the leadership of Brigham Young, members of the community sought a home far beyond the reach of those who did not wish them well. They selected the desert wilderness of the Salt Lake Valley in Utah, where a small group settled in 1847. Over the next few decades, through determination and hard labor, the thousands of Latter-day Saints who followed helped in the communal effort to dig irrigation canals and clear the fields for planting. Soon the area was producing sufficient vegetables, fruits, and beef to provide not only for their own needs, but for the needs of travelers passing through on the way to California.

Since the Mormon Church attracted members from all parts of Europe and beyond, its kitchens reflect no single style of immigrant cooking. However, what all Mormon homes shared was a strong sense of independence from the outside world. Theirs has always been a frugal kitchen, typical of all pioneers who realize that the waste-not, want-not approach to cooking is the only one that makes sense.

As might be expected, Mormon cooks became very skilled at food preservation, whether it was drying tomatoes or canning fish, pork, peaches, or applesauce. Most every member of the community had a garden and was asked to tithe ten percent of its yield to the church. This excess was distributed to those who could not provide for themselves.

The Basques

One of the most distinctive regional cuisines of the West was introduced by the Basques, who immigrated to this country from the rugged Pyrenees Mountains bordering Spain and France. An

Brigham Young and his band of Mormons faced indescribable hardship as they journeyed across prairies and plains toward their goal, the Salt Lake Valley. They finally founded Salt Lake City on July 24, 1847. Majestic Wellsville Mountains (left) reflect at sunset into Logan River pools in northern Utah.

intense pride plus a history of cultural isolation made the Basques ideally suited to solitude, and they were quite naturally drawn to the lonely life of the sheepherder on vast arid plateaus of Nevada and Idaho (and to a lesser extent California and Colorado).

One of the most ancient ethnic groups in Europe, the Basques have preserved not only their unique language but their unique style of cookery. Basque men, in particular, have a passion for both cooking and eating. Back in Europe, they had traditionally formed culinary clubs where they prepared meals for each other and ate communally whenever possible. Such clubs inspired retired American sheepherders to build boardinghouses in towns that grew up along the edges of the grazing lands. Here, from time to time, the shepherds could gather for the bountiful and flavorful repasts they had known back home.

The precise approach to cooking a Basque meal depends upon whether the cook hails from the Spanish or the French side of the Pyrenees. However, there are a number of ingredients that all Basque cooks use with abandon. There is mutton, of course, and either fresh fish or bacalao (salt cod). Chicken is also popular, as is cured ham and various forms of highly seasoned sausage known as chorizo.

Basque cooks love garlic and olive oil and use these as a starting point for a variety of colorful sauces based on tomatoes and red peppers (red sauce), parsley (green sauce), and squid ink (black sauce).

If you are lucky enough to find yourself dining in a Basque hotel today—a handful still thrive in this part of the world—you are likely to begin the meal with an apertif known as *picon* punch, a potent amalgam of homemade herb wine and brandy mixed with some soda water. You will then be invited to sit down at a long table and dine family style.

A few of the dishes will reveal a bow to your presence in the western United States, perhaps some pasta rather than bread cubes in your garlic soup, perhaps a basket of soft white bread rather than a crusty peasant loaf. But most of the food will be unmistakably Basque. There might be a paella with chicken and chorizo, fried codfish balls, and perhaps a hearty lamb stew heavily laced with garlic and red peppers and dotted with ham. A green salad, potatoes, and vegetables are typical accompaniments, and dessert is often an egg-rich custard similar to the Spanish flan. By all accounts, prices are reasonable and quantities are awesome.

The lonely, rigorous existence of a shepherd was a traditional way of life for immigrant Basques. A young Basque and his dog tend their flock in the eastern Sierra Nevada of California (above). Cattle still graze on the rolling hills of California's inland valleys, like these near Mt. Diablo in the northern part of the state (right).

Idaho Potatoes

*N*o state can be more proud of the fruits of its land than Idaho is of its potatoes. License plates read "Famous Potatoes," and the Idaho Potato Commission has published a two-hundred-page treatise called *Aristocrat in Burlap: A History of the Potato in Idaho.*

Nowadays Idaho produces about one-third of the U.S. fall potato crop. Most of the those potatoes are Russet Burbanks, a variety developed by Luther Burbank in 1872. Burbank was seeking a potato that was not only superior in taste and texture, but also resistant to potato blight and other common tuber diseases.

Originally developed in Maine, the seed ball that was eventually to be called the Russet Burbank was grown in experimental batches in California, Colorado, and Idaho, but the climate and growing conditions of the latter state—warm days and cool nights, rich volcanic soil, and fresh mountain water carried by the Snake River—conspired to create the finest specimen.

Idaho's first potato grower was Henry Spalding, a Presbyterian missionary who settled in the Gem State in 1836 to bring Christianity to the Nez Percé Indians. Recognizing that the buffalo was a rapidly vanishing source of food for the Indians, he sought alternatives and settled upon the potato as a likely possibility.

After several years of hard work, Spalding and the Indians reaped a successful potato harvest in 1838. The earliest Idaho potatoes were sold to pioneers crossing the country in wagon trains. Over the ensuing decades, with more sophisticated irrigation and marketing techniques, the harvest grew dramatically, and before long the American public completely forgot they were getting a Russet Burbank when they ordered an Idaho baked potato.

California Here I Come

As the cable car clangs its way from Union Square toward Fisherman's Wharf, few visitors to San Francisco are likely to recall that this famous town is named for the Franciscan friars who founded twenty-one missions along the coast from San Diego to Sonoma. Beginning with their first mission in 1769, these gentle padres—as local historians often refer to them—built hostelries and churches about a day's journey apart along a road they called El Camino Real (The Royal Road).

In California the padres encountered Indians of the Hupa, Pomo, and Mohave tribes eating an abundant diet that included wild game, greens, seeds, and berries. Their staple food was numerous varieties of acorn, processed to leach out the nut's natural tannic acid. As the padres converted these Native Americans to Christianity, they also introduced them to many new foods.

The Indians were brought into the missions to work the soil and plant the many types of trees that now form the basis of California agriculture—olives, figs, pomegranates, apricots, pistachios, oranges, and lemons. The Fransciscans also introduced wheat, corn, beans, sugar, tomatoes, tomatillos, chocolate, and chili peppers. Since California was then a part of Mexico, wealthy landowners established huge ranches for grazing sheep and cattle—the latter two animals also introduced to the New World from Spain via Mexico.

The food cooked in the Spanish missions reflected a subtle blend of the new food crops and indigenous ingredients. For example, there might be a hearty beef stew spiked with chili peppers and served with a salad of wild greens. Dishes like *chiles rellenos* (stuffed peppers) and enchilladas became known in California at this time. Although the mission movement was brought to an end in 1823, the Spanish influence still lives on, not only in the architecture of southern California, but in restaurant and home kitchens from San Diego to Eureka.

Such an indelible impression was

Magnificent stands of California coastal redwoods offer a glimpse of the wilderness that once existed before the Gold Rush of 1849 changed everything. Below: Chinese came to California by the thousands to work on the transcontinental railroad in the mid-1800s. This nineteenth-century drawing of Chinese immigrants panning gold showed that they were as susceptible to gold fever as any other forty-niner.

left in part because, until the adventurous John Bidwell made it across the Sierra Nevada in 1841, very few newcomers followed the padres into the wilds of California. Indeed, it was not until the termination of the Mexican War in 1848 that California even became a United States territory.

That same fateful year brought another event that would forever change California's history. The discovery of gold in the area around Sacramento set into motion a cross-country human stampede of extraordinary proportions. Immigrants came not only from the East and Midwest, but from all over Europe, swelling the populations of all of the states where gold had been sighted, including Colorado, Montana, Idaho, and Nevada.

The forty-niners arrived to find the crudest imaginable living conditions and the cost of food and drink inflated to absurd proportions. In

those days gold dust was common tender, and the many lucky ones who had found their fortunes in streams "made of gold" did not complain much about the high cost of living.

Hangtown Fry is the only famous dish associated with this rough-and-tumble era. According to leg-

end, a lucky miner swaggered into Hangtown (so named after five men were found hanged there on the same day!), his pockets swelling with gold dust. He demanded the best meal money could buy, and a mountain of fried oysters, eggs, and bacon was set before him. From then on, ordering

San Francisco's Chinatown remains a district of small shops much like it was in this 1900 photograph.

Hangtown Fry became the symbolic way for a miner to celebrate striking it rich.

As the century progressed, streams were "panned out" and gold fever ebbed. Many men turned to farming or became tradesmen in the growing cities. As a major port, San Francisco felt a keen influence of the Chinese who arrived to complete the last leg of the transcontinental railroad. Many of them settled in the city's world-famous Chinatown, where they introduced Americans to specialties like egg foo yung, chop suey, and chow mein. When the railroad was completed in 1869, the Far West opened its doors to a second large wave of immigrants. Many newly settled Italians became fishermen and introduced San Francisco to a fish stew laced with garlic and tomatoes that became known as cioppino. Cioppino is a famous specialty served in restaurants along Fisherman's Wharf to this day.

California Wines

Although there were two varieties of wild grape indigenous to California, by all accounts they made terrible wine. Indeed, the Indians brewed their fermented beverage from wild cherries blended with wild tobacco, powdered shells, and water. Apparently, this potent libation never won any converts among the missionaries.

Taking matters into their own

hands, the padres planted the seeds of mission grapes they brought from Mexico, tending them lovingly to create wine for their mass and for the table. This was done at the insistence of Father Junípero Serra, founder of the San Diego mission and acknowledged father of California winemaking. By 1830, almost all of the missions had flourishing vineyards. Los Angeles was in the lead with approximately one hundred thousand vines.

A French vintner family named Vignes had already established a small commercial winemaking company by that time, but the great boon to the industry came after the Gold Rush, when many disappointed miners were lured by the potential profits of "liquid gold." They were encouraged by a state legislature offering four-year tax exemptions to new vineyards. According to wine historian Leon D. Adams, 12 million vines had been planted by 1863.[3] Before long, California vintners were exporting wines as far away as Europe, Russia, the Orient, and South America.

News of the California winemaking paradise quickly reached Frenchmen, who came to investigate, reporting back that California was "capable of entering competition with the wines of Europe . . . in the distant future."[4] That distant future arrived sooner than the French anticipated, primarily because California vintners began growing varieties of grape more delicious than the mission variety. These were cultivated from the fine varietal cuttings brought by numerous European vintners over the final four decades of the nineteenth century.

But the success of the early industry was checked by the spread of the destructive pest called the phylloxera, which attacked vines both in France and in California around the turn of the century. The pestilence was ultimately checked by grafting European vines onto Native American vines that were phylloxera-resistant.

The history of California winemaking reads like a good saga of

Abalone: An American Original

*A*balone is quite possibly the most expensive indigenous American food—easily fifty dollars per pound for a wild specimen, if you can get it at all. A native to the Pacific waters along the coast of California, this conchlike shellfish is available in fine restaurants from San Diego to San Francisco, but nowadays is most closely associated with Monterey. (Over the last decade, abalone has been commercially farmed under controlled conditions; farmed abalone is likely to be the type available in restaurants today.)

Abandoned abalone shells found in ancient middens suggest that the earliest California Indians appreciated this delicacy, which in this century became so popular that an abalone harvester is permitted to take a maximum of four per day.

The abalone has a concave oval top shell that is iridescent on the inside and often used for making jewelry. With its large, fleshy foot, the abalone adheres to rocks and feeds upon sea kelp. It is this muscular foot that is cut into steaks, pounded until thin and tender, and then dipped into batter and quickly fried. A squirt of lemon on top enhances the delicate, slightly fishy taste of the meltingly soft meat—a feast for seafood lovers who can afford the splurge and are lucky enough to find the genuine item.

California vineyards were almost almost wiped out by phylloxera at the turn of the century, but were revived after hardy stock was grafted onto disease-resistant vines.

the wild, wild west, full of intrigue and roller-coaster rides from boom to bust and back to boom again. But luckily the story has a happy ending. With approximately four hundred wineries and twelve thousand vineyards dotting the state, winemaking has become a major tourist attraction, particularly in counties like Sonoma and Napa in northern California.

Some of the vintners are gentlemen farmers from San Francisco; others are Frenchmen with sister wineries abroad. But whatever their lineage, some of the wines produced over the last few decades have been so fine that they've won prizes over their French cousins in blind tastings. Just what Gallic visitors had predicted over 150 years ago!

Flavors from the West

California

ALMOND-AVOCADO SPREAD

Almond trees were planted in the gardens of the Spanish missions in California in the eighteenth century, although almonds weren't successful as a crop for at least another hundred years. Avocados arrived in California in the mid-1800s, but didn't flourish until after the turn of the century. (Pictured on page 226)

1 large ripe avocado, seeded, peeled, and mashed
1 tablespoon lime juice
¼ teaspoon chili powder
¼ teaspoon seasoned salt
¼ cup toasted chopped almonds
2 tablespoons diced green chilies
2 slices bacon, crisp-cooked, drained, and crumbled
3 medium shrimp, peeled, cooked, and chopped
2 tablespoons toasted sliced *or* slivered almonds
Toasted tortilla wedges

Mix avocado, lime juice, chili powder, salt, and ¼ teaspoon *pepper*. Stir in the ¼ cup almonds, chilies, and bacon. Cover surface with plastic wrap; chill up to 4 hours. To serve, sprinkle with shrimp and remaining almonds. If desired, garnish with whole shrimp. Serve with tortilla wedges. Makes 1 cup.

Nutrition information per tablespoon: 50 calories, 2 g protein, 2 g carbohydrate, 4 g total fat (1 g saturated), 10 mg cholesterol, 57 mg sodium, 120 mg potassium

Mormon Fish Chowder, top (see recipe, page 227), and Kolaches (see recipe, page 244)

Idaho

POTATO SKINS WITH MUSHROOM FILLING

In the early 1870s, when Luther Burbank first tried to sell seedlings for what was to become the famous Idaho Russet potato, few farmers were interested. He finally found a buyer, but only for a fraction of his asking price. (Pictured on page 226)

3 medium baking potatoes, baked
2 tablespoons margarine *or* butter, melted
1½ cups chopped fresh mushrooms
¼ cup sliced green onion
¼ cup finely chopped red sweet pepper
1 garlic clove, minced
1 tablespoon margarine *or* butter
2 tablespoons finely chopped walnuts
2 tablespoons snipped parsley
1 slightly beaten egg yolk
Dash ground red pepper

Cut potatoes in half lengthwise. Scoop out pulp, leaving ¼- to ½-inch-thick shells. Brush with the 2 tablespoons margarine. Sprinkle with salt. Place cut side up on a baking sheet. Bake in a 425° oven about 10 minutes or till crisp. Cook mushrooms, onion, sweet pepper, and garlic in remaining margarine till tender and most liquid evaporates. Remove from heat. Stir in walnuts, parsley, egg yolk, and red pepper. Fill potato with mushroom mixture. Bake 5 to 7 minutes or till hot. Makes 6 appetizers.

Nutrition information per appetizer: 142 calories, 3 g protein, 16 g carbohydrate, 8 g total fat (1 g saturated), 35 mg cholesterol, 102 mg sodium, 277 mg potassium

Almond-Avocado Spread, top left (see recipe, page 225), Potato Skins with Mushroom Filling, top right (see recipe, page 225), and Goat Cheese, Tomato, and Oregano Boboli Pizza

California

GOAT CHEESE, TOMATO, AND OREGANO BOBOLI PIZZA

Goat cheese appeared on the menus of a few California restaurants in the early 1970s. Its inclusion was part of a great experiment by young chefs to interpret classic French cuisine using the bounty of fresh foods available locally. Since then, goat cheese has become inseparably linked with this new cooking style.

1 **16-ounce (12-inch) Italian bread shell (Boboli)**
1 **tablespoon olive oil *or* cooking oil**
1 **clove garlic, minced**
⅛ **teaspoon pepper**
2 **medium tomatoes, thinly sliced**
½ **of a medium onion, thinly sliced and separated into rings**
3 **tablespoons sliced pitted ripe olives**
4 **ounces chèvre (goat cheese)**
1 **tablespoon snipped fresh oregano *or* 1 teaspoon dried oregano, crushed**
2 **tablespoons toasted pine nuts**

Place Italian bread shell on a lightly greased baking sheet. In small mixing bowl combine olive oil or cooking oil, garlic, and pepper. Brush generously over the bread shell. Bake in a 400° oven for 5 minutes.

Arrange tomato slices, without overlapping them, in a circular pattern on top of the bread shell; top with sliced onion and ripe olives.

Crumble or dollop the chèvre over the tomato slices; sprinkle with oregano. Bake in the 400° oven about 8 minutes more or till warm and cheese softens. Remove from oven; sprinkle with pine nuts. Cut into wedges. Makes 12 servings.

Nutrition information per serving: 159 calories, 7 g protein, 18 g carbohydrate, 7 g total fat (2 g saturated), 9 mg cholesterol, 274 mg sodium, 75 mg potassium

Utah

MORMON FISH CHOWDER

The Mormons, in establishing the Mormon Trail, traveled 1,400 miles from Nauvoo, Illinois, to the Salt Lake Valley. Their cooking was simple and satisfying, and reflected their midwestern and eastern way of cooking. (Pictured on page 224)

1½ pounds fresh *or* frozen haddock fillets *or* other fish fillets
4 ounces salt pork, diced, *or* 3 strips bacon, diced
1 cup chopped onion
4 cups cubed, peeled potatoes (6 medium)
2 cups water
¾ teaspoon salt
¼ teaspoon pepper
2 cups milk
1 12-ounce can evaporated milk
2 tablespoons all-purpose flour

Thaw fish, if frozen. Cut fish into 1-inch pieces. Set aside. In a Dutch oven cook salt pork or bacon slowly till golden brown. Drain, reserving *1 tablespoon* drippings in pan; set salt pork or bacon aside.

Add onion to pan; cook till tender but not brown. Stir in potatoes, water, salt, and pepper. Bring to boiling; reduce heat. Simmer, covered, about 15 minutes or till potatoes are tender. Add fish. Simmer, covered, about 3 minutes or till fish just flakes when tested with a fork.

Combine milk and evaporated milk. Slowly stir milk mixture into flour till smooth; add to fish mixture. Cook and stir till thickened and bubbly. Add cooked salt pork or bacon; heat through. Makes 6 servings.

Nutrition information per serving: 384 calories, 30 g protein, 41 g carbohydrate, 11 g total fat (5 g saturated), 88 mg cholesterol, 505 mg sodium, 1,080 mg potassium

Caesar Salad with Bagel Croutons (see recipe, page 240), and Cioppino

California

CIOPPINO

The men who fished commercially in San Francisco Bay were primarily Italians from Genoa. They prepared this seafood stew with their catch. Cioppino is still closely associated with the city's Fisherman's Wharf area. Most of the restaurants there offer it on their menus.

8 fresh *or* frozen clams in shells
8 ounces fresh *or* frozen fish fillets (red snapper, perch, sea bass, *or* halibut)
8 ounces fresh *or* frozen peeled and deveined shrimp
½ cup sliced fresh mushrooms
⅓ cup chopped green *or* red sweet pepper
¼ cup chopped onion
2 cloves garlic, minced
1 tablespoon olive oil *or* cooking oil

1 16-ounce can tomatoes, cut up
⅓ cup dry red *or* white wine
¼ cup water
2 tablespoons snipped parsley
2 tablespoons tomato paste
1 tablespoon lemon juice
1½ teaspoons snipped fresh basil *or* ½ teaspoon dried basil, crushed
1½ teaspoons snipped fresh oregano *or* ½ teaspoon dried oregano, crushed
1 teaspoon sugar
¼ teaspoon salt
⅛ teaspoon crushed red pepper

Thaw clams, if frozen. Scrub clam shells under cold running water using a stiff brush. Combine 8 cups *water* and 3 tablespoons *salt*. Add clams; soak 15 minutes. Drain and rinse. Discard water. Repeat the soaking, draining, and rinsing steps two more times.

Partially thaw fish and shrimp, if frozen. Remove and discard fish skin, if present. Cut fish into 1½-inch pieces; set aside. Cover and refrigerate fish pieces and shrimp till needed.

In a large saucepan cook mushrooms, green or red sweet pepper, onion, and garlic in hot oil till tender but not brown. Stir in *undrained* tomatoes, wine, water, parsley, tomato paste, lemon juice, basil, oregano, sugar, salt, and crushed red pepper. Bring to boiling; reduce heat. Simmer, covered, 20 minutes.

Add clams, fish pieces, and shrimp. Simmer, covered, for 5 to 10 minutes or till clams open, fish flakes easily, and shrimp are opaque. Discard any unopened clams. Makes 4 servings.

Nutrition information per serving: 202 calories, 25 g protein, 11 g carbohydrate, 5 g total fat (1 g saturated), 110 mg cholesterol, 527 mg sodium, 805 mg potassium

Pasta with Artichoke Sauce, top (see recipe, page 241), and Marsala-Marinated Trout

Idaho

MARSALA-MARINATED TROUT

There must be something special about Idaho's rivers and streams. Almost all of the rainbow trout available in markets across the country are farmed from these waters.

4	8- to 10-ounce fresh *or* frozen pan-dressed rainbow trout *or* lake perch
½	cup dry marsala *or* other white wine
1	tablespoon lemon juice
½	teaspoon dried thyme, crushed
½	cup sliced fresh mushrooms
½	cup chopped carrot
⅓	cup chopped onion
1	clove garlic, minced
2	tablespoons cooking oil
¼	cup chicken broth

Thaw fish, if frozen. Place fish in a shallow baking dish. Sprinkle with salt and pepper.

For marinade, stir together the marsala, lemon juice, and thyme; pour over fish. Cover and marinate in the refrigerator for 2 hours. Drain fish, reserving marinade. Pat fish dry.

In a 12-inch skillet cook mushrooms, carrot, onion, and garlic in hot oil till tender but not brown. Push to the edges of the skillet. Add fish and cook 4 minutes on each side. Add marinade and broth. Cover, simmer about 4 minutes or till fish flakes easily with a fork. Remove fish and vegetables.

Simmer marinade mixture till it is reduced to ¼ cup; spoon over fish. Makes 4 servings.

Nutrition information per serving: 263 calories, 31 g protein, 4 g carbohydrate, 12 g total fat (2 g saturated), 83 mg cholesterol, 95 mg sodium, 870 mg potassium

Colorado

ROCKY MOUNTAIN TROUT

Pioneer families that settled near water depended on fish to supplement their meager diet until they could plant crops or a vegetable garden. The clear waters of Rocky Mountain streams are particularly renowned for their trout.

4	8- to 10-ounce fresh *or* frozen pan-dressed rainbow trout
¼	cup finely chopped red onion
¼	cup finely chopped green pepper
2	teaspoons tarragon vinegar *or* white wine vinegar
1	teaspoon snipped fresh basil
¼	teaspoon salt
¼	teaspoon cumin
⅛	teaspoon pepper
1	tablespoon grated Parmesan cheese
2	tablespoons cooking oil
	Whole tiny new potatoes (optional)
	Fresh basil sprigs (optional)

Thaw fish, if frozen. For stuffing, in a mixing bowl stir together the onion, green pepper, vinegar, basil, salt, cumin, and pepper. Add Parmesan cheese; mix well.

Rinse fish and pat dry with paper towels. Brush the outsides and cavities of fish with oil. Spoon *one-fourth* of the stuffing mixture into each fish cavity.

Brush a wire grill basket with cooking oil. Place fish in basket. Grill fish on an uncovered grill directly over *medium-hot* coals for 7 to 11 minutes or till fish flakes easily with a fork, turning once.

If desired, serve with new potatoes and garnish with basil sprigs. Makes 4 servings.

Nutrition information per serving: 234 calories, 30 g protein, 1 g carbohydrate, 12 g total fat (2 g saturated), 84 mg cholesterol, 201 mg sodium, 737 mg potassium

Rocky Mountain Trout

Stir-Fried Seafood with Linguine, top left, Fresh Tuna with Fettuccine, top right, and Crab Louis

California

STIR-FRIED SEAFOOD WITH LINGUINE

Californians have enjoyed stir-fries since the first Chinese chop suey parlors opened their doors after the 1849 gold rush. Customers at these restaurants thought they were eating authentic Chinese dishes, but actually the food was modified to appeal to western tastes. Chop suey doesn't exist in China.

1 **pound fresh *or* frozen sea scallops**
½ **pound fresh *or* frozen peeled and deveined medium shrimp**
10 **ounces linguine**
2 **cups fresh pea pods *or* one 6-ounce package frozen pea pods, thawed**
⅔ **cup chicken broth**
¼ **cup dry sherry**
3 **tablespoons soy sauce**
4 **teaspoons cornstarch**
1 **teaspoon toasted sesame oil**
¼ **teaspoon crushed red pepper**
1 **tablespoon cooking oil**
4 **cloves garlic, minced**
6 **green onions, bias-sliced into 1-inch pieces (¾ cup)**
⅓ **cup dried tomatoes (oil-packed), drained and cut into thin strips**
3 **tablespoons finely shredded Parmesan cheese**

Thaw scallops and shrimp, if frozen. Cook linguine according to package directions; drain. Cut any large scallops in half. In a medium bowl combine the scallops and shrimp; set aside. Cut pea pods diagonally in half. For sauce, in a small bowl stir together chicken broth, sherry, soy sauce, cornstarch, sesame oil, and crushed red pepper. Set sauce aside.

Pour cooking oil into a wok or 12-inch skillet. (Add more oil as necessary during cooking.) Preheat over medium-high heat. Stir-fry garlic in hot oil for 15 seconds. Add green onions and, if using, fresh pea pods; stir-fry for 2 minutes. Remove vegetables from the wok.

Add *half* of the scallop mixture to the hot wok. Stir-fry for 2 to 3 minutes or till scallops are opaque and shrimp turn pink.

Remove from wok. Repeat with remaining scallop mixture. Transfer entire scallop mixture to wok; push from center of wok. Add sauce to center of wok. Cook and stir till thickened and bubbly.

Add cooked vegetables, linguine, thawed pea pods, if using, and tomatoes. Stir all ingredients together to coat with sauce. Cook and stir about 1 minute more or till heated through. Transfer to a large serving dish. Top with cheese. Makes 6 servings.

Nutrition information per serving: 368 calories, 26 g protein, 46 g carbohydrate, 8 g total fat (2 g saturated), 86 mg cholesterol, 850 mg sodium, 580 mg potassium

Veal with Sherry and Olives, left (see recipe, page 232), and Stuffed Artichokes (see recipe, page 242)

California

FRESH TUNA WITH FETTUCCINE

Some 300 species of fish and shellfish are harvested from California waters, including tuna, swordfish, sole, and many varieties of rockfish.

1   pound fresh *or* frozen tuna
     or swordfish steaks
     (1 inch thick)
½   cup chopped onion
2   cloves garlic, minced
1   tablespoon olive oil *or*
     cooking oil
2   14½-ounce cans diced
     tomatoes
2   tablespoons snipped fresh
     basil *or* 1½ teaspoons
     dried basil, crushed
2   tablespoons tomato paste
¼   teaspoon salt
¼   teaspoon crushed red
     pepper
1   9-ounce package frozen
     artichoke hearts, thawed
     and cut into quarters
2   tablespoons capers, drained
3   cups hot cooked spinach
     fettuccine
     Fresh oregano (optional)

Thaw fish, if frozen. Cut fish into 1-inch cubes, discarding any skin and bones. Set aside.

For sauce, in a large skillet cook onion and garlic in hot olive oil or cooking oil till onion is tender but not brown. Stir in the *undrained* tomatoes, basil, tomato paste, salt, and crushed red pepper. Bring to boiling. Reduce heat and simmer, uncovered, about 20 minutes or till very thick. Add fish cubes. Cover and cook about 6 minutes or till fish flakes easily with a fork.

Gently stir artichokes and capers into sauce; heat through. Serve sauce over fettuccine. If desired, garnish with oregano. Serves 4.

Nutrition information per serving: 411 calories, 35 g protein, 46 g carbohydrate, 10 g total fat (2 g saturated), 42 mg cholesterol, 637 mg sodium, 1,078 mg potassium

California

CRAB LOUIS

Who is Louis? He may have been San Francisco chef Louis Coutard, but no one is quite sure. Whoever the creator, he gave his name to this dressing for crab salad. It's pronounced Louie *not* Lewis, *by the way.*

¼   cup whipping cream
½   cup mayonnaise *or* salad
     dressing
¼   cup sliced green onion
2   tablespoons chili sauce
1   teaspoon prepared
     horseradish
½   teaspoon finely shredded
     lemon peel
1   teaspoon lemon juice
⅛   teaspoon salt
     Dash ground red pepper
1   to 2 tablespoons milk
     (optional)
     Red-tip leaf lettuce leaves
4   cups shredded Chinese
     cabbage *and/or* romaine
½   cup shredded carrot
12   ounces coarsely flaked,
     cooked crabmeat (2¼ cups)
     or three 4-ounce packages
     frozen, crab-flavored,
     salad-style fish

1½   cups red *and/or* yellow baby
     pear tomatoes, halved
2   hard-cooked eggs, sliced
1   medium avocado, seeded,
     peeled, and sliced
     lengthwise
     Paprika
     Lemon wedges

For dressing, in a small bowl beat whipping cream till soft peaks form. Fold in mayonnaise or salad dressing, green onion, chili sauce, horseradish, lemon peel, lemon juice, salt, and ground red pepper. Cover and chill for 2 to 24 hours. (If necessary, thin dressing with 1 to 2 tablespoons milk before serving.)

To serve, line 4 salad plates with lettuce leaves. Toss together shredded Chinese cabbage or romaine and shredded carrot; pile atop lettuce leaves. Arrange crabmeat atop shredded cabbage mixture. Arrange tomatoes, egg slices, and avocado slices around crabmeat. Drizzle with chilled dressing. Sprinkle with paprika. Garnish with lemon wedges. Makes 4 servings.

Nutrition information per serving: 493 calories, 24 g protein, 14 g carbohydrate, 40 g total fat (9 g saturated), 228 mg cholesterol, 677 mg sodium, 1,056 mg potassium

California

VEAL WITH SHERRY AND OLIVES

Spanish priests carried olive cuttings from Mexico into what is now southern California in the early eighteenth century. Olive trees were planted in the orchards of their missions. (Pictured on page 231)

1   pound boneless veal leg top round steak *or* lean boneless pork, cut into thin bite-size strips
3   tablespoons margarine *or* butter
1   cup thinly bias-sliced carrot
3   green onions, bias-sliced into 1-inch pieces (¼ cup)
3   tablespoons all-purpose flour
1   teaspoon instant chicken bouillon granules
¼   teaspoon coarsely cracked black pepper
2   cups half-and-half *or* light cream
¾   cup sliced pitted ripe olives
¼   cup dry sherry
3   cups hot cooked spinach fettuccine
2   tablespoons snipped fresh parsley

In a large skillet cook and stir *half* the veal or pork at a time in margarine or butter about 3 minutes or till brown. Remove veal or pork from skillet, reserving drippings.

In the same skillet, cook and stir carrots and green onions for 3 to 4 minutes or till crisp-tender. Stir in flour, bouillon granules, and pepper. Add half-and-half or light cream all at once. Cook and stir till thickened and bubbly. Cook and stir for 1 minute more.

Stir in cooked veal, olives, and dry sherry; heat through. Spoon veal mixture over pasta. Sprinkle with parsley. Makes 4 servings.

Nutrition information per serving: 578 *calories, 35 g protein, 44 g carbohydrate, 29 g total fat (11 g saturated), 133 mg cholesterol, 644 mg sodium, 694 mg potassium*

Montana

MARINATED VENISON LOIN WITH FRIED GRAPES

Before the great surge of settlers moved in, deer, bear, and elk were abundant on the frontier. The hunter lucky enough to shoot one could feed his family for a long time.

1   5- to 6-pound loin end saddle of venison
2   medium onions, quartered
2   medium tomatoes, cut up
6   juniper berries, crushed
1   to 2 bay leaves
¾   cup red wine
¼   cup margarine *or* butter, melted
¼   cup whipping cream
2   tablespoons cranberry jelly *or* currant jelly
2   tablespoons catsup
1   teaspoon prepared mustard
¼   cup dairy sour cream
    Fried Grapes
    Fresh Grapes (optional)
    Parsley (optional)

Wash venison and pat dry. Trim off excess fat. Place in a roasting pan, bone side down. Sprinkle with salt and pepper. Place onions, tomatoes, juniper berries, and bay leaves around venison. Pour wine and melted margarine or butter over venison. Insert a meat thermometer into the thickest portion of the meat. Roast in a 375° oven about 1 hour or till thermometer registers 140° (medium-rare); baste with pan juices every 20 minutes. Transfer meat to a platter; cover and let stand about 15 minutes.

Meanwhile, for sauce, strain pan juices into a saucepan (should be about 1 cup). Cook mixture down till it measures ½ cup. Stir in whipping cream. Cook and stir till thickened and bubbly. Stir in jelly, catsup, and mustard. Cook and stir till jelly is dissolved. Stir in sour cream and heat through. *(Do not boil.)* Spoon sauce over venison and garnish with Fried Grapes and, if desired, fresh grapes and parsley. Makes 12 servings.

Fried Grapes: Rinse 1½ cups *grapes* and remove stems. Toss with ⅓ cup *all-purpose flour* to coat well. Dip the grapes in 1 beaten *egg*, then in ¾ cup *fine dry bread crumbs*. In a large skillet fry grapes in 2 tablespoons hot *margarine or butter* and 1 tablespoon *cooking oil* about 5 minutes or till coating is golden, turning frequently.

Nutrition information per serving: 336 *calories, 33 g protein, 17 g carbohydrate, 14 g total fat (4 g saturated), 138 mg cholesterol, 206 mg sodium, 507 mg potassium*

Twice-Baked Potatoes, top left (see recipe, page 242), Avocado and Fruit Salad, lower left (see recipe, page 241), and Marinated Venison Loin with Fried Grapes

Wyoming

COWPUNCHER STEW

In the dining halls of large western ranches, eating was the main order of business for the hands. There was little conversation during meals that typically included dishes like cowpuncher stew. After supper, however, if the cook permitted, the crew might hang around to swap some tales. (Pictured on page 234)

1½ pounds beef stew meat, cut in 1-inch cubes
3 tablespoons all-purpose flour
2 tablespoons cooking oil
1½ cups strong coffee
2 tablespoons molasses
1 clove garlic, minced
1 teaspoon Worcestershire sauce
½ teaspoon dried oregano, crushed
⅛ teaspoon ground red pepper
4 carrots, cut in ½-inch slices
4 small onions, quartered
3 medium potatoes, peeled and cut up
3 tablespoons all-purpose flour

Coat beef cubes with a mixture of 3 tablespoons flour and ½ teaspoon salt. In a Dutch oven brown *half* of the meat at a time in hot oil. Return all meat to pan. Stir in the coffee, molasses, garlic, Worcestershire sauce, oregano, red pepper, and ½ teaspoon salt. Cover; simmer 1½ hours or till meat is nearly tender.

Add the carrots, onion, potatoes, and 1½ cups *water.* Simmer, covered, about 30 minutes or till vegetables are tender. Combine the 3 tablespoons flour and ¼ cup cold *water;* stir into the stew mixture. Cook and stir till mixture is thickened and bubbly. Cook and stir for 1 minute more. Makes 6 servings.

Nutrition information per serving: 359 calories, 31 g protein, 32 g carbohydrate, 12 g total fat (4 g saturated), 86 mg cholesterol, 445 mg sodium, 814 mg potassium

233

Cowboy Beans (see recipe, page 243), and Cowpuncher Stew (see recipe, page 233)

utes. Stir in potatoes, mushrooms, carrots, and onion. Return to boiling; reduce heat. Cover and simmer about 30 minutes or till tender. Discard bay leaf. Combine the ¼ cup flour and remaining broth. Stir into meat mixture. Cook and stir till thickened and bubbly. Stir in cubed cream cheese and parsley. Stir gently till cheese melts. Keep warm.

Meanwhile, for pastry, in a bowl combine the 1 cup flour and onion salt. Cut in margarine and shortening till mixture resembles coarse crumbs. Stir in beaten egg till well blended. Form into ball. Roll pastry into a rectangle 1 inch larger than a 2-quart rectangular baking dish or a circle 1 inch larger than diameter of a 1½-quart casserole. Transfer meat mixture into the baking dish or casserole. Place pastry atop. Cut slits in pastry. Seal and flute edge. Bake in a 375° oven about 20 minutes or till golden. Serves 4.

Nutrition information per serving: 715 calories, 29 g protein, 60 g carbohydrate, 38 g total fat (12 g saturated), 138 mg cholesterol, 853 mg sodium, 916 mg potassium

Nevada

MINER'S CAMP PIE

This stew must have fed a miner whose claim panned out. According to one report from an 1849 camp, potatoes sold for $30 a bushel, an unheard of amount at the time.

1 pound lamb shoulder, trimmed and cut in ¾-inch cubes
1 tablespoon cooking oil
1⅓ cups beef broth
⅓ cup dry red wine *or* beef broth
2 cloves garlic, minced
1 teaspoon dried marjoram, crushed
½ teaspoon dried thyme, crushed
1 bay leaf
¼ teaspoon salt

¼ teaspoon pepper
2 cups peeled potatoes, cut into ½-inch cubes
1½ cups whole small fresh mushrooms
1 cup sliced carrots
1 cup onion wedges
¼ cup all-purpose flour
1 3-ounce package cream cheese, cubed
¼ cup snipped parsley
1 cup all-purpose flour
½ teaspoon onion salt
¼ cup margarine *or* butter
2 tablespoons shortening
1 egg, beaten

In a large saucepan brown *half* of the meat at a time in hot oil. Drain fat. Return all meat to pan. Add ⅔ *cup* of the broth, the wine, garlic, marjoram, thyme, bay leaf, salt, and pepper. Bring to boiling; reduce heat. Cover and simmer for 30 min-

Wyoming

CHICKEN POTPIES

Life became easier once pioneers established their homesteads, and the meagerness of the meals of those early days disappeared. Familiar dishes like meat pies made with fresh-killed poultry and vegetables from home gardens began to appear on the dinner table. (Pictured on page 237)

Pastry for Double-Crust Pie (see recipe, page 274)
1 10-ounce package frozen peas and carrots
½ cup chopped onion
½ cup chopped fresh mushrooms
¼ cup margarine *or* butter
⅓ cup all-purpose flour
½ teaspoon salt
½ teaspoon dried sage, marjoram, *or* thyme, crushed

Miner's Camp Pie

⅛ teaspoon pepper
2 cups chicken broth
¾ cup milk
3 cups cubed cooked chicken
or turkey
¼ cup snipped parsley
¼ cup chopped pimiento

Prepare pastry; set aside. Cook peas and carrots according to package directions; drain. In a saucepan cook onion and mushrooms in margarine or butter till tender. Stir in flour, salt, herb, and pepper. Add chicken broth and milk all at once. Cook and stir till thickened and bubbly. Stir in drained peas and carrots, chicken or turkey, parsley, and pimiento; heat till bubbly. Pour chicken mixture into six 10-ounce round casseroles. (*Or*, use a 2-quart rectangular baking dish.)

Roll pastry into a 15x10-inch rectangle. Cut into six 5-inch circles, and place atop the 10-ounce casseroles. (*Or*, roll pastry into a 13x9-inch rectangle. Place over the 2-quart rectangular baking dish.)

Flute edges of pastry and cut slits in the top for steam to escape. Bake in a 450° oven for 12 to 15 minutes or till pastry is golden brown. Makes 6 servings.

Nutrition information per serving: 631 calories, 31 g protein, 46 g carbohydrate, 35 g total fat (8 g saturated), 62 mg cholesterol, 788 mg sodium, 506 mg potassium

Split Pea and Sausage Soup, and Sourdough Bread (see recipe, page 244)

leaves. Divide asparagus spears, baby corn, kiwi fruit or carambola, and apricots, nectarines, or peaches among salad plates. Pour Jalapeño Dressing over salads. Serves 4.

Jalapeño Dressing: In a blender container or food processor bowl combine ½ cup *mayonnaise or salad dressing*, 2 tablespoons *honey*, 1 tablespoon *lime juice or lemon juice*, 1 coarsely chopped (not seeded) *jalapeño pepper*, ¼ teaspoon *dry mustard*, and ¼ teaspoon *paprika*. Cover and blend or process till smooth. Cover and chill.

Nutrition information per serving: 475 calories, 30 g protein, 24 g carbohydrate, 30 g total fat (5 g saturated), 89 mg cholesterol, 392 mg sodium, 677 mg potassium

California

CALIFORNIA CHICKEN SALAD WITH JALAPEÑO DRESSING

Californians have always loved spicy flavors, a heritage of the early cooking that developed on the huge Spanish colonial land-grant ranchos. They've also been quick to integrate the new with the old. Exotics like kiwi fruit, once grown only in China and New Zealand and now a major California crop, are commonplace in markets throughout the state.

4   **large skinless, boneless chicken breast halves (about 1 pound total)**
2   **tablespoons lemon juice**
1   **jalapeño pepper, finely chopped**
1   **tablespoon cooking oil**
½   **teaspoon lemon-pepper seasoning**
12   **ounces asparagus spears Boston *or* Bibb lettuce leaves**
1   **5-ounce can baby corn, drained**

2   **kiwi fruit *or* carambola (star fruit), sliced**
2   **apricots, nectarines, *or* peaches, pitted and cut into wedges Jalapeño Dressing**

Rinse chicken; pat dry. Combine the lemon juice, jalapeño pepper, cooking oil, and lemon-pepper seasoning; brush over both sides of chicken breasts. Grill chicken on an uncovered grill directly over *medium* coals for 12 to 15 minutes or till no longer pink, turning once.

Cool chicken about 5 minutes or till cool enough to handle. (*Or,* broil chicken 4 to 5 inches from heat for 12 to 15 minutes, turning once.)

Meanwhile, cook the asparagus, covered, in a small amount of boiling water for 4 to 8 minutes or till crisp-tender.

To serve, line 4 salad plates with lettuce leaves. Diagonally cut the chicken breast halves into slices; reassemble halves atop lettuce

Utah

SPLIT PEA AND SAUSAGE SOUP

A typical meal for Mormons traveling westward in the mid-1800s might have included a big kettle of split pea soup, whole wheat bread with comb honey, and a lettuce salad with whipped cream dressing.

1½   **cups green split peas**
6   **cups chicken broth**
1   **clove garlic, minced**
1   **tablespoon snipped fresh oregano *or* ¾ teaspoon dried oregano, crushed**
⅛   **teaspoon pepper**
1   **bay leaf**
½   **pound bulk pork sausage**
1   **cup chopped carrot**
¾   **cup chopped onion**
¾   **cup peeled potato, cut in ¼-inch cubes**
½   **cup chopped celery**

Rinse peas. In a large saucepan or kettle combine split peas, broth, garlic, oregano, pepper, and bay leaf. Bring to boiling; reduce heat. Cover and simmer for 1 hour, stirring occasionally.

California Chicken Salad with Jalapeño Dressing, top left, Chicken Potpies, top right (see recipe, page 234), and Cobb Salad

Meanwhile, form pork sausage into twenty-five ½- to ¾-inch balls; place in a 13x9x2-inch baking pan. Bake in a 400° oven for 10 to 15 minutes or till no pink remains. Remove from pan; place on paper towels to drain.

Stir carrot, onion, potato, celery, and sausage balls into soup. Return to boiling; reduce heat. Cover and simmer for 20 minutes. Uncover; simmer 10 to 15 minutes more or till desired consistency and vegetables are tender. Discard bay leaf. Makes 5 servings.

Nutrition information per serving: 480 calories, 27 g protein, 56 g carbohydrate, 16 g total fat (6 g saturated), 23 mg cholesterol, 1,224 mg sodium, 1,433 mg potassium

California

COBB SALAD

Patrons of the Brown Derby Restaurant in Los Angeles, where this salad originated in 1936, never needed to ask how the restaurant got its name. The original site on Wilshire Boulevard was built in the shape of a gargantuan hat.

6   **cups shredded red Swiss chard *or* shredded lettuce**
3   **cups chopped cooked chicken**
1½ **cups chopped, seeded tomatoes (2 medium)**
¾   **cup crumbled blue cheese (3 ounces)**
6   **slices bacon, crisp-cooked, drained, and crumbled**
3   **hard-cooked eggs, chopped**
1   **small head Belgian endive**
1   **medium avocado, seeded, peeled, and cut into wedges**

Brown Derby French Dressing

Place shredded Swiss chard or lettuce in 6 salad bowls. Evenly divide chicken, tomatoes, blue cheese, bacon, and eggs among bowls.

Separate the Belgian endive into leaves. Place a few endive leaves and avocado wedges in each bowl. Serve with Brown Derby French Dressing. Makes 6 servings.

Brown Derby French Dressing: In a screw-top jar combine ½ cup *olive oil or salad oil*, ⅓ cup *red wine vinegar*, 1 tablespoon *lemon juice*, 1 teaspoon *Worcestershire sauce*, ½ teaspoon *salt*, ½ teaspoon *sugar*, ½ teaspoon *dry mustard*, ½ teaspoon *pepper*, and 1 clove *garlic*, minced. Cover and shake well. Shake before serving. Makes about 1 cup.

Nutrition information per serving: 496 calories, 32 g protein, 11 g carbohydrate, 36 g total fat (9 g saturated), 181 mg cholesterol, 597 mg sodium, 726 mg potassium

Summer Ratatouille, left (see recipe, page 242), and Chicken with Black Bean Sauce

California

CHICKEN WITH BLACK BEAN SAUCE

In the 1850s Chinese arrived in California by the thousands to build the transcontinental railroad. Later they opened restaurants and worked as cooks in mining camps and in private homes. West Coast cuisine reflects continued immigration from Asia even today.

4   large skinless, boneless chicken breast halves (1 pound total)
⅓   cup water
1   tablespoon soy sauce
2   teaspoons cornstarch
½   teaspoon sugar
½   teaspoon instant chicken bouillon granules
1   tablespoon cooking oil
2   cloves garlic, minced
1   pound fresh asparagus, cut into 2-inch pieces (3 cups), *or* one 10-ounce package frozen cut asparagus, thawed
1   medium onion, cut into thin wedges (¾ cup)
1   tablespoon fermented black beans, chopped
3   cups hot cooked rice

Rinse chicken and pat dry. Cut into ¾-inch pieces. For sauce, in a small bowl stir together the water, soy sauce, cornstarch, sugar, and chicken bouillon granules. Set aside.

Pour cooking oil into a wok or large skillet. (Add more oil as necessary during cooking.) Preheat over medium-high heat. Stir-fry garlic in hot oil for 15 seconds. If using fresh asparagus, stir-fry for 1 minute. Add thawed asparagus (if using), onion, and black beans; stir-fry about 3 minutes more or till vegetables are crisp-tender. Remove vegetables from the wok.

Add *half* of the chicken to the hot wok. Stir-fry for 2 to 3 minutes or till no pink remains. Remove the chicken from the wok. Repeat with remaining chicken. Return all chicken to the wok. Push the chicken from the center of the wok. Stir sauce. Add the sauce to the center of the wok. Cook and stir till thickened and bubbly.

Return the cooked vegetables to the wok. Stir all ingredients together to coat with sauce. Cook and stir about 1 minute more or till heated through. Serve immediately over hot cooked rice. Makes 4 servings.

Nutrition information per serving: 420 calories, 35 g protein, 51 g carbohydrate, 8 g total fat (2 g saturated), 72 mg cholesterol, 588 mg sodium, 629 potassium

Nevada

MARINATED GRILLED LAMB

Most Basques came to the West from the mountains between Spain and France in answer to a call from American sheep ranchers for herders. Not surprisingly, lamb in every form was part of their cooking.

1   5- to 7-pound leg of lamb, boned and butterflied
1   cup dry red wine
⅓   cup soy sauce
⅓   cup Dijon-style mustard
2   tablespoons olive oil

Remove fell (paper-thin, reddish pink layer), if present, from outer surface of leg of lamb. Trim excess fat from lamb. Place lamb in a plastic bag set in a deep bowl.

For marinade, in a mixing bowl combine wine, soy sauce, Dijon-style mustard, and olive oil. Pour marinade over lamb; seal bag. Marinate in the refrigerator for 8 to 24 hours, turning bag occasionally to distribute marinade. Drain lamb; discard marinade.

To keep the lamb flat during cooking, insert two 18-inch wooden or metal skewers through meat at right angles, making a cross.

In a covered grill arrange *medium* coals around a drip pan. Test for *medium-slow* heat over the drip pan. Place lamb on the grill rack over the drip pan but not over the coals. Lower the grill hood. Grill about 1¼ hours for medium doneness. Remove skewers. Let stand for 15 minutes.

To serve, thinly slice lamb across the grain. Makes 12 to 16 servings.

Nutrition information per serving: 257 calories, 35 g protein, 1 g carbohydrate, 11 g total fat (4 g saturated), 109 mg cholesterol, 399 mg sodium, 437 mg potassium

Colorado

HUNTER'S LEG OF LAMB

Despite the range wars that were common occurrences between cattlemen and sheepherders, Colorado ranches still managed to develop a fine reputation for high-quality beef and lamb.
(Pictured on page 240)

1 **4- to 6-pound leg of lamb, boned and butterflied**
¾ **cup dry red wine**
⅛ **cup Worcestershire sauce**
1 **6-ounce package dried apricots, chopped**
½ **cup water**
1 **6-ounce package long grain and wild rice mix**

Marinated Grilled Lamb, and Pasta Salad with Chèvre and Tomatoes (see recipe, page 241)

1 **cup finely chopped onion**
1 **teaspoon lemon-pepper seasoning**
¼ **cup snipped fresh basil or 1 tablespoon dried basil, crushed**
   Watercress (optional)

Remove fell (paper-thin, pinkish red layer), if present, from outer surface of lamb. Place lamb in a 3-quart rectangular baking dish. Stir together the red wine and Worcestershire sauce; pour over lamb. Cover and marinate in refrigerator for 6 hours or overnight. Turn meat over once or spoon marinade over meat occasionally.

Remove meat from dish, reserving marinade. In a small bowl combine chopped apricots and water. Bring to boiling. Remove from heat; cover and let stand 5 minutes.

Prepare rice mix according to package directions, adding chopped onion to mix. In a large bowl combine cooked rice and onions, undrained apricots, basil, and lemon-pepper seasoning. Mix well.

Trim fat. Place meat, boned side up, between 2 pieces of plastic wrap; pound meat with a meat mallot to an even thickness. Spread *half* of the rice mixture over roast. Roll up; tie securely.

Place roast, seam side down, on a rack in a shallow roasting pan. Insert a meat thermometer into thickest portion of meat. Roast in a 325° oven for 1¾ to 2½ hours or till thermometer registers 150°. Baste lamb with reserved marinade several times during cooking. (Do not brush during the last 5 minutes.) Let stand 15 minutes before carving. Meanwhile, put remaining rice mixture in a 1-quart casserole; cover. Bake with lamb during the last 25 to 30 minutes of meat's roasting and standing time. Remove strings. If desired, garnish with watercress. Makes 10 servings.

Nutrition information per serving: 320 calories, 32 g protein, 27 g carbohydrate, 8 g total fat (3 g saturated), 91 mg cholesterol, 539 mg sodium, 700 mg potassium

Green Goddess Dressing, top left, and Hunter's Leg of Lamb (see recipe, page 239)

(see recipe, page 239)

California

GREEN GODDESS DRESSING

In the early part of this century, George Arliss starred in a San Francisco production of The Green Goddess, *a play by William Archer. In honor of the actor, the famed Palace Hotel created this dressing.*

¾ cup packed parsley leaves
⅓ cup mayonnaise *or* salad dressing
⅓ cup dairy sour cream *or* plain yogurt
1 green onion, cut up
1 tablespoon vinegar
1 teaspoon anchovy paste *or* 1 anchovy fillet, cut up
¼ teaspoon dried basil, crushed
⅛ teaspoon garlic powder
⅛ teaspoon dried tarragon, crushed
1 to 2 tablespoons milk

In a blender container or food processor bowl combine parsley, mayonnaise, sour cream, green onion, vinegar, anchovy paste, basil, garlic powder, and tarragon. Cover and blend or process till smooth. Cover and store in the refrigerator for up to 2 weeks.

Before serving, stir in some milk to make the dressing the desired consistency. Makes about 1 cup.

Nutrition information per tablespoon: *45 calories, 0 g protein, 1 g carbohydrate, 5 g total fat (1 g saturated), 5 mg cholesterol, 39 mg sodium, 30 mg potassium*

California

CAESAR SALAD WITH BAGEL CROUTONS

Like so many California dishes, this one has its roots in Mexico, although by way of Italy. It was the creation of Caesar Cardini for his restaurant in Tijuana, which is just across the border from San Diego.
(Pictured on page 227)

(Pictured on page 227)

1 egg
⅓ cup chicken broth
2 anchovy fillets *or* 1 teaspoon anchovy paste
3 tablespoons olive oil
1 teaspoon finely shredded lemon peel
2 tablespoons lemon juice
1 teaspoon Dijon-style mustard
¼ teaspoon white wine Worcestershire sauce
1 clove garlic, halved
10 cups torn romaine lettuce
1 cup Bagel Croutons
¼ cup grated Parmesan cheese
Whole black peppercorns

For dressing, in a blender container or food processor bowl combine egg, chicken broth, anchovy fillets or paste, olive oil, lemon peel, lemon juice, mustard, and Worcestershire sauce. Cover and blend or process till smooth. Transfer dressing to a small saucepan. Cook and stir dressing over low heat for 8 to 10 minutes or till thickened. Do not boil. Transfer to a bowl. Cover surface with plastic wrap; chill for 2 to 24 hours.

To serve, rub the inside of a wooden salad bowl with the cut sides of the garlic clove; discard garlic clove. Add romaine, Bagel Croutons, and Parmesan cheese to salad bowl. Pour dressing over salad. Toss lightly to coat. Transfer to individual salad plates. Grind peppercorns over each serving. Makes 6 servings.

Bagel Croutons: Split 2 *onion bagels.* With the cut side down, slice each bagel half into ¼-inch-thick half moons. In a large skillet combine 3 tablespoons *margarine or butter,* 1 tablespoon *olive oil,* and 2 small cloves *garlic,* minced. Cook and stir till margarine or butter melts. Remove from heat. Stir bagel pieces into margarine mixture. Spread pieces in a single layer in a shallow baking pan. Bake in a 300° oven for 10 minutes. Stir; bake 10 to 15 minutes more or till dry and crisp. Cool croutons. Store in an airtight container for up to 1 week. Makes about 2 cups.

Nutrition information per serving: *241 calories, 7 g protein, 14 g carbohydrate, 18 g total fat (3 g saturated), 40 mg cholesterol, 343 mg sodium, 336 mg potassium*

California

PASTA SALAD WITH CHÈVRE AND TOMATOES

In recent years, California chefs have developed a cuisine inspired in part by the foods of Mediterranean countries. They recognize that California's warm, gentle climate mirrors that of southern France and Italy, as does the wonderful abundance of fresh ingredients available to them.
(Pictured on page 239)

1½	cups tricolor corkscrew macaroni
1	6-ounce jar marinated artichoke hearts
2	ounces sliced salami, cut into strips
⅓	cup sliced pitted ripe olives
2	tablespoons olive oil *or* salad oil
2	tablespoons red wine vinegar
1	tablespoon snipped fresh basil *or* 1 teaspoon dried basil, crushed
1	tablespoon snipped fresh oregano *or* 1 teaspoon dried oregano, crushed
4	ounces chèvre (goat cheese), cut into chunks, *or* crumbled feta cheese
½	cup halved red *and/or* yellow cherry tomatoes

Cook macaroni according to package directions; drain. Rinse with cold water; drain again.

Meanwhile, drain the artichoke hearts, reserving the marinade. Coarsely chop the artichokes.

In a large mixing bowl combine cooked macaroni, artichokes, salami, and ripe olives.

For dressing, in a screw-top jar combine the reserved artichoke marinade, olive or salad oil, wine vinegar, basil, and oregano. Cover and shake well. Pour over pasta mixture and toss lightly to coat. Cover and chill for 4 to 24 hours.

To serve, toss in chèvre or feta cheese and tomatoes. Makes 4 to 6 servings.

Nutrition information per serving: 387 calories, 14 g protein, 38 g carbohydrate, 21 g total fat (7 g saturated), 22 mg cholesterol, 570 mg sodium, 274 mg potassium

California

PASTA WITH ARTICHOKE SAUCE

Castroville, some 100 miles south of San Francisco, describes itself as the artichoke center of the world. In fact, more artichokes are grown in the Mediterranean area, but California produces all of the commercial crop in the United States.
(Pictured on page 228)

½	cup chopped onion
1	clove garlic, minced
1	tablespoon olive oil *or* cooking oil
2	tablespoons all-purpose flour
1	tablespoon snipped fresh basil *or* oregano *or* 1 teaspoon dried basil *or* oregano, crushed
⅛	teaspoon salt
1¼	cups milk
1	13¾-ounce can artichoke hearts, drained and cut up
2	tablespoons finely shredded asiago cheese *or* Parmesan cheese
4	ounces spinach fettucine, carrot fettucine, *or* whole wheat fettuccine, cooked and drained
	Coarsely ground pepper

For sauce, in a saucepan cook onion and garlic in hot oil till tender but not brown. Stir in flour, basil or oregano, and salt. Add milk all at once. Cook and stir till thickened and bubbly. Cook and stir for 1 minute more. Stir in artichoke hearts and cheese; heat through.

To serve, spoon sauce over hot fettuccine. Sprinkle with pepper. Makes 4 servings.

Nutrition information per serving: 238 calories, 10 g protein, 35 g carbohydrate, 7 g total fat (2 g saturated), 9 mg cholesterol, 211 mg sodium, 420 mg potassium

California

AVOCADO AND FRUIT SALAD

In 1911 a nurseryman from southern California traveled throughout Mexico looking for avocado stock that would adapt to the California soil and climate. All but one of the cuttings he brought back failed to flourish. The one that survived was named fuerte, Spanish for "strong." That tree was the start of California's avocado industry.
(Pictured on page 232)

¼	cup walnut oil *or* salad oil
¼	cup raspberry vinegar
	Boston *or* Bibb lettuce leaves
2	medium red grapefruit, peeled and sectioned
1	medium avocado, seeded, peeled, and sliced lengthwise
1	medium papaya, seeded, peeled, and sliced lengthwise
2	tablespoons toasted chopped walnuts
½	cup raspberries (optional)

For dressing, in a screw-top jar combine walnut oil or salad oil and raspberry vinegar. Cover and shake well. Chill for at least 1 hour.

Line 4 salad plates with Boston or Bibb lettuce leaves. Place grapefruit sections in center. Fan avocado and papaya slices on opposite sides of grapefruit. Sprinkle with toasted walnuts.

If desired, sprinkle the salads with raspberries. Shake dressing well; pour over each salad. Makes 4 servings.

Nutrition information per serving: 290 calories, 3 g protein, 22 g carbohydrate, 24 g total fat (3 g saturated), 0 mg cholesterol, 8 mg sodium, 679 mg potassium

Idaho

TWICE-BAKED POTATOES

Idaho homesteaders used potatoes as a cash crop in the mid-1800s. They sold the tubers to miners who rushed to the state looking for lead, gold, and silver. (Pictured on page 232)

2   **large baking potatoes (10 to 12 ounces each)**
½   **cup sour cream dip with toasted onion**
¼   **cup finely shredded cheddar cheese (1 ounce)**
¼   **cup finely shredded zucchini**
¼   **cup finely shredded carrot**
⅛   **teaspoon salt**
⅛   **teaspoon white pepper *or* black pepper**
1   **to 2 tablespoons milk (optional)**

Scrub potatoes thoroughly with a brush. Pat dry, and prick with a fork. Bake in a 425° oven for 40 to 60 minutes or till tender.

Cut potatoes in half lengthwise. Gently scoop out potato, leaving a thin shell. Place the potato pulp in a small mixing bowl.

With an electric mixer on low speed or a potato masher, beat or mash potato pulp. Add the sour cream dip, cheddar cheese, zucchini, carrot, salt, and pepper; beat till smooth. (If necessary to reach desired consistency, stir in 1 to 2 tablespoons milk.)

Spoon mashed potato mixture into potato shells. Place in a 1½-quart rectangular baking dish. Bake in a 425° oven for 20 to 25 minutes or till lightly browned. Serves 4.

Nutrition information per serving: 261 calories, 6 g protein, 41 g carbohydrate, 9 g total fat (5 g saturated), 20 mg cholesterol, 140 mg sodium, 735 mg potassium

California

STUFFED ARTICHOKES

California's artichoke industry got its start at the end of the nineteenth century. The first commercial acreage was developed by Italian immigrants who settled in the coastal area south of San Francisco. The thistly plant thrived in the foggy, damp climate. Today, about 12,000 acres are under cultivation in four counties. (Pictured on page 231)

4   **small artichokes (about 8 ounces each)**
1   **tablespoon lemon juice**
4   **dried tomato halves (not oil-packed)**
¾   **cup finely chopped zucchini**
⅓   **cup fine dry bread crumbs**
⅓   **cup grated Parmesan cheese *or* Romano cheese**
¼   **cup crumbled feta cheese**
2   **tablespoons margarine *or* butter, melted**
2   **teaspoons snipped fresh oregano *or* ½ teaspoon dried oregano, crushed**
⅛   **teaspoon pepper**

Wash artichokes; trim stems and remove loose outer leaves. Cut off 1 inch from each top; snip off the sharp leaf tips. Brush the cut edges with lemon juice.

In a large saucepan or Dutch oven bring a large amount of water to boiling. Add artichokes. Return to boiling; reduce heat. Cover and simmer for 20 to 30 minutes or till a leaf pulls out easily. Drain artichokes upside down on paper towels. Spread leaves apart.

When cool enough to handle, use a spoon to remove center leaves (cone) and choke; discard.

Meanwhile, place dried tomatoes in a small bowl. Add enough boiling water to cover tomatoes; soak for 10 to 15 minutes or till softened. Drain and pat dry. Finely chop tomatoes; set aside.

In a medium mixing bowl combine zucchini, bread crumbs, Parmesan or Romano cheese, feta cheese,

melted margarine or butter, oregano, pepper, and chopped tomatoes. Add enough water to moisten.

Place artichokes upright in a 2-quart square baking dish. Spoon zucchini mixture into artichoke centers and between leaves. Bake, loosely covered with foil, in a 350° oven about 25 minutes or till heated through. Makes 4 servings.

Nutrition information per serving: 278 calories, 13 g protein, 34 g carbohydrate, 12 g total fat (5 g saturated), 20 mg cholesterol, 599 mg sodium, 870 mg potassium

California

SUMMER RATATOUILLE

The Asian twist to this classic French eggplant casserole is very typical of current California cooking, which has become an increasingly cross-cultural mélange. (Pictured on page 238)

2   **tablespoons olive oil *or* cooking oil**
1   **small onion, cut into wedges**
2   **Japanese eggplants, cut into ¼-inch-thick slices**
1   **cup sliced fresh shiitake mushrooms *or* other mushrooms**
1   **small zucchini *or* yellow summer squash, halved lengthwise and cut into ¼-inch-thick slices (1 cup)**
½   **cup red *and/or* yellow sweet pepper strips**
2   **cloves garlic, minced**
2   **medium tomatoes, cut into wedges**
3   **tablespoons snipped fresh basil *or* 2 teaspoons dried basil, crushed**
¼   **teaspoon salt**
¼   **teaspoon coarsely ground pepper**
⅓   **cup finely shredded asiago cheese *or* Parmesan cheese**

Heat olive oil or cooking oil in a large skillet. Add onion, eggplant, mushrooms, zucchini or yellow summer squash, sweet pepper strips, and garlic. Cook and stir over medium heat about 10 minutes or till vegetables are tender. Add tomatoes, basil, salt, and pepper. Cook, stirring occasionally, for 5 minutes more. Sprinkle with cheese. Makes 4 to 5 servings.

Nutrition information per serving: 173 calories, 6 g protein, 18 g carbohydrate, 10 g total fat (3 g saturated), 6 mg cholesterol, 299 mg sodium, 568 mg potassium

Colorado

COWBOY BEANS

No range cook would start out on the trail without a good supply of dried beans. In fact, mealtime was often referred to as bean time.
(Pictured on page 234)

½   **pound dry pinto beans (1¼ cups)**
½   **cup chopped smoked ham *or* salt pork**
1   **cup chopped onion**
1   **8-ounce can tomato sauce**
1   **4-ounce can diced green chilies**
¼   **cup packed brown sugar**
1   **to 1½ teaspoons chili powder**
½   **teaspoon salt**
½   **teaspoon dry mustard**

Rinse beans. In a large saucepan combine beans and 4 cups *water.* Bring to boiling; reduce heat. Simmer for 2 minutes. Remove from heat. Cover and let stand for 1 hour. *(Or,* skip boiling the water and soak beans overnight in a covered bowl.)

Drain and rinse beans. In the same pan combine beans and 4 cups *fresh water.* Bring to boiling; reduce heat. Cover and simmer

Western Pepper Jelly

about 1¼ hours or till beans are tender, stirring occasionally. Drain beans, reserving liquid.

In a 1-quart casserole combine the beans, ham, and onion. Stir together ½ *cup* of the bean liquid, tomato sauce, chili peppers, brown sugar, chili powder, salt, and mustard. Stir into bean mixture. Bake, covered, in a 325° oven about 1 hour. Uncover and bake about 45 minutes more or to desired consistency, stirring occasionally. Makes 6 servings.

Nutrition information per serving: 198 calories, 12 g protein, 37 g carbohydrate, 1 g total fat (0 g saturated), 6 mg cholesterol, 788 mg sodium, 721 mg potassium

California

WESTERN PEPPER JELLY

When westerners put up their pickles and preserves, they revised their treasured recipes to include regional flavors and ingredients like spicy jalapeños. This jelly is offered as a condiment for meat, or as an hors d'oeuvre spread on crackers and topped with cheese.

2   **medium cooking apples, cored and coarsely chopped (2 cups)**
1   **medium green pepper, coarsely chopped (¾ cup)**
6   **to 8 jalapeño peppers, halved**
5   **cups sugar**
1½   **cups cider vinegar**
½   **of a 6-ounce package (1 foil pouch) liquid fruit pectin**
¼   **cup finely chopped green pepper**
¼   **cup finely chopped red sweet pepper**
1   **small banana pepper, finely chopped**

In a 4- or 5-quart Dutch oven combine apples, coarsely chopped green pepper, jalapeño peppers, sugar, vinegar, and ¼ cup *water.* Bring to boiling; reduce heat. Boil gently, uncovered, for 10 minutes.

Strain mixture through a sieve, pressing with back of a spoon to remove all liquid (you should have about 4 cups). Discard pulp. Return liquid to Dutch oven; bring to boil. Add pectin; bring to a full, rolling boil. Boil hard for 1 minute, stirring occasionally. Remove from heat. Stir in the finely chopped green pepper, red sweet pepper, and banana pepper.

Pour into hot, sterilized half-pint jars, leaving ¼-inch headspace. Wipe the rims and adjust the lids. Process in boiling-water canner for 5 minutes (start timing after water boils). Remove and cool on a wire rack till set. (Jelly will take 2 to 3 days to set. Chopped pepper pieces will float to top on standing.) Makes about 5 half-pints.

Note: If you would like to use antique canning jars, ladle the hot jelly into sterilized jars, leaving ½-inch headspace. Adjust lids; cool and then store in refrigerator.

Nutrition information per tablespoon: 47 calories, 0 g protein, 13 g carbohydrate, 0 g total fat (0 g saturated), 0 mg cholesterol, 0 mg sodium, 15 mg potassium

California

SOURDOUGH BREAD

Like their Alaska counterparts, California miners during the gold rushes of 1849 and later kept a bubbling crock of sourdough starter to use for baking. San Francisco is still famous for its sourdough bread, which has a unique flavor that no one has been able to duplicate anywhere else. (Pictured on page 236)

1	cup Sourdough Starter (see recipe, right)
5½	to 6 cups all-purpose flour
1	package active dry yeast
1½	cups water
3	tablespoons sugar
3	tablespoons margarine *or* butter
1	teaspoon salt
	Cornmeal

Bring Sourdough Starter to room temperature. In a large mixing bowl combine *2½ cups* of the flour and yeast; set aside. In a saucepan heat and stir water, sugar, margarine or butter, and salt *just till warm* (120° to 130°) and margarine almost melts. Add to flour mixture. Add Sourdough Starter. Beat with an electric mixer on low to medium speed for 30 seconds, scraping bowl. Beat on high speed for 3 minutes. Stir in as much of the remaining flour as you can.

On a lightly floured surface, knead in enough of the remaining flour to make a moderately stiff dough that is smooth and elastic (6 to 8 minutes total). Shape into a ball. Place dough in a lightly greased bowl, turning once to grease the surface. Cover and let rise in a warm place till double (45 to 60 minutes).

Punch dough down. Turn out onto a lightly floured surface. Divide in half. Cover and let rest for 10 minutes. Meanwhile, lightly grease a large baking sheet. Sprinkle with cornmeal. Shape *each* half of dough into a ball. Place on prepared baking sheet. Flatten

slightly to 6 inches in diameter. With a sharp knife, make crisscross slashes about ¼ inch deep across the tops of the loaves. Cover and let rise in a warm place till *nearly* double (about 30 minutes).

Bake in a 375° oven for 30 to 35 minutes or till bread tests done (if necessary, cover loosely with foil the last 15 minutes of baking to prevent overbrowning). Cool on a wire rack. Makes 2 loaves (24 servings).

Nutrition information per serving: 144 calories, 4 g protein, 28 g carbohydrate, 2 g total fat (0 g saturated), 0 mg cholesterol, 102 mg sodium, 45 mg potassium

SOURDOUGH STARTER

1	package active dry yeast
2½	cups warm water (105° to 115°)
2	cups all-purpose flour
1	tablespoon sugar *or* honey

In a bowl dissolve yeast in *½ cup* of the warm water. Stir in the remaining water, flour, and sugar or honey. Stir till smooth. Cover bowl with 100 percent cotton cheesecloth. Let stand at room temperature (75° to 85°) 5 to 10 days or till the mixture has a sour, fermented aroma, stirring 2 or 3 times each day. (Fermentation time depends upon the room temperature; a warmer room hastens fermentation.)

When fermented, transfer starter to a 1-quart jar. Cover with cheesecloth; refrigerate. Do not cover jar with a tight-fitting lid. If starter isn't used within 10 days, stir in 1 teaspoon *sugar or honey*. Repeat every 10 days till used.

To use starter, bring desired amount to room temperature. For every 1 cup used, stir ¾ cup *all-purpose flour*, ¾ cup *water*, and 1 teaspoon *sugar or honey* into the remaining amount. Cover and let stand at room temperature at least 1 day or till bubbly. Then refrigerate for later use. Makes about 2 cups.

Montana

KOLACHES

For the Bohemians who settled in Montana, these yeast-raised sweet rolls were a fragrant reminder of home. There are a number of traditional fillings, including one made of ground poppy seed, milk, and honey. (Pictured on page 224)

3¾	to 4¼ cups all-purpose flour
1	package active dry yeast
1	cup milk
¾	cup margarine *or* butter
½	cup sugar
½	teaspoon salt
4	egg yolks
1	teaspoon finely shredded lemon peel
	Apricot Filling
2	tablespoons margarine *or* butter, melted, *or* milk
	Powdered sugar

In a large mixing bowl stir together *2 cups* of the flour and the yeast. Set aside.

In a medium saucepan heat and stir the 1 cup milk, the ¾ cup margarine or butter, sugar, and salt *just till warm* (120° to 130°) and margarine almost melts. Add to the flour mixture. Add the egg yolks. Beat with an electric mixer on low to medium speed for 30 seconds, scraping the sides of the bowl constantly. Then beat on high speed for 3 minutes. Using a wooden spoon, stir in the lemon peel and as much of the remaining flour as you can.

Turn dough out onto a lightly floured surface. Knead in enough of the remaining flour to make a moderately soft dough that is smooth and elastic (3 to 5 minutes total). Place dough in a greased bowl, turning once to grease the surface. Cover and let rise in a warm place till double (1 to 1½ hours). Meanwhile, prepare desired filling. Set aside to cool.

Punch down dough. Turn the dough out onto a lightly floured surface. Divide in half. Cover and let rest for 10 minutes. Grease baking sheets. Shape *each* half of dough into 12 balls, pulling the edges under to make smooth tops. Place the balls 3 inches apart on the prepared baking sheets. Flatten each ball to 2½ inches in diameter. Cover; let rise till *nearly* double (about 35 minutes).

Using your thumb or two fingers, make an indentation in the center of each dough circle. Spoon about *2 teaspoons* filling into each indentation. Lightly brush the 2 tablespoons melted margarine or milk around the edges of rolls.

Bake in a 375° oven for 10 to 12 minutes or till rolls are golden brown. Remove rolls from baking sheets and cool on a wire rack. Lightly sift powdered sugar over the tops. Makes 24 kolaches.

Apricot Filling: In a small saucepan combine 1 cup snipped dried *apricots* and enough *water* to come 1 inch above the apricots. Bring to boiling. Reduce heat. Cover and simmer for 10 to 15 minutes or till apricots are very soft. Drain, reserving *2 tablespoons* cooking liquid.

In a blender container or food processor bowl place apricots, reserved liquid, ¼ cup *sugar,* 1 teaspoon *lemon juice,* and ¼ teaspoon ground *nutmeg.* Cover and blend or process till smooth, stopping to scrape down the sides as necessary. Makes 1 cup.

Nutrition information per kolache: 188 calories, 3 g protein, 26 g carbohydrate, 8 g total fat (1 g saturated), 36 mg cholesterol, 108 mg sodium, 124 mg potassium

California

DATE PINWHEEL COOKIES

Date palms need the hot, dry climate of the desert to survive, so it's not surprising that those planted by the Spanish missionaries along the California coast did poorly. Early in this century, experiments with an Algerian variety in the state's inland valleys finally proved successful.

Date Pinwheel Cookies

Date Filling
½	**cup margarine *or* butter**
½	**cup shortening**
3	**cups all-purpose flour**
½	**cup sugar**
½	**cup packed brown sugar**
1	**egg**
3	**tablespoons milk**
1	**teaspoon vanilla**
½	**teaspoon baking soda**
¼	**teaspoon salt**

Prepare Date Filling; set aside.

Beat margarine or butter and shortening with an electric mixer about 30 seconds or till softened. Add about *half* of the flour. Then add the sugars, egg, milk, vanilla, baking soda, and salt. Beat till thoroughly combined, scraping the sides of the bowl occasionally. Beat or stir in the remaining flour. Cover and chill about 1 hour or till easy to handle.

To shape, divide the dough in half. Place each half of the dough between 2 sheets of waxed paper. Using a rolling pin, roll each half into a 12x10-inch rectangle. Remove top sheets of waxed paper.

Spread Date Filling over each half of the dough. From a long side, roll up each half jelly-roll style, removing bottom sheet of paper as you roll. Moisten and pinch edges to seal each roll. Wrap each in waxed paper or plastic wrap. Chill for 4 to 48 hours.

Grease a cookie sheet; set aside. Cut the dough into ¼-inch-thick slices. Place slices 2 inches apart on the prepared cookie sheet. Bake in a 375° oven for 10 to 12 minutes or till done. Remove cookies from cookie sheet and cool on a wire rack. Makes about 84 cookies.

Date Filling: In a small saucepan snip one 8-ounce package (1⅓ cups) pitted whole *dates.* Stir in ½ cup *water* and ⅓ cup *sugar.* Bring to boiling, then reduce heat. Cook and stir about 2 minutes or till thickened. Then stir in 2 tablespoons *lemon juice* and ½ teaspoon *vanilla.* Set filling aside to cool. Makes about 2 cups.

Nutrition information per cookie: 56 calories, 1 g protein, 8 g carbohydrate, 2 g total fat (0 g saturated), 2 mg cholesterol, 22 mg sodium, 27 mg potassium

GRAPEFRUIT MERINGUE PIE

California is a main producer of citrus fruit, including oranges, lemons, and grapefruit. The citrus industry faced a unique crisis after the San Francisco earthquake of 1906: so much lumber was needed to rebuild the city that none was left to make crates for boxing citrus fruit.

1	cup sugar
3	tablespoons all-purpose flour
3	tablespoons cornstarch
	Dash salt
1½	cups water
3	eggs
2	tablespoons margarine *or* butter
1½	teaspoons finely shredded grapefruit peel
⅓	cup grapefruit juice
	Pastry for Single-Crust Pie (see recipe, page 55)
	Meringue for Pie

For filling, in a medium saucepan combine sugar, flour, cornstarch, and salt. Gradually stir in water. Cook and stir over medium-high heat till thickened and bubbly. Reduce heat; cook and stir for 2 minutes more. Remove from heat.

Separate egg yolks from whites; set whites aside to come to room temperature for meringue. Beat egg yolks slightly. Gradually stir *1 cup* of the hot filling into yolks; return all to saucepan. Bring to a gentle boil. Cook and stir 2 minutes more. Remove from heat. Stir in margarine or butter and grapefruit peel. Gradually stir in grapefruit juice, gently mixing well. Pour hot filling into Baked Pastry Shell.

Immediately spread meringue over *hot* pie filling, carefully spreading to edge of pastry to seal and prevent shrinkage.

Bake in a 350° oven for 15 minutes. Cool for 1 hour on a wire rack. Cover and chill. Makes 8 servings.

Creamy Fresh Apricot Tart, left, Grapefruit Meringue Pie, right, and Pioneer Fruit Candy

Meringue for Pie: Let the 3 *egg whites* stand at room temperature for 30 minutes. In a large mixing bowl combine the egg whites, ½ teaspoon *vanilla*, and ¼ teaspoon *cream of tartar*. Beat with an electric mixer on medium speed about 1 minute or till soft peaks form (tips curl). Gradually add 6 tablespoons *sugar*, 1 tablespoon at a time, beating on high speed about 4 minutes more or till mixture forms stiff, glossy peaks and sugar dissolves.

Nutrition information per serving: 430 calories, 7 g protein, 60 g carbohydrate, 19 g total fat (4 g saturated), 80 mg cholesterol, 306 mg sodium, 70 mg potassium

CREAMY FRESH APRICOT TART

Apricots were reportedly grown in Virginia in the seventeenth century, but even that gentle climate was too harsh for the delicate fruit. Commercial orchards were successfully established in the Santa Clara Valley near San Jose as early as 1792. Today the Golden State leads the nation and the world in apricot production.

1¼	cups all-purpose flour
¼	cup sugar
½	cup ground toasted pistachio nuts *or* almonds
½	cup cold margarine *or* butter
2	beaten egg yolks
1	tablespoon water
½	cup sugar
3	tablespoons cornstarch

vanilla. Cover surface with plastic wrap; cool to room temperature (*do not stir*). Spread filling in cooled pastry shell. Arrange apricot quarters, cut sides up, in a circle atop filling. Press fruit gently into filling till flush with filling surface. Cover; chill 1 to 3 hours. Before serving, sprinkle with toasted nuts. Serves 8.

Nutrition information per serving: *418 calories, 9 g protein, 46 g carbohydrate, 23 g total fat (4 g saturated), 138 mg cholesterol, 145 mg sodium, 356 mg potassium*

Utah

PIONEER FRUIT CANDY

A shortage of food was a familiar hardship to the first Mormon settlers in Utah. To be prepared for any emergency, Mormons still follow the practice of stockpiling a year's worth of provisions. Canned and preserved foods, like the dried fruits used for this candy, are pantry staples.

1⅓	cups raisins
¾	cup dried figs
⅔	cup pitted dates
½	cup chopped pitted prunes
1	teaspoon finely shredded orange peel
½	cup finely chopped walnuts
1	tablespoon frozen orange juice concentrate, thawed
8	ounces chocolate *or* white candy coating, chopped
1	tablespoon shortening

Finely chop first four ingredients. *Or,* process in a food processor.

Mix fruit, orange peel, walnuts, and juice concentrate. Shape into balls about 1-inch in diameter. Chill several hours or overnight.

In a saucepan melt candy coating and shortening over low heat, stirring constantly. Dip candies in chocolate to coat evenly. Place on waxed paper. Let harden on a wire rack. Makes about 42 candies.

Nutrition information per candy: *76 calories, 1 g protein, 13 g carbohydrate, 3 g total fat (1 g saturated), 0 mg cholesterol, 1 mg sodium, 107 mg potassium*

2	cups milk
3	beaten egg yolks
1	tablespoon margarine *or* butter
1	teaspoon vanilla
8	fresh whole apricots, pitted and quartered
3	tablespoons chopped toasted pistachio nuts *or* toasted slivered almonds

For pastry, stir together the flour, the ¼ cup sugar, and ground nuts. Cut in the ½ cup margarine till pieces are the size of small peas. Combine the 2 egg yolks and water; gradually stir the egg yolk mixture into the flour mixture. Using your fingers, gently knead dough just till a ball forms. If necessary, chill 30 to 60 minutes or till easy to handle.

On a lightly floured surface roll dough from center to edges, forming a 12-inch circle. Wrap pastry around a rolling pin; unroll pastry onto a 10-inch tart pan with a removable bottom. Ease pastry into tart pan, being careful not to stretch it. Press pastry into the fluted sides of the tart pan and trim edges. Using the tines of a fork, prick bottom and sides of pastry generously.

Line pastry shell with a double thickness of foil. Bake in a 375° oven 10 minutes. Remove foil. Bake 8 to 10 minutes more or till golden. Completely cool pastry shell in pan.

Meanwhile, for filling, in a saucepan mix the ½ cup sugar and the cornstarch; stir in milk. Cook and stir over medium heat till mixture is bubbly. Cook and stir 2 minutes more. Remove from heat. Gradually stir about *1 cup* of the milk mixture into the 3 egg yolks. Stir egg yolk mixture into milk mixture in saucepan. Bring to a gentle boil; reduce heat. Cook and stir 2 minutes. Remove from heat. Stir in the 1 tablespoon margarine and

California

POACHED FIGS WITH CRÈME ANGLAISE

California provides all of America's commercially grown figs. The first variety planted in the state came to be known as the Black Mission as it was brought here by the Spanish padres. Along with the amber-colored Calimyrna, it is still one of the most popular.

⅔   **cup whipping cream**
1   **egg yolk**
⅓   **cup sugar**
½   **teaspoon vanilla**
1   **cup port**
4   **light *or* 8 dark fresh whole figs *or* 2 large pears, cored and halved**
    Fresh mint sprigs

For crème anglaise, in a small, heavy saucepan bring cream just to boiling, stirring frequently. Remove saucepan from heat.

In a bowl combine about *2 tablespoons* of the hot cream, the egg yolk, and sugar. Beat with an electric mixer on high speed 2 to 3 minutes or till thick and lemon-colored.

Gradually stir about *half* of the remaining cream mixture into the egg yolk mixture. Transfer the egg yolk mixture to the saucepan. Cook and stir over medium heat about 5 minutes or till mixture *nearly* returns to boiling. Remove from heat. Stir in vanilla. Cover surface with plastic wrap. Chill in the refrigerator till serving time.

To poach figs or pears, in a skillet bring port to boiling; add figs or pears. Return to boiling; reduce heat. Cover; simmer over low heat about 5 minutes or till tender. Using a slotted spoon, remove fruit from port. Return port to boiling; cook over medium heat 4 to 5 minutes or till liquid is reduced to about ½ cup. Chill fruit and port separately.

To serve, spoon crème anglaise onto 4 dessert plates. Place figs or pear half in the center of each plate. Drizzle with the port. Garnish with fresh mint. Makes 4 servings.

Poached Figs with Crème Anglaise

Nutrition information per serving: 381 calories, 2 g protein, 44 g carbohydrate, 16 g total fat (10 g saturated), 108 mg cholesterol, 23 mg sodium, 320 mg potassium

California

CALIFORNIA ALMOND SHORTBREAD COOKIES

Virtually all of this country's almonds are from California. While attempts were made to grow the nut elsewhere, few states could provide the proper climatic conditions for the trees to thrive. Almonds are also California's largest food export.

2   **cups all-purpose flour**
½   **cup sugar**
½   **cup ground toasted almonds**
1   **cup butter**
¾   **cup semisweet chocolate pieces**
1½   **teaspoons shortening**
    About 40 blanched whole almonds

In a bowl combine flour, sugar, and ground almonds. Cut in butter till mixture resembles fine crumbs and starts to cling. Shape into a ball and knead till smooth. Divide in half.

On an ungreased cookie sheet pat or roll *half* of the dough into a 9x5-inch rectangle. Repeat with other half of dough.

Bake in a 325° oven for 20 to 25 minutes or till bottom of the dough just starts to turn brown. Cool about 5 minutes. While shortbread is still warm, cut each rectangle into 3x1 inch sticks; cool on a wire rack.

In a small heavy saucepan melt chocolate and shortening together over low heat, stirring occasionally. Dip half of each cookie into chocolate mixture. Place an almond in the center of each glazed half. Place cookies on waxed paper and let stand till chocolate is set. (*Or*, refrigerate cookies about 5 minutes or till chocolate is set.) Makes about 40 cookies.

Nutrition information per cookie: 110 calories, 1 g protein, 10 g carbohydrate, 7 g total fat (4 g saturated), 12 mg cholesterol, 48 mg sodium, 45 mg potassium

California

CAPPUCCINO

San Francisco has always been known as a coffee-drinking town. The coffeehouses in the North Beach section, home to much of the city's Italian population, were famous as gathering places in the 1950s for poets, writers, and artists.

1½   **cups half-and-half, light cream, *or* milk**
2   **cups brewed espresso coffee**
    Unsweetened cocoa powder *or* ground cinnamon

In a saucepan heat half-and-half till almost boiling. Remove from heat and beat with a rotary beater or wire whisk till foamy. To each of 4 coffee cups add ½ *cup* of espresso coffee and ½ *cup* of half-and-half. Sprinkle with cocoa powder. Makes four 8-ounce servings.

Nutrition information per serving: 121 calories, 3 g protein, 4 g carbohydrate, 10 g total fat (6 g saturated), 33 mg cholesterol, 39 mg sodium, 185 mg potassium

Cappucino, and California Almond Shortbread Cookies

The Pacific Northwest and Beyond

Before the Oregon Territory began to attract settlers during the mid–nineteenth century, the wilderness that now comprises the states of Washington and Oregon was inhabited by numerous groups of Native Americans, including the Tlingit, Salish, Chinook, and Haida.

The impressive Cascade Range traverses this region from north to south, producing coastal lowlands to the west and an arid region to the east. Further diversity is created by Oregon's high desert and the rich fertility and temperate climate of the Willamette Valley just south of Portland. The Native Americans of this region enjoyed a diet of plenty, with an abundance of seafood, game, and wild berries. For their starch, they relied primarily upon the wild camas bulb, which they dug up with sticks, baked, and then sun-dried for winter use.

Salmon was the staple of most Indians of the Pacific Northwest, who would migrate each summer to spear these delicious fish in the mighty Columbia River (which acts as a natural border between Washington and Oregon). What they didn't eat fresh, they would air-dry in the gusty river winds to create jerky. Often, they would simultaneously smoke the salmon over

an alder-wood fire—a practice that has lasted until this day and given the region one of its most famous specialties. A wide variety of mollusks were preserved for winter in similar fashion.

The social relations among the many tribes were regulated by a ceremonial feast known by the Chinook word *potlatch*, meaning "gift." During the course of several days of festivities, food would be exchanged and offered as "take-away" gifts. In this way, a more equal distribution of natural wealth was created, and all groups had an adequate store of food for survival during an unexpectedly harsh winter.

As any visitor to Seattle's Pike Place Market (established in 1907 and still going strong!) can tell at a glance, the bounty of this region remains as impressive now as it was during the era of the great potlatch. With its temperate climate, long growing season, and fertile valleys, the area produces magnificent produce and very fine tree fruit.

Washington is famous for its glorious apples and cherries, including Bings, Lamberts, and Royal Annes. Washington cherries are extraordinary when in season and are even more intensely flavored in their dried form. Oregon produces fine plums and approximately ninety-five percent of the country's pears—Boscs, Seckels, Comice, and Anjou, to name but a few varieties. And the locally produced jams, jellies, and fruit butters sold at the market are fine reminders of the extensive harvest.

The dairy cases are also full of finely crafted regional cheeses, including Oregon blue, Tillamook cheddar, Cougar gold (a white cheddar), and Yakima gouda. But a stroller through the market will inevitably be drawn to the seafood stalls, where huge red just-boiled Dungeness crabs are set in layers twelve deep. There are mussels, smelts, shrimp, razor clams, and at least a half-dozen variety of oysters. And if you spot a gargantuan clam with a two-foot syphon protruding from its shell, it will no doubt be the geoduck (pronounced *GOO-ee-duck*), with each single specimen weighing in at two to three pounds. The neck (syphon) of the geoduck is used for

Previous pages: Oregon Territory must have resembled paradise to weary pioneers. Lilies bloom at the base of Mt. Ranier, Washington.
Right: Fruit trees flourish on both sides of the Cascade Range, although the climate to the west is wet and to the east is dry. Mt. Hood looms from a distance over an Oregon pear orchard.

How the Pacific Northwest Was Won— By an Apple Tree

When settlers brought the first apple seedlings with them to the Pacific Northwest during the mid–nineteenth century, the trees immediately prospered, finding a climate so ideally suited to their needs that before long Washington growers developed a fine reputation for their handsome fruit. Indeed, Washington apples were so highly esteemed by the time of the Gold Rush that the sale of four bushels of them in California brought the extraordinary price of $500 back in 1852.

Like snowflakes, there are no two apple trees alike. For this reason, the history of apple varieties reads like the Who's Who of Noble Fruit, and each type has its own unique biography. Take Washington's Golden Delicious variety, for example. Its transplanted life began in the 1880s when Anderson Mullen of Clay County, West Virginia, bought some Golden Russet seedlings from an itinerant peddler. Over the next few decades the seedlings grew into a small orchard, but one particular tree captured Mullen's attention because of the unusual look, crisp texture, and delicious taste of the fruit. The mutant tree quickly became famous throughout the county, and in 1914 the famous Stark Nursery in Missouri purchased the rights to Mullen's Yellow Seedlings, renaming them Golden Delicious.

Over the next few decades, apple growers in the Wenatchee area east of the Cascades began to notice how well this variety did in their dry, sunny orchards. By the mid-1940s, the crop size averaged close to 17 million pounds per year. Nowadays, Washington supplies the country with more than half a billion pounds of Golden Delicious apples annually.

chowders while the more delicate body meat is either fried or "acid-cooked" in lemon juice for ceviche.

Although the geoduck is an interesting oddity, in this part of the world it's ultimately the salmon that steal the show. And it's not just a matter of saying, "I'll have a pound of salmon, please." It's a matter of knowing if you want Chinook salmon, with its intense flavor and high fat content, or silver salmon, which is not quite as flavorful or rich. Or perhaps you prefer sockeye salmon, with its bright red flesh and melt-in-the-mouth texture, or even chum or pink salmon if you're on a budget or planning to mix the cooked salmon with mayonnaise for a salad.

Salmon is, of course, featured in many Northwest restaurants. You might find, for example, grilled or poached salmon in a seafood restaurant, or perhaps an elegant dish of gravlax, a dill-flecked pickled salmon introduced by the large number of Scandinavians who settled in the region. Alternatively,

Wild mushrooms thrive in the forests of the northwestern states (above). Right: Dense woodlands like those of Oregon's Silver Creek National Park and Washington's misty rain forests are classic images of the region. Below: Huge tracts of unclaimed land and the opportunity to work its vast timber forests lured restless easterners like these loggers to the Oregon Territory.

you might prefer a plate of salmon sushi, where the raw fish is surrounded by vinegared rice and wrapped in seaweed—an approach introduced by the Japanese.

The strong Asian influence felt throughout the Pacific Northwest began in the 1850s when large numbers of Chinese immigrants came to work on the railroads, and in the logging camps and seafood canning factories. The Japanese followed soon thereafter. The minimalist approach that characterizes Asian cooking was ideally suited to the high-quality indigenous ingredients, and in many of the region's finest restaurants the scent of ginger or the sizzle of stir-fry cooking is clearly evident.

In the fog-shrouded Northwest, the frequent drizzle rewards poncho-draped mycologists with thousands of varieties of wild mushrooms. Among the edible treasures of the damp and shady forests are porcini (cèpes), chanterelles, oysters, morels, and Oregon white truffles.

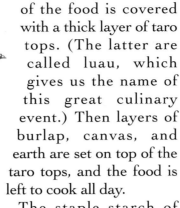

The region is also noted for its profusion of wild berries, including huckleberries, blackberries, and blueberries. These are often made into pies and cobblers, betraying a strong English influence in the area's kitchens. This influence was transported across country by settlers who came from New England to set down new roots along the Pacific Coast, and who gave towns names like Portland and Salem to remind them of their former homes.

Aloha Cookery

Countless years after the volcanic islands known as Hawaii emerged from the Pacific Ocean, they were inhabited by seafaring Polynesians who introduced three foods that became the basic staples of the island diet: pigs, taro, and coconuts. The Polynesians also brought their traditional technique of pit cooking, a method for preparing food that developed in the absence of fireproof cooking pots.

Pit cooking evolved into the memorable feast we now know as the luau. A luau must be planned in advance so that the pit can be dug and lined with wood and lava rock. After the wood is burned and the rocks have become red-hot, a layer of banana tree stumps is placed in the pit to create steam and to protect the food from burning by direct contact with the rocks.

A large pig is essential to any luau. After the pig is stuffed with sizzling-hot rocks, it is covered with ti leaves and then lowered into the pit. Taro, breadfruit, and a variety of whole fish are set around the pig before all

of the food is covered with a thick layer of taro tops. (The latter are called luau, which gives us the name of this great culinary event.) Then layers of burlap, canvas, and earth are set on top of the taro tops, and the food is left to cook all day.

The staple starch of Hawaii is poi, a simple porridgelike dish made by pounding baked taro root with water to create a purplish paste. Traditionally eaten with the hands, "two-finger" poi is quite thick, while "three-finger" poi is further thinned with water, requiring an additional finger for scooping it up. For Hawaiians, a meal isn't quite complete without a helping of poi. Visitors seem to find this bland dish more interesting than delicious.

It wasn't until Captain James Cook discovered the Hawaiian islands in 1778 that thousands of years of isolation were ended. Over the course of the next century, immigrants arrived from the Philippines, Japan, China, and Korea, creating a hybrid Asian-Polynesian cooking style. The Chinese introduced stir-fry cooking and their love of rice and soy sauce. The Koreans brought their beloved pickled cabbage, kimchi. With the Japanese came hibachi grilling and a devotion to sea vegetables. The standard Hawaiian pupu platter of mixed appetizers—including such specialties as dim sum, sushi, Korean meatballs, and tidbits of marinated, grilled steak—reveals the eagerness with which island cooks embraced all of these culinary influences.

Hawaii is a major producer of macadamias. These very rich and flavorful nuts that resemble filberts were introduced from their native Australia about a century ago.

Freshly harvested macadamias have a subtle sweetness. When roasted, they develop a robust crunch that makes them most welcome additions to cakes, pies, and fruit salads.

Hawaii is a veritable paradise for fruit lovers. When Hawaii became the fiftieth state in 1959, it brought

Kauai is one of the wettest spots on earth, so the lushness of Kalalau Valley isn't surprising. Sugar and pineapple are important crops on this and other Hawaiian islands.

into the United States the luscious fruits of the tropical sun: the star fruit called carambola, the crimson Natal plum called carissa, and the ohelo berry. Cultivated pineapple is probably the most famous export, but strawberry guavas, papayas, and coconuts grow wild, there for the picking by any hungry passerby.

Coconut is much loved by Hawaiian cooks, who use it to prepare *malihini*, made by simmering chicken and pineapple chunks in coconut milk. A pudding made of taro and coconut called *haupia* is a traditional island dessert, and grated coconut and coconut cream are both used extensively in pies and cakes. And if your fresh fruit salad or piña colada is presented to you in a hollowed-out coconut shell, you can be pretty sure that you're in Hawaii.

To the lower forty-eight, Alaska will always be the frontier because of its relative isolation and vast expanses of wilderness.

Talking Coffee In Seattle

Latte-land.

That's how Seattleites have recently begun referring to their hometown, and with good reason. You can hardly walk a block in any direction without inhaling the deep, dark, delicious scent of freshly brewing coffee.

Sidewalk coffee carts, espresso kiosks, bakeries, even the local health-food store, all sell a mind-boggling array of coffee-to-go. There are even drive-though coffee bars with names like Motor Moka. Perish the thought that someone may not have a cupful of foaming brew at arm's reach.

A visitor to Seattle who wants to join in the fun immediately encoun-ters a language and educational barrier. What is a "Double Dry Short," for example, or a "Harm-less"? How are you supposed to know if you want Guatemalan cof-fee or Kenyan? Denizens of Latte-land talk about coffee with the same degree of connoisseurship that Californians have developed about wine, and it's hard getting what you want if you don't know the lingo.

Here is a preview of the forth-coming course on conversational coffee:

Barista—the person behind the counter who prepares and serves the coffee

Cappuccino—espresso blended with steamed milk and topped with foamed milk

Double Cher—espresso with steamed skim milk, sweetened with the sugar substitute called Equal

Double Dry Short—double shot of espresso in a small cup without any foam

Drip Brew Grande—large cup of good old American coffee

Espresso—intense, dark-roasted coffee served black in a small cup

Espresso con Panna—espresso topped with whipped cream

Harmless—decaf with nonfat milk

Latte—coffee topped with steamed milk and a layer of foamed milk, short for *caffè latte*

Alaska—the Last Frontier

It's easy to think of Alaska as eternally "frozen under," but this vast state—over twice the size of Texas—actually has numerous richly agricultural regions. The best known is Matanuska Valley, about fifty miles north of Anchorage. Here, during the short but intense summer growing season, twenty-three hours of daily sunlight commonly create sixty-pound cabbages and three-pound radishes.

Alaska is also blessed with magnificent wild berries, including blueberries, elderberries, and crowberries (better known as lingonberries). These are frequently used to make cakes, preserves, and a wide variety of relishes to accompany wild game.

For the native Indians, Eskimos, and Aleuts, eating has always been more about survival than about refinement. Salmon was the staple food for Indians living in the more temperate Panhandle and along the southern coast. They supplemented their abundant diet with seal, sea otter, and game as well as wild roots and berries. Foods readily available in spring and summer were dried to last over the long winter months.

Life was not as easy for the Eskimos who inhabited northern and western Alaska. Their main source of food—seal, whale, and walrus—was the frigid waters of the Arctic Ocean and Bering Sea. Since firewood was scarce, these meats were typically eaten raw, and the high fat content of such fare as whale blubber provided much-needed fuel for keeping the body warm in subzero temperatures.

The diet of Alaskan Eskimos depended on what was available to them. In the more temperate south, it was interesting and varied. In the frigid north and west, there were few choices. Whale was one.

Wild game was also a major source of calories for the nomadic Eskimos, who ate moose, bighorn sheep, musk-ox, mountain goat, caribou, polar bear, geese, and eider ducks. In these parts of the world, it was a simple matter to quick-freeze for storage whatever meat wasn't eaten fresh.

The name Alaska comes from the Aleut word *Al-ay-ek-sa*, meaning "Great Land." Like the Eskimos, the Aleuts of southwestern Alaska depended upon the seal as a main form of sustenance, supplemented by fish, wildfowl, and berries. Their marginal existence was further challenged when the Russian fur trappers colonized the Aleutian Islands in 1741. The result after more than a century was the near extinction of both sea otters and the Aleut population.

But Alaska was not to remain desolate for long. Around the turn of the century, boomtowns like Juneau, Nome, and Fairbanks sprung up to answer to the needs of prospectors who had struck gold.

Gold dust became the medium of exchange, and meals cost a small fortune, but during this time many of the basic foods of the lower forty-eight were introduced: eggs, milk, ham, and beef. And every good restaurant had a bubbling crock of sourdough starter for biscuits and bread. By the time Alaska became the forty-ninth state in 1959, many mainstream American foods were already available in the larger cities, particularly canned foods, coffee, and sugar.

Like Washington and Oregon, Alaska today is best known to gastronomes for its extraordinary range of seafood. Leading the list is inevitably salmon, with the Alaskan king crab following a close second. Lesser known are the surviving pockets of ethnic cooking, a legacy of immigration during the nineteenth century. In the Panhandle city of Sitka, Russian specialties are washed down with hot tea, and in Petersburg the Norwegian influence is keenly felt.

Although visitors may be curious to taste native favorites like seal or walrus, the federal Marine Mammal Protection Act of 1972 made it illegal for all but native Alaskans to hunt these animals for food. Nowadays, the meat is still frequently eaten raw, but on occasion it is cooked. For example, here's a sampling of recipe titles from the hefty collection *Cooking Alaskan*, published in 1983: fried seal liver ("tastes better than the finest calves' liver!"), sea lion meatballs and spaghetti, walrus meat loaf, and Arctic muktuk chowder (muktuk is the blubber and skin of the whale). And what's for dessert? Whale oil sugar cookies, to be sure.[1]

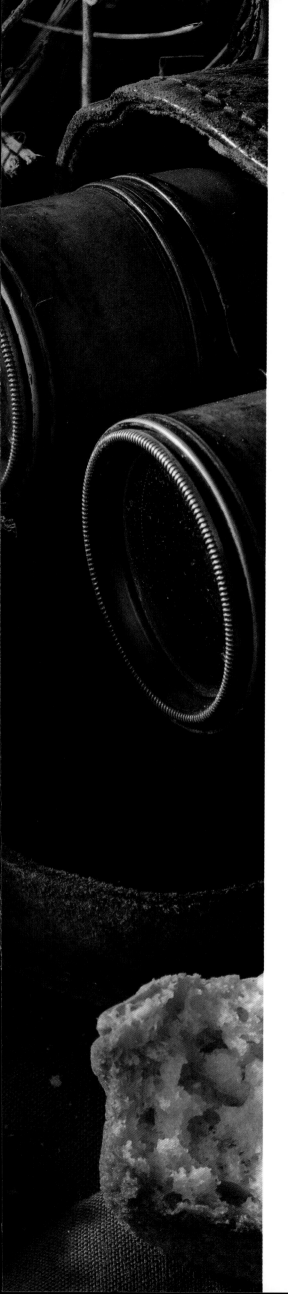

Flavors from the Pacific Northwest & Beyond

Oregon

PEAR, PROSCIUTTO, AND BLUE CHEESE APPETIZERS

Washington and Oregon, along with California, produce virtually all of the nation's commercial pear crop. The first Bartlett pear tree was planted in Oregon in 1854 in the Rogue River Valley. That valley is also the birthplace of Oregon's acclaimed blue cheese. (Pictured on page 262)

3 to 4 ounces very thinly sliced prosciutto
1 ripe pear, cored and cut into 12 wedges
½ cup crumbled blue cheese
2 tablespoons soft-style cream cheese
2 teaspoons milk

Cut prosciutto lengthwise into 12 strips (each about 6x1½ inches). Combine blue cheese, cream cheese, and milk.

Spread about *½ tablespoon* of the blue cheese mixture on a prosciutto strip. Wrap the strip around one pear wedge. Repeat with remaining ingredients.

To serve, place seam side down on a lettuce-lined platter. Chill up to 2 hours. Makes 12 appetizers.

Nutrition information per appetizer: 48 calories, 3 g protein, 2 g carbohydrate, 3 g total fat (2 g saturated), 11 mg cholesterol, 181 mg sodium, 59 mg potassium

Pumpkin Soup (see recipe, page 269), and Oatmeal-Prune Muffins (see recipe, page 271)

Washington

FRESH HERB AND CHÈVRE SPREAD

Although California gets the lion's share of attention for its justly famous goat cheeses, the Puget Sound area of Washington produces a fine local product. (Pictured on page 262)

1 8-ounce package cream cheese, softened
8 ounces chèvre (goat cheese)
2 tablespoons finely chopped green onion
1 tablespoon snipped fresh tarragon *or* 1 teaspoon dried tarragon, crushed
1 tablespoon snipped fresh rosemary *or* ½ teaspoon dried rosemary, crushed
¼ teaspoon ground white pepper
2 dried tomato halves (oil-packed)
   Fresh tarragon *or* rosemary (optional)
   Assorted crackers

Beat together the cream cheese, chèvre, green onion, tarragon, rosemary, and white pepper.

Pat tomatoes with paper towels to remove excess oil. Finely chop tomatoes; stir into cheese mixture.

If desired, press cheese mixture into a 2- to 2½-cup mold lined with plastic wrap. Cover and chill for several hours or overnight.

Unmold onto a serving platter. (*Or*, chill spread in a bowl and spoon onto a serving platter to serve.) If desired, garnish with fresh tarragon or rosemary. Serve with crackers. Makes 2 cups.

Nutrition information per tablespoon: 46 calories, 2 g protein, 5 g carbohydrate, 4 g total fat (3 g saturated), 11 mg cholesterol, 49 mg sodium, 26 mg potassium

Fresh Herb and Chèvre Spread, top, and Pear, Prosciutto, and Blue Cheese Appetizers (see recipes, page 261)

Oregon

BASQUE LAMB SHANKS

Before the turn of the century, Basque sheepherders came from Spain to settle in the mountainous areas of the West. Their families followed later. Retired sheepherders and their wives opened boardinghouses that became famous for their home cooking.

3 or 4 lamb shanks
    (about 3½ pounds total)
1 tablespoon cooking oil
2 14½-ounce cans stewed
    tomatoes
½ cup chopped onion
½ cup water
½ teaspoon dried thyme,
    crushed
½ teaspoon dried basil,
    crushed
¼ teaspoon salt
¼ teaspoon pepper
1 15-ounce can garbanzo
    beans, drained
3 cups hot cooked rice *or*
    couscous

In a Dutch oven brown lamb shanks on all sides in hot oil. Drain off fat. Add *undrained* tomatoes, onion, water, thyme, basil, salt, and pepper. Bring to boiling, reduce heat. Cover and simmer for 1½ hours or till lamb is tender. Skim excess fat from pan juices. Stir in garbanzo beans and heat through.

Serve over hot cooked rice or couscous. Makes 4 to 6 servings.

Nutrition information per serving: 546 calories, 39 g protein, 62 g carbohydrate, 16 g total fat (6 g saturated), 108 mg cholesterol, 603 mg sodium, 889 mg potassium

Oregon

PHEASANT IN ORANGE-HONEY SAUCE

For the early immigrants to the Northwest, there were no crops to harvest nor animals to spare for butchering. They depended on hunting and gathering for their food. Fortunately, there was an abundance of choices, including wild game birds.

1 2½- to 3-pound pheasant *or*
    broiler-fryer chicken,
    quartered
1 tablespoon margarine *or*
    butter
1 tablespoon oil

1 cup chopped onion
¼ cup frozen orange juice con-
    centrate, thawed
¼ cup water
2 tablespoons snipped parsley
1 tablespoon lemon juice
1 teaspoon grated fresh
    gingerroot *or* ¼ teaspoon
    ground ginger
¼ teaspoon salt
¼ teaspoon pepper
¼ teaspoon ground nutmeg
2 tablespoons honey
    Kale (optional)

Rinse poultry; pat dry with paper towels.

In a 12-inch skillet heat margarine or butter and oil; add poultry and onion. Cook over medium heat about 10 minutes or till browned, turning occasionally to brown evenly. Turn meaty side up. Combine orange juice concentrate, water, parsley, lemon juice, gingerroot or ginger, salt, pepper, and nutmeg; add to skillet. Bring to boiling; reduce heat and simmer, covered, 35 to 40 minutes or till tender.

Transfer poultry to a platter; cover and keep warm. Increase heat and boil juices gently about 5 minutes or till reduced to 1 cup. Stir in honey. Serve over poultry. If desired, garnish with kale. Makes 4 servings.

Nutrition information per serving: 416 calories, 36 g protein, 20 g carbohydrate, 21 g total fat (6 g saturated), 111 mg cholesterol, 223 mg sodium, 587 mg potassium

Alaska

CHILLED SALMON STEAKS WITH LEMON-DILL DRESSING

The Indians of the Northwest would offer prayers of thanksgiving in celebration of the arrival of the first salmon in the spring.
The combination of salmon and dill is not Native American, but typically Scandinavian. Danes, Swedes, and Norwegians immigrated to the Oregon Territory from the Midwest.
(Pictured on page 264)

Basque Lamb Shanks, top, Mushroom Medley au Gratin, lower left (see recipe, page 270), and Pheasant in Orange-Honey Sauce, lower right

1½	**cups water**
¼	**cup lemon juice**
1	**medium onion, sliced**
10	**whole black peppercorns**
3	**sprigs parsley**
2	**bay leaves**
6	**fresh *or* frozen salmon steaks, cut 1 to 1¼ inches thick (about 2 pounds)**
¾	**cup mayonnaise *or* salad dressing**
3	**tablespoons buttermilk**
2	**tablespoons snipped fresh dill *or* 2 teaspoons dried dillweed**
1	**tablespoon snipped fresh chives**
½	**teaspoon finely shredded lemon peel**
2	**teaspoons lemon juice Fresh dill (optional) Lemon wedges (optional)**

In a 12-inch skillet combine water, lemon juice, onion, peppercorns, parsley, bay leaves, and ½ teaspoon *salt*. Bring to boiling; add salmon steaks. Cover; simmer 8 to 12 minutes (12 to 18 minutes for frozen) or till fish flakes easily with a fork.

Remove salmon from skillet; discard poaching liquid. Cover; refrigerate salmon 2 hours or till chilled.

For dressing, in a small mixing bowl combine mayonnaise or salad dressing, buttermilk, dill, chives, lemon peel, and lemon juice. Cover and chill about 1 hour. Serve salmon steaks topped with dressing. If desired, garnish with dill and lemon wedges. Makes 6 servings.

Nutrition information per serving: 458 calories, 32 g protein, 4 g carbohydrate, 34 g total fat (5 g saturated), 115 mg cholesterol, 419 mg sodium, 510 mg potassium

263

Alaska

SALMON IN PHYLLO WITH MUSTARD-CREAM SAUCE

In the last century, salmon was so plentiful in the Columbia River that it was harvested during low tide with nets pulled by teams of horses. Five species of salmon return to Pacific waters each year, including the chinook, which reaches sixty pounds or more.

1	pound skinless salmon fillets
¼	cup dairy sour cream
2	tablespoons snipped fresh dill _or_ 1 teaspoon dried dillweed
8	sheets frozen phyllo dough (18x14-inch rectangles), thawed
⅓	cup margarine _or_ butter, melted
	Mustard Cream Sauce
	Green onion strips (optional)

Cut salmon into 4 portions. Spread _1 tablespoon_ of the sour cream over one side of each fish portion. Sprinkle with dill or dillweed, dash _salt_, and dash _pepper_. Set aside.

Unfold phyllo dough; cover with a damp towel or clear plastic wrap. Lay 1 sheet of phyllo dough flat. Brush with some of the melted margarine or butter. Top with another sheet of phyllo dough. Brush with more melted margarine or butter. Add 2 more sheets of dough, making a total of 4 sheets, brushing each sheet with margarine or butter.

Fold the rectangle of dough in half crosswise to form a 9x14-inch rectangle; brush top with margarine or butter. Cut in half crosswise, making 2 smaller rectangles, each about 9x7 inches. Place a salmon fillet upside down on each dough

Salmon in Phyllo with Mustard-Cream Sauce, top, Wilted Spinach and Dungeness Crab Salad, center (see recipe, page 272), and Chilled Salmon Steaks with Lemon-Dill Dressing (see recipe, page 262)

Gooseberry Relish, top left (see recipe, page 270), Pineapple Salsa, top right (see recipe, page 269), and Grilled Veal Chops with Walla Walla Onion Marmalade

rectangle. Fold the top portion of the dough up over the salmon; then bring bottom portion over salmon, brushing dough with margarine and pressing lightly. Bring dough edges together and seal.

Repeat with remaining phyllo dough, margarine or butter, and salmon for a total of 4 salmon-phyllo bundles.

Arrange bundles on a baking sheet. Brush tops with margarine. Bake in a 375° oven for 15 to 18 minutes or till phyllo dough is golden and fish flakes easily with a fork. Serve with Mustard Cream Sauce. If desired, garnish bundles with long green onion strips. Serves 4.

Mustard Cream Sauce: Combine ⅓ cup _dry white wine_ and 3 tablespoons finely chopped _shallots_. Bring to boiling; reduce heat. Simmer, uncovered, for 8 to 10 minutes or till liquid is reduced to about 3 tablespoons, stirring occasionally.

Combine 1 cup _light cream_ and 4 teaspoons _all-purpose flour_. Stir into wine mixture with ⅛ teaspoon _white pepper_. Cook and stir over medium heat till bubbly. Stir in 1 tablespoon _Dijon-style mustard_. Cook and stir for 1 minute more.

Nutrition information per serving: 626 calories, 29 g protein, 29 g carbohydrate, 42 g total fat (13 g saturated), 120 mg cholesterol, 534 mg sodium, 499 mg potassium

Washington

GRILLED VEAL CHOPS WITH WALLA WALLA ONION MARMALADE

The Walla Walla Valley in southeastern Washington is a major agricultural area. Probably its most famous crop is the Walla Walla onion, which is almost a third again as sweet as a regular onion. Locals say they prefer to eat the onions raw, like apples. They're that good.

2	large Walla Walla onions _or_ other onions, thinly sliced and separated into rings (2 cups)
1	teaspoon grated gingerroot
2	tablespoons margarine _or_ butter
1½	cups chicken broth
1	tablespoon white wine vinegar
½	teaspoon coarsely cracked black pepper
½	cup dry white wine
1	cup whipping cream
4	veal loin chops, cut ¾ inch thick
	Italian parsley (optional)

For onion marmalade, cook onions and gingerroot in margarine till tender but not brown. Add _1 cup_ of the chicken broth, the vinegar, pepper, and ½ teaspoon _salt_. Cook, uncovered, over high heat about 15 minutes or till liquid evaporates. Add remaining broth and the wine. Return to boiling; simmer, uncovered, about 5 minutes or till liquid is reduced by two-thirds. Stir whipping cream into onion mixture. Cook and stir over medium heat about 15 minutes or till thickened.

Meanwhile, grill veal chops on an uncovered grill directly over _medium-hot_ coals for 5 minutes. Turn and grill for 5 to 7 minutes more or to desired doneness. Serve onion marmalade with veal chops. If desired, garnish with Italian parsley. Makes 4 servings.

Nutrition information per serving: 541 calories, 28 g protein, 8 g carbohydrate, 42 g total fat (20 g saturated), 176 mg cholesterol, 695 mg sodium, 468 mg potassium

Marinated Venison Chops, top left, and Grilled Elk Burgers (see recipe, page 269)

(see recipe, page 269)

Washington

MARINATED VENISON CHOPS

Dr. John McLoughlin, chief agent of the Hudson's Bay Company outpost in Fort Vancouver in the early nineteenth century, fancied the pleasures of the table. His dinners were formal, complete with bagpipe accompaniment, and often showcased wild game like venison.

4   boneless venison chops *or* steaks, cut ¾ inch thick (about 1 pound)
¼   cup red wine vinegar
2   tablespoons cooking oil
¼   cup catsup
2   teaspoons Worcestershire sauce
1   teaspoon sugar
1   clove garlic, minced
½   teaspoon dry mustard
¼   teaspoon salt
    Dash pepper
    Fresh mint *or* basil sprigs

Place venison chops or steaks in a plastic bag set in a deep bowl or shallow baking dish. For marinade, combine the wine vinegar, cooking oil, catsup, Worcestershire sauce, sugar, garlic, dry mustard, salt, and pepper. Pour marinade over meat in the plastic bag; close bag. Refrigerate for 6 hours or overnight, turning bag occasionally.

Drain venison, reserving marinade; pat dry. Place marinated chops on the rack of an unheated broiler pan. Broil 4 inches from heat for 6 to 8 minutes; brush with marinade. Turn and continue broiling to desired doneness. (Allow about 10 minutes total time for medium-rare, 12 minutes for medium, and 14 minutes for well-done.) Place broiled chops on a serving platter. Heat remaining marinade to boiling and skim off fat; serve with chops. Makes 4 servings.

Nutrition information per serving: 217 calories, 26 g protein, 6 g carbohydrate, 10 g total fat (2 g saturated), 95 mg cholesterol, 395 mg sodium, 397 mg potassium

Hawaii

GINGER-ORANGE SHRIMP STIR-FRY

Chinese and Japanese laborers moved to the Pacific Northwest to work on the railroads and to cook in the lumber camps. After the railroads were built, many of these workers stayed on. Asian ingredients and cooking techniques are very much a part of this region's cuisine.

1   pound fresh *or* frozen peeled and deveined medium shrimp
3   tablespoons soy sauce
½   teaspoon finely shredded orange peel
2   tablespoons orange juice
2   teaspoons cornstarch
1   teaspoon sugar
½   teaspoon crushed red pepper *or* ⅛ teaspoon black pepper
2   tablespoons cooking oil
1   teaspoon grated gingerroot
4   green onions, bias-sliced into 1-inch pieces
2   medium red sweet peppers, cut into ¾-inch pieces
3   oranges, peeled and sectioned
3   cups hot cooked rice

Thaw shrimp, if frozen. For sauce, in a bowl stir together soy sauce, orange peel, orange juice, cornstarch, sugar, and crushed red pepper or black pepper. Set aside.

Pour *1 tablespoon* of the cooking oil into a wok or large skillet. Preheat over medium-high heat. Stir-fry gingerroot for 15 seconds. Add green onions and red sweet peppers. Stir-fry about 3 minutes or till crisp-tender. Remove vegetables from wok.

Add remaining oil to wok. Add *half* of the shrimp to the hot wok. Stir-fry 2 to 3 minutes or till shrimp turn pink; remove. Repeat with remaining shrimp.

Return all shrimp to wok. Push shrimp from center of wok. Stir sauce; add to center of wok. Cook and stir till thickened and bubbly.

Ginger-Orange Shrimp Stir-Fry, top left, Halibut Steaks with Thyme and Tomato Coulis, right, and Mahimahi with Honey-Ginger Glaze (see recipe, page 268)

Stir vegetables into the sauce; cook and stir about 1 minute more or till heated through. Stir in oranges. Serve immediately with hot cooked rice. Makes 4 servings.

Nutrition information per serving: 416 calories, 23 g protein, 62 g carbohydrate, 8 g total fat (1 g saturated), 152 mg cholesterol, 948 mg sodium, 499 mg potassium

Alaska

HALIBUT STEAKS WITH THYME AND TOMATO COULIS

More halibut is fished from Alaskan waters than anywhere else. The size of the catch is enormous, measured in the millions of pounds, even though the season is very short. The Native Americans liked to steam halibut gently in stone-lined cooking pits with seaweed.

4   **fresh *or* frozen halibut steaks, cut 1 inch thick (about 1½ pounds total)**
1   **shallot, finely chopped**
1   **tablespoon olive oil *or* cooking oil**
1   **tablespoon margarine *or* butter, melted**
1   **teaspoon snipped fresh thyme *or* ¼ teaspoon dried thyme, crushed**
    Tomato Coulis

Thaw fish, if frozen. In a small mixing bowl stir together shallot, olive oil or cooking oil, melted margarine or butter, and thyme.

Place fish on the greased unheated rack of a broiler pan; sprinkle with salt and pepper. Broil 4 inches from the heat for 7 minutes; turn fish. Brush each fish steak with some of the thyme mixture. Broil 3 to 5 minutes more or till fish flakes easily with a fork.

Spoon Tomato Coulis onto 4 plates. Top with fish. Serves 4.

Tomato Coulis: In a medium saucepan cook ¼ cup chopped *onion* and 1 clove *garlic*, minced, in 1 tablespoon *olive oil or cooking oil* till onion is very tender. Stir in 1 pound ripe fresh *tomatoes*, peeled, seeded, and coarsely chopped (2½ cups); ¼ teaspoon *salt*; and ⅛ teaspoon *pepper*. Bring to boiling. Reduce heat; simmer, uncovered, for 15 to 20 minutes or till sauce is slightly reduced and thickened.

Transfer tomato mixture to a blender container or food processor bowl. Cover and blend or process till puréed. Return purée to saucepan and stir in 1 tablespoon snipped *parsley*. Cook and stir over medium heat till heated through.

Nutrition information per serving: 286 calories, 33 g protein, 7 g carbohydrate, 13 g total fat (2 g saturated), 49 mg cholesterol, 252 mg sodium, 985 mg potassium

Geoduck Clam Chowder

Hawaii

MAHIMAHI WITH HONEY-GINGER GLAZE

Until recently, mahimahi was best enjoyed in the islands where it was served as fresh as possible. Improvements in refrigeration and transportation now allow mainland fanciers of this tropical fish to savor its sweet, moist flesh. (Pictured on page 267)

4   4-ounce skinless mahimahi
    fillets (about 1 inch thick)
3   tablespoons honey
3   tablespoons sherry vinegar
1   teaspoon grated gingerroot
½   teaspoon finely shredded
    orange peel
2   cloves garlic, minced
1   tablespoon cooking oil
½   teaspoon cornstarch
    Lemon wedges (optional)
    Endive (optional)

Place mahimahi in a shallow dish. For marinade, stir together honey, sherry vinegar, gingerroot, orange peel, and garlic. Pour marinade over fish. Turn fish to coat with marinade. Cover; marinate for 30 minutes, turning fish occasionally.

Drain fish, reserving marinade. In a large skillet cook fish in hot oil over medium-high heat about 6 minutes. Turn fish and cook about 6 minutes more or till fish flakes easily when tested with a fork. Remove from skillet; keep warm.

For glaze, in the same skillet stir together the reserved marinade and cornstarch. Scrape bottom of pan to loosen browned bits. Bring mixture to boiling. Cook and stir over medium-high heat about 1 minute or till glaze thickens. Spoon glaze over fish fillets. If desired, garnish with lemon wedges and endive. Makes 4 servings.

Nutrition information per serving: 191 calories, 19 g protein, 15 g carbohydrate, 6 g total fat (1 g saturated), 88 mg cholesterol, 76 mg sodium, 312 mg potassium

Washington

GEODUCK CLAM CHOWDER

Northwesterners know to say gooey-duck when they order this huge (about three-pound) bizarre-looking Pacific clam. A large water-spouting neck, or siphon, protrudes from its shell like a periscope, providing a clue for clam diggers. The body meat is sliced for steaks, the neck ground for chowder.

2   medium potatoes, peeled
    and chopped (2 cups), *or*
    2 cups loose-pack frozen
    hash brown potatoes
1   cup chicken broth

½ cup chopped onion
½ cup chopped celery
1¼ cups milk
2 tablespoons all-purpose flour
⅛ teaspoon pepper
¾ cup ground *or* minced geoduck clams *or* one 6½-ounce can minced clams
2 slices bacon, crisp-cooked and crumbled
Snipped chives (optional)

In a medium saucepan combine chopped potatoes or frozen hash brown potatoes, chicken broth, onion, and celery. Bring to boiling, reduce heat. Cover and simmer about 10 minutes or till potatoes are tender. *Do not drain.* Slightly mash the potatoes.

In a small mixing bowl stir together the milk, flour, and pepper. Stir into potato mixture. Cook and stir till thickened and bubbly. Stir in *undrained* clams; heat through. Sprinkle each serving with bacon and, if desired, chives. Makes 4 to 6 side-dish servings.

Nutrition information per serving: 214 calories, 14 g protein, 31 g carbohydrate, 4 g total fat (2 g saturated), 25 mg cholesterol, 375 mg sodium, 749 mg potassium

Alaska

GRILLED ELK BURGERS

Elk was hunted by northwestern Native Americans and by immigrants in the early years. Although no longer a necessity, hunting is still a favorite form of recreation in the Northwest.
(Pictured on page 266)

1 beaten egg
3 tablespoons catsup
1 teaspoon Worcestershire sauce
¼ cup soft bread crumbs
1 small onion, finely chopped (¼ cup)
1 teaspoon prepared horseradish

1½ pounds ground elk *or* ground buffalo
6 hamburger buns, split and toasted
Assorted condiments

In a bowl combine the egg, catsup, and Worcestershire sauce. Stir in the bread crumbs, onion, horseradish, and ½ teaspoon *salt*. Add the ground meat; mix well. Shape into six ¾-inch-thick burgers.

Grill over *medium-hot* coals till no pink remains, turning once (15 to 18 minutes). Serve burgers on toasted buns with assorted condiments. Makes 6 servings.

Nutrition information per serving: 292 calories, 31 g protein, 27 g carbohydrate, 6 g total fat (2 g saturated), 131 mg cholesterol, 419 mg sodium, 407 mg potassium

Washington

PUMPKIN SOUP

When pumpkin seeds from England arrived at the Hudson's Bay Company, they were not for human consumption. They were ordered to provide food for the pigs!
(Pictured on page 260)

¼ cup chopped onion
1 tablespoon margarine *or* butter
1 14½-ounce can chicken broth
½ cup finely chopped, peeled potato *or* loose-pack, frozen, hash brown potatoes
½ cup loose-pack frozen corn
¼ cup finely chopped red *or* green sweet pepper
½ of a 16-ounce can (1 cup) pumpkin
¼ teaspoon salt
⅛ teaspoon pepper
1 cup half-and-half, light cream, *or* milk
Sliced green onion *or* chives (optional)

In a large saucepan cook onion in hot margarine or butter till tender but not brown. Stir in chicken broth, finely chopped potato or frozen hash brown potatoes, corn, and red or green sweet pepper. Cover and simmer about 15 minutes or till vegetables are tender.

Stir pumpkin, salt, and pepper into broth mixture. Slowly add half-and-half, light cream, or milk, stirring constantly. Heat through. Ladle soup into individual bowls. If desired, garnish with sliced green onion or chives. Makes 4 side-dish servings.

Nutrition information per serving: 178 calories, 6 g protein, 17 g carbohydrate, 11 g total fat (5 g saturated), 23 mg cholesterol, 523 mg sodium, 406 mg potassium

Hawaii

PINEAPPLE SALSA

Pineapples are thought to be as Hawaiian as the hula. They aren't. The fruit didn't appear in the islands until the end of the eighteenth century and didn't prove successful commercially until James Dole organized the Hawaiian Pineapple Company on Oahu in 1901.
(Pictured on page 265)

⅔ cup fresh *or* canned chopped pineapple
⅓ cup fresh *or* canned chopped peaches
⅓ cup chopped green *or* red sweet pepper
2 tablespoons sliced green onion
2 tablespoons lime juice
1 teaspoon snipped fresh cilantro *or* parsley

In a medium bowl combine pineapple, peaches, green or red sweet pepper, and green onion. Add lime juice and cilantro or parsley, tossing to coat. Serve with chicken, turkey, or fish. Makes 4 servings.

Nutrition information per serving: 24 calories, 0 g protein, 6 g carbohydrate, 0 g total fat (0 g saturated), 0 mg cholesterol, 1 mg sodium, 89 mg potassium

Oregon

MUSHROOM MEDLEY AU GRATIN

Thousands of varieties of wild mushrooms grow in the damp forests of Oregon and Washington, although only relatively few are safe to forage for and eat. Asian shiitake and oyster mushrooms are also cultivated.
(Pictured on page 263)

2	tablespoons grated Parmesan cheese
2	tablespoons fine dry bread crumbs
2	teaspoons margarine *or* butter, softened
8	ounces shiitake mushrooms
4	ounces oyster mushrooms
16	ounces button mushrooms, sliced
1	clove garlic, minced
2	tablespoons margarine *or* butter
2	tablespoons all-purpose flour
2	teaspoons Dijon-style mustard
½	teaspoon dried thyme, crushed
¼	teaspoon salt
⅔	cup milk
	Kale (optional)

In a small bowl combine Parmesan cheese, bread crumbs, and the 2 teaspoons margarine; set aside.

Separate caps and stems from shiitake and oyster mushrooms. Reserve stems to use in stocks or discard. Slice mushroom caps.

In a large skillet cook button mushrooms and garlic in the 2 tablespoons margarine or butter over medium-high heat about 4 minutes or till tender and most of the liquid has evaporated. Remove mushrooms, reserving drippings. Add shiitake and oyster mushrooms; cook for 7 to 8 minutes or till tender and most of the liquid has evaporated. Stir in flour, mustard, thyme, and salt. Add milk all at once. Cook and stir till thickened and bubbly. Cook and stir 1 minute more. Stir in button mushrooms.

Transfer to a 1-quart casserole. Sprinkle with crumb mixture. Bake in a 350° oven about 20 minutes or till bubbly. If desired, serve atop kale. Makes 4 servings.

Nutrition information per serving: 200 calories, 7 g protein, 22 g carbohydrate, 10 g total fat (2 g saturated), 5 mg cholesterol, 386 mg sodium, 677 mg potassium

Oregon

GOOSEBERRY RELISH

Attempts by colonists in New England to plant gooseberry seeds from Europe failed because of disease. Indigenous varieties were found to carry white pine blight, so cultivation wasn't pursued. A new hybrid of the English and American strains was eventually developed and is under cultivation in Washington and Oregon.
(Pictured on page 265)

2	cups gooseberries
1	cup packed brown sugar
¼	cup vinegar
2	tablespoons port wine *or* sweet marsala
1	teaspoon finely shredded orange peel
¼	teaspoon ground cinnamon
⅛	teaspoon ground cloves
⅛	teaspoon ground allspice
⅛	teaspoon ground nutmeg

Remove tops and stems from gooseberries; rinse and drain. In a 2-quart saucepan stir together berries, brown sugar, vinegar, wine, and orange peel. Bring to boiling; reduce heat. Simmer, uncovered, for 5 minutes, stirring frequently.

Stir cinnamon, cloves, allspice, and nutmeg into the hot gooseberry mixture. Simmer, uncovered, for 5 minutes more, stirring often.

Serve warm or chilled on ham, pork, or chicken. To store, cool to room temperature. Cover and chill for up to 2 weeks. Makes 1½ cups.

Nutrition information per tablespoon: 42 calories, 0 g protein, 11 g carbohydrate, 0 g total fat (0 g saturated), 0 mg cholesterol, 3 mg sodium, 60 mg potassium

Alaska

SOURDOUGH PANCAKES

Miners working in the goldfields of Alaska depended on sourdough starter to leaven bread. These rugged settlers came to be called sourdoughs themselves because the starter was so much a part of their lives in the wilderness.

1¼	cups Sourdough Starter (see recipe, page 244)
1	cup all-purpose flour
1	tablespoon sugar
1	teaspoon baking powder
½	teaspoon baking soda
¼	teaspoon salt
1	beaten egg
2	tablespoons cooking oil

Bring Sourdough Starter to room temperature. In a mixing bowl stir together flour, sugar, baking powder, baking soda, and salt. In another mixing bowl combine Sourdough Starter, egg, and cooking oil. Add to flour mixture all at once. Stir mixture just till blended but still slightly lumpy.

For each pancake, pour about *¼ cup* batter onto a hot lightly greased griddle or heavy skillet. (*Or,* for each silver-dollar-size pancake pour about *1 tablespoon* batter onto hot griddle.)

Cook till pancakes are golden brown, turning to cook second sides when pancakes have bubbly surfaces and slightly dry edges. Makes 8 to 10 pancakes.

Nutrition information per pancake: 179 calories, 5 g protein, 30 g carbohydrate, 4 g total fat (1 g saturated), 27 mg cholesterol, 167 mg sodium, 46 mg potassium

Hawaii

Banana-Macadamia Nut Muffins

The hard-shell macadamia nut isn't native to the islands, but was brought there in 1881 from Australia where it grows wild. The nut was named for Dr. John MacAdam, an Australian scientist, who was so enamored of its rich, addictive flavor that he became one of its most vocal promoters.

1¾ cups all-purpose flour
⅓ cup chopped macadamia nuts
⅓ cup packed brown sugar
2 teaspoons baking powder
¼ teaspoon baking soda
¼ teaspoon salt
¼ teaspoon ground nutmeg
1 beaten egg
¾ cup mashed banana
½ cup orange juice
⅓ cup cooking oil
Streusel Topping

In a large mixing bowl combine the flour, nuts, brown sugar, baking powder, baking soda, salt, and nutmeg. Make a well in the center of the dry ingredients.

Combine the egg, mashed banana, orange juice, and cooking oil; add all at once to flour mixture. Stir just till moistened (batter should be lumpy). Lightly grease muffin cups or line them with paper bake cups; fill ⅔ full. Sprinkle with the Streusel Topping.

Bake in a 400° oven about 20 minutes or till golden. Remove from pan; serve warm. Makes 12 to 14 muffins.

Streusel Topping: In a small mixing bowl stir together 2 tablespoons *all-purpose flour* and 2 tablespoons *sugar.* Cut in 1 tablespoon *margarine or butter* till mixture resembles coarse crumbs. Stir in ⅓ cup chopped *macadamia nuts.*

Nutrition information per muffin: *231 calories, 3 g protein, 26 g carbohydrate, 13 g total fat (2 g saturated), 18 mg cholesterol, 86 mg sodium, 139 mg potassium*

Sourdough Pancakes, Banana-Macadamia Nut Muffins, and Blackberry Jam (see recipe, page 272)

Oregon

Oatmeal-Prune Muffins

Cuttings for prune trees were brought to the Willamette Valley by French settlers in the mid-1850s. Pioneer cooks used them in preserves, baked goods, puddings, and stuffings. (Pictured on page 260)

1⅓ cups all-purpose flour
¾ cup rolled oats
2 teaspoons baking powder
½ teaspoon baking soda
¼ teaspoon salt
1 beaten egg
¾ cup milk
½ cup packed brown sugar
¼ cup cooking oil
½ teaspoon vanilla
1 cup snipped, dried, pitted prunes

Grease eighteen 1¾-inch or twelve 2½-inch muffin cups or line them with paper bake cups; set aside. In a bowl stir together flour, oats, baking powder, soda, and salt. Make a well in center of dry mixture.

In a bowl combine the egg, milk, brown sugar, oil, and vanilla. Add egg mixture all at once to the dry mixture. Stir just till moistened (batter should be lumpy). Fold prunes into the batter.

Spoon *half* of the batter into the prepared 1¾-inch muffin cups, filling each ¾ full. *Or,* divide all of the batter among the 2½-inch muffin cups. Bake in a 400° oven for 10 to 12 minutes for 1¾-inch muffins or 16 to 18 minutes for 2½-inch muffins or till done. Cool in muffin cups on a wire rack 5 minutes; remove muffins from cups. Repeat with remaining batter. Serve warm. Makes thirty-six 1¾-inch or twelve 2½-inch muffins.

Nutrition information per muffin: *58 calories, 1 g protein, 9 g carbohydrate, 2 g total fat (1 g saturated), 6 mg cholesterol, 49 mg sodium, 55 mg potassium*

WILTED SPINACH AND DUNGENESS CRAB SALAD

The Dungeness crab represents Washington state much as the cod does Massachusetts. Although found in Pacific waters from Alaska to California, it was named for the Dungeness Bay of Washington's Olympic Peninsula. (Pictured on page 264)

1½   pounds fresh *or* frozen cooked crab claws *or* 12 ounces fresh *or* frozen cooked crabmeat
6   cups torn fresh spinach
1   cup sliced fresh mushrooms
¼   cup sliced green onion
3   slices bacon
¼   cup white wine vinegar
1   tablespoon sugar
¼   teaspoon salt
1   11-ounce can mandarin orange sections, drained
¼   cup toasted sliced almonds

Thaw crabmeat, if frozen. Drain well. In a large bowl combine spinach, mushrooms, and green onion. Set aside.

In a 12-inch skillet cook bacon till crisp. Drain bacon on paper towels, reserving drippings in skillet. Crumble bacon; set aside.

Stir wine vinegar, sugar, and salt into drippings. Heat to boiling. Add spinach mixture and crabmeat to skillet, tossing 30 to 60 seconds or till spinach is just wilted. Remove from heat.

Gently stir in the orange sections. Sprinkle with the almonds and bacon. Serve immediately. Makes 4 servings.

Nutrition information per serving: 307 calories, 25 g protein, 15 g carbohydrate, 17 g total fat (6 g saturated), 79 mg cholesterol, 659 mg sodium, 1,041 mg potassium

*lackberry Pie with Hazelnut Glaze, left, and Apple-Cherry Pie (see recipe, page 274)*

BLACKBERRY JAM

Oregon is the nation's blackberry patch. Most of the berries used commercially in the United States come from Oregon vines. Jams and preserves were one way for early settlers to extend the season for fresh fruit. (Pictured on page 271)

4   cups blackberries
4   cups sugar
¼   teaspoon finely shredded lemon peel *or* orange peel
½   of a 6-ounce package (1 foil pouch) liquid fruit pectin
2   tablespoons lemon juice

BLACKBERRY PIE WITH HAZELNUT GLAZE

Berry pies were favorite desserts for pioneer cooks. They knew that blackberry vines grew in logged-over areas, and during the summer months would set out, pails in hand, for a day of berry picking.

¾ cup sugar
¼ all-purpose flour
½ teaspoon finely shredded
    lemon peel
4 cups fresh *or* frozen
    unsweetened blackberries
    Pastry for Double-Crust Pie
    (see recipe, page 274)
    Hazelnut Glaze (optional)

In a large mixing bowl combine the sugar, flour, and lemon peel. Add fresh or frozen blackberries; toss gently till coated. (If using frozen blackberries, before adding let them stand 15 to 30 minutes or till berries are *partially* thawed but still icy.)

Transfer berry mixture to a pastry-lined 9-inch pie plate. Add top crust; cut slits in top crust. Trim, seal, and flute edge. To prevent overbrowning, cover edge of pie with foil.

Bake in a 375° oven for 25 minutes for fresh berries (50 minutes for frozen berries). Remove foil. Bake for 20 to 25 minutes more for fresh berries (20 to 30 minutes for frozen berries) or till top is golden. If desired, top hot pie with Hazelnut Glaze. Cool. Serves 8.

Hazelnut Glaze: In a small saucepan combine ⅓ cup packed *brown sugar* and 3 tablespoons *half-and-half or light cream*. Cook and stir over low heat till sugar melts. Stir in ⅓ cup chopped toasted *hazelnuts*. Pour over hot pie.

Nutrition information per serving: 450 calories, 5 g protein, 61 g carbohydrate, 21 g total fat (5 g saturated), 2 mg cholesterol, 139 mg sodium, 228 mg potassium

Crush blackberries. Measure *2 cups* berries. In a bowl combine berries, sugar, and lemon peel or orange peel. Let stand 10 minutes.

Combine pectin and lemon juice. Add to berry mixture; stir for 3 minutes.

Ladle at once into jars or freezer containers, leaving a ½-inch headspace. Seal, label, and let stand at room temperature about 2 hours or till jam is set. Store up to 3 weeks in the refrigerator or 1 year in the freezer. Makes 4 half-pints.

Nutrition information per tablespoon: 53 calories, 0 g protein, 14 g carbohydrate, 0 g total fat (0 g saturated), 0 mg cholesterol, 0 mg sodium, 22 mg potassium

Washington

APPLE-CHERRY PIE

Apples from the Wenatchee Valley of Washington formed the basis of the state's gigantic apple industry. Washington is also well known for its cherries, like the dark, black-red, sweet Bing and the Royal Anne. The Bing cherry is a transplant from Oregon, however. It was developed in orchards near Portland in the mid-1800s. (Pictured on page 273)

2 cups fresh *or* frozen pitted tart red cherries
1 cup sugar
2 tablespoons all-purpose flour
1 teaspoon ground cinnamon
¼ teaspoon ground nutmeg
3 cups peeled, cored, and thinly sliced apples
  Pastry for Double-Crust Pie (see recipe, right)
2 tablespoons margarine *or* butter
1 tablespoon milk
½ teaspoon sugar
  Dash ground cinnamon

If using frozen cherries, let stand at room temperature 30 minutes or till partially thawed. Stir together the 1 cup sugar, the flour, the 1 teaspoon cinnamon, and nutmeg; set aside.

In a large bowl combine cherries and apple slices. Add sugar mixture. Toss to coat. Transfer to pastry-lined 9-inch pie plate. Dot fruit with margarine or butter. Adjust top crust. Seal and flute edge. If desired, cut decorative shapes from dough scraps. Brush the back sides of the shapes with milk and arrange on the top crust. Cut slits in the top crust. Brush top crust with milk. Combine the ½ teaspoon sugar and the dash cinnamon; sprinkle over crust. Cover edge with foil.

Bake in a 375° oven for 25 minutes (50 minutes if using frozen cherries). Remove foil. Bake for 20 to 25 minutes more or till the top is golden and fruit is tender. Makes 8 servings.

Pear Cobbler

Nutrition information per serving: 459 calories, 4 g protein, 61 g carbohydrate, 21 g total fat (5 g saturated), 0 mg cholesterol, 160 mg sodium, 136 mg potassium

PASTRY FOR DOUBLE-CRUST PIE

2 cups all-purpose flour
½ teaspoon salt
⅔ cup shortening *or* lard
6 to 7 tablespoons cold water

In a mixing bowl stir together flour and salt. Cut in shortening or lard till pieces are the size of small peas.

Sprinkle *1 tablespoon* of the water over part of the mixture; gently toss with a fork. Push to side of bowl. Repeat till all is moistened. Divide dough in half. Form each half of dough into a ball.

On a lightly floured surface, flatten each ball of dough with your hands. Roll out dough from center to edges, forming a circle about 12 inches in diameter. Wrap pastry around a rolling pin. Unroll pastry onto a 9-inch pie plate. Ease pastry into pie plate, being careful not to stretch pastry. Trim pastry even with rim of pie plate.

For top crust, repeat rolling remaining dough. Cut slits to allow steam to escape. Fill pastry in pie plate with desired filling. Place top crust on filling. Trim top crust to ½ inch beyond edge of plate. Fold top crust under bottom crust; flute edge. Bake as directed in individual recipes.

Oregon

PEAR COBBLER

Harry and David Rosenberg thought that the Royal Riviera pears from their Bear Creek Orchards near Medford, Oregon, were something special. In 1934, they carefully packed some samples and hit the road. They returned with hundreds of orders, the start of their now world-famous mail-order company.

4 cups sliced, peeled pears
⅓ cup packed brown sugar
2 tablespoons water
1 tablespoon lemon juice
2 tablespoons water
1 tablespoon cornstarch
⅓ cup all-purpose flour
2 tablespoons finely crushed graham crackers
1 tablespoon finely chopped pecans
1 tablespoon brown sugar
¾ teaspoon baking powder
2 tablespoons margarine *or* butter
1 slightly beaten egg white
2 tablespoons milk
1½ teaspoons sugar
⅛ teaspoon ground cinnamon
  Half-and-half, light cream, *or* vanilla ice cream (optional)
  Red currants (optional)

In a large saucepan, bring pears, the ⅓ cup brown sugar, 2 tablespoons water, and lemon juice to boiling, stirring to dissolve sugar. Reduce heat. Cover and simmer for 5 minutes or till fruit is almost tender, stirring occasionally. Combine 2 tablespoons water and the cornstarch; add to pear mixture. Cook and stir till thickened and bubbly.

Hawaiian Upside-Down Cake, left (see recipe, page 276), Frosty Hawaiian Nog, right, and Cream Cheese-Macadamia Pie, (see recipe, page 276)

Meanwhile, for biscuit topping, in a mixing bowl stir together the flour, crushed graham crackers, pecans, the 1 tablespoon brown sugar, and baking powder. Cut in the margarine or butter till the mixture resembles coarse crumbs. In another mixing bowl combine egg white and milk. Add all at once to the flour mixture, stirring just till moistened.

Spoon the hot fruit mixture into a 2-quart square baking dish. Immediately spoon the biscuit topping into 6 mounds atop the hot fruit mixture. Combine the sugar and cinnamon. Sprinkle sugar-cinnamon mixture over the biscuit mounds.

Bake in a 400° oven for 12 to 15 minutes or till a wooden toothpick inserted in the center of a biscuit comes out clean. Serve warm If desired, serve with half-and-half, light cream, or ice cream. Serves 6.

Nutrition information per serving: 194 calories, 2 g protein, 36 g carbohydrate, 5 g total fat (1 g saturated), 0 mg cholesterol, 97 mg sodium, 207 mg potassium

Hawaii

FROSTY HAWAIIAN NOG

The Smooth Cayenne variety, brought to Hawaii from Jamaica in 1886 for its superior flavor, is the foundation of the canned pineapple industry. While it was sweet and delicious, it didn't ship well fresh. Pineapple growers learned that canning was the best way to preserve the fruit.

3   cups buttermilk
1   8-ounce can crushed
    pineapple (juice pack),
    chilled
¼   cup sugar *or* honey

1   teaspoon vanilla
¼   teaspoon salt
5   ice cubes *or* 1 cup small
    ice cubes
    Pineapple leaves *or* fresh
    mint sprigs (optional)

In a blender container place buttermilk, *undrained* pineapple, sugar or honey, vanilla, and salt. Cover and blend about 30 seconds or till combined. With blender running, add ice cubes, one at a time, through opening in lid. Blend till mixture is nearly smooth and frothy.

Pour into 5 chilled mugs or tall glasses. If desired, garnish each serving with pineapple leaves or a sprig of mint. Makes about five 8-ounce servings.

Nutrition information per serving: 126 calories, 5 g protein, 24 g carbohydrate, 1 g total fat (1 g saturated), 5 mg cholesterol, 155 mg sodium, 278 mg potassium

275

CREAM CHEESE-MACADAMIA PIE

The macadamia is one tough nut to crack. In fact, its shell is so difficult to remove that the nut was never popular in its native Australia. It didn't become viable commercially in Hawaii either for almost fifty years, until someone invented a machine that could crack the almost impenetrable casing.
(Pictured on page 275)

2	3-ounce packages cream cheese, softened
½	cup sugar
4	eggs
2	teaspoons vanilla
¼	teaspoon salt
	Pastry for Single-Crust Pie (see recipe, page 55)
1¼	cups chopped macadamia nuts
¾	cup light corn syrup
3	tablespoons sugar
3	tablespoons margarine *or* butter, melted

In a mixing bowl beat cream cheese with an electric mixer on medium speed till smooth. Add the ½ cup sugar, *one* of the eggs, *1 teaspoon* of the vanilla, and salt; beat just till combined. Spread cream cheese mixture onto bottom of a pastry-lined 9-inch pie plate. Sprinkle nuts over cream cheese mixture.

Use a rotary beater or wire whisk to lightly beat the remaining eggs just till mixed. Stir in the corn syrup, the 3 tablespoons sugar, margarine, and remaining vanilla.

Place the partially filled pie plate on a baking sheet on the oven rack. Slowly pour the syrup mixture over nuts. To prevent overbrowning, cover the pie edge with foil.

Bake in a 375° oven for 20 minutes. Remove foil. Bake for 25 to 30 minutes more or till edges puff and center is nearly set. Cool completely Cover and chill to store. Serves 10.

Nutrition information per serving: 455 calories, 6 g protein, 44 g carbohydrate, 30 g total fat (8 g saturated), 104 mg cholesterol, 286 mg sodium, 97 mg potassium

Hazelnut Crunch Ice Cream, top (see recipe, page 279), Pineapple Daiquiri Ice, right (see recipe, page 279), and Baked Custard with Coffee Sauce

HAWAIIAN UPSIDE-DOWN CAKE

This cake is a true showcase of Hawaiian agriculture. Sugar, pineapple, and macadamia nuts are Hawaii's top three crops, in that order. Coconut and ginger are other hallmarks of island cooking.
(Pictured on page 273)

2	tablespoons margarine *or* butter
⅓	cup packed brown sugar
1	tablespoon rum *or* 1 tablespoon water plus a few drops rum extract
1	8-ounce can pineapple slices, drained and halved
½	cup chopped toasted macadamia nuts
2	tablespoons flaked coconut, toasted
1⅓	cups all-purpose flour
⅔	cup sugar
2	teaspoons baking powder
¼	teaspoon ground ginger

BAKED CUSTARD WITH COFFEE SAUCE

The gospel and the muumuu weren't all that the missionaries brought to the Hawaiian islands. They get the credit for planting the first coffee trees along the Kona Coast of the Big Island.

6   **eggs**
3   **cups milk**
½   **cup sugar**
1½   **teaspoons vanilla**
¼   **teaspoon salt**
    Coffee Sauce

In a large mixing bowl use a rotary beater or wire whisk to lightly beat eggs just till mixed. Stir in milk, sugar, vanilla, and salt.

Place an ungreased 4½- or 5-cup ovenproof ring mold (about 8 inches in diameter) in a 13x9x2-inch baking pan. (*Or,* place eight 6-ounce custard cups or individual molds in a large roasting pan.) Set the baking or roasting pan on the oven rack. Pour the egg mixture into the mold(s). Pour boiling or very hot tap water into the pan around the mold to a depth of 1 inch. Bake in a 325° oven for 35 to 45 minutes or till a knife inserted near the center come out clean.

Remove mold(s) from water in pan. Cool custard in the mold(s) on a wire rack. Cover and chill in the refrigerator for at least 2 hours before serving.

To serve, prepare sauce. Remove custard from mold(s). Serve sauce with chilled custard. Serves 8.

Coffee Sauce: In a saucepan combine ½ cup *water,* ¼ cup *light corn syrup,* 2 teaspoons *cornstarch,* and 1 teaspoon *instant coffee crystals.* Cook and stir over medium heat till mixture is bubbly. Cook and stir for 2 minutes more. Remove from heat.

Stir in ¼ teaspoon *vanilla* and, if desired, 1 teaspoon *coffee liqueur.* Cover and chill sauce in the refrigerator till serving time.

Nutrition information per serving: 243 calories, 10 g protein, 34 g carbohydrate, 7 g total fat (3 g saturated), 222 mg cholesterol, 140 mg sodium, 196 mg potassium

⅔   **cup milk**
¼   **cup margarine *or* butter, softened**
1   **egg**
1   **teaspoon vanilla**
    Whipped cream (optional)

Melt the 2 tablespoons margarine or butter in a 9x1½-inch round baking pan. Stir in brown sugar and rum or water and rum extract. Arrange pineapple slices in pan; fill in the spaces with chopped macadamia nuts and coconut. Set pan aside.

Combine flour, sugar, baking powder, and ginger. Add milk, the ¼ cup margarine, egg, and vanilla. Beat for 1 minute. Spoon into pan.

Bake in a 350° oven 30 to 35 minutes or till a toothpick inserted near center comes out clean. Cool 5 minutes. Loosen sides; invert cake onto a plate. Serve warm; if desired, top with whipped cream. Serves 8.

Nutrition information per serving: 342 calories, 4 g protein, 45 g carbohydrate, 16 g total fat (3 g saturated), 28 mg cholesterol, 174 mg sodium, 142 mg potassium

Washington

APPLE-BERRY CIDER

Settlers in the Pacific Northwest who had a yen for the cider they so enjoyed back east pressed it from locally grown apples. The inclusion of berries picked from the bushes that grew wild throughout the Northwest gave the sweet drink a new taste.

8   cups apple cider *or* apple
      juice
1   10-ounce package frozen
      red raspberries *or* frozen
      sliced strawberries
4   inches stick cinnamon
1½ teaspoons whole cloves
      Cinnamon sticks (optional)
1   medium apple, cut into
      8 wedges (optional)

In a large saucepan combine the apple cider or juice, raspberries or strawberries, cinnamon, and cloves. Bring to boiling; reduce heat. Cover and simmer for 10 minutes. Strain through a sieve lined with 100 percent cotton cheesecloth.

To serve, pour the cider into 8 heat-proof glasses or cups. If desired, garnish each serving with a cinnamon stick and apple wedge. Makes eight 8-ounce servings.

Nutrition information per serving: 163 calories, 0 g protein, 41 g carbohydrate, 0 g total fat (0 g saturated), 0 mg cholesterol, 8 mg sodium, 355 mg potassium

Apple-Berry Cider

Oregon

HAZELNUT CRUNCH ICE CREAM

You say filbert, I say hazelnut. It's a regional difference: hazelnut in the East, filbert in the West. Or it was anyway, until the industry adopted hazelnut as the official market name. Oregon is the nation's largest producer of these tasty nuts. Washington is not far behind.
(Pictured on page 277)

⅔   cup chopped hazelnuts
      (filberts)
¼   cup sugar
1   tablespoon margarine *or*
      butter
4   cups half-and-half *or*
      light cream
1½ cups sugar
1   tablespoon vanilla
2   cups whipping cream
      Cookies (optional)

In a small heavy skillet cook hazelnuts, the ¼ cup sugar, and margarine or butter over medium heat (*do not stir*) till sugar begins to melt, shaking skillet occasionally. Reduce heat to low and cook till sugar turns golden, stirring frequently with a wooden spoon. Immediately spread coated nuts on a baking sheet lined with greased foil. Cool and break into chunks. Set aside.

In a large mixing bowl combine half-and-half or light cream, the 1½ cups sugar, and vanilla. Stir till sugar dissolves. Stir in whipping cream and nut chunks. Freeze in a 4- or 5-quart ice cream freezer according to the manufacturer's directions. If desired, serve with cookies. Makes 2 quarts (16 to 20 servings).

Nutrition information per serving: 303 calories, 3 g protein, 26 g carbohydrate, 22 g total fat (11 g saturated), 63 mg cholesterol, 42 mg sodium, 123 mg potassium

Hawaii

PINEAPPLE DAIQUIRI ICE

Frozen daiquiris are refreshing tropical coolers. The drink was first concocted in Cuba and named after a town there. Hawaiian bartenders give it local flavor with island-grown fruits like pineapple, guava, or bananas.
(Pictured on page 277)

2   20-ounce cans pineapple
      chunks (juice pack) *or* one
      3- to 3½-pound pineapple,
      cleaned, cored, and cut
      into chunks
¾   cup sugar
¼   cup lime juice
¼   cup rum
      Pineapple leaves (optional)

If using canned pineapple, drain juice from *one* can of pineapple chunks. Combine drained, canned pineapple and *undrained*, canned pineapple, or fresh pineapple, with sugar, lime juice, and rum.

In a blender container or food processor bowl place about *one-third* of the pineapple mixture. Cover and blend or process till mixture is almost smooth. Repeat with remaining pineapple mixture, one-third at a time.

Freeze in a 2-quart ice-cream freezer according to manufacturer's directions. If desired, garnish each with pineapple leaves. Makes 12 servings.

Nutrition information per serving: 87 calories, 0 g protein, 20 g carbohydrate, 0 g total fat (0 g saturated), 0 mg cholesterol, 1 mg sodium, 58 mg potassium

Notes

Introduction

1. Richard Hooker, *Food and Drink in America* (Indianapolis: Bobbs-Merrill, 1981), 307.

2. Hooker, *Food and Drink in America*, 97. The explanation for the American way of handling the knife and fork is also from Hooker, 97–98.

Chapter 2

1. Peter G. Rose, ed. and trans., *The Sensible Cook* (New York: Syracuse University Press, 1989), 28.

2. Gilbert Chinard, ed., *Benjamin Franklin on the Art of Eating* (Princeton: American Philosophical Society, 1958), 16.

3. Chinard, *Benjamin Franklin on the Art of Eating*, 43–45.

4. Lorna J. Sass, "The Great Nosh: Some Landmark New York Delis," *Journal of Gastronomy 4*, no.1 (Spring 1988), 37–48.

Chapter 3

1. John Egerton, *Southern Food* (New York: Knopf, 1987), 14.

2. Karen Hess, *The Carolina Rice Kitchen* (Columbia: University of South Carolina Press), 1.

3. Marshall Fishwick, "Southern Cooking," in *The American Heritage Cookbook*, eds. American Heritage (New York: Simon & Schuster, 1964), 131.

4. Fishwick, "Southern Cooking," 131.

5. Egerton, *Southern Food*, 155.

Chapter 4

1. Raymond Sokolov, *Fading Feast* (New York: Farrar, Straus, Giroux, 1981), 37.

2. Kay Graber, *Nebraska Pioneer Cookbook* (Lincoln: Univeristy of Nebraska Press, 1974), 98–102.

3. Graber, *Nebraska Pioneer Cookbook*, 100.

4. Shifra Stein and Rich Davis, *Bar.B.Q. Kansas City Style* (Kansas City: Barbacao Press, 1985), 8.

Chapter 5

1. Frank Cushing, *Zuni Breadstuff* (New York: Museum of the American Indian, 1974 reprint), 53.

2. The book that resulted from this research is *Hopi Cookery* by Juanita Tiger Kavena (Tuscon: University of Arizona Press, 1987).

3. Frank X. Tolbert, *A Bowl of Red* (New York: Doubleday, 1972), 11.

4. Tolbert, *A Bowl of Red*, 31.

Chapter 6

1. Bridger Canyon Women's Club, *Canyon Cookery* (Bozeman: privately published, 1978), 22.

2. Bridger Canyon Women's Club, *Canyon Cookery*, 22.

3. Leon D. Adams, *The Wines of America* (New York: McGraw-Hill, 1978), 228.

4. Adams, *The Wines of America*, 22.

Chapter 7

1. Editors and Friends of *Alaska* magazine, *Cooking Alaskan* (Anchorage: Alaska Northwest Publishing Company, 1983), 152–62.

Picture Credits

The Publishers would like to thank the following photographers and organizations for permission to reproduce their photographs:

(Abbreviations: b=below, c=center, l=left, r=right, t=top)

Abby Aldrich Rockefeller Folk Art Center 27b

J. C. Allen and Son 16t

Archive Photos/A.E. French 18b

H. Armstrong Roberts 15, 17, 29, 215; H. Armstrong Roberts/K. Vreeland 6–7; H. Armstrong Roberts/J. Irwin 62t; H. Armstrong Roberts/G. Ahrens 64t; H. Armstrong Roberts/David Muench 94–95; H. Armstrong Roberts/W. Metzen 98t, 99; H. Armstrong Roberts/F. Gordon 102; H. Armstrong Roberts/R. Krubner 143

Better Homes & Gardens 142b

The Bettmann Archive 65, 105, 145b, 214t, 217, 221b, 222t, 223; UPI/Bettmann 68t

Courtesy, Bishop Hill State Historic Site, Illinois 145t

Courtesy of the Bostonian Society/Old State House 31

Comstock/Art Gingert 14, 136–37; Comstock/Stuart Cohen 63; Comstock/Georg Gerster 141

Culver Pictures Inc. 67b

FPG International 19, 66, 257; FPG International/Ron Thomas 20–21, 22t, 212–13, FPG; International/Clyde H. Smith 27t; FPG International/Peter Gridley 30t; FPG International/ Willard Clay 60–61; FPG International/Kenneth Garrett 101; FPG International/Tom Algire 181

From the collections of Henry Ford Museum and Greenfield Village 62b

The Granger Collection, New York 18t, 23t, 23b, 140, 144, back jacket

Courtesy, Historic Hudson Valley 69

Hubener, George (attrib. to) *Dish*, 1785–86, Philadelphia Museum of Art: Purchased: Baugh-Barber Fund 67t

Prints and Photographs Division, Library of Congress 16b, 30b, 64b, 96t, 104c, 146, 180b, 184

Monticello, Thomas Jefferson Memorial Foundation, Inc. 100

Mountain Light Inc./Galen Rowell 183, 218, 219, 254t

David Muench 2–3, 138b, 139, 179, 216–17, 250–51

Collection of the Museum of Early Southern Decorative Atrs, Winston-Salem, N.C. 24b, 104b

North Wind Picture Archives 24t, 98b, 103, 138t, 254b, endpapers

George Catlin, *The Corn Dance*, Rare Books and Manuscripts Division, The New York Public Library, Astor, Lenox and Tilden Foundations 182b

Plimoth Plantation/Ted Curtin 28

The Cowboy, Frederic Remington, oil on canvas, 1902 186

Schlesinger Library, Radcliff College 142t

Schwenkfelder Library, Pennsburg Pa. 68b

Tony Stone Worldwide/Doris De Witt 97; Tony Stone Worldwide/H. Richard Johnston 253, 255

Courtesy, the Strong Museum, Rochester, New York© 1993 26

Harald Sund 176–77, 221t

The University Museum, University of Pennsylvania 185t, 259

David Wakely 178, 180t

Tom Wallis 182t, 185b

Westlight/Jim Zuckerman 25; Westlight/Annie Griffiths Belt 96b; Westlight/Steve Chen 258t

Acknowledgments

The publishers would like to thank the following people and organizations for their assistance in the preparation of this book:

Norman Kolpas, Richard VanOosterhout, John Bull, Steven Lee, Simon Gompertz, Katharina Vitols, Tara Brown, Sigrid Chase, Diana Reiss-Koncar, Ken DellaPenta, Wendely Harvey, Fee Ling Tan, Roger Smoothy, Anne Dickerson, Laurie Wertz, Tori Ritchie, Dawn Low, Janique Poncelet, Patty Hill, Thomas Wear, Khristy Benoit, Carla Horner, Cindy Slobaszewski, Heidi Kaisand, Sara Jane Treinen, Michael Treinen, Deb Felton, Patricia Beebout, Marilyn Cornelius, Kay Cargill, Jennifer Peterson, Colleen Weeden, Lori Wilson, Judy Comstock, Lynn Blanchard, Maryellen Krantz, Sharon Stilwell, B. J. Martell, Michell Barton, Barbara Whalen

Nutrition Analysis
When a recipe gives an ingredient substitution, we use the first choice in the analysis. If it makes a range of servings (such as 4 to 6), we used the smallest number. Ingredientes listed as optional weren't included in the calculations.

Metric Cooking Hints

By making a few conversions, cooks in Australia, Canada, and the United Kingdom can use the recipes in Better Homes and Gardens® *Heritage of America Cookbook* with confidence. The charts on this page provide a guide for converting measurements from the U.S. customary system, which is used throughout this book, to the imperial and metric systems. There also is a conversion table for oven temperatures to accommodate the differences in oven calibrations.

Volume and Weight: Americans traditionally use cup measures for liquid and solid ingredients. The chart (top right) shows the approximate imperial and metric equivalents. If you are accustomed to weighing solid ingredients, here are some helpful approximate equivalents.
★ 1 cup butter, sugar, or rice = 8 ounces = about 250 grams
★ 1 cup flour = 4 ounces = about 125 grams
★ 1 cup icing sugar = 5 ounces = about 150 grams
    Spoon measures are used for smaller amounts of ingredients. Although the size of the tablespoon varies slightly among countries. However, for practical purposes and for recipes in this book, a straight substitution is all that's necessary.
    Measurements made using cups or spoons should always be level, unless stated otherwise.

Product Differences: Most of the ingredients called for in the recipes in this book are available in English-speaking countries. However, some are known by different names. Here are some common American ingredients and their possible counterparts:
★ Sugar is granulated or caster sugar.
★ Powdered sugar is icing sugar.
★ All-purpose flour is plain household flour or white flour. When self-rising flour is used in place of all-purpose flour in a recipe that calls for leavening, omit the leavening agent (baking soda or baking powder) and salt.
★ Light corn syrup is golden syrup.
★ Cornstarch is cornflour.
★ Baking soda is bicarbonate of soda.
★ Vanilla is vanilla essence.

Useful Equivalents

⅛ teaspoon = 0.5ml	⅔ cup = 5 fluid ounces = 150ml
¼ teaspoon = 1ml	¾ cup = 6 fluid ounces = 175ml
½ teaspoon = 2 ml	1 cup = 8 fluid ounces = 250ml
1 teaspoon = 5 ml	2 cups = 1 pint
¼ cup = 2 fluid ounces = 50ml	2 pints = 1 litre
⅓ cup = 3 fluid ounces = 75ml	½ inch =1 centimetre
½ cup = 4 fluid ounces = 125ml	1 inch = 2 centimetres

Baking Pan Sizes

American	Metric
8x1½-inch round baking pan	20x4-centimetre sandwich or cake tin
9x1½-inch round baking pan	23x3.5-centimetre sandwich or cake tin
11x7x1½-inch baking pan	28x18x4-centimetre baking pan
13x9x2-inch baking pan	32.5x23x5-centimetre baking pan
12x7½x2-inch baking dish	30x19x5-centimetre baking pan
15x10x2-inch baking pan	38x25.5x2.5-centimetre baking pan (Swiss roll tin)
9-inch pie plate	22x4- or 23x4-centimetre pie plate
7- or 8-inch springform pan	18- or 20-centimetre springform or loose-bottom cake tin
9x5x3-inch loaf pan narrow loaf pan or paté tin	23x13x6-centimetre or 2-pound
1½-quart casserole	1.5-litre casserole
2-quart casserole	2-litre casserole

Oven Temperature Equivalents

Farenheit Setting	Celsius Setting*	Gas Setting
300°F	150°C	Gas Mark 2
325°F	160°C	Gas Mark 3
350°F	180°C	Gas Mark 4
375°F	190°C	Gas Mark 5
400°F	200°C	Gas Mark 6
425°F	220°C	Gas Mark 7
450°F	230°C	Gas Mark 8
Broil		Grill

*Electric and gas ovens may be calibrated using Celsius. However, increase the Celsius setting 10 to 20 degrees when cooking above 160°C with an electric oven. For convection or forced-air ovens (gas or electric), lower the temperature setting 10°C when cooking at all heat levels.